The Complete
MUMPS®

An Introduction and Reference Manual for the MUMPS® Programming Language

JOHN M. LEWKOWICZ

New York State College of Veterinary Medicine
Cornell University
Ithaca, New York

Prentice Hall
Englewood Cliffs, New Jersey 07632

Library of Congress Cataloging-in-Publication Data

Lewkowicz, John M.
    The complete MUMPS : an introduction and reference manual for the
MUMPS programming language / John M. Lewkowicz.
      p.   cm.
    Bibliography: p.
    Includes index.
    ISBN 0-13-162125-4
    1. MUMPS (Computer program language)   I. Title.
QA76.73.M85L48 1989
005.13'3—dc19
                                    88-28855
                                      CIP

Editorial/production supervision and
  interior design: Laura Cleveland
Cover design: Lundgren Graphics, Ltd.
Manufacturing buyer: Mary Ann Gloriande

© 1989 by Prentice-Hall, Inc.
A Division of Simon & Schuster
Englewood Cliffs, New Jersey 07632

Printed in the United States of America

10 9 8 7 6 5 4 3

ISBN   0-13-162125-4

Prentice-Hall International (UK) Limited, *London*
Prentice-Hall of Australia Pty. Limited, *Sydney*
Prentice-Hall Canada Inc., *Toronto*
Prentice-Hall Hispanoamericana, S.A, *Mexico*
Prentice-Hall of India Private Limited, *New Delhi*
Prentice-Hall of Japan, Inc., *Tokyo*
Simon & Schuster Asia Pte. Ltd., *Singapore*
Editora Prentice-Hall do Brasil, Ltda., *Rio de Janeiro*

MUMPS is a registered trademark of
Massachusetts General Hospital.

Contents

Preface   xi

Chapter 1   Introduction to MUMPS   1

1.1 How to Use This Book   1
1.2 Introduction to MUMPS   3
1.3 A Brief History of MUMPS   8
    1.3.1 The MUMPS Development Committee (MDC)   8
    1.3.2 MUMPS Users' Group   10
    1.3.3 Availability of MUMPS   10
1.4 How to Use MUMPS   10
    1.4.1 Signing onto MUMPS   11
    1.4.2 Issuing MUMPS Commands from the Keyboard   12
    1.4.3 Entering and Editing Programs   12
    1.4.4 Loading a Program from Disk   14
    1.4.5 Executing a Program   14
    1.4.6 Exiting MUMPS   14
1.5 Chapter Highlights   15

Chapter 2   The MUMPS Environment   **16**

2.1   Interpreters   17
2.2   Concept of Directories and Partitions   17
    2.2.1   Partitions   18
    2.2.2   Directories   20
    2.2.3   Name Spaces: Local and Global   21
2.3   Jobs (Processes)   23
2.4   Chapter Highlights   23

Chapter 3   MUMPS Commands   **24**

3.1   Assignment Commands   27
    3.1.1   SET Command   27
    3.1.2   KILL Command   30
    3.1.3   NEW Command   35
3.2   Conditional Commands   38
    3.2.1   IF Command   39
    3.2.2   ELSE Command   41
    3.2.3   FOR Command   42
3.3   Flow Control Commands   46
    3.3.1   GOTO Command   47
    3.3.2   DO Command   51
    3.3.3   QUIT Command   58
    3.3.4   HALT Command   61
    3.3.5   XECUTE Command   62
3.4   Input/Output Commands   64
    3.4.1   OPEN Command   66
    3.4.2   USE Command   69
    3.4.3   READ Command   70
    3.4.4   WRITE Command   77
    3.4.5   CLOSE Command   81
    3.4.6   PRINT Command   82
3.5   System and Miscellaneous Commands   83
    3.5.1   BREAK Command   84
    3.5.2   HANG Command   85
    3.5.3   JOB Command   86
    3.5.4   LOCK Command   89
    3.5.5   VIEW Command   94
    3.5.6   ZLOAD Command   96
    3.5.7   ZINSERT Command   96
    3.5.8   ZREMOVE Command   97
    3.5.9   ZPRINT Command   97

3.5.10 ZSAVE Command   97
3.5.11 Miscellaneous Z Commands   98
3.6 Summary   98

Chapter 4   Data Structures   99

4.1 Strings   100
4.2 Numbers   101
   4.2.1 Exponential Notation   102
   4.2.2 Numeric Interpretation of Strings   103
4.3 Boolean (True/False)   104
4.4 Variables   104
   4.4.1 Local Variables   106
   4.4.2 Arrays   107
   4.4.3 Globals   114
   4.4.4 System Variables   115
4.5 Chapter Highlights   118

Chapter 5   Expressions   120

5.1 Numeric Operators: $+$, $-$, $*$, $**$, $/$, $\backslash$, and $\#$ 122
   5.1.1 Unary Operators: $+$ and $-$ 122
   5.1.2 Binary Numeric Operators   123
5.2 String Operators: Concatenate, _(Underscore)   125
5.3 Logical and Relational Operators: $>$, $<$, $=$ [,], ?, &, !, and '   125
   5.3.1 Numeric Relational Operators   125
   5.3.2 String Relational Operators   126
   5.3.3 Logical Operators   130
5.4 Combined Operator Types   132
5.5 Chapter Highlights   134

Chapter 6   MUMPS Syntax   135

6.1 Commands   136
   6.1.1 Command Arguments   136
   6.1.2 Implied Commands   138
   6.1.3 Command Abbreviation and Command Case   139
   6.1.4 Conditional Execution of Commands   141
   6.1.5 Timed Commands   145
   6.1.6 Comments   147
6.2 Lines   148

Contents

6.3 Subroutines (Parts) 151
6.4 Routines 151
6.5 Programs 152
6.6 Block Structuring 153
6.7 Chapter Highlights 155

Chapter 7 Indirection 157

7.1 XECUTE Command 158
7.2 Indirection Operator @ 159
   7.2.1 Name Indirection 159
   7.2.2 Argument Indirection 161
   7.2.3 Pattern Indirection 163
   7.2.4 Subscript Indirection 165
7.3 Dynamic Routine Linking 166
7.4 Indirection: Cautions and Caveats 167
7.5 Chapter Highlights 168

Chapter 8 Intrinsic Functions 169

8.1 String Functions 170
   8.1.1 $EXTRACT 170
   8.1.2 $PIECE Function 172
   8.1.3 $LENGTH Function 176
   8.1.4 $FIND Function 178
   8.1.5 $TRANSLATE Function 179
   8.1.6 $JUSTIFY Function 182
   8.1.7 $FNUMBER Function 183
   8.1.8 $ASCII Function 186
   8.1.9 $CHAR Function 186
   8.1.10 $TEXT Function 188
8.2 Data Functions 191
   8.2.1 $DATA Function 191
   8.2.2 $ORDER Function 192
   8.2.3 $NEXT Function (OBSOLETE) 195
   8.2.4 $QUERY Function 195
   8.2.5 $GET Function 197
8.3 Other Functions 198
   8.3.1 $SELECT Function 198
   8.3.2 $RANDOM Function 199
   8.3.3 $VIEW Function 200
8.4 $Z. . . Functions 201
8.5 Summary 202

Chapter 9   Parameter Passing and Extrinsic Functions   203

9.1   Parameter Passing with the DO Command   203
     9.1.1   Passing Parameters by VALUE   206
     9.1.2   Parameter Passing by REFERENCE   207
9.2   Extrinsic Functions   210
9.3   Extrinsic Variables   213
9.4   Subroutine Libraries   213
     9.4.1   Conversion of $H Time and Date to Readable Format   213
     9.4.2   Check and Conversion of Numbers   216
     9.4.3   Numeric Conversion between Bases   217
     9.4.4   Simple Statistics   217
     9.4.5   An Extrinsic Function to Replace Strings   219
9.5   Parameter Passing with the JOB Command   221
9.6   Technique and Style   222
9.7   Chapter Highlights   223

Chapter 10   Advanced Global Techniques   225

10.1   Introduction to Globals   226
10.2   Subscripts   227
     10.2.1   Subscript Collating Sequence   227
     10.2.2 $ORDER and $DATA Functions   233
10.3   Naked Global References   236
10.4   The LOCK Command   238
10.5   Global Extensions   240
     10.5.1   Distributed Databases   240
     10.5.2   Replication   241
     10.5.3   Journaling   241
     10.5.4   Global Security   242
10.6   Advanced Examples: Global Dumps and Copy Utilities   243
10.7   Database Design   246
     10.7.1   Inverted or Key Indexes   250
     10.7.2   Reference Files   253
10.8   Searching and Sorting   255
10.9   Chapter Highlights   257

Chapter 11   MUMPS Internals   259

11.1   Global Disk Files   260
     11.1.1   Adding Data to a B-Tree   261
     11.1.2   B-Tree Variants   268
     11.1.3   Multiple Subscript Levels   271

11.1.4   Key Compression   272
11.1.5   Deleting Data from a B-Tree   273
11.1.6   Buffering   273
11.1.7   Storage Efficiency Considerations   274
11.1.8   Database Errors   276
11.2   MUMPS Program Execution   277
11.3   Chapter Highlights   284

Chapter 12   Device Input/Output   286

12.1   General I/O Environment   286
12.2   The Principal Device   288
12.3   System Variables Associated with I/O Operations   290
12.4   Devices   292
12.4.1   Video Terminals   293
12.4.2   Printing Terminals   299
12.4.3   Magnetic Tape Drives   299
12.4.4   Sequential Disk Files   303
12.4.5   Print Spool Devices   306
12.4.6   Miscellaneous Devices   306
12.5   Advanced Topics on Device I/O   307
12.5.1   Screen Handling Utilities   308
12.5.2   Keyboard Input: Single-Character READ Function   315
12.5.3   Option Lists and Multiple-Choice Questions   322
12.5.4   Editing Keyboard Read   327
12.5.5   Question Driver   328
12.5.6   Summary of Advanced I/O Topics   335
12.6   Chapter Highlights   336

Chapter 13   Error Processing   337

13.1   Trapping Errors   338
13.2   Debugging Programs   345
13.3   Chapter Highlights   346

Chapter 14   MUMPS: The Evolving Language   347

14.1   Networking   348
14.1.1   Networking between MUMPS Implementations   348
14.1.2   Networking with Non-MUMPS Environments   349
14.2   Enhanced Device Control   349
14.3   Access to Other Languages   350

14.4 Use of Alternative Character Sets   351
14.5 Standardized Error Processing   352
14.6 Miscellaneous Language Changes   352
14.7 Concluding Remarks   353

Appendix A   ASCII Character Set   354

Appendix B   Selected MUMPS References   356

Appendix C   Summary of MUMPS Commands   358

Appendix D   Summary of MUMPS Intrinsic Functions   364

Appendix E   Summary of MUMPS Operators   371

Appendix F   Summary of System Variables   373

Appendix G   Documentation for Selected Subroutines   375

Appendix H   RS-232 Devices   380

Appendix I   Terminal Functions   384

Index   397

To Alicia, Matthew, Mark, and Jill

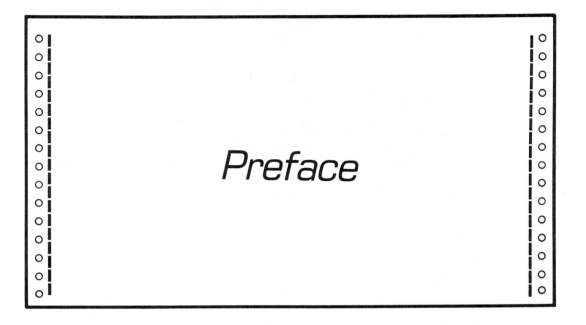

Preface

I was first introduced to the MUMPS language in 1971 after almost 10 years of scientific programming using FORTRAN, BASIC, and a variety of assembler languages. At that time, the clinics at the New York State College of Veterinary Medicine were facing a data crisis of major proportions. Managing the vast quantities of information associated with the teaching hospital, communicating between widely separated functional units, and processing data retrieval requests were becoming all but impossible. MUMPS appeared to offer the best and most cost-effective computer solution for our record-management needs. I must confess, though, I was not pleased with the idea of trading the real environment of laboratory computing for the dull world of database computing.

What a difference 15 years can make, both in terms of the impact of MUMPS on the database management needs of the college and on my attitude. My early trepidations concerning database programming were soon replaced with enthusiasm. The MUMPS language turned out to be an excellent tool for managing data and communicating information between widely separated units within the college. MUMPS provides an ideal blend of power, economy, and ease of use, and our initial efforts rapidly expanded beyond the clinics to administrative and research computing needs.

MUMPS is usually labeled as a database management language and, while it certainly lives up to that definition, it is also considerably more. As an inherent feature of the language, MUMPS supports a unique file structure in which data are stored on disk in the form of arrays. These arrays are hierarchical and sparse in nature, providing an excellent means for organizing and retrieving data in an efficient manner. The arrays can also be shared simultaneously by all applications in a multiuser MUMPS environment. In addition, MUMPS supports powerful string functions for manipulating text-oriented data and an extremely flexible input/output environment.

I still program with other languages (Pascal, C, APL, LISP, and so on), but almost always find myself saying, "but it's so much easier in MUMPS!" These excursions into other languages are usually short-lived; it's just plain quicker and easier to implement most applications in MUMPS. MUMPS is a powerful computing language designed to solve real-world problems. As the saying goes: "Try it, you'll like it."

Acknowledgments

It would have been impossible to finish this book without the help and support of many individuals. First and foremost, I wish to thank my good friend and colleague, Dr. Richard F. Walters. Dick has suffered through the agonizing process of bringing this book to print with countless hours of review, a torrent of corrections and suggestions, and, most important, a continuing sense of optimism and humor. His support has been invaluable.

The text was reviewed by a variety of experts in the MUMPS community for both content and organization. Among those who reviewed the numerous drafts, and contributed significantly to the final product, were Holly Boyd, Richard Davis, Bruce Douglas, Frederick L. Hiltz, Don Piccone, and Thomas Salander. One interesting aside of the review process concerns the suggestions made by these reviewers: of the hundreds of comments, corrections, and suggested additions, only 12 items were cited by two or more individuals. Apparently, the reviewers' points of reference were as diverse as the applications to which MUMPS is applied.

Additional thanks must be expressed to the entire staff of the Computing Center at the College of Veterinary Medicine at Cornell University. These individuals suffered (mostly silently) through "the book" and contributed to its content and my sanity. Although it may be unfair to single out individuals, I would like to express special thanks to John Godfrey, Katherine Earle, Tom Fredericks, Cindy Hannah-White, and Victor Silva for their help.

I would like to thank Peter Beaman for his efforts in explaining the internals of compiled MUMPS. His tutelage helped reduce a complex subject to meaningful terms.

Finally, I wish to thank my family, to whom this book is dedicated. Their understanding and encouragement were essential ingredients in completing this text.

Introduction to MUMPS

This book is designed to serve two basic and often conflicting purposes: the first is to provide a learning text for the MUMPS programming language, and the second is to serve as a reference manual for those proficient in the language. It is aimed both at individuals with no previous experience using MUMPS and the experienced MUMPS programmer needing detailed information on specific language features. It is not designed as a text for those individuals with no previous programming experience; such readers are advised to start with either the *MUMPS Primer, Revised* or the *Introduction to Standard MUMPS* (see Appendix B).

Appendix B presents a brief listing of some other MUMPS texts that are currently available. The introductory guides provide an excellent starting point for the beginning MUMPS programmer but are less effective as reference manuals for the intermediate or experienced programmer. The more advanced texts serve as good reference manuals, but they often fail to convey the general flavor of this unique language and can be too technical for the beginning or intermediate-level programmer.

1.1 How to Use This Book

As a reader wishing to realize the full potential of MUMPS, you should approach reading this text as a collaborative effort between you and me. We can examine the basic mechanics of the language and demonstrate its use with numerous examples, but many of the nuances must be left to the reader to explore. The examples are designed to stimulate the reader, not to be an exhaustive description of all the possibilities. MUMPS is such a powerful and flexible language that, even after 15 years of programming experience, I am constantly delighted to discover new revelations or techniques while developing applications. You should keep an open mind as you are reading and explore the possibilities beyond those that are demonstrated; most of all, enjoy yourself.

Every attempt has been made to make this book function as both a learning tool and reference manual. The text is accompanied with numerous examples of MUMPS code that demonstrate the concepts discussed. Beginning MUMPS programmers are advised to experiment with the examples as they read the book, since exercising the examples will lead to a much better understanding of the concepts being presented. Section 1.4 will explain how to execute MUMPS commands directly from the keyboard and also how to create and invoke programs. The accompanying appendixes and index should provide the more experienced programmer with direct access to specific information needed for developing complex applications.

As you read the book you may encounter certain redundancies; the same concept or definition may be developed in more than one location. This duplication stems, in part, from the two differing goals of the text. To serve as a learning text, it must be organized in such a fashion that new concepts are explained as they are encountered. On the other hand, when used as a reference for specific language features, it is desirable to have a complete definition in a single location to avoid the need to thumb through the book to find all relevant information on a given topic. The beginning MUMPS programmer should be consoled by the understanding that repeated definitions imply the importance of a particular concept (real or imagined) and should serve to reinforce these.

Two basic formats will be used throughout the book to convey special information. Examples of MUMPS code will be highlighted with a box similar to the following:

```
o|>WRITE "Example"←                                      |o
 |                                                       |
o|Example                                                |o
```

EXAMPLE 1.1. Example format

In these examples, keyboard input by a user will be <u>underlined</u> and computer output will be printed in **boldface**. The special character ← will be used to represent pressing the <ENTER> key. A second format is used for displaying important concepts and will be boxed in the following manner:

```
Important Concept
```

The final section of each chapter is labeled *Chapter Highlights* and summarizes the important concepts that have been developed in the chapter.

Sections that explain aspects of MUMPS that are not necessary to gain a basic working knowledge of the language (such as Chapter 11, MUMPS Internals) are identified so that the beginning programmer can skip them initially, and then return to them as time allows or as needs dictate.

The beginning MUMPS programmer should read the first two chapters thoroughly, and then scan Chapter 3 (especially the sections covering the SET, WRITE, and DO commands). After reading Chapters 4, 5, and 6, you can return to Chapter 3 and examine the commands in greater detail. Chapter 7 on *indirection* can initially be skipped, as it is a fairly complex subject and is not needed for a basic understanding of MUMPS. The remaining chapters can be read in sequence, as each chapter builds on the material presented in previous chapters. Chapter 11 provides some detail on the internal workings of the language, especially on how data are organized and stored on disk and the rudiments of how MUMPS compilers work. It is designed to give the advanced reader an insight into the language and can be skipped by the beginning programmer.

1.2 Introduction to MUMPS

What is MUMPS? In the simplest of terms, MUMPS is a computer language like FORTRAN, COBOL, BASIC, or Pascal. It was first developed at the Laboratory of Computer Science at Massachusetts General Hospital in 1967 specifically to process string-oriented data and support random-access databases. These features were not available in other languages and were deemed to be essential for developing general-purpose hospital database management systems. The acronym MUMPS stands for **M**assachusetts **G**eneral **H**ospital **U**tility **M**ulti-**P**rogramming **S**ystem.

While MUMPS was originally developed to support medical applications, it is a general-purpose database management system and is not limited to the medical environment. Extensive MUMPS programs have been written for library information systems, banking and accounting applications, inventory and scheduling systems, and many other nonmedical packages. MUMPS combines built-in database management features and powerful commands for manipulating character-oriented data, while incorporating highly efficient data storage techniques. These features make MUMPS an attractive and cost-effective language for developing almost any database application.

As a language, MUMPS provides many string-oriented primitives (operators and functions), which allow it to process character-oriented data and text fields efficiently. It also supports hierarchical and sparse data arrays as the primary method for data storage. Data arrays can either be temporary and maintained only in local memory, or they can be automatically mapped to disk. When mapped to disk, these virtual arrays replace the more traditional disk file structures (sequential files, linked lists, and the like) found in other languages. Virtual arrays residing on disk are called GLOBALS in MUMPS. The use of GLOBALS as the primary method for storing data is a major departure from traditional languages and has a profound effect on all aspects of programming in the MUMPS environment.

> MUMPS uses arrays automatically mapped to disk as its primary form of data storage. These arrays are called GLOBALS.

MUMPS arrays and globals can be created dynamically with any number of levels (subscripts). Unlike arrays in most other languages, MUMPS arrays do *not* map into a matrix, but instead map into a tree structure in which each subscript can represent the beginning of a subtree (branch). All pathways below a particular branch node are related to the parent node. By means of this tree structure, MUMPS globals assume a hierarchical structure.

> MUMPS globals are hierarchical in structure.

In addition, subscripts in MUMPS are *not* limited to numbers but can also be strings of characters. A valid array reference might be **SET ARRAY("Name") = "Peter Rabbit"**, where the string of characters "Name" is used as the subscript into ARRAY pointing to a data node containing the characters "Peter Rabbit".

> Array subscripts can be either numeric, alpha, or alphanumeric.

Global arrays can be sparse in nature; only data nodes that are actually defined require space on disk. This permits the efficient storage of information, especially when the data are intermittent in nature. Consider storing information on patient visits to a clinic. For example, a patient may visit the clinic an arbitrary number of times; each visit may be associated with an arbitrary number of procedures, diagnoses, and so on. If we had to reserve space for all possible visits, procedures, and so on, we would have difficulty finding enough space even on the largest of disk systems. In MUMPS, on the other hand, disk space is only allocated when a data node is created; a global array dynamically grows and shrinks as new data elements are added or deleted.

GLOBALS are sparse arrays: only those nodes defined are allocated storage space.

Most implementations of MUMPS permit more than one simultaneous user. In these multiuser MUMPS environments, GLOBALS can be shared by all users *simultaneously*; therefore many different processes can access the same data at the same time.

GLOBALS can be shared simultaneously by multiple users.

MUMPS also has many attributes of an operating system. Indeed, the original versions of MUMPS were specifically designed to run on minicomputers and took complete control of the hardware, handling all functions (input/output, task scheduling, and so on) that are usually associated with an operating system. It is only recently that MUMPS has been made into a layered product that will run under the control of other operating systems. Even in such layered implementations, MUMPS still performs many basic operating system functions, such as scheduling MUMPS tasks and managing all virtual array disk files.

MUMPS is an *interpreted* language. The original versions were pure interpreters; to execute a MUMPS program, it was necessary to interpret each line of source code as the program ran. Since this added significant overhead, many implementors now offer versions of MUMPS that compile the source code before it is executed. The type of compilation performed is quite different from what is found in a FORTRAN or COBOL environment. In those environments, the compilers usually convert the source code to machine language instructions to form stand-alone programs; once compiled, these programs no longer need the original compiler to execute. MUMPS compilers, on the other hand, do *not* reduce source code to the machine language level. Rather, they compile the source code to a level intermediate between the original source and the assembler language of the computer. At run time, the code must still be interpreted, but interpretation is much faster. Compiling MUMPS programs is usually transparent to the programmer, with the source code compiled automatically as it is saved on disk.

```
┌─────────────────────────────────────────────┐
│                                               │
│        MUMPS is an interpreted language.      │
│                                               │
│                                               │
└─────────────────────────────────────────────┘
```

Programmers can execute MUMPS commands directly from the keyboard as well as initiate (run) programs written in MUMPS. Once initiated, program execution can be interrupted, and the programmer can examine the current status of the variable environment and even modify the variables. When the interactive activity is finished, program execution can be resumed.

```
┌─────────────────────────────────────────────┐
│                                               │
│     MUMPS commands can be executed directly   │
│     from the keyboard                         │
│     or be made into routines for subsequent   │
│     execution.                                │
│                                               │
└─────────────────────────────────────────────┘
```

Finally, in the MUMPS language environment, there is no need to declare or type variables. Many languages require that each variable to be used must first be identified and classified as to type (integer, string, boolean, and so on). When working with arrays in other languages, the programmer is required to define the maximum size of each array (for example, the DIMENSION statement in FORTRAN) and the type of data to be held in the array. In MUMPS these steps are not necessary. As MUMPS encounters commands that create variables (for example, **SET A = 22**), it checks to see if the referenced variable is defined. If it is undefined, MUMPS will automatically create space for the variable and its value. All subsequent references to the variable will be mapped to the correct location. MUMPS does not establish requirements about the type of data associated with a variable.

```
┌─────────────────────────────────────────────┐
│                                               │
│     It is not necessary to either DECLARE or  │
│     TYPE                                      │
│     variables in MUMPS programs.              │
│                                               │
└─────────────────────────────────────────────┘
```

While a given value may be a number (integer or floating point) or a string, MUMPS automatically and invisibly converts between these forms as necessary.

MUMPS handles calculations involving data strings *in context*. For example, we can issue the following MUMPS commands to create two variables A and B:

```
o|>SET A="500 Miles"←            |o
 |>SET B="25 Gallons"←           |
 |>                              |
o|                               |o
```

EXAMPLE 1.2.   Creating variables

In this example, the > character starting each line is the MUMPS prompt requesting keyboard (command) input and the special character ← represents pressing the <ENTER> key. As the commands are executed, MUMPS will reserve space for the variables named A and B and associate the strings "500 Miles" and "25 gallons" with them. Look what happens when we use these variables in calculations:

```
o|>WRITE A/B←                    |o
 |                               |
o|20                             |o
 |>                              |
```

EXAMPLE 1.3.   Arithmetic calculations by context

In this example, we instruct MUMPS to write out the results of a calculation dividing the contents of variable A by the contents of variable B. Even though both variables appear to be strings, MUMPS evaluates them (from left to right, insofar as possible) as numbers, since the requested operation was arithmetic. In the next example, we use the same two variables, but this time use the *concatenate* operator (represented by the underscore character, _) instead of the divide operator (/). The concatenate operator instructs MUMPS to append the characters associated with the expression on the *right* side of the operator to the characters associated with the expression on the *left* side of the operator.

```
o|>WRITE A_B←                    |o
 |                               |
o|500 Miles25 Gallons            |o
 |>                              |
```

EXAMPLE 1.4.   String calculations by context

In Example 1.4, do not confuse the underlined text representing input from the keyboard with the character "_", which is used to represent the concatenate operator. The method in which MUMPS interprets the data is totally dependent on the context in which the data are used. Arithmetic operators force numeric interpretation of data, whereas string operators force a string interpretation of the same data elements.

MUMPS interprets data value types in context.

1.3 A Brief History of MUMPS

MUMPS was first developed at the Laboratory of Computer Science at Massachusetts General Hospital in 1967. The original goals were to design an on-line, multiuser computer system with shared-file capabilities and powerful string primitives to handle the textual data being processed in the hospital environment. In addition, it was designed to run on minicomputers to provide a cost-effective alternative to more expensive mainframe systems. Because of the intermittent nature of the data to be processed (for example, patients with varying numbers of visits, lab tests, diagnoses, and the like) it was necessary to define a file structure that would accept such sparse data and store them efficiently. It was from these early design considerations that the MUMPS language and globals originated.

With the availability of the MUMPS language came the potential for developing large-scale database management systems on relatively inexpensive hardware. Use of the MUMPS language expanded as the early prospects of cost-effective database management were realized, and a number of new MUMPS dialects began to appear. By 1972 there were over 14 different versions of MUMPS, and the continued expansion of MUMPS dialects seemed inevitable.

1.3.1 The MUMPS Development Committee (MDC)

The MUMPS Development Committee (MDC) was established in 1972 to define a MUMPS standard to be submitted to the American National Standards Institute (ANSI). The original standardization efforts were financed jointly by the National Bureau of Standards and by the National Center for Health Sciences Research. Formal definition of a MUMPS standard was finished in 1975 and was submitted to ANSI, receiving approval in 1977.

The MDC remains an active organization whose responsibility is to evaluate new language proposals for inclusion within the standard. The MUMPS language continues evolving to meet the changing requirements of its user community. New language proposals can be submitted to the MDC by any interested party. A proposal goes through a series of defined steps before it can become part of the *MUMPS Language Standard*. These steps are listed next for those interested in the formal process by which the language changes.

1.3.1.1 Type C Proposal The MDC meets twice a year to consider new proposals for extensions to the language. When a proposal is first submitted, it is discussed in an open session and, if the majority of MDC members decide it merits further consideration, it is elevated to the status of a Type C Proposal. This status simply means that the proposal is being actively considered and further discussions will ensue.

1.3.1.2 Type B Proposal The next step in the chain is upgrading a type C proposal to a type B. This level indicates that the majority of MDC members think that the proposal adds a needed functionality to the language and that it is well enough defined for testing by MUMPS implementors. Many implementors include type B proposals within their implementations and test the proposed changes for deficiencies or unexpected problems.

1.3.1.3 Type A Proposal After being tested in a number of implementations, a proposal can be elevated to type A. Type A proposals are generally considered sure candidates for inclusion in the *MUMPS language standard*, which is updated at four- to five-year intervals. If the implementors have problems in implementation of a type B proposal, it can be held at that level until the difficulties have been resolved, or its status can be reduced (even to the point of dropping the proposal altogether). Almost all vendors include type A proposals in their implementation, and the de facto standard becomes the current standard plus all the type A proposals. All type A proposals in this book are clearly marked, since some implementations that adhere to the current standard do not include all of them.

1.3.1.4 The MUMPS Standard Final inclusion of type A proposals to the MUMPS standard requires canvassing a representative sample of the MUMPS community and other interested parties. Final decision on which type A proposals are to be included in the standard is based on arguments for and against each proposal. If the MDC cannot effectively resolve to the satisfaction of ANSI any questions concerning a specific proposal from those canvassed, the proposal in question will *not* be included in the new standard.

The *MUMPS language standard* represents the minimal requirement to which all implementors must adhere if their version of MUMPS is to conform to the ANSI standard. It defines the basic language elements, but does not address issues such as the size of routines or local work spaces or a variety of other factors that relate directly to the portability of applications between various versions of MUMPS.

A second document produced by the MDC, the *Portability Standard*, is a set of conventions defining some of these parameters. This standard defines a *minimum* set of specifications for implementors and a *maximum* for portable applications; applications written to this standard should run on all MUMPS implementations. Individual implementors do *not* have to follow the portability standard to be called an ANSI standard version of MUMPS, but it is in their best interest to do so, and all current versions do adhere to the limits defined in this document. Subsequent discussions in this book will try to differentiate between restrictions imposed by the language standard and those imposed by the portability standard.

1.3.2 MUMPS Users' Group

An excellent source of current information concerning the MUMPS language is the MUMPS Users' Group (MUG). MUG is an international, nonprofit organization designed to promote the MUMPS language through a variety of avenues, including periodic publications (*MUG Quarterly*), annual meetings, continuing education seminars and tutorials, and a public domain library of application programs.

```
MUMPS Users' Group
4321 Hartwick Road, Suite 510
College Park, Maryland 20740
(301) 779-6555
```

MUG provides a central repository of information on the most current implementations of MUMPS, including hardware and operating systems that support MUMPS. They also sell all the major MUMPS texts at discounted prices for MUG members; all the publications listed in Appendix B are available through MUG.

The main MUG organization also coordinates activities through a number of international MUMPS support groups including MUG Europe, MUG Japan, and MUG Brazil.

1.3.3 Availability of MUMPS

MUMPS is currently available on a wide range of computer systems, both as stand-alone packages and as layered products that will run under other operating systems. Current versions are available for a variety of microcomputer systems (including MS-DOS), for minicomputer systems such as Digital Equipment Corporation PDP-11s and VAX computers, and for large mainframe computing systems such as the IBM 370 series. The best source of information concerning the hardware and operating systems under which MUMPS runs can be obtained through the MUMPS Users' Group.

1.4 How to Use MUMPS

This section deals with the basics of signing into MUMPS, executing direct mode commands, and creating programs. It is intended primarily for those individuals who have never used MUMPS before.

In the previous section we mentioned the desirability of exercising the examples accompanying this text at a MUMPS terminal in order to gain a better comprehension of the concepts being presented. To do so, you will need a quick explanation on how to sign into MUMPS, how to issue direct commands to the MUMPS interpreter, how to enter programs, and how to execute programs that have been previously entered.

1.4.1 Signing onto MUMPS

Getting into the MUMPS computing environment requires different approaches, depending on the computer hardware and software under which you are running. We can categorize the general computing environment with which you will likely be dealing into two broad classifications: (1) dedicated MUMPS environments where MUMPS is the only process running on the computer, and (2) shared environments where the MUMPS process is just one of many possible applications.

When signing onto a *dedicated MUMPS computer*, it is usually necessary to perform one or more of the following steps:

1. Get the attention of MUMPS. This is usually accomplished either by pressing the <BREAK> key on the keyboard or by pressing the <ENTER> key (the <ENTER> key is labeled <RETURN> on some keyboards). The MUMPS operating system will respond by typing out an identification message (usually identifying the MUMPS implementation being used and often displaying the internal MUMPS terminal number).

2. You will then be prompted for a password or access code authorizing your use of the system. This request may be a specialized password program or a general log-on procedure supplied with most versions of MUMPS. Often you will be asked for a **UCI**: and a **PAC**; the UCI, in MUMPS jargon, stands for User Class Identifier, a fancy term for a directory, and PAC stands for **Programmer Access Code** (or password).

    Before proceeding beyond this point, you will have to get both a UCI and a password from the system manager. At the UCI and password prompts, make your entry at the keyboard and press the <ENTER> key. If your entry is incorrect or invalid, you will be given a message to that effect and you should try again. If you still have trouble signing on, get additional directions from the individual who assigned your password.

    If the password is acceptable, MUMPS will type out a special prompt character requesting input. This prompt is usually the ">" character, although some implementations use other prompts. When you see the prompt character, you are signed onto MUMPS and should skip ahead to Section 1.4.2. If you don't get a prompt, seek help.

The technique for signing onto a general-purpose or *shared computer system* is similar to signing onto a dedicated MUMPS system except that you must first inform the general-purpose operating system that you want to run in the MUMPS environment. This usually involves entering a command such as "MUMPS" in response to the operating system prompt. However, it is sometimes necessary to change disks or disk directories before initiating MUMPS, so it is worth your while to talk to the system manager before attempting to start a MUMPS process. Once you have established the method for initiating MUMPS, do so and then follow the steps listed previously to sign into the MUMPS operating environment.

1.4.2 Issuing MUMPS Commands from the Keyboard

MUMPS allows users to enter commands from the keyboard and will interpret these commands and execute them immediately. Commands entered in this mode of interaction are often referred to as *direct mode commands*, and a programmer entering such commands is usually referred to as being in *direct mode*.

When the MUMPS prompt appears, you can enter any valid line of MUMPS commands for execution. The command(s) are not evaluated or executed until the <ENTER> key is pressed. Mistakes in the line can be corrected before the <ENTER> key is pressed by deleting the characters and then retyping the corrected entry. Pressing the <ENTER> key signifies that the command line entry is finished and MUMPS can evaluate it and begin execution. The length of a single command line is limited to the maximum supported string length (the *Portability Standard* defines this as 255 characters long). In actual practice, direct mode commands are usually much shorter; in the event of a mistake, the programmer must usually reenter the entire command.

> MUMPS command lines can be up to 255 characters in length.

If MUMPS detects an error in the command line (such as a command syntax error), it will display an error message before issuing the next prompt. Error messages vary from system to system; you should refer to the implementation manual for help in understanding the nature of the error.

1.4.3 Entering and Editing Programs

In addition to being able to enter and execute individual command lines directly from the keyboard, most versions of MUMPS also permit keyboard entry of command lines to form a program. These lines are not immediately executed and can be stored and retrieved from disk for later execution.

Unfortunately, while MUMPS provides a rich and well-defined programming language, there is no established standard on how to enter, edit, load, or store routines. On the other hand, an informal convention has been adopted by most implementors, and all supply one or more program editors for entering or editing routines. The MUMPS standard provides for the inclusion of implementor-specific commands. All these commands must start with the letter **Z** and, while they differ in minor ways, almost all implementations do provide commands for loading routines into the temporary work area (partition), inserting new lines of code into the routine, and saving the routine to disk. The commands usually used to accomplish these functions are **ZLOAD**, **ZINSERT**, and **ZSAVE**. These commands are discussed in more detail in Chapter 3.

Because of the many different conventions used to enter, edit, and save routines using the **Z** commands, it is strongly advised that the reader take a few minutes to become familiar with the routine editor supplied with the system. Using the editor to create and modify routines is usually more efficient than issuing implementation-specific commands from the keyboard. This editor will allow you to enter command lines, edit existing lines, insert new lines, and save and retrieve the program from disk. Each implementation supplies at least one editor, and editors differ significantly from system to system; check the users' manual for your system for directions on using the editor.

In this book, examples of programs will be presented in a slightly different format from those representing direct mode commands issued from the keyboard (see Example 1.1). Programs, and any output they may generate, will be displayed as follows:

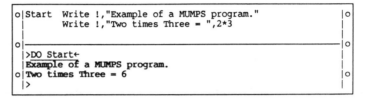

EXAMPLE 1.5. Program example format

In Example 1.5, the horizontal line separates the MUMPS program (upper part of the display) from the direct mode commands and program output (lower part of display). As with examples of direct mode commands, keyboard input below the horizontal line will be <u>underlined</u> and computer output will be in **boldface**. The character ← used in examples represents pressing the <ENTER> key.

We will try to limit the early examples to relatively simple and straightforward samples of code. The <u>WRITE</u> command in the previous example instructs the computer to display strings of characters (for example, "<u>Example of a MUMPS</u> <u>program</u>") or the result of a calculation (for example, <u>2*3</u> to multiply the value 2 by 3) on the terminal. The exclamation mark associated with the WRITE command (Write !) is used to instruct the computer to move down one line on the screen.

Unlike direct mode commands issued from the keyboard, program lines must start with either a line **LABEL** or a <SPACE> or <TAB> character. LABELS consist of one to eight alphabetic characters, which can be either upper- or lowercase; MUMPS distinguishes between upper- and lowercase characters so that **START** and **Start** represent two different labels. Line LABELS are separated from the rest of the commands on the line by one or more SPACE or TAB characters.

The DO command is used to start the execution of a program and requires an argument that consists of the label at which execution is to start. Consequently, the first line of a program should include a LABEL so that it can be referenced.

Program names are assigned when using the editor. Like line labels, they are from one to eight alphabetic characters and can be either upper- or lowercase. As with labels, MUMPS differentiates between the case of a name such that **MYPROG** and **MyProg** represent different program names.

1.4.4 Loading a Program from Disk

Programs saved on disk with the editor can be loaded back into your work area with the **ZLOAD** command. The ZLOAD command requires an argument that defines the name of the program to be loaded. Before the program is loaded into the work area, MUMPS automatically clears the area of any existing program lines.

```
o|>ZLOAD MYPROG←                                              |o
 |>DO Start←                                                  |
 |Example of a MUMPS program.                                 |
o|Two times Three = 6                                         |o
 |>                                                           |
```

EXAMPLE 1.6.   Loading a program from disk

1.4.5 Executing a Program

As we have seen in Example 1.6, you can initiate execution of a program by loading it into your work area (with the ZLOAD command), and then by issuing a **DO** command (DO Start). Alternatively, you can execute the program directly from disk by giving the DO command the name the program is stored under, rather than a label.

```
o|>DO ^MYPROG←                                                |o
 |Example of a MUMPS program.                                 |
 |Two times Three = 6                                         |
o|>                                                           |o
```

EXAMPLE 1.7.   Executing a program from disk

Notice that the program name (MYPROG) is preceded by the special character up-arrow (^). This character tells MUMPS that the argument to the DO command is the name of a program residing on disk, rather than the label of a program in the work area. MUMPS will then load the program from disk into your work area and begin execution at the first line of the program.

1.4.6 Exiting MUMPS

To **TERMINATE** a session with MUMPS (that is, end the MUMPS session and release the partition and terminal), issue a **HALT** command (which can also be abbreviated to the single letter **H**) in response to the MUMPS prompt character.

```
o|>HALT←                                                          |o
 |                                                                |
o|EXIT - End of MUMPS session.                                    |o
```

EXAMPLE 1.8. Terminating a MUMPS session.

> The HALT command is used to terminate a MUMPS session.

When the HALT command is issued, both the terminal and the temporary work area associated with that terminal are released back to the MUMPS operating system for use by other processes. When MUMPS is running as a layered product, the terminal is released back to the operating system.

1.5 Chapter Highlights

- MUMPS uses arrays automatically mapped to disk as its primary form of data storage. These arrays are called GLOBALS (1.2).
- MUMPS globals are hierarchical in structure (1.2).
- Array subscripts can be either numeric, alpha, or alphanumeric (1.2).
- Globals are sparse arrays: only those nodes defined are allocated storage space (1.2).
- Globals can be shared simultaneously by multiple users (1.2).
- MUMPS is an interpreted language (1.2).
- MUMPS commands can be executed directly from the keyboard or be made into routines for subsequent execution (1.2).
- It is not necessary to either DECLARE or TYPE variables in MUMPS programs (1.2).
- MUMPS interprets data value types in context (1.2).
- MUMPS command lines can be up to 255 characters in length (1.4.2).
- The HALT command is used to terminate a MUMPS session (1.4.6).

2

The MUMPS Environment

This chapter explores the general MUMPS computing environment, including the characteristics of an interpreted language, the concepts of disk directories, working partitions, name spaces, and MUMPS jobs. The programmer who has previously used MUMPS and is familiar with these concepts may wish to skip this chapter.

MUMPS is more than just a computer language; it also encompasses many characteristics usually associated with a general-purpose operating system in order to provide a uniform environment for developing application programs. Aside from providing a language interpreter, there is also an inherent database management system, as well as an interface to input/output (I/O) devices. In addition, most MUMPS implementations support a multiuser environment that permits running of more than one task at the same time (time-sharing). In these instances MUMPS also assumes the responsibility of scheduling the tasks, communicating between the tasks, and arbitrating between the various concurrent processes.

Often MUMPS runs under the auspices of another general-purpose operating system, such as VM, VMS, or MS-DOS, but, for the most part, the MUMPS programmer is unaware of this fact. MUMPS provides a layer of insulation between individual MUMPS processes and the physical computer environment under which they are running.

2.1 Interpreters

MUMPS has the outward appearance of an interpreted language; it interprets instructions at the time of execution. This is in contrast to many other languages, which require that the instructions first be converted to machine language before they can be executed (a step usually referred to as compilation). Interpreted languages have certain advantages over compiled languages. Because the commands are decoded at the time of execution, most interpreted languages permit a direct mode of operation in addition to a mode for running existing programs. Direct mode operation allows a programmer to execute commands directly from the keyboard, rather than having to go through the process of first writing a program, compiling, and then executing it. Direct mode command entry permits the programmer to easily test language constructs, and also provides an ideal environment for debugging programs, which is not typically available to the users of compiled languages.

Interpreted languages also have disadvantages, the chief of which is the reduced speed of execution due to the overhead of interpreting each command at the time of execution. To reduce this overhead, many MUMPS implementations partially compile MUMPS code before it is executed. The instructions are not reduced to assembler language; instead, they are reduced to a level intermediate between the source code and the actual machine instructions necessary to perform the task. It is still necessary for MUMPS to interpret the compiled instructions before execution, but much of the overhead (checking for correct syntax, and the like) has already been performed and, consequently, program execution is faster. In most cases this compilation phase is transparent to the programmer; when saving the program to disk, MUMPS automatically compiles the source code and saves both source and compiled versions. As far as programmers are concerned, they are still dealing with an interpreted language, and MUMPS still allows immediate execution of commands entered from the keyboard.

2.2 Concept of Directories and Partitions

This section examines some of the operating system characteristics of MUMPS, especially the manner in which the system manages multiple processes. As we explore the concepts of job partitions, name spaces, and directories, we will use logical models of the environment. Various versions of MUMPS may be implemented using altogether different approaches, but the overall concepts and limiting factors are covered in the model presented. A general model of the MUMPS environment can be depicted as in Figure 2.1.

The operating system represents the control program under which the computer is operating, such as VM, VMS, UNIX, or MS-DOS, and the various tasks represent programs that are overseen by the operating system. These tasks are usually independent programs, often tied to different users on the computer. The operating system is responsible for ensuring that the different tasks are given

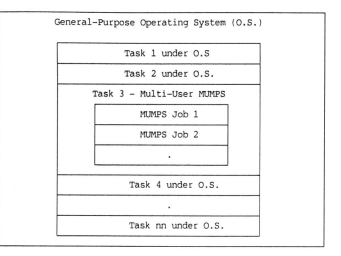

```
┌─────────────────────────────────────────────────┐
│                                                   │
│       General-Purpose Operating System (O.S.)     │
│                                                   │
│    ┌─────────────────────────────────────────┐   │
│    │          Task 1 under O.S               │   │
│    ├─────────────────────────────────────────┤   │
│    │          Task 2 under O.S.              │   │
│    ├─────────────────────────────────────────┤   │
│    │      Task 3 - Multi-User MUMPS          │   │
│    │   ┌─────────────────────────────────┐   │   │
│    │   │        MUMPS Job 1              │   │   │
│    │   ├─────────────────────────────────┤   │   │
│    │   │        MUMPS Job 2              │   │   │
│    │   ├─────────────────────────────────┤   │   │
│    │   │              .                  │   │   │
│    │   └─────────────────────────────────┘   │   │
│    ├─────────────────────────────────────────┤   │
│    │          Task 4 under O.S.              │   │
│    ├─────────────────────────────────────────┤   │
│    │              .                          │   │
│    ├─────────────────────────────────────────┤   │
│    │          Task nn under O.S.             │   │
│    └─────────────────────────────────────────┘   │
│                                                   │
└─────────────────────────────────────────────────┘
```

FIGURE 2.1. MUMPS model

appropriate slices of time in which to be executed and is also responsible for interfacing with all the devices (terminals, disks, magnetic tape, and so on) on the system. Most tasks make requests for devices through the operating system; they do not address them directly.

MUMPS is simply another task in this model. It competes with other tasks for resources on the computer (execution time, devices, and so on). On the other hand, MUMPS can also manage, independently from the operating system, a number of MUMPS jobs or processes. Each of these processes is analogous to a task under the operating system, but one that operates under the control of MUMPS rather than under the direct control of the system. Typically, each MUMPS job is an independent process that is often directly associated with an end user.

In some MUMPS implementations there is no other operating system. In these cases the model compresses one level with the operating system and the other tasks being removed. MUMPS then takes on all the responsibilities normally handled by the operating system.

2.2.1 Partitions

Each MUMPS job is assigned a partition or work space in which to operate (Figure 2.2). This partition is used to hold all the necessary data for a single MUMPS job, including space for the program, for local variables, and for system information related to that job. Partitions in MUMPS are generally on the order of 10,000 bytes (a byte is equivalent to a character) in size. This is usually divided into a fixed area for system information related to the job and two other areas: one for temporary variable storage and one for program code. Often these two latter areas compete for space; that is, the more space taken up for MUMPS code, the less is available for variables.

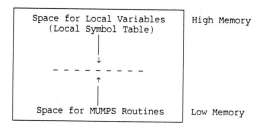

```
┌─────────────────────────────┐
│  Space for Local Variables  │  High Memory
│    (Local Symbol Table)     │
│              │              │
│              ↓              │
│     - - - - - - - - -       │
│              ↑              │
│              │              │
│   Space for MUMPS Routines  │  Low Memory
└─────────────────────────────┘
```

FIGURE 2.2. A MUMPS partition

As new local variables are created by a MUMPS process, they are added to the variable area known as the *local symbol table*. When routines are called or loaded from disk, they are moved from disk into the partition for execution. The actual MUMPS interpreter is usually shared by all MUMPS jobs and resides outside the partition area.

While the model depicted in Figure 2.2 represents how partitions are often implemented, it may be somewhat misleading; the *Portability Standard* developed by the MUMPS Development Committee defines variable and program space in somewhat different terms. In the following discussions on portability issues, the numbers given represent the current *type B* proposals to the *Portability Standard*. Almost all implementations currently support partitions well in excess of the definitions in the current *Portability Standard*.

There are separate limits for program and variable space, each of which is 5,000 bytes long. That is, a program that consists of 5,000 or fewer bytes of source code and uses 5,000 bytes or less of variable space should run on all implementations of MUMPS. By this definition, the space reserved for local variables and routines may be considered separate areas, and it may not be possible to trade off between program size and variable space. In general, programmers should keep the amount of code for an individual routine to less than 5,000 bytes and the amount of space required for local, temporary variables to less than 5,000 bytes.

┌───┐
│   │
│ Individual routines should be held to   │
│ under 5,000 bytes in length.   │
│   │
└───┘

┌───┐
│   │
│ The total amount of space taken up by local │
│ variables should be less than 5,000 bytes.   │
│   │
└───┘

The portability limitation of 5,000 bytes of source code for any MUMPS routine does not mean that an application is limited to this size. Usually an application consists of many routines that are invoked by other routines. As each subroutine is called, the status of the calling routine is saved, the new routine is loaded from disk into the partition, and execution continues with the called subroutine. When the subroutine is finished, the original calling routine is loaded back into the partition, and execution continues after the command that invoked the subroutine. This is a simplification of the actual process, but it illustrates the general concept of routine swapping. A given application may be very large, consisting of hundreds of routines, but individual routines should be limited in size to 5,000 bytes.

In many other languages it is necessary to link all the routines that comprise a package before they can be run. When the application is invoked, the main routine and all its subroutines are loaded into memory for execution. Loading all related programs makes execution of the application relatively fast, since no additional disk reads are required as subroutines are called, but it requires substantially more memory, as enough space must be reserved for all the routines used in the application. In contrast, MUMPS uses an *overlay* philosophy where called routines are loaded from disk *on top of* the calling routine each time they are invoked. This reduces the memory requirements for each application at the expense of the time required to load subroutines from disk as they are invoked. To reduce the time required for loading subroutines from disk, most implementations employ sophisticated routine buffering schemes that keep frequently called subroutines resident in memory buffers.

Note that, in the discussion of swapping in routines, we made no mention of the area reserved for temporary variables in the partition. When a new routine is loaded into the partition, the variable area *remains intact*. That is, the variables available to the calling routine are available to the invoked routine; variables established by the called routine will be available to the calling routine when control is passed back. In this aspect, MUMPS is quite different from most other languages, because the called routine becomes an extension of the calling routine. Most other languages define a new variable environment when a subroutine is called. This can also be done in MUMPS (see Chapter 9 on parameter passing and the NEW command), but the general philosophy is that all routines that share a partition also share a common variable area.

> Temporary local variable space (*local symbol table*) is shared between all routines called within a single partition (or Job).

2.2.2 Directories

In MUMPS, each job or process (that is, an activity that has been assigned a partition) runs independently of other MUMPS jobs or processes. Certainly, there are methods of communication between tasks, but, for the most part, they run as if alone on the computer. In addition, most MUMPS systems provide for directories to hold disk files (programs and databases). The directory used by a given process is usually determined at sign-on time when a partition is assigned. Use of multiple disk directories permits the programmer to modify routines or databases in one directory while, at the same time, applications are using other copies of the routines and databases that reside in a separate directory. Directories are also referred to as user class identifiers (UCIs), name spaces, or data sets under different implementations of MUMPS, but their functions are the same, regardless of the name.

> Each directory in MUMPS is unique from other directories; separate directories can hold different versions of programs and databases with the same names.

In addition, there is usually a library directory (often called the manager's directory) that contains library routines and databases. The names of library routines and databases all start with a special character (the percent sign, %), and references to these routines or databases are automatically mapped by MUMPS to the library directory. Routines and databases beginning with a % are usually permitted *only* in the library directory, but they can be accessed from all other directories.

2.2.3 Name Spaces: Local and Global

We have discussed, in general, how MUMPS handles temporary or local variables; when MUMPS encounters a reference to a variable name, it searches the local symbol table in the partition for that variable. Local variables are available only to the process running in that partition and, as soon as the process finishes and relinquishes the partition, all local variables associated with that partition are lost.

> Local variables are transient. Once the process using them terminates, they are deleted.

There is another type of variable in MUMPS that overcomes this limitation and forms the heart of MUMPS databases. This variable is called a **GLOBAL** variable and is mapped not to the local symbol table, but rather to disk under the directory associated with the process. Local variable names all begin with an alphabetic character or with the percent character (%), and all such variable references are mapped to the local symbol table within the partition. Global variables are identified by the special character up-arrow (^), which is appended to the front of the variable name. All global variables are mapped to disk and become available to *all* MUMPS processes sharing the same directory. These variables are not automatically deleted on completion of the process, but remain on disk until they are specifically removed. The use of global arrays (that is, arrays in which the first character of the name is an up-arrow, ^) is the basic structure of databases in MUMPS.

Global variables are mapped to disk where they remain until specifically removed. Global variables are available to all other processes within the same directory.

The global storage area can be viewed as a more permanent form of a local symbol table. In MUMPS there is no need to OPEN and CLOSE global data files. In addition, there is no limit to the number of files (global variables) that can be open at any given time.

There is no limit on the number of global files that can be open at a given time. Global variables can be considered an extension of local variables.

Clearly, there are many advantages to this type of file structure, although there are also some disadvantages. Since global nodes can be accessed at any time, by any process, it is necessary to provide a mechanism whereby access to sections of the databases can be limited during critical periods. This is provided in MUMPS by the LOCK command, which is discussed in Sections 3.5.4 and 10.4.

Additionally, there is no limitation on the maximum file size of a global array imposed by the language. However, some versions of MUMPS, especially layered implementations running under the control of another operating system, have size limitations that are imposed by that operating system. Additional information on arrays, globals, and variable naming conventions is provided in Chapter 4.

2.3 Jobs (Processes)

A job or process in MUMPS is a computing activity that is associated with a partition. It can be an executing application program or a programmer working in direct mode. Each job is isolated from other jobs in that all local variables used by a job are unique to a partition and cannot be examined or changed by other jobs. For the most part, different processes run independently, although they can communicate with each other through the use of global variables. It is possible for an application to spawn another process by starting another job in a new partition using the JOB command (Section 3.5.3). These started or background tasks are assigned their own partition. Communications between the starting and started tasks are usually accomplished through global variables.

2.4 Chapter Highlights

- Individual routines should be held to under 5,000 bytes in length (2.2.1).
- The total amount of space taken up by local variables should be less than 5,000 bytes (2.2.1).
- Temporary local variable space (local symbol table) is shared between all routines called within a single partition (or job) (2.2.1).
- Each directory in MUMPS is unique from other directories; separate directories can hold different versions of routines and databases with the same names (2.2.2).
- Local variables are transient. Once the process using them terminates, they are deleted (2.2.3).
- Global variables are mapped to disk, where they remain until specifically removed. Global variables are available to all other processes using the same directory (2.2.3).
- There is no limit to the number of global files that can be open at any given time. Global variables can be considered an extension of local variables (2.2.3).

3

MUMPS Commands

This chapter examines both the function and the syntax of all MUMPS commands. Individuals already familiar with MUMPS might benefit from a quick review of each of the commands in their various forms, especially some of the more recent additions to the language, such as the NEW command, use of the DO command with parameters, and the QUIT command when used to terminate an extrinsic function. A brief summary of the commands (with examples) can be found in Appendix C.

The beginning MUMPS programmer is advised to at least skim through the entire list of commands, paying particular attention to the introductory sections of the various command types (Sections 3.1 through 3.5). You should examine in greater detail the **SET**, **WRITE**, and **DO** commands, as they will be used extensively in examples in Chapters 4 and 5. Then come back and examine the remaining commands in greater detail as they are encountered in other sections of the text. Don't worry initially about some of the extended syntactical constructs such as *indirection* or *postconditioning*; these concepts will be covered in Chapters 6 and 7.

In describing the MUMPS commands, we use a uniform format for defining the basic syntax, as well as the additional syntactical forms that are permitted (such as postconditioning, indirection, and others). The basic command definition will be in the following format:

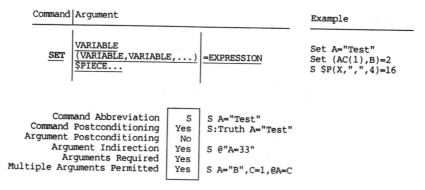

FIGURE 3.1. Command definition format

Each command definition consists of two parts: (1) a definition of the basic syntax with examples, and (2) a table summarizing whether or not the command can use some of the broader syntactical constructions such as postconditioning or indirection. Figure 3.1 depicts these two parts as defined for the **SET** command.

In the first part of the definition, the vertical bars separate the various elements that, together, make up a command. The leftmost field is the command being defined (the **SET** command in this example), and the fields to the right of the first vertical bar are additional elements needed to complete the command. In cases where an element can be of more than one form [for example, the second field in Figure 3.1 can be either **VARIABLE** or **(VARIABLE,VARIABLE,...)** or **$PIECE...**], each possible choice is displayed on a separate line. If an element is optional, then it will be enclosed in square brackets [...] (for example, the PARAMETER field for the DO command defined in Section 3.3.2). In essence, we have something that resembles a menu at a Chinese restaurant; pick one item from the first column, one from the second, and so on, to build a complete command. Unless a column is enclosed in square brackets or one of the optional choices is **—no arguments—**, then an entry from that column is *required* to make a complete command. As an example using the definition pictured in Figure 3.1, the following formats of the **SET** command are permitted:

SET VARIABLE = EXPRESSION	Set A = "Test"
SET (VARIABLE,VARIABLE,...) = EXPRESSION	Set (A,C(1),B) = 2
SET $PIECE... = EXPRESSION	Set $P(X,",",4) = 16

The second part of the definition elaborates on syntactical constructs that may or may not be allowed for a given command. Each valid syntactical form also has an example to demonstrate its use. For the present, the beginning programmer should ignore the second, third, and fourth entries in this table defining postconditioning and indirection; as mentioned earlier, these will be covered in more detail in succeeding chapters.

There are many possible ways to organize and present the individual commands (alphabetically, in order of increasing complexity, by overall function, and so on). In order to establish some organization, we group the commands into broad categories that define their primary function. Traditional groupings of computer language elements include the following

1. *Declaration commands*: These commands are used to define the variable environment, such as the type of values that can be associated with a particular variable name (integer, floating point, string, and so on), statements that reserve space for arrays, and statements that define common, shared variables. The MUMPS language dynamically manages the variable environment during program execution and neither requires nor supports declaration commands.

MUMPS neither requires nor supports declaration commands.

---

2. *Assignment commands*: Assignment commands are used to alter the variable environment by linking data values to variable names, deleting variables, or temporarily redefining the variable environment during the execution of a subroutine.

3. *Conditional commands*: Conditional commands are those used to alter the normal sequential execution of commands [that is, if a given condition exists, execute the following command(s), otherwise don't execute them].

4. *Flow control commands*: These commands are used to alter the normal, sequential execution of program steps. They include commands to invoke subroutines and to perform logic branching.

5. *Input/output commands*: Commands of this type are used to attach peripherals, such as terminals, printers, and magnetic tapes to a process and to transfer information to and from the process and the device.

6. *System and miscellaneous directives*: This is a catchall category for commands that cannot easily be categorized in any of the preceding groups. MUMPS commands can be organized in the traditional groupings as follows

Assignment	Conditional	Flow Control	Input/ Output	System and Misc.
3.1.1 SET	3.2.1 IF	3.3.1 GOTO	3.4.1 OPEN	3.5.1 BREAK
3.1.2 KILL	3.2.2 ELSE	3.3.2 DO	3.4.2 USE	3.5.2 HANG
3.1.3 NEW	3.2.3 FOR	3.3.3 QUIT	3.4.3 READ	3.5.3 JOB
		3.3.4 HALT	3.4.4 WRITE	3.5.4 LOCK
		3.3.5 XECUTE	3.4.5 CLOSE	3.5.5 VIEW

In many instances, commands have attributes such that they could be placed in more than one group. Consider the READ command. This command is used to read information from a peripheral device such as a keyboard or a magnetic tape and associate the results of the input operation with a variable name. As such, it could be placed in either the ASSIGNMENT or the INPUT/OUTPUT group. In instances of this nature, the command will be arbitrarily assigned to a logically consistent group (the READ command is included in the INPUT/OUTPUT category).

In addition, MUMPS provides a rich syntactic environment where the execution of virtually all commands can be made conditional based on the run-time environment. This syntax is noted in the descriptions of the individual commands in the chapter and is explored in greater detail in Section 6.1.4.

3.1 Assignment Commands

Assignment statements are used to alter the variable environment by establishing linkages between variable names and data values. In addition, they are used to delete variables from the operating environment or to temporarily alter the variable environment for the scope of a given process.

All the commands described in this section are used to associate data values with variable names or to delete (permanently or temporarily) variables from the run-time environment. Variables are defined in greater detail in Chapter 4. For use in this chapter, consider a variable to be a symbolic name that is used to reference a data value. All variable names start with an alphabetic character (upper- or lowercase) or the special characters ˆ or %, which can then be followed by additional alpha or numeric characters. Variable names can be of any length, but only the first eight characters are used in resolving names. Variable names are case sensitive (that is, "MILES" is different from "Miles").

The following commands are covered in this section:

SET command	Assigns a data value to a variable name.
KILL command	Deletes a variable and its associated data value from the current variable environment.
NEW command	Temporarily redefines the variable environment for specific variables for the duration of a process (i.e., during the execution of a subroutine).

3.1.1 SET Command

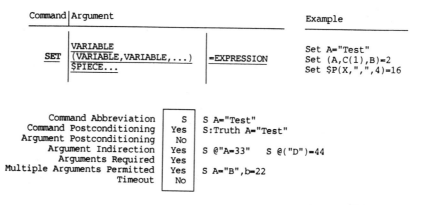

The SET command provides one of the two means available in MUMPS for setting the contents of a variable name equal to a value (the other being the READ command). The VARIABLE being set does not have to be defined before execution of the SET command, but all VARIABLEs encountered in EXPRESSION on the right side of the equals sign (=) must have been previously defined. The KILL command is the logical opposite of the SET command and is used to delete local and global variables. In addition, both the NEW command and parameter passing can affect the local symbol table. Chapter 4 defines, in considerable detail, how an EXPRESSION is evaluated.

The beginning programmer should concentrate on the first form of the SET command (SET VARIABLE = ARGUMENT; Section 3.1.1.1); the remaining two forms, while useful, are not essential in understanding MUMPS and will not be used in the examples in the following three chapters.

3.1.1.1 VARIABLE = EXPRESSION This is the most common format of the SET command. VARIABLE is any valid variable name and can be a simple local variable or a subscripted array element (either local or global). If the VARIABLE is undefined before the SET command, MUMPS will create a new variable and assign the value of EXPRESSION to it. If the variable is already defined, the value of EXPRESSION will replace the value originally associated with the variable name. Consider the following example:

```
o|>Set A=12,B=2,C=A*B Write A," Times ",B," = ",C↵        |o
 |12 Times 2 = 24                                         |
 |>                                                       |
```

EXAMPLE 3.1. Set VARIABLE = EXPRESSION

In this example, we use the SET command to initialize the variable <u>A</u> to the value of <u>12</u>, the variable <u>B</u> to the value of <u>2</u>, and the variable <u>C</u> to the product of <u>A</u> times <u>B</u>. The WRITE command following the SET command is used to display the three variables; arguments to the WRITE command that are enclosed in quotes (" Times ") are output as strings of characters.

3.1.1.2 (VARIABLE,VARIABLE,...) = EXPRESSION This is an extension of the simple SET VARIABLE = EXPRESSION, which is a useful shorthand when setting a number of VARIABLEs equal to a common value (EXPRESSION). Each variable in the list surrounded by parentheses is set to the value of EXPRESSION.

```
o|>S (Count,Sum,Average)=0 W "The COUNT is : ",Count,!↵     |o
 |The COUNT is : 0                                          |
 |>Write "Average=",Average," Sum=",Sum↵                    |
o|Average=0   Sum=0                                         |o
 |>                                                         |
```

EXAMPLE 3.2. Set (VARIABLE,VARIABLE) = EXPRESSION

Special note should be taken of the similarity of this syntax and the syntax of the exclusive KILL [for example, KILL (VARIABLE,VARIABLE,...)] that is described in the next section. While the SET and KILL are complementary commands, the functional difference between the two commands when parentheses are used is quite different. The effect of a KILL (VARIABLE,VARIABLE,...) command is to KILL all local variables *except* those enclosed within the parentheses, while the SET (VARIABLE,VARIABLE,...) syntax is used to establish a value for the variables enclosed in parentheses.

3.1.1.3 $PIECE... = EXPRESSION

The term $PIECE refers to a MUMPS FUNCTION used to manipulate pieces of text within a string. Functions, and more particularly the $PIECE function, are described in more detail in Section 8.1.2.4, but a summary of that function will be provided here so that we can examine its use in the SET command.

$PIECE, when used as part of a general expression, returns one or more substrings from a target string based on a specified delimiter and position. Consider the following example:

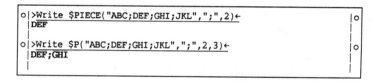

```
o|>Write $PIECE("ABC;DEF;GHI;JKL",";",2)←
 |DEF
 |
o|>Write $P("ABC;DEF;GHI;JKL",";",2,3)←
 |DEF;GHI
 |
```

EXAMPLE 3.3. $PIECE Function

In both examples the target string consists of the characters "ABC;DEF;GHI;JKL", and the delimiter we have defined is the semicolon character (";"). In the first example, MUMPS has been instructed to "write out the second piece of the target string using the semicolon character to define how the string is to be delimited." The second example shows a case where an optional fourth parameter is included in the $PIECE function. It instructs MUMPS to "write the second through third piece of the target string using the semicolon character as a string delimiter." Note, in the second case, the semicolon separating the second and third pieces of the target string is also retrieved.

When $PIECE is used as part of a general expression (that is, whenever it is used on the right side of the equal sign in a SET command), it *extracts* characters from the target string. When used on the left side of the equals sign (=) in a SET command, it has the opposite effect: the results of EXPRESSION are *inserted* into the target string. Consider the following examples:

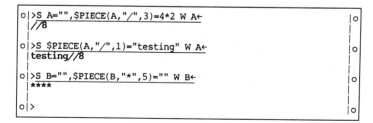

```
o|>S A="",$PIECE(A,"/",3)=4*2 W A←
 |//8
 |
o|>S $PIECE(A,"/",1)="testing" W A←
 |testing//8
 |
o|>S B="",$PIECE(B,"*",5)="" W B←
 |****
 |
o|>
```

EXAMPLE 3.4. Set $PIECE

The English equivalent of the first command in Example 3.4 is "set the third piece of the variable A using the character "/" as a delimiter to the results of the calculation 4*2; it is implied in the command that if the variable A does not contain enough "/" characters to define the third field, append the appropriate number of "/" characters to the end of variable A before executing the command."

When the $PIECE function is used on the left side of an equal sign (=) in a SET command, the first argument in the $PIECE function *must* evaluate to a legal VARIABLE name (simple variable or array element, local or global). Notice that only *four* asterisks were inserted in the target variable; the fifth piece of the string follows the fourth delimiting character.

In all examples, the target variable is changed by inserting EXPRESSION at the appropriate place determined by the delimiting string and the position(s) defined by the third argument. If the target variable does not contain enough delimiters, they are automatically appended to the end of the target variable before EXPRESSION is inserted. If the target variable does not exist at the time of execution, it is created and initialized to null before the SET is executed. One further example demonstrates the use of the $PIECE function with the fourth optional argument.

```
o|>S A=";;;;;",$P(A,";",2,4)="replace" W A←        |o
 |;replace;;                                        |
 |>Set $P(A,";",2)="REPLACE" Write A←               |
o|;REPLACE;;                                        |o
 |>                                                 |
```

EXAMPLE 3.5. Set $PIECE, 4 argument

Note that, in the first part of this example, we have requested that the second through fourth piece of the target variable A be replaced with "replace"; since the replacement string did *not* contain the delimiting character (;), the resulting string contains *two* fewer semicolons than before the SET $PIECE was executed.

3.1.2 KILL Command

Command	Argument		Example
KILL	—no arguments—		KILL S A=1
	VARIABLE		KILL A K ^C(3)
	(LOCAL VARIABLE,LOCAL VARIABLE,...)		KILL (A,B,C)

Command Abbreviation	K	K A
Command Postconditioning	Yes	K:Truth A,B,C
Argument Postconditioning	No	
Argument Indirection	Yes	S A="B" K @A
Arguments Required	No	K S A=1
Multiple Arguments Permitted	Yes	K A,B,^XYZ,D
Timeout	No	

The KILL command is the logical opposite of the SET command and is used to delete variables from the local symbol table as well as from the disk (global variables). It does have a few subtle differences from the SET command. When KILLing an array node (local or global), that node *and all its descendants* are killed. If the name of an array (local or global, without subscripts) is used as an argument to a KILL command, then the *entire* array is KILLed. Also, the parenthesized form of the KILL command has a different functional meaning than the parenthesized form of the SET command.

Additional MUMPS commands and language features such as the NEW command and parameter passing also have an effect on the local variable environment. Both of these features initiate sequences that will invoke a temporary *implied KILL* (see the definition of the NEW command in this chapter and a discussion of parameter passing in Chapter 9).

3.1.2.1 Argumentless KILL   The KILL command with *no* arguments will kill all *local variables*. This must be taken in the context of the current local variable environment and how that environment is affected by both the NEW command and parameter passing (which performs an implied NEW command). Detailed discussion of this environment is deferred until the definition of the NEW command (Section 3.1.3 and Chapter 9).

We examine command and line syntax in more detail in Chapter 6, but note that an argumentless KILL command *must* be separated from the next command on the same line with *two* spaces (one for the missing argument and one to separate the KILL command from the next command on the line); if there are no additional commands on the line, then no spaces are required after the KILL command.

```
o|>Set A=22,B=3 Kill   Write A*B←               |o
 |<UNDEFINED> ERROR                             |
 |>                                             |
```

EXAMPLE 3.6.   Argumentless KILL

In this example, the KILL command deletes the two variable names that were established with the SET command. When the expression A*B is evaluated for the WRITE command, we encounter an UNDEFINED error; neither the variable A nor the variable B are defined after the KILL command. Also note the *two* spaces between the KILL command and the WRITE command; if we had used only one space to separate these commands, we would have gotten a ⟨SYNTAX⟩ ERROR.

3.1.2.2 Inclusive KILL   The inclusive KILL command, that is, **Argument = VARIABLE,VARIABLE,...**, specifically deletes those VARIABLES in the argument list. No error occurs if a variable in the argument list is undefined.

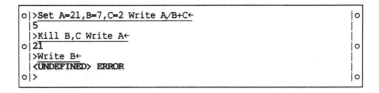

```
o|>Set A=21,B=7,C=2 Write A/B+C←       |o
 |5                                    |
 |>Kill B,C Write A←                   |
o|21                                   |o
 |>Write B←                            |
 |<UNDEFINED> ERROR                    |
o|>                                    |o
```

EXAMPLE 3.7. Inclusive KILL

3.1.2.3 Exclusive KILL The exclusive KILL command, that is, **Argument = (LOCAL VARIABLE,LOCAL VARIABLE,...)**, deletes all LOCAL VARIABLES *except* those specifically listed within the parentheses. Again, as with all forms of the KILL command, this is done within the context of the current variable environment, especially as this environment relates to the NEW command. Global variables are *not* affected by the exclusive KILL.

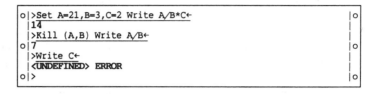

```
o|>Set A=21,B=3,C=2 Write A/B*C←       |o
 |14                                   |
 |>Kill (A,B) Write A/B←               |
o|7                                    |o
 |>Write C←                            |
 |<UNDEFINED> ERROR                    |
o|>                                    |o
```

EXAMPLE 3.8. Exclusive KILL

It is *illegal* to use a subscripted array reference as arguments for the exclusive KILL. However, the unsubscripted array name may be used. See Section 3.1.2.4 for more information on this constraint.

3.1.2.4 Advanced Considerations Two additional areas should be explored in conjunction with the KILL command: (1) how the KILL works with arrays, and (2) some interesting effects when KILLing variables that are passed in as parameters to subroutines.

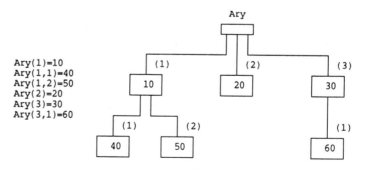

Ary(1)=10
Ary(1,1)=40
Ary(1,2)=50
Ary(2)=20
Ary(3)=30
Ary(3,1)=60

FIGURE 3.2. Hierarchical array structure

KILLing Arrays and Array Branches MUMPS arrays (both local and global) are hierarchical in structure; they are often referred to as tree-structured and resemble the root structure of a plant. The MUMPS KILL command can be used to kill the entire array or selected branches of the array. Consider the MUMPS array structure in Figure 3.2, which represents a hypothetical MUMPS array in which the boxes contain data values and the pathways to each value are identified by subscripts (enclosed in parentheses). For example, the array element Ary(1,2) has an associated data value of 50.

The MUMPS KILL command can either be used to kill the *entire* array (Example 3.9) or *selected branches* (Example 3.10).

```
o|>Write Ary(1,2)←                                              |o
 |50                                                            |
 |>Kill Ary←                                                    |
o|>Write Ary(1,2)←                                              |o
 |<UNDEFINED> ERROR                                             |
 |>Write Ary(1)←                                                |
o|<UNDEFINED> ERROR                                             |o
 |>                                                             |
```

EXAMPLE 3.9. KILL entire array

```
o|>Write Ary(1),",",Ary(1,2),",",Ary(3,1)←                     |o
 |10,50,60                                                      |
 |>Kill Ary(1,2),Ary(3)←                                        |
o|>Write Ary(1)←                                                |o
 |10                                                            |
 |>Write Ary(1,2)←                                              |
o|<UNDEFINED> ERROR                                             |o
 |>Write Ary(3,1)←                                              |
 |<UNDEFINED> ERROR                                             |
o|>Write Ary(1,1)←                                              |o
 |40                                                            |
 |>                                                             |
```

EXAMPLE 3.10. KILL of selected array branches

When KILLing selected branches of an array, the data node defined by the subscripts, *all descendant data nodes*, and *all immediate predecessor nodes containing only pointers to the deleted node* (that is, up to, but not including, the next highest node in the path defined by the subscripts that contains data or that points to other branches) are also deleted. If there is only one data node in an array, killing that node would result in killing the entire array.

It is important to note, again, that it is *illegal* to use a subscripted array element as an argument for an exclusive KILL command. You may use the name of an entire array, but you cannot do an exclusive KILL on only a branch of the array.

```
o|>Kill (Ary)←                                                |o
 |>Write Ary(1)←                                              |
 |10                                                          |
o|>Kill (Ary(1))←                                             |o
 |<SYNTAX> ERROR                                              |
 |>                                                           |
```

EXAMPLE 3.11. Exclusive KILL of arrays

KILLing Parameters within a Subroutine There are some interesting implications that are encountered when the KILL command is used within a subroutine to kill parameters that have been passed to the subroutine. Normally, a subroutine does not kill the variables in the FORMAL parameter list (see Section 3.3.2.2 and Chapter 9 for details on parameter passing); there is an implied NEW performed on all variable names in the formal parameter list, which ensures that the original values, if any, of these variables will be automatically restored when the subroutine QUITs.

There are two methods for passing data into a subroutine, by VALUE and by REFERENCE (see Sections 9.1.1 and 9.1.2). Passing by VALUE simply initializes a variable name in the formal parameter list with a value passed by the calling program. Passing by REFERENCE, on the other hand, forms an internal linkage between the variable named in the formal parameter list with the corresponding variable name in the actual parameter list. Changes made to the contents of the variable name in the formal list are also reflected back to the corresponding variable named in the actual list.

KILLing a variable name in a subroutine whose contents were initialized by VALUE has no impact on the variable environment of the calling routine. However, KILLing a variable name from the formal parameter list that has been initialized by REFERENCE in the actual list has the effect of killing *both* the variable named in the formal list *and* the associated variable name in the actual list. On return to the calling routine, the original variable name passed by reference *no longer exists*. Variable names passed by reference in the actual list of parameters are identified by a period preceding the variable name.

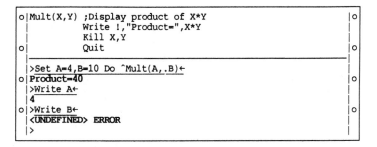

```
o|Mult(X,Y) ;Display product of X*Y                          |o
 |          Write !,"Product=",X*Y                           |
 |          Kill X,Y                                         |
o|          Quit                                             |o
 |_____|
 |>Set A=4,B=10 Do ^Mult(A,.B)←                              |
o|Product=40                                                 |o
 |>Write A←                                                  |
 |4                                                          |
o|>Write B←                                                  |o
 |<UNDEFINED> ERROR                                          |
 |>                                                          |
```

EXAMPLE 3.12. KILLing subroutine parameters

It should be reemphasized that one does not normally KILL variable names from the formal parameter list in a subroutine; the implied NEW that is performed on all variable names in the formal parameter list at the beginning of subroutine execution eliminates the need to delete these variable names at the end of the subroutine.

3.1.3 NEW Command[1]

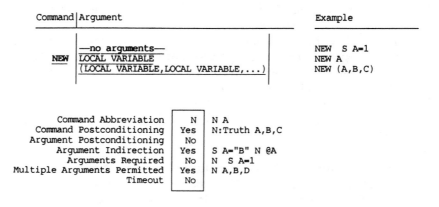

Command	Argument	Example
NEW	—no arguments— LOCAL VARIABLE (LOCAL VARIABLE, LOCAL VARIABLE,...)	NEW S A=1 NEW A NEW (A,B,C)

Command Abbreviation	N	N A
Command Postconditioning	Yes	N:Truth A,B,C
Argument Postconditioning	No	
Argument Indirection	Yes	S A="B" N @A
Arguments Required	No	N S A=1
Multiple Arguments Permitted	Yes	N A,B,D
Timeout	No	

A complete understanding of the NEW command assumes an understanding of how subroutines and extrinsic functions are handled in MUMPS. The beginning programmer is advised to review the function of the DO command (especially Section 3.3.2.2, DO command with parameter passing) before proceeding with the definition of the NEW command. The NEW command is also covered in considerably more detail in Chapter 9.

The NEW command permits the reuse of variable names within the scope of a DO command (that is, within a subroutine), extrinsic functions, and XECUTEd strings. All local variable names and associated data values (including entire arrays) specified by the NEW command are saved, and the variables become undefined. The variable names that have been NEWed can then be used internally within the subroutine. On encountering either an implicit or an explicit QUIT command at the subroutine level, all variables that have been NEWed at that level are KILLed, and any of those defined before the NEW(s) was executed are restored to their original values.

When using parameter passing with either the DO command or with extrinsic functions, there is an implied NEW performed for each variable name in the *formal* list of parameters. However, the implicitly NEWed variable names are not left undefined but, rather, assume the values (or addresses in the case of calls by reference) of the variables in the actual list. If the *actual* list of parameters is *shorter* than the *formal* list, each variable in the formal list without a corresponding entry in the actual list is *undefined* when execution of the subroutine starts. Some care

---

[1]MDC Type A release, January 1987.

must be taken when NEWing variables defined in the formal list of parameters. Since all variables in the formal list are implicitly NEWed, an explicit NEW command with their names makes them undefined in the subroutine.

It is possible to have more than one NEW command at any given subroutine level. The terminating QUIT command for the subroutine counteracts all NEW commands issued at that subroutine level.

Normally, all variables in the partition's local symbol table are available to the called subroutine. All variable names that have not been NEWed can still be used or set by the subroutine; any changes to these variables will be passed back to the calling routine through the common, shared, variable environment. To create an independent subroutine that does not inadvertently alter the variable environment of the calling routine(s), *all* variables whose values are changed within the subroutine should be either implicitly or explicitly NEWed.

It is *illegal* to use a subscripted variable name as an argument to a NEW command, although it is legal to NEW an entire array (that is, the array name *without* subscripts).

3.1.3.1 Argument = —no argument— The NEW command with *no* arguments causes an explicit NEW for *all* variables in the partition's local symbol table. Care should be exercised when using this form of the NEW, especially when using parameter passing. In these cases, there is already an implicit NEW performed on the formal list of parameters, and an argumentless NEW will make these variable names unavailable to the called subroutine.

Also remember that, as in the argumentless form of the KILL command, the argumentless form of the NEW requires two spaces between the NEW command and the next command on the line (see Chapter 6 for a more detailed discussion of command and line syntax).

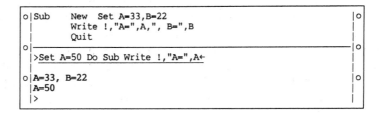

```
o|Sub    New  Set A=33,B=22                               |o
 |       Write !,"A=",A,", B=",B                          |
 |       Quit                                             |
o|-------------------------------------------------------|o
 |>Set A=50 Do Sub Write !,"A=",A←                        |
 |                                                        |
o|A=33, B=22                                              |o
 |A=50                                                    |
 |>                                                       |
```

EXAMPLE 3.13. NEW all

3.1.3.2 Argument = LOCAL VARIABLE This form of the NEW is referred to as the *inclusive NEW* and causes the LOCAL VARIABLE name(s) in the argument list to be NEWed. It is allowed to NEW a variable name that is currently *not* defined; upon encountering a QUIT at the current subroutine level, variable names that were undefined on entering the subroutine will become undefined when control is returned back to the calling routine.

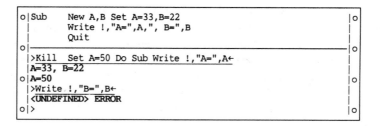

```
o|Sub     New A,B Set A=33,B=22                                  |o
 |              Write !,"A=",A,", B=",B                           |
 |              Quit                                              |
o|---------------------------------------------------------------|o
 |>Kill   Set A=50 Do Sub Write !,"A=",A←                         |
 |A=33, B=22                                                      |
o|A=50                                                            |o
 |>Write !,"B=",B←                                                |
 |<UNDEFINED> ERROR                                               |
o|>                                                               |o
```

EXAMPLE 3.14. Inclusive NEW

3.1.3.3 Argument = (LOCAL VARIABLE,LOCAL VARIABLE,...) This form of
the NEW command is also known as the *exclusive NEW*; all local variable name(s)
not explicitly listed are NEWed. It is similar in function to the argumentless NEW
command in that all variables in the partition's local symbol table *except* those
given in the argument list are NEWed.

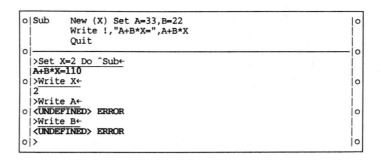

```
o|Sub     New (X) Set A=33,B=22                                  |o
 |              Write !,"A+B*X=",A+B*X                            |
 |              Quit                                              |
o|---------------------------------------------------------------|o
 |>Set X=2 Do ^Sub←                                               |
 |A+B*X=110                                                       |
o|>Write X←                                                       |o
 |2                                                               |
 |>Write A←                                                       |
o|<UNDEFINED> ERROR                                               |o
 |>Write B←                                                       |
 |<UNDEFINED> ERROR                                               |
o|>                                                               |o
```

EXAMPLE 3.15. Exclusive NEW

While it might seem desirable to use this form of the NEW command for
subroutines with parameters, there can be considerable execution overhead in the
use of this syntax. For that reason it is advised that subroutines explicitly NEW
only those variables altered within the subroutine using the inclusive form of the
NEW command (3.1.3.2).

3.1.3.4 Advanced Considerations In understanding exactly what happens to
variables used as arguments to a NEW command, it is also necessary to examine
the context in which they are used (subroutines) and the concept of subroutine
levels. Subroutines are invoked either as the result of executing a DO command
or by evaluating an extrinsic function. A called subroutine can, in turn, call additional subroutines, and they can invoke other subroutines, and so on. This is
often referred to as *nesting* of subroutines and is somewhat analogous to nesting
FOR loops.

Each time a subroutine is invoked, we can picture the process as entering a new level or plane of operation; each time a subroutine QUITs, the process falls back one level to that of the calling routine. NEW commands issued within a subroutine effectively stack the current contents of the named variables and make the variable UNDEFINED. The variables can then be assigned new values and used freely within the level. When a QUIT command is executed to terminate the subroutine and fall back one operating level, all variables that were NEWed at the current level are restored to the value (or undefined status) they had immediately prior to entering the current level. This basically amounts to stacking and unstacking variables, depending on the level of operation.

What happens if one NEWs the same variable more than once at a given level? Each time the variable is NEWed, its status (undefined or associated data value) is stacked, and the variable is made undefined. On QUITting the current level, the variable is restored to the value it had immediately prior to entering that level, which is *not* necessarily the value it had prior to the most recently executed NEW command. The following example demonstrates some of these concepts.

```
o|Sub      New i                                               |o
 |          For i=1:1 New A Set A=i Write " ",A Quit:A=5        |
 |          Write !,"A=",A                                      |
o|          Quit                                                |o
 |_____   |
 |>Set A=100 Do ^Sub←                                          |
o| 1 2 3 4 5                                                    |o
 |A=5                                                           |
 |>Write A←                                                    |
o|100                                                           |o
 |>                                                             |
```

EXAMPLE 3.16.   NEW command issued at same level

Notice that the QUIT command that terminates the FOR loop does not cause the value of the variable A to be altered in any way; only QUIT commands that terminate a subroutine cause an unstacking of NEWed variables. Also notice how the QUIT that terminates the subroutine causes the value of A to be correctly restored to 100 rather than the value saved by the last NEW command (A = 4).

3.2 Conditional Commands

Conditional commands are used to alter the normal sequential execution of instructions based on run-time considerations, usually depending on the values associated with one or more variables. As mentioned earlier, the MUMPS language permits the programmer to *condition* virtually every MUMPS command. This is often referred to as *command postconditioning* or *argument postconditioning* and is covered in detail in Chapter 6.

This section concerns itself only with those commands specifically designed to evaluate run-time conditions and alter execution depending on these conditions. In evaluating these commands, it is important to understand that MUMPS is a line-oriented language; each MUMPS command line can contain one or more individual MUMPS commands. Normally, MUMPS executes commands sequentially; it executes lines from the top of a program down and commands within the line from left to right. In the absence of the commands IF, ELSE, or FOR, it makes little difference if individual commands are strung together on one line or if each command is placed on a separate line.

The commands IF, ELSE, and FOR, however, determine whether or not the rest of the commands on the line are executed; the scope or range of commands affected by these commands is limited to those that follow them on the same line. For our purposes, we will define *conditional commands* as those that determine if, and how often, the remaining commands on the same *line* are executed. Using this definition, the following commands will be covered in this section:

IF command — This command is used to check the condition of one or more variables (or the success of a previously executed command such as a timed READ or LOCK) and enable or disable execution of the rest of the commands on the line.

ELSE command — Similar to the IF command, but checks the inverse (false) status of a previously evaluated expression or command.

FOR command — This command is the primary iteration command in the MUMPS language. It permits repetitive execution of code depending on run-time conditions.

The IF command sets an internal system variable named **$TEST** (Section 4.4.4.5) to a TRUE/FALSE value based on the evaluation of the expression used as the argument to the command. It is this system variable that is used as the *implicit argument* to an ELSE command (which has no argument). It is also important to note that the $TEST system variable can also be set by other types of command operations, such as a timed READ command or a timed LOCK.

3.2.1 IF Command

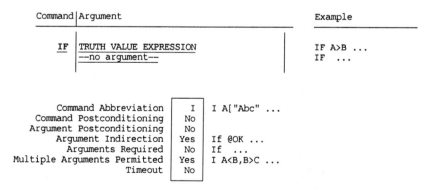

The IF command evaluates a TRUTH VALUE EXPRESSION and, if the results are TRUE (nonzero), execution continues with the next instruction on the command line; if FALSE, the rest of the commands on the line are ignored. The argumentless form is an implied test on the contents of the system variable $TEST, which holds the results of the most recently tested evaluation (via an IF with arguments or a READ, LOCK, JOB, or OPEN command with TIMEOUT syntax).

3.2.1.1 Argument = TRUTH VALUE EXPRESSION In this form of the IF command, the TRUTH VALUE EXPRESSION is evaluated and, if TRUE, the rest of the line is executed; if FALSE, the rest of the commands on the line are ignored. In addition, the system variable $TEST is set to the TRUE/FALSE evaluation of the EXPRESSION and can subsequently be tested with an IF command, an ELSE command, or any other command permitting postconditioning (for example, **DO:$TEST ...**). If you are unfamiliar with either the *contains* or the *greater than* operators, [and > , used in the next example, refer to Sections 5.3.2.2 and 5.3.1.1.

```
o|>Set A=1234,B=123←                                          |o
 |>If B[A Write "B contains A"←                               |
 |                                                            |
o|>If A>B,A[B W "A greater than B and A contains B."←         |o
 |A greater than B and A contains B.                          |
 |>                                                           |
o|                                                            |o
```

EXAMPLE 3.17. If ARGUMENT = TRUTH VALUE EXPRESSION

3.2.1.2 Argument = —no argument— This form is a shorthand method of saying **IF $TEST** and tests the TRUTH status of the system variable $TEST. $TEST is set whenever an IF command with arguments is executed or when a READ, LOCK, JOB, or OPEN command with TIMEOUT has been executed.

```
o|>Set Low=22,Test=14←                                        |o
 |>If Test<Low Set Low=Test←                                  |
 |>If  Write "New Low value = ",Low←                          |
o|New Low value = 14                                          |o
 |>                                                           |
 |                                                            |
```

EXAMPLE 3.18. If ARGUMENT = —no argument—

It is probably worthwhile to note that command and argument postconditional statements do *not* alter the value of $TEST.

```
o|>Set A=1,B=2←                                               |o
 |>If A<B Write "A less than B"←                              |
 |A less than B                                               |
o|>Set:A=B B=B*B←                                             |o
 |>If  Write "$TEST still TRUE"←                              |
 |$TEST still TRUE                                            |
o|>                                                           |o
```

EXAMPLE 3.19. Effect of postconditionals on $T

The conditional SET command ($\underline{\text{Set:A}=B\ B=B*B}$) does *not* alter the value of $TEST established by the preceding IF command.

The related command $\underline{\text{ELSE}}$ is similar to the argumentless IF command except it checks the opposite TRUTH VALUE of $TEST and is equivalent to the command $\underline{\text{IF '\$TEST}}$. The command $\underline{\text{IF '\$TEST}}$, however, would invert the value of $TEST, while the ELSE command does not alter its value.

Remember, like all argumentless commands, *two spaces* are required between the IF command and the next command on the line.

3.2.2 ELSE Command

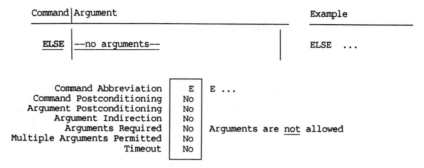

The ELSE command tests the TRUTH status of the system variable $TEST and, if FALSE ($TEST = 0$), execution continues, beginning with the next command on the line; if TRUE ($TEST = 1$), the rest of the commands on the line are ignored. $TEST is set on execution of an IF command with arguments or a READ, LOCK, JOB, or OPEN command with a TIMEOUT specified. The ELSE command is equivalent to an $\underline{\text{IF '\$TEST}}$ command except that it does not alter the value of $TEST ($\underline{\text{IF '\$TEST}}$ reverses the truth value of $TEST).

```
o|>Set A=500,B=250←                                    |o
 |>If A<B Write "A less than B"←                        |
 |>Else  Write "A greater than B"←                      |
o|A greater than B                                      |o
```

EXAMPLE 3.20. ELSE command

Note that there is a mistake in *logic* in this example. If $\underline{\text{A} = B}$ it will be erroneously reported as "A greater than B."

Note, also, that it makes no sense to include an ELSE statement on the same line as an IF statement checking the same value; in the case where the IF fails (and thus the ELSE will succeed), the ELSE will never be executed.

```
o|>Set A="Bcd",B="abc"←                                 |o
 |>If A]B Write "A follows B" Else  W "B follows A"←     |
 |>Write "Oops, ELSE command never executed !"←          |
o|Oops, ELSE command never executed !                   |o
 |>                                                      |
```

EXAMPLE 3.21. ELSE following an IF command

3.2.3 FOR Command

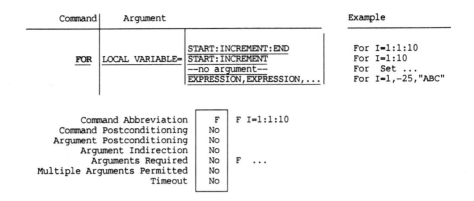

Command	Argument		Example
FOR	LOCAL VARIABLE=	START:INCREMENT:END START:INCREMENT —no argument— EXPRESSION,EXPRESSION,...	For I=1:1:10 For I=1:10 For Set ... For I=1,-25,"ABC"

Command Abbreviation	F	F I=1:1:10
Command Postconditioning	No	
Argument Postconditioning	No	
Argument Indirection	No	
Arguments Required	No	F ...
Multiple Arguments Permitted	No	
Timeout	No	

The FOR command is the primary loop control command in MUMPS with a basic format of For Argument(s) ;execute the remainder of the command line. In English, the FOR command translates to: "For the scope of the arguments, execute the rest of the commands on the line. Terminate execution of the line when the arguments are satisfied or when a QUIT or GOTO command is executed."

3.2.3.1 Argument = START:INCREMENT:END This form of the FOR loop with a START:INCREMENT:END argument is shown in the next example:

```
o|>For i=1:1:5 Set Sqr=i*i Write i," Squared is ",Sqr,!←    |o
 |1 Squared is 1                                             |
 |2 Squared is 4                                             |
o|3 Squared is 9                                            |o
 |4 Squared is 16                                            |
 |5 Squared is 25                                            |
o|>                                                         |o
```

EXAMPLE 3.22. FOR START:INCREMENT:END

We can break down the execution of the FOR loop in this example into the following four steps.

1. Evaluate the START, INCREMENT, and END expressions.
2. Initialize the loop counter **i** to the START value specified in the FOR argument (1).
3. Check the value of the loop counter **i** against the END value (5). If it is greater than the END value, STOP the FOR loop (all done). Otherwise, continue to step 4.
4. Execute the remainder of the MUMPS code on the line following the FOR command.
5. Increment the loop counter **i** by the specified INCREMENT (1). Go to step 3.

In both forms of the FOR command with a START and INCREMENT

specification, all three parameters (START, INCREMENT, and END) are evaluated as numbers *once at the beginning of the loop*. If variables are used as part of these expressions, changing the value of the variable within the scope of the loop will *not* affect execution of the loop. They can be integer or real, positive or negative. In the case of negative INCREMENTS, the English equivalent of the third step listed previously would have to be changed to:

3. Check the value of loop counter **I** against the END value. If it is *less than* the END value, STOP the FOR loop. Otherwise, continue to step 4.

Positive increments cause a check on the loop counter being *greater* than the END value, while negative increments check for the loop counter being *less* than the END value.

```
o|>For LC=-3:-0.1:-3.3 Write LC,","←                    |o
 |-3,-3.1,-3.2,-3.3,                                    |
 |Write LC←                                             |
o|-3.3                                                  |o
 |>                                                     |
```

EXAMPLE 3.23. FOR loop with negative increments

On terminating the loop, the loop counter <u>LC</u> contains the value of the last valid pass through the loop, *not* the value that failed the check in the FOR command (which would have been −**3.4**). Also notice that, if the START value is initialized such that it already exceeds the END value (dependent on the sign of the IN-CREMENT), the <u>FOR</u> loop will *not* be executed, and the loop counter will be left set to the START value.

```
o|>Set Start=20,Increment=1,End=15←                    |o
 |>For I=Start:Increment:End Write !,I←                 |
 |                                                      |
o|>Write "Loop Counter is ",I←                          |o
 |Loop Counter is 20                                    |
 |>                                                     |
```

EXAMPLE 3.24. Value of FOR index on completion of loop

Notice that the values for *start*, *increment*, and *end* are calculated only *once*, at the beginning of the loop. Changing the values of variables used in these expressions within the loop will *not* affect the scope of the loop.

```
o|>Set x="abc" For i=1:1:$L(x) Write $E(x,i) Set x=x_i←  |o
 |abc                                                    |
 |>Write x←                                              |
o|abc123                                                 |o
 |>                                                      |
```

EXAMPLE 3.25. Changing value of END during FOR loop

Normally, the FOR loop will continue until the loop counter exceeds the END value, but there are two other ways to terminate a FOR loop prematurely: (1) execution of a QUIT command, or (2) execution of a GOTO command. The QUIT command will cause the FOR loop to terminate with the loop counter intact at its last assigned value. Execution will continue at the next MUMPS instruction outside the range of the loop (it could be the next line or even on the same line if there are nested FOR loops). The GOTO command unconditionally transfers control of execution to a specified LABEL elsewhere in the program. Consider the following example using nested FOR loops.

```
o|>F L1=1:5:20 W ! F L2=2:2:8 W L1*L2,"," QUIT:L1*L2>50←       |o
 |2,4,6,8,                                                      |
 |12,24,36,48,                                                  |
o|22,44,66,                                                     |o
 |32,64,                                                        |
 |>                                                             |
```

EXAMPLE 3.26. Nested FOR loops

In this example, the QUIT command conditionally terminates the second FOR command, returning control to the outer FOR loop just as if the inner loop had terminated normally. *Note* that some of the values printed *exceed* the loop terminating value of 50; the QUIT command is executed *after* the WRITE command. It is also possible to change the value of the loop counter in the instructions being executed under the control of the FOR loop, but doing so can be dangerous. Both of the following examples change the value of the primary loop counter and will result in the dreaded endless loop since neither example offers an alternative method for terminating the loop.

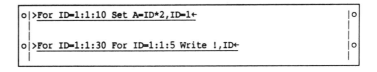

```
o|>For ID=1:1:10 Set A=ID*2,ID=1←                              |o
 |                                                             |
 |                                                             |
o|>For ID=1:1:30 For ID=1:1:5 Write !,ID←                      |o
 |                                                             |
```

EXAMPLE 3.27. Changing the FOR loop index within the loop

3.2.3.2 Argument = START:INCREMENT This form of the FOR loop is similar to the previous form except that no END value is specified and loop termination relies on a QUIT or GOTO command within the loop. This form is frequently used when searching databases with the $ORDER function (described in Chapter 8), where the end condition (that is, the number of subscripts defined at a given level in the global) may be unknown. The reader is referred to the description of the $ORDER function for examples of this type of use. The following example also demonstrates the use of this form of the FOR loop:

```
o|>For I=1:1 Read !,": ",A(I) Quit:A(I)=""←
 |: 10←
 |: 20←
o|: 30←
 |: ←
 |>
```

EXAMPLE 3.28.   FOR START:INCREMENT

3.2.3.3 Argument = —no argument—[2]   The FOR command with *no* argument is a further reduction of the general form FOR LOCAL VARIABLE = START:INCREMENT:END. However, no loop counter is specified in the FOR command and, like the previous form, the loop requires an explicit command (QUIT or GOTO) within the range of the FOR command to terminate loop execution. This form is commonly used when searching databases with the $ORDER function and is demonstrated in the next example.

```
o|>Set sub="",^TEST(20)=1,^TEST(10)=1,^TEST(30)=1←
 |>For  Set sub=$Order(^TEST(sub)) Quit:sub=""  Write !,sub←
 |10
o|20
 |30
 |>
```

EXAMPLE 3.29.   FOR command with no argument

3.2.3.4 Argument = EXPRESSION,EXPRESSION,...   The FOR loop does *not* permit multiple arguments. For example, the command:

For I = 1:1:10,J = 2:2:6 Write !,I*J←

is *illegal*. On the other hand, there is a format that permits a list of discrete elements to be used as the loop variable. Each of these elements can be any EXPRESSION, including a string of characters, as can be seen in the following examples.

```
o|>Set Sum=0,N=0 For I=230,20,-50,100 Set Sum=Sum+I,N=N+1←
 |>Write "The SUM is ",Sum,". The Average is ",Sum/N,"."←
 |The SUM is 300. The average is 75.
o|>
```

EXAMPLE 3.30.   FOR EXPRESSION,EXPRESSION

```
o|>Set N=2 For X="Start","By","End" Set @X=N,N=N*N←
 |>Write Start,", ",By,", ",End←
 |2, 4, 16
o|>
```

EXAMPLE 3.31.   String values in FOR loop argument

[2]MDC Type A release, January 1987.

3.2.3.5 Mixed Arguments While multiple arguments to the FOR command are illegal (for example, For I = 1:1:10,J = 2:2:6 ... is *illegal*), each *parameter* in the argument list can take any of the forms described previously. Mixed argument types are demonstrated in the following example.

```
o|For i=1,5,10:1:13,"ABC",2:2:6 Write !,i←        |o
 |1                                               |
 |5                                               |
o|10                                              |o
 |11                                              |
 |12                                              |
o|13                                              |o
 |ABC                                             |
 |2                                               |
o|4                                               |o
 |6                                               |
 |>                                               |
```

EXAMPLE 3.32. Mixed expression types in FOR command list

3.3 Flow Control Commands

Flow control commands, for purposes of this book, are those used to transfer command execution to code falling outside the scope of the current line. The transfer of control can either be temporary (as in the DO and XECUTE commands), in which control is ultimately returned to the command following the flow control command, or permanent, as in the case of the GOTO command. Note that the distinctions between flow control and conditional commands are somewhat arbitrary. Both control the flow of execution, and it is the scope of the resulting execution that determines into which category the command falls.

Flow control commands that will be discussed in the following section are:

GOTO command	Transfers program execution to another labeled command line or routine. Control is *not* returned to the command following a GOTO after the code branched to has finished.
DO command	This is similar to a CALL subroutine found in many other languages and temporarily transfers control to another labeled MUMPS line or routine. On completion of the code that was invoked, control is returned to the command that follows the original DO command.
QUIT command	The command used to terminate the most recently issued DO or FOR command. Control is transferred back to the command or argument following the original DO command or, in the case of a FOR command, to the first command outside the range of the invoking FOR.
HALT command	Initiates a sequence that results in the unconditional termination of the current process. All devices owned by the process are released back to the system, the current proc-

ess is stopped, and the partition is released back to the system.

XECUTE command   Similar in function to the DO command; however, the MUMPS code to be executed is held as a variable rather than as part of a MUMPS routine. As with the DO command, when the invoked code is finished, control is returned to the command or argument following the initiating XECUTE command.

3.3.1 GOTO Command

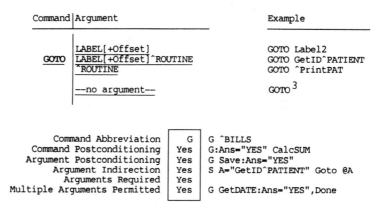

Command	Argument		Example
GOTO	LABEL[+Offset] LABEL[+Offset]^ROUTINE ^ROUTINE		GOTO Label2 GOTO GetID^PATIENT GOTO ^PrintPAT
	—no argument—		GOTO [3]

Command Abbreviation	G	G ^BILLS
Command Postconditioning	Yes	G:Ans="YES" CalcSUM
Argument Postconditioning	Yes	G Save:Ans="YES"
Argument Indirection	Yes	S A="GetID^PATIENT" Goto @A
Arguments Required	Yes	
Multiple Arguments Permitted	Yes	G GetDATE:Ans="YES",Done

The GOTO command transfers program control to a specified label or routine. The transfer of control is absolute; control will *not* be returned to the command following the GOTO.

```
o|Start   Read !,"Do you really want to HALT (Y or N): ",ans  |o
 |        If ans'="Y"&(ans'="N") Write " ??" Goto Start        |
 |        If ans="N" Goto Cont                                 |
o|        Halt                                                 |o
 |Cont    Write !,"Continuing..."                              |
 |          .                                                  |
o|          .                                                  |o
 |_____|
 |>Do Start←                                                   |
o|Do you really want to HALT (Y or N): Maybe← ??               |o
 |Do you really want to HALT (Y or N): N←                      |
 |Continuing...                                                |
```

EXAMPLE 3.33.   GOTO command

When issued while in the scope of a DO command, a GOTO has the effect of extending the range of the DO to the code where control is transferred. Upon executing a QUIT command, regardless of the number of GOTOs performed, control is "popped" back to the command following the initiating DO command.

---

[3]The argumentless form of the GOTO command is *not* defined by the MUMPS standard. Many implementations use a ZGO command instead.

Refer to Section 6.6 for a more detailed discussion concerning *execution levels* and where the GOTO command is and is not allowed.

```
o|Start   Write !,"Enter POSITIVE scores to be Averaged"      |o
 |         Kill Array Set n=0                                  |
 |         For  Do Geta Quit:a="" If a>0 Set n=n+1,Array(n)=a  |
o|         Goto CalcAvg                                        |o
 |Geta     Read !,": ",a If a<0 Goto Error                     |
 |         Quit                                                |
o|Error    Write " ?? - POSITIVE values only." Set a=-1        |o
 |         Quit                                                |
 |_____|
o|>Do Start←                                                  |o
 |Enter POSITIVE scores to be Averaged                         |
 |5←                                                          |
o|15←                                                         |o
 |-3← ?? - POSITIVE values only.                              |
 |3←                                                          |
o|  .                                                         |o
 |  .                                                         |
 |  .                                                         |
```

EXAMPLE 3.34. GOTO extending the range of a DO command

Notice in Example 3.34, when a value of -3 is entered, control is transferred to the part labeled Error. The GOTO extends the range of the part Geta, and the QUIT command on the line Error + 1 has the same effect as the QUIT command in line Geta + 1.

When issued within the scope of a FOR loop, that loop and *all other FORs to the left of the GOTO* in the same line are terminated with the transfer of control.

```
o|Start   W ! F i=1:1:10 F j=1:1:10 W " ",i*j G:i*j>8 Done    |o
 |         W " This line never executed."                      |
 |Done     W " Done."                                          |
o|         Quit                                                |o
 |_____|
 |>Do Start←                                                  |
o|                                                            |o
 | 1 2 3 4 5 6 7 8 9 Done.                                     |
 |>                                                           |
```

EXAMPLE 3.35. GOTO used to terminate a FOR loop

Example 3.35 presents a different format than earlier examples. MUMPS commands can be abbreviated to the first character of the command name ("FOR" = "F") and the command case (upper- or lowercase characters) is immaterial. For the most part, the commands will be spelled out in examples to improve readability, but occasionally they will be abbreviated as in this example. Most older code you will examine will look more like this example, and it is probably wise to expose you to this style. Chapter 3 explores command syntax in greater detail.

Notice that the FOR loop terminates when the expression i*j evaluates to a value that is greater than 8, yet the result of 9 is displayed. The WRITE command precedes the test that terminates the loop. Also notice that the GOTO command in the first line terminates *both* of the FOR loops on that line.

3.3.1.1 Argument = LABEL In this form of the GOTO command, control is transferred to the line defined by LABEL. The labeled line is assumed to be defined in the current routine resident in the partition; if no line with the indicated LABEL is found, an error is generated. If in direct mode, a routine can be loaded into the partition (for example, ZLOAD ROUTINE), and a GOTO LABEL can be issued. Borrowing from the previous example, we could also initiate execution in the following manner:

```
o|>ZLOAD TEST  Goto Start←            |o
 |                                     |
 | 1 2 3 4 5 6 7 8 9 Done.             |
o|>                                   |o
```

EXAMPLE 3.36.   GOTO LABEL

3.3.1.2 Argument = LABEL^ROUTINE The GOTO command in which the argument is LABEL^ROUTINE is similar to the previous form except that the line referenced by LABEL resides in a routine on disk. The routine indicated by ROUTINE is loaded from disk into the partition and execution continues at the designated LABEL.

```
o|>Goto Start^TEST←                    |o
 |                                     |
 | 1 2 3 4 5 6 7 8 9 Done.             |
o|>                                   |o
```

EXAMPLE 3.37.   GOTO LABEL^ROUTINE

3.3.1.3 Argument = ^ROUTINE This syntax is a reduction of the GOTO LABEL^ROUTINE syntax, where the LABEL is not specified and execution begins with the first line of executable code in the specified ROUTINE. As in the previous form, ROUTINE is automatically loaded from disk into the partition before execution continues.

3.3.1.4 Argument = —no argument— The argumentless form of the GOTO command is *not* part of the MUMPS standard but is so often used in MUMPS implementations that it deserves coverage. It is often used in conjunction with the BREAK command (see Section 3.5.1) or when processing errors (Chapter 13) to resume program execution. The BREAK command is used primarily for program debugging and temporarily interrupts the execution of a program and returns to direct mode. While in direct mode, the programmer can examine and/or change the current variable environment before continuing program execution. There is no consistent method for continuing execution of the paused routine, but many implementors have adopted the argumentless form of the GOTO command to achieve program restart. In this aspect, the command could be more aptly defined as a GO command rather than a GOTO.

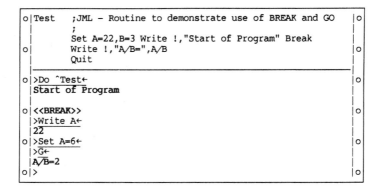

```
o|Test    ;JML - Routine to demonstrate use of BREAK and GO   |o
 |        ;                                                    |
 |        Set A=22,B=3 Write !,"Start of Program" Break        |
o|        Write !,"A/B=",A/B                                   |o
 |        Quit                                                 |
 |_____|
o|>Do ^Test←                                                  |o
 |Start of Program                                            |
 |                                                            |
o|<<BREAK>>                                                   |o
 |>Write A←                                                   |
 |22                                                          |
o|>Set A=6←                                                   |o
 |>G←                                                         |
 |A/B=2                                                       |
o|>                                                           |o
```

EXAMPLE 3.38. Argumentless GOTO

Notice that execution of the BREAK command initiates a message indicating that the computer is now in BREAK mode, and MUMPS shifts into direct mode (indicated by the prompt character after the <<BREAK>> message). While in direct mode, the programmer can examine variables (Write A) and even change their values (Set A = 6). To resume program execution, the argumentless form of the GOTO command is issued in direct mode (abbreviated in the previous example to G). On receipt of the direct mode GO command, program execution continues. In implementations supporting this syntax, the argumentless form of the GOTO is only valid when issued from direct mode and only during the execution of a BREAK command.

Not all implementations use this method for resuming program execution after a BREAK. Some use a ZGO or QUIT command, and others use special function keys; check your documentation for the appropriate command sequence required to resume program execution after a BREAK command.

Section 13.1 explores trapping errors in MUMPS and, more to the point, the use of the argumentless form of the GOTO command to resume execution after an error.

3.3.1.5 GOTO Command with Offset In all forms of the GOTO command with arguments (GOTO LABEL, GOTO LABEL^ROUTINE, or GOTO ^ROUTINE) it is also possible to include an optional Offset to the labeled line to which control is being transferred. Offset is interpreted as a nonnegative integer (zero is allowed) representing the number of lines after the designated LABEL at which program execution will be transferred.

```
o|Test    ;JML - Routine demonstrating GOTO with OFFSETS        |o
 |         Write !,"0-Quit, 1-Option1, 2-Option2, 3-Option3"     |
 |Loop     Read !,"Enter Option (0-3): ",opt                     |
o|         If opt<0!(opt>3) Write " ??" Goto Test                |o
 |         Goto Branch+opt                                       |
 |Branch Write " End of program." Quit                           |
o|         Write " This is Option A" Goto Loop                   |o
 |         Write " This is Option B" Goto Loop                   |
 |         Write " This is Option C" Goto Loop                   |
o|                                                               |o
 |_____|
 |>Do ^Test←                                                     |
o|0-Quit, 1-OptionA, 2-OptionB, 3-OptionC                        |o
 |Enter Option (0-3): 2← This is Option B                        |
 |Enter Option (0-3): 0← End of program.                         |
o|>                                                              |o
```

EXAMPLE 3.39. GOTO LABEL + Offset

Care should be taken when using this syntax as it is not always clear when examining the code being branched to that the relative line positioning after the LABELed line is critical to proper execution. It is all too easy to make relatively minor changes (such as breaking a long command line into two or more lines) that may have significant and adverse effects on subsequent program execution.

3.3.2 DO Command

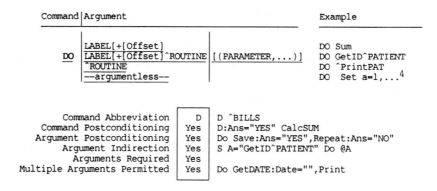

Command	Argument		Example
DO	LABEL[+[Offset]		DO Sum
	LABEL[+[Offset]^ROUTINE	[(PARAMETER,...)]	DO GetID^PATIENT
	^ROUTINE		DO ^PrintPAT
	--argumentless--		DO Set a=1,...[4]

Command Abbreviation	D	D ^BILLS
Command Postconditioning	Yes	D:Ans="YES" CalcSUM
Argument Postconditioning	Yes	Do Save:Ans="YES",Repeat:Ans="NO"
Argument Indirection	Yes	S A="GetID^PATIENT" Do @A
Arguments Required	Yes	
Multiple Arguments Permitted	Yes	Do GetDATE:Date="",Print

The DO command provides the basic function of calling subroutines in MUMPS. The entry point of the subroutine is defined by the argument and is identified in the called subroutine by a line LABEL. The subroutine executes one or more MUMPS commands and terminates when a QUIT is encountered. On termination of the subroutine, control is passed back to the calling routine at the command following the DO that invoked the subroutine, where execution continues.

The invoked subroutine can be a routine (or a *part* of a routine) residing on disk or a *part* of the routine currently resident in the partition. In either case, the

[4]MDC Type A proposal, *Block Structuring.*

invoked routine has the *same* variable environment as existed before the DO was executed. Any variables set by the subroutine and not explicitly KILLed are available to the calling routine. This is a significant departure from the way most languages handle subroutine calls. In most other languages, a called subroutine is given a new variable environment, and only those data elements passed as parameters by the calling routine are available to the subroutine.

3.3.2.1 DO Command without Parameter Passing

In the following section we examine how the DO command works in a relatively simple environment, that is, without parameter passing. We assume that the program named DEMO (Example 3.40) has already been created and filed on the disk. In the listing of the program that follows, we have also included a line number to the left of each line so that we can conveniently refer to command lines in the text description that follows.

```
 1  o|DEMO       ;JML-NYSCVM ; 12/22/86 06:35              |o
 2   |           ;Routine to demonstrate the use of DO command |
 3   |           Kill  For i=1:1:10 Set Ary(i)=i*2         |
 4  o|           Do Average Write "The AVERAGE is ",AVG    |o
 5   |           Kill Ary,AVG,i                            |
 6   |           Quit                                      |
 7  o|Average    Set Sum=0                                 |o
 8   |           For i=1:1:10 Set Sum=Sum+Ary(i)           |
 9   |           Set AVG=Sum/i Kill Sum,i                  |
10  o|           Quit                                      |o
```

EXAMPLE 3.40. DO command without parameters

This is an example of a relatively simple routine. Lines 1 to 6 form the main body of the routine, while lines 7 to 10 represent a small subroutine used to calculate the average of the ten values in the array Ary. Let's examine what the routine does, line by line.

Main Body of the Routine

1: This is the first line in the program and, by convention, starts with a label identical to the program name. The remainder of the line is a comment containing the author(s) initials and the date and time the routine was last edited.

2: The second line is, again by convention, a comment line that describes the purpose of the routine.

3: The third line starts off by KILLing all local variables and then defining ten data nodes in the array Ary.

4: The fourth line invokes the subroutine Average and then prints out the results calculated by that subroutine. Note that the results are returned in the variable AVG, which was created in the subroutine. The programmer must be aware of the variable environment in both the calling routine and the subroutine. If the subroutine inadvertently uses or KILLs variables needed by the main body of the routine, unexpected errors can occur later in the program.

5: The fifth line cleans up the local variable environment by killing off all variables it no longer needs. While this is not essential to the running of the program, it represents good programming style.

6: The sixth line QUITs the main routine DEMO and returns control back to the invoking routine. If the program was invoked in direct mode (as we will demonstrate shortly), control would be returned back to the direct mode prompt.

The Subroutine Average

7: Line seven starts out with the label of the procedure (<u>Average</u>) and initializes the variable <u>Sum</u> to zero. Note that it is necessary for the programmer to know that the subroutine <u>Average</u> uses (Sets) the variables <u>Sum</u>, <u>i</u>, and <u>AVG</u> and that these variables will be altered by invoking the subroutine.

8: Line eight loops through the array <u>Ary</u>, adding each array element to the running total held in <u>Sum</u>.

9: Line nine sets the variable <u>AVG</u> to the calculated average and then KILLs off all the variables created within the subroutine except <u>AVG</u>, which is used to pass back the results of the calculation.

10: The last line of the subroutine <u>Average</u> is a QUIT statement used to terminate the subroutine. Control is returned to the WRITE command following the DO in line 4.

To execute the program, we would issue the following direct mode MUMPS command:

```
o|>Do ^DEMO←
 |The AVERAGE is 11
 |>
```

EXAMPLE 3.41.   Initiating a routine

The command <u>Do ^DEMO</u> instructs MUMPS to load the routine DEMO from disk into the partition and to begin execution of the routine with the first line of code. The steps outlined previously are performed, the main body of the routine writes out the results, and control is returned to direct mode. In the command to start DEMO, the up-arrow (^) informs MUMPS that the routine resides on disk and must be loaded into the partition before it can be executed. If the program already was in the partition (that is, a command of <u>ZLOAD DEMO</u> had already been issued), the program could also have been started with a <u>Do DEMO.</u> In that case, execution initiates with the line labeled <u>DEMO</u> from the routine currently in the partition.

It must be emphasized that, with this format of the DO command, both the calling routine *and* the called routine (or part) must be fully cognizant of the variable environment in which they are running; both share the same variable environment. Any changes to that environment by the called subroutine affect the calling routine.

We need to examine precisely how the called subroutine QUITs back to the called subroutine. Subroutine calls can be *nested*: a called subroutine can call additional subroutines, which can call additional subroutines, and so on. Chained subroutine calls are referred to as nesting or stacking routines. But how does each nested subroutine know when to quit? We mentioned that a subroutine returns control to the calling routine when it executes a QUIT command. We should extend this definition to include "executes a QUIT command *at the same level* as the invoked subroutine." Consider the following example:

```
 1   o|DEMO      ;JML-NYSCVM ; 12/22/86 - 07:10              |o
 2    |          ;Demonstration of "nested" DO commands       |
 3    |          Kill  For i=1:1:10 Set Ary(i)=i*2            |
 4   o|          Do Average Write !,"Average=",AVG           |o
 5    |          Kill Ary,AVG,i                               |
 6    |          Quit                                         |
 7   o|Average   Set Sum=0                                   |o
 8    |          For i=1:1:10 Set X=Ary(i) Do Value          |
 9    |          Set AVG=Sum/i Kill i,Sum,X                   |
10   o|          Quit                                        |o
11    |Value     Write !,"Data Value ",i," = ",X             |
12    |          Set Sum=Sum+X                                |
13   o|          Quit                                        |o
      |                                                       |
```

EXAMPLE 3.42.   Quitting a subroutine

In this example, the subroutine Average calls a second subroutine Value, which prints each data value before adding it into the accumulating Sum. The QUIT command in line 13 returns flow control to line 9, which then goes to line 10. The QUIT on line 10 returns flow control to line 4. It should be emphasized that not all QUIT commands encountered in a subroutine will initiate a return of program execution to the calling routine. QUIT commands within the range of a FOR loop terminate execution of that loop but *not* execution of the subroutine.

```
 1   o|DEMO      ;JML-NYSCVM ; 12/22/86 - 07:10              |o
 2    |          ;Demonstration of "nested" DO commands       |
 3    |          Kill  For i=1:1:10 Set Ary(i)=i*2            |
 4   o|          Do Average Write !,"Average of values >10 ",AVG |o
 5    |          Kill Ary,AVG,i                               |
 6    |          Quit                                         |
 7   o|Average   Set Sum=0,N=0                               |o
 8    |          For i=1:1:10 Set X=Ary(i) Quit:X>10  Do Value |
 9    |          Set AVG=Sum/N Kill i,Sum,X,N                 |
10   o|          Quit                                        |o
11    |Value     Write !,"Data Value ",i," = ",X             |
12    |          Set Sum=Sum+X,N=N+1                          |
13   o|          Quit                                        |o
      |                                                       |
```

EXAMPLE 3.43.   Quit commands terminating either a FOR loop or a Subroutine

In Example 3.43 we have modified Average so that it will only consider those values in Ary until it finds a value that exceeds 10. At that time, the FOR loop terminates with a QUIT. This QUIT applies to the FOR loop, *not* to the subroutine Average.

The QUIT in line 6 is used to terminate the main body of the program; if omitted, the part labeled Average would be executed after Ary, AVG, and i are KILLed, and an <UNDEFINED> error would occur. The QUIT in line 10 ends the subroutine Average; omitting it would erroneously cause the subroutine Value to be executed each time the subroutine Average is invoked. The postconditioned QUIT in line 8 is used to prematurely terminate the FOR loop. The QUIT in line 13 terminates the subroutine Value. It could be left out since there is always an implied QUIT at the end of a routine, but that is poor programming practice. Section 3.3.3 contains an expanded description of the QUIT command.

3.3.2.2 DO Command with Parameter Passing[5]

MUMPS also has provisions for avoiding the potential problems associated with a variable name space that is shared between calling and called routines. This provision includes the ability to pass parameters with the DO command and also use of the NEW command. These topics, as well as extrinsic functions, are described in considerably more detail in Chapter 9.

The NEW command is intimately linked to the DO and QUIT commands. The programmer needs to understand the concept of nesting and DO levels before the effects of the NEW command can be fully appreciated. On the other hand, passing parameters with a DO command performs an implied NEW, and we need some understanding of this command before we can fully explore parameter passing with DO. We will briefly describe the NEW command at this point, but the reader is referred to the more complete definition in Section 3.1.3.

The NEW command has a syntax similar to the KILL command and, indeed, it has many of the outward appearances of the KILL command. This command lets the programmer selectively reuse a variable name and have the original contents of the variable automatically restored at the end of the process. Most frequently, the NEW command is issued at the beginning of a subroutine and requests a new copy of all "scratch" variables that are used within the subroutine. The data values of all NEWed variables (which can also be the names of local arrays) are saved; those variables become undefined in the new environment. The named variables can then be used within the subroutine without conflicting with variable names in the calling environment. Upon encountering a QUIT at the end of the current subroutine level (when control would normally be passed back to the calling routine), all variables that were NEWed during the subroutine are implicitly KILLed, and their old values (if any) are restored before control is passed back to the calling routine. Variables used as arguments to a NEW command that were undefined prior to the NEW will remain undefined on return to the calling program.

This eliminates one of the bottlenecks to writing environment-independent subroutines. With use of the NEW command, the subroutine can ensure that none of the locally created and used variables affect the calling routine. However, the subroutine must still know enough about the variable environment of the calling program to pick up data values from the original environment. One way around

[5]MDC Type A release, January 1987.

this problem is to pass data values to the subroutine as parameters, allowing the parameters to assume new names within the subroutine.

With parameter passing, a list of parameters to be passed to the subroutine is enclosed in parentheses immediately following the name of the subroutine (LABEL, LABEL^ROUTINE, or ^ROUTINE) used as part of the DO command. Additionally, the subroutine LABEL must have a corresponding list of parameters enclosed in parentheses.

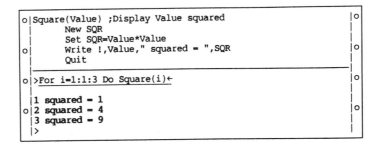

```
Square(Value) ;Display Value squared
        New SQR
        Set SQR=Value*Value
        Write !,Value," squared = ",SQR
        Quit

>For i=1:1:3 Do Square(i)←

1 squared = 1
2 squared = 4
3 squared = 9
>
```

EXAMPLE 3.44. DO command with parameters

Each parameter in the DO list of parameters is called an *actual parameter*, while each parameter following the subroutine label is called a *formal parameter*. The names used in the actual parameter list can be different from those in the formal parameter list. Indeed, the parameters in the actual list do not even have to be variable names but can also be expressions. Each formal parameter must be a simple variable or unsubscripted array name. In the example, **i** [Square(i)] is the *actual* parameter and **Value** [Square(**Value**)] is the *formal* name of the parameter.

When execution of the subroutine starts, each variable name in the formal list is automatically NEWed. That is, if there are already variables with the names defined in the formal list, the values for those variables are saved. The variables are then initialized to the values associated with the actual list of parameters by position; the first variable in the formal list gets the value of the first parameter in the actual list, and so on.

In addition, the variable SQR has been NEWed in this example, since it is a scratch variable created in the subroutine and we wish to avoid possible variable name conflicts between the subroutine and the general local variable environment.

Parameters in the actual list can be passed to the subroutine either by *value* or by *reference*. A parameter passed by *value* can be any valid MUMPS expression; a parameter passed by *reference* must be the name of a local variable. Variable names passed by reference can be the name of an entire array, but *cannot* be a subscripted array element or a reference to a global variable (either simple or subscripted).

Parameters passed by reference are identified in the actual parameter list by the presence of a leading period (.). When passed by reference, the variable name in the formal list of parameters is bound to the corresponding variable name in the actual list. Any changes to the variable name in the formal list within the subroutine are reflected back to the original variable as well; on return from the subroutine, the variable named in the actual list will reflect any changes made to the variable named in the formal list within the subroutine. The reader is referred to Chapter 9 for a more detailed discussion of these concepts.

Even when passing no parameters to a subroutine with a formal parameter list, it is necessary to include the parentheses in the DO command. The parentheses need not enclose any actual parameters, but they are required.

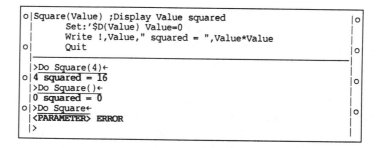

```
o|Square(Value) ;Display Value squared                              |o
 |        Set:'$D(Value) Value=0                                     |
 |        Write !,Value," squared = ",Value*Value                    |
o|        Quit                                                       |o
 |_____
 |>Do Square(4)←                                                     |
o|4 squared = 16                                                     |o
 |>Do Square()←                                                      |
 |0 squared = 0                                                      |
o|>Do Square←                                                        |o
 |<PARAMETER>  ERROR                                                 |
 |>                                                                  |
```

EXAMPLE 3.45. Actual and formal parameter lists

Also notice that it is necessary to check within the subroutine to determine whether or not a parameter has been passed. If there are no actual parameters passed, then the formal variable name will be undefined in the subroutine. The $DATA function (Section 8.2.1) in line 2 is used to determine whether or not a variable is defined. If *not* (function returns a zero), the variable can be initialized to a default value. Alternatively, the $GET function (Section 8.2.5) can be used to initialize parameters.

3.3.2.3 DO Command with Offsets

As with the GOTO command, an optional Offset value can be appended to the LABEL, LABEL^ROUTINE, or ^ROUTINE argument, as long as parameters are not being passed; the DO command with offset is *not* permitted with parameter passing. The Offset is interpreted as a nonnegative integer (zero is permitted) that indicates the number of physical lines *after* the LABELed line at which execution of the subroutine is to start.

As with the GOTO command with Offsets, care should be exercised when using this feature. Refer to Section 3.3.1.5 for additional information and caveats concerning the use of offsets.

3.3.2.4 Argumentless DO Command (Block Structuring)[6]

The argumentless form of the DO command is used to initiate execution of *inner blocks* of routine lines. The use of this syntax requires an understanding of line syntax and execution levels that are covered in subsequent chapters. Therefore, a full description of the argumentless DO command and block structuring is deferred until Section 6.6.

[6]MDC Type A proposal, January 1987.

3.3.3 QUIT Command

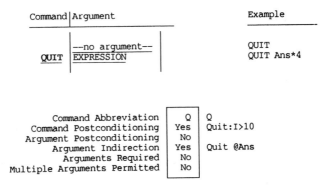

Command	Argument		Example
QUIT	—no argument—		QUIT
	EXPRESSION		QUIT Ans*4

Command Abbreviation	Q	Q
Command Postconditioning	Yes	Quit:I>10
Argument Postconditioning	No	
Argument Indirection	Yes	Quit @Ans
Arguments Required	No	
Multiple Arguments Permitted	No	

The QUIT command is used to terminate a process that was started either with a DO, XECUTE, or FOR command, as well as to terminate extrinsic functions. When executing a QUIT command within the scope of a FOR loop, the QUIT forces termination of the current FOR loop and control is returned to the first command outside the range of that loop. When executed outside the range of a FOR loop, the QUIT command terminates the most recently issued DO or XE-CUTE command or the most recently invoked extrinsic function. There is always an implied QUIT at the end of each routine, although it is recommended that programmers insert explicit QUITs at the end of all routines for clarity.

QUIT commands that terminate a DO, XECUTE, or extrinsic function automatically undo all NEW commands (whether implicit or explicit) that have been issued at the DO or XECUTE level being terminated. All variables that were NEWed at the level being terminated are KILLed, and those that were defined before the NEW command(s) was issued are restored to their original values.

3.3.3.1 Argument = —no argument— The argumentless form of the QUIT is used to terminate FOR loops and DO or XECUTE commands. When encountered within the scope of a FOR command, it causes termination of the innermost FOR loop, and control is returned to the first command outside the range of this loop.

```
o|Test     For   Read !,"Number=",num Quit:num=""  Do Square  |o
 |          Quit                                               |
 |Square Write " squared is ",num*num                          |
o|          Quit                                               |o
 |----------------------------------------------------------- |
 |>Do ^Test←                                                   |
o|Number=2← squared is 4                                       |o
 |Number=6← squared is 36                                      |
 |Number=←                                                     |
o|>                                                            |o
```

EXAMPLE 3.46. Argumentless QUIT command terminating a subroutine

Example 3.46 demonstrates the use of the QUIT command both to terminate a FOR loop and to terminate a subroutine. The FOR loop in the first line of code (label = Test) will continue to execute indefinitely until the postconditioned QUIT command is executed. This command will only be executed when the postconditioned argument evaluates to TRUE (that is, when the user makes no keyboard entry other than the <ENTER> key). If the postconditioned argument evaluates to FALSE, the QUIT command is ignored and execution continues with the next command on the line (Do Square).

Note the fact that there are *two* spaces between the QUIT command on the first line and the DO command that follows it. Argumentless commands (the postconditional :num = """ is *not* considered an argument, but rather a command modifier) require two spaces separating them from the next command on the line, one space for the missing argument and one separating the two commands. Command and line syntax is discussed in greater detail in Chapter 6.

A further example demonstrating the effect of a QUIT command within nested FOR loops is appropriate.

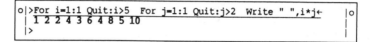

```
o|>For i=1:1 Quit:i>5  For j=1:1 Quit:j>2  Write " ",i*j←   |o
|  1 2 2 4 3 6 4 8 5 10                                     |
|>                                                          |
```

EXAMPLE 3.47. QUIT command to terminate a FOR loop

Again note that both of the QUIT commands in Example 3.47 are separated from the next command on the line by two spaces. The outer FOR loop (For i = 1:1) will be executed until the value of the variable i exceeds 5 (that is, i = 1,2,3,4,5). The inner loop (For j = 1:1) will be executed twice for each time the outer loop is executed. The second QUIT (Quit: j>2) terminates the most recently executed FOR loop (inner loop), but does *not* affect the outer loop.

When encountered outside the direct range of a FOR loop (i.e., not contained in the remainder of the line following a FOR command), the QUIT is applied to the most recently issued DO or XECUTE command and that process is terminated; control is returned to the command following the DO or XECUTE whose process was just terminated. If the DO or XECUTE command terminated was issued in direct mode, control is returned to direct mode.

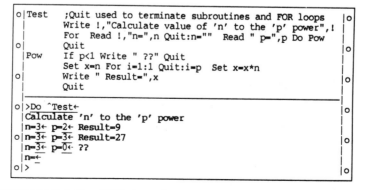

```
o|Test    ;Quit used to terminate subroutines and FOR loops  |o
|         Write !,"Calculate value of 'n' to the 'p' power",! |
|         For  Read !,"n=",n Quit:n=""  Read " p=",p Do Pow   |
o|        Quit                                                |o
|Pow      If p<1 Write " ??" Quit                             |
|         Set x=n For i=1:1 Quit:i=p  Set x=x*n               |
o|        Write " Result=",x                                  |o
|         Quit                                                |
|_____|
o|>Do ^Test←                                                 |o
|Calculate 'n' to the 'p' power                              |
|n=3← p=2← Result=9                                          |
o|n=3← p=3← Result=27                                        |o
|n=3← p=0← ??                                                |
|n=←                                                         |
o|>                                                          |o
```

EXAMPLE 3.48. FOR loop QUIT does not terminate a subroutine

This example should be relatively self-explanatory, but note how the QUIT command in the second line of the subroutine Pow terminates the FOR loop, not the subroutine. Also note that the QUIT in line Test + 3 returns control back to direct mode.

3.3.3.2 Argument = EXPRESSION[7]   The second form of the QUIT command has an EXPRESSION as its argument. This form is used to return a value for an EXTRINSIC function. Extrinsic functions represent a variation of the DO command with parameter passing but return an expression directly, rather than having the expression passed back to the calling routine through a variable. An extrinsic function is invoked with the following syntax:

$$EXTFUNC(PARAMETER,PARAMETER,...)

where EXTFUNC is the name (LABEL, ˆROUTINE, or LABELˆROUTINE) of the function and PARAMETER,PARAMETER,... is the list of parameters being passed to the function. As with the DO command with parameters (refer to Section 3.3.3.2), the label associated with EXTFUNC must also have a list of parameters. The parameter list associated with $$EXTFUNC is called the *actual* list of parameters, while the parameter list associated with the function label is called the *formal* list. As in parameter passing with the DO command, there is an implied NEW command on all variables in the formal list of parameters when the extrinsic function is entered. In addition, the code used to perform the extrinsic function can issue additional NEW commands to ensure that the original variable environment is not compromised.

The primary difference between an extrinsic function and a DO command with parameters is that the extrinsic function returns the result directly back to the expression invoking the function rather than through a parameter. Consider the following example:

```
o|Start   For i=1:1:4 Write !,$$Cube(i)          |o
 |         Quit                                    |
 |Cube(Data) ;Return Data cubed                    |
o|         Set Data=Data*Data*Data                 |o
 |         Quit Data                               |
 |                                                 |
o|_____|o
 |>Do Start←                                       |
 |                                                 |
 |1                                                |
o|8                                                |o
 |27                                               |
 |64                                               |
o|>                                                |o
```

EXAMPLE 3.49.   QUIT with arguments to terminate extrinsic functions

In this example, when the $$Cube(i) function is encountered, control is passed

[7]MDC Type A release, January 1987.

to the label <u>Cube</u> with the parameter i. The function then calculates the cube of the value, which is used as the returned value (the argument to the QUIT command for the subroutine <u>Cube</u>). When executing the Write command, it is the *returned* argument that is printed in place of the string "$$Cube(i)". The function <u>Cube(Data)</u> shown could be written in a simpler fashion as follows:

```
o|Cube(Data) Quit Data*Data*Data                                      |o
```

EXAMPLE 3.50.   Simplified cube function

The reader is also referred to the more detailed discussions of extrinsic functions found in Chapter 9.

3.3.4 HALT Command

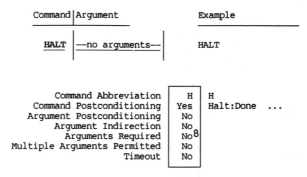

Command	Argument		Example
HALT	--no arguments--		HALT

Command Abbreviation	H	H
Command Postconditioning	Yes	Halt:Done ...
Argument Postconditioning	No	
Argument Indirection	No	
Arguments Required	No[8]	
Multiple Arguments Permitted	No	
Timeout	No	

The HALT command terminates a process, releases all devices owned by the process, releases all LOCKed variables, and returns the active partition to the system. The command can be postconditioned, but remember, as with all argumentless commands, two spaces are required after the command and postconditional expression and before the next command on the line.

There is an implied CLOSE of all devices currently owned by the process before the partition is released, including the principal I/O device.

```
o|ChkDon Read !,"Really STOP? (Y or N): ",ans               |o
 |       If ans="Y" Halt                                     |
 |       Quit                                                |
o|----------------------------------------------------------|o
 |>Do ChkDon←                                                |
 |Really STOP? (Y or N): N←                                  |
o|>Do ChkDon←                                                |o
 |Really STOP? (Y or N): Y←                                  |
 |<<EXIT>>                                                   |
o|                                                          |o
```

EXAMPLE 3.51.   Halt command

[8]The HALT command may *not* have an argument. Lack of an argument when abbreviating to the single character **H** differentiates a HALT from a HANG command.

3.3.5 XECUTE Command

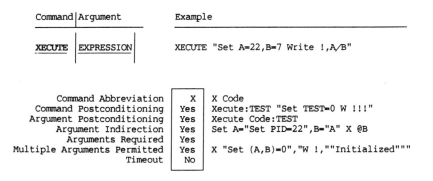

Command	Argument	Example
XECUTE	EXPRESSION	XECUTE "Set A=22,B=7 Write !,A/B"

Command Abbreviation	X	X Code
Command Postconditioning	Yes	Xecute:TEST "Set TEST=0 W !!!"
Argument Postconditioning	Yes	Xecute Code:TEST
Argument Indirection	Yes	Set A="Set PID=22",B="A" X @B
Arguments Required	Yes	
Multiple Arguments Permitted	Yes	X "Set (A,B)=0","W !,""Initialized"""
Timeout	No	

The XECUTE command is used to execute the line of code in EXPRESSION. EXPRESSION is evaluated as a line of MUMPS instructions as if it had been entered in direct mode. EXPRESSION can be a variable (local or global, simple or subscripted array element) or a string literal, as long as it contains a valid line of MUMPS code. The XECUTE command is also discussed in Section 7.1.

Execution of the XECUTE command is similar to the execution of a DO command. There is an implied QUIT command at the end of the line to be executed, and any explicit QUIT commands executed during the execution of EXPRESSION (except those within the range of a FOR command) terminate the XECUTE. Control is automatically returned to the command [or additional argument(s)] immediately following the argument just XECUTEd. If a $TEXT (8.1.10) function is encountered in a XECUTE expression, it refers to lines of code in the routine that initiated the XECUTE command.

```
o|>Set Z="Set PID=Ans Quit:Ans'?1N.N  Write Ans"←          |o
 |>Set Ans=1234 Write !,Z,!,"Patient ID = " Xecute Z←      |
 |                                                          |
o|Set PID=Ans Quit:Ans'?1N.N Write Ans                      |o
 |Patient ID = 1234                                         |
 |                                                          |
o|>Set Ans="Good Morning" Write !,"Answer = " Xecute Z←     |o
 |                                                          |
 |Answer =                                                  |
o|                                                          |o
 |>                                                         |
```

EXAMPLE 3.52. XECUTE command

Notice that the second time the XECUTE command is executed, the value for Ans is not displayed since the postconditioned QUIT command terminates the XECUTE argument before the WRITE is executed.

A common use of the XECUTE command is to hold device or system-specific commands. These can be initialized at the beginning of an application and used throughout the program to provide a level of device or system independence. Consider the MUMPS code needed to position the cursor to a specified location on a CRT screen. Many (but not all) CRT terminals permit the cursor to be moved to any arbitrary position on the screen, yet often they use different ESCape sequences (see the discussion of the WRITE command in Section 3.4.4 and Chapter 12) to accomplish this function. In addition to writing out an ESCape sequence to the terminal, it is also necessary to update the system variables $X and $Y to reflect the new cursor location. The following code demonstrates how to establish an XECUTE argument to position the cursor on a VT-100 terminal. By changing the ESCape sequence in the XECUTEd argument (variable XY), this argument could be adjusted for other terminal types at the beginning of an application.

```
o|>Set XY="Write *27,*91,DY+1,DX+1,*102 Set $X=DX,$Y=DY"←     |o
 |>Set DX=15,DY=7 X XY W "Cursor=(",$X,",",$Y,")"←            |
 |                                                            |
o|                                                            |o
 |                                                            |
 |                                                            |
o|            Cursor=(23,7)                                   |o
 |>                                                           |
```

EXAMPLE 3.53.   Cursor positioning with XECUTE command

In Example 3.53, we assume that the screen has just been cleared and that the upper-left corner of the screen has the coordinates $X=0 and $Y=0. The displayed value for $X at the new cursor position is *not* 15, since $X was updated by MUMPS as the characters "Cursor = (" were output. While we could have output the control sequence needed by the terminal to position the cursor to location DX,DY as an indirect argument to a WRITE command, we could *not* have performed the necessary update of $X and $Y.

An argument to an XECUTE command can evaluate to an empty string (""), in which case the XECUTE performs no action and processing continues as if the argument were not there.

The XECUTE command is similar to the DO command except that the DO command transfers control to a specified routine line, whereas the XECUTE command temporarily transfers control to the contents of a variable or a string literal. While the DO command may initiate execution of multiple lines of MUMPS code (until a QUIT command is encountered), the XECUTE command automatically returns control after the string of commands is exhausted; there is an implied QUIT command at the end of the string being executed.

Like the DO command, it is possible to use the NEW command within the argument being executed. The NEW command operates in a fashion similar to that encountered in the DO environment, and the reader is referred to the sections concerning the DO command with parameter passing, the NEW command, and Chapter 9 on parameter passing and the NEW command.

The command string used as an argument can contain additional XECUTE commands, but things get a little confusing as XECUTEs are nested. As with the use of argument indirection, care should be exercised when incorporating XECUTE commands in routines. It is often difficult to tell from static program listings the code that is actually being executed during a command, making maintenance of programs more difficult. Arguments to XECUTE commands should be well documented.

```
o|>Set XY="Write *27,*91,DY+1,*59,DX+1,*102 Set $X=DX,$Y=DY"←|o
 |>Set ErMsg="S DX=0,DY=8 Xecute XY Write ""Error"""←
 |>Xecute ErMsg←
o|                                                            |o
 |
 |
o|                                                            |o
 |
 |Error
o|>                                                           |o
```

EXAMPLE 3.54. Xecuting code within an XECUTE string

Imagine that you encountered the command **Xecute ErMsg** in a complicated program and you didn't know where the variables XY and ErMsg had been set or what they contained. You could spend considerable time tracking down the contents of these variables to understand what function the XECUTE was performing.

Note that all MUMPS commands are allowed in the string being executed, including additional XECUTE commands, DO commands, and so on. The line being executed behaves like any short subroutine; a NEW command encountered in a line of code being executed behaves just as a NEW command would in any other subroutine.

There is at least one additional caveat in the use of the XECUTE command that should be brought to the reader's attention. Execution time, especially for compiled versions of MUMPS, may be considerably slower when code is XECUTEd in contrast to the same code held as part of a routine. This is because the source code held in a variable must be compiled at execute time before it can be invoked. To reduce this overhead, some implementations keep around compiled versions of variables that have been used as an argument to an XECUTE command, so that subsequent XECUTEs using the same argument are faster. Others provide special **Z** commands that can be used to compile the code held in a variable once, and then XECUTE this compiled version rather than the source.

3.4 Input/Output Commands

Input and output commands are used to manage various peripheral devices in the MUMPS environment and to initiate the transfer of information between a MUMPS process and a device. There are six MUMPS commands that fall into this category:

OPEN command   This command is used to establish ownership of a device. Each process in MUMPS can own many devices, but, for

	the most part, a given device can only be owned by a single process at any given time.
USE command	While each MUMPS process can own multiple devices, only one of these is active at any given time. All READ and WRITE operations are directed from or to the currently active device. The USE command is used to make a currently owned device the active device.
READ command	This command is used to read information from the currently active device into a variable for further processing.
WRITE command	The WRITE command is used to transfer data to the currently active device.
CLOSE command	The CLOSE command is used to terminate input or output operations to an owned device and to release that device for other MUMPS processes.
PRINT command	The PRINT command is not part of the MUMPS standard, but is implemented in most versions and will be described in this section. The PRINT command is used to output routine lines to the current device.

A detailed explanation of input and output operations in MUMPS is deferred to Chapter 12, but a brief review is presented here for the beginning programmer.

MUMPS maintains a list of device identifiers (often as integer numbers) for all supported devices. These include terminals (CRTs and serial printers), line printers, magnetic tapes, sequential disk files, and so on. Each MUMPS implementation has a different set of device identifiers, and it will be necessary to check your documentation to determine which devices are available and their internal designation. For the most part, only one process (partition) can own a particular device at a given time. While that process owns the device, no other process can gain access to it. Device ownership is established with the OPEN command and devices are released back to MUMPS with the CLOSE command (that is, ownership is relinquished). More than one device can be owned by a process at any given time.

Once device ownership has been established, the process can then direct I/O to that device. Input and output to a device are initiated with the READ and WRITE commands. I/O using these commands is directed to the current device; the current device is established with the USE command. The USE command specifies to which of the currently owned devices I/O will be directed. The current device remains in effect until another USE or a CLOSE command is executed, or, if in direct mode, until MUMPS prompts for another direct mode command.

In addition to the commands listed here, there are a number of nonstandard commands that can be used to perform input or output operations. Commands such as **ZLOAD** and **ZSAVE** are intended primarily for loading and saving routines to disk but can also be used with other devices. Discussion of these commands is deferred to Sections 3.5.6 and 3.5.10.

3.4.1 OPEN Command

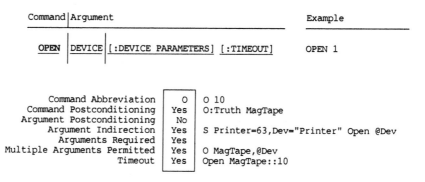

Command	Argument	Example
OPEN	DEVICE [:DEVICE PARAMETERS] [:TIMEOUT]	OPEN 1

Command Abbreviation	O	O 10
Command Postconditioning	Yes	O:Truth MagTape
Argument Postconditioning	No	
Argument Indirection	Yes	S Printer=63,Dev="Printer" Open @Dev
Arguments Required	Yes	
Multiple Arguments Permitted	Yes	O MagTape,@Dev
Timeout	Yes	Open MagTape::10

The OPEN command is used to gain ownership of an input/output (I/O) device in the MUMPS environment for subsequent input or output operations (READ and WRITE). A given process may establish ownership of more than one device using the OPEN command and then select between the owned devices with the USE command.

If a process attempts to gain ownership of a device that is already owned by another job, the OPEN will hang (that is, execution will temporarily suspend) until the specified device is released (CLOSEd) by the other process. The optional [:TIMEOUT] parameter to the OPEN command allows the programmer to regain control of the OPEN process and avoid situations where the OPEN command might hang for an indefinite period of time. When specified, TIMEOUT represents the number of seconds to wait while trying to establish device ownership before continuing execution of the process. On return from an OPEN command with a TIMEOUT specified, the system variable $TEST will be TRUE if ownership was established or FALSE if the device could not be allocated to the current process. If no TIMEOUT is specified, the value of $TEST is not altered.

The OPEN command is specific to individual implementations. Each implementor specifies the possible values for DEVICE and the actual devices available in the implementation. In addition, there are optional DEVICE PARAMETERS that can be associated with each device or device class. The syntax and functions performed by these DEVICE PARAMETERS are also implementor specific, and you should check your documentation to see what is allowed.

One DEVICE is always available to a process. By definition, DEVICE number zero (0) always refers to the principal device associated with a given process. The principal device is defined as the device under which the partition was first granted and is typically the terminal that was used to sign onto MUMPS. This device usually has a system-assigned DEVICE identifier as well, but 0 can always be used as a DEVICE identifier when addressing the principal device (that is, argument to a USE command). When signing onto MUMPS, the principal device is automatically OPENED by MUMPS using whatever default DEVICE PARAMETERS are in effect for the system. On terminating the process (that is, relinquishing the partition with a HALT command), MUMPS automatically CLOSEs the principal device as well as any other devices that were OPEN for that process.

The OPEN command does *not* direct input or output to a specific device; rather, it establishes a partition's ownership of that device. The USE command is necessary to establish the current device and is discussed in the next section.

3.4.1.1 Argument = DEVICE This use of the OPEN command establishes simple ownership of a device. If the device specified in DEVICE is not currently owned by another process, ownership is established for this process and execution continues. If the device is already owned by another process, execution will hang (that is, suspend execution) on the OPEN command until the other process has relinquished control of the device. Multiple processes can be competing for the same device at the same time. How requests are processed is implementor specific and may not be in the form "first requested, first serviced."

While there may be one or more DEVICE PARAMETERS to be established with a device, it may be advisable to first establish ownership and then establish the DEVICE PARAMETERS with the USE command to ensure you get all necessary devices. Check the documentation for your implementation to see if this is permitted.

```
o|>Open 67,68←                                                    |o
 |>                                                                |
```

EXAMPLE 3.55. OPEN command

3.4.1.2 Argument = DEVICE:DEVICE PARAMETERS This form is similar to the previous form but also includes a list of device-specific parameters that are used to establish certain operating characteristics of the device. These might include items such as right margin, echo ON/OFF, magnetic tape density, and so on. Again, check the documentation for your specific implementation.

Since both the syntax and content of the DEVICE PARAMETER list are implementor specific, it is *strongly* recommended that code using these features be well identified and documented. Attempting to move MUMPS code between implementations can be made excruciatingly difficult if each routine must be examined for use of implementation-specific features such as the DEVICE PARAMETERS.

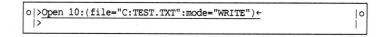
```
o|>Open 10:(file="C:TEST.TXT":mode="WRITE")←                      |o
 |>                                                                |
```

EXAMPLE 3.56. OPEN command with parameters

Example 3.56 could be used on *some* micro-based version of MUMPS to open a sequential disk file on drive C̲ named TEST.TXT for output (mode = "WRITE").

3.4.1.3 Argument = DEVICE::TIMEOUT The optional TIMEOUT argument to the OPEN command specifies the number of seconds to wait while attempting to gain ownership of a device. TIMEOUT is evaluated as an integer; if less than zero (0), then zero (0) is used. If the device is not currently owned by another process, ownership for this process is established and control is returned immediately with the system variable $TEST set to TRUE (1). If the DEVICE is currently owned by another process, the system will continue to try to gain ownership for TIMEOUT seconds. If ownership is established within this time period, control is returned to the program with $TEST set to TRUE. If, at the end of TIMEOUT, ownership has not been established, control is returned to the program with $TEST set to FALSE (0). If *no* TIMEOUT is specified, the value associated with $TEST is left unchanged.

Note, especially, the need for *two colons* in the OPEN command when TIMEOUT is specified. Even if no DEVICE PARAMETERS are specified, the colons used to delimit that field from the TIMEOUT field *must* be entered to allow MUMPS to differentiate between the two argument parts.

```
o|>Open 51:("AV":0:1024):10←                                      |o
 |>Open 40::30←                                                   |
 |>                                                               |
```

EXAMPLE 3.57. Timed OPEN command

The first line of Example 3.57 attempts to OPEN device number 51 with the DEVICE PARAMETERS of ("AV":0:1024) and a TIMEOUT of 10 seconds. The second line attempts to OPEN device number 40 with no special parameters but with a TIMEOUT of 30 seconds. The colons within the DEVICE PARAMETER list are *not* counted as argument separators to the OPEN command.

```
o|Print ;Print Stock Inventory to Line Printer (Device #3)    |o
 |      Open 3::0 Else  Write "Can't get Printer." Quit        |
 |      Use 3                                                  |
o|       .                                                     |o
 |       .                                                     |
 |       .                                                     |
o|       .                                                     |o
```

EXAMPLE 3.58. Timed OPEN command without parameters

The ELSE command in the second line of Example 3.58 checks the status of the system variable $TEST. The value of $TEST will reflect whether or not the timed OPEN command was successful. If $TEST is FALSE (0), the error message will be printed. Otherwise, execution will continue with the next line of code.

3.4.2 USE Command

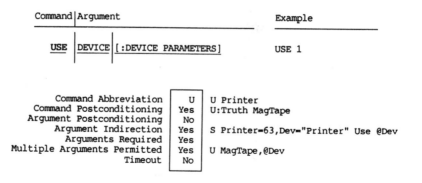

Command	Argument		Example
USE	DEVICE	[:DEVICE PARAMETERS]	USE 1

Command Abbreviation	U	U Printer
Command Postconditioning	Yes	U:Truth MagTape
Argument Postconditioning	No	
Argument Indirection	Yes	S Printer=63,Dev="Printer" Use @Dev
Arguments Required	Yes	
Multiple Arguments Permitted	Yes	U MagTape,@Dev
Timeout	No	

The USE command is invoked to make a device that has already been OPENED by the process the current device. A brief description of devices and the OPEN, USE, and CLOSE commands is given at the beginning of this section and a detailed description of input/output operations is presented in Chapter 12. The USE command directs all subsequent I/O operations (using READ or WRITE commands) to the device associated with DEVICE until another USE command is encountered or until the DEVICE is CLOSEd. Each implementor is responsible for defining both the DEVICEs and the syntax and content of the optional DEVICE PARAMETER list; check the documentation for more information on these values.

If the DEVICE is currently owned by the process (via the OPEN command), then that device is made the current device and the system variables $IO, $X, and $Y will be updated to reflect the current status of DEVICE. The system variable $IO always contains the DEVICE designator of the current device. The variables $X and $Y contain the X position (column) and Y position (row) of the current device and are updated on each READ or WRITE operation.

If the DEVICE was not owned by the process, an error results when code to USE it is executed.

3.4.2.1 Argument = DEVICE   This form of the USE command establishes the current DEVICE from the list of OPENed devices for a given process. Note that, while it is possible to include multiple DEVICEs as arguments, only the last DEVICE in the list becomes the current device. There can only be one current device active at a given time for a given process.

3.4.2.2 Argument = DEVICE:DEVICE PARAMETERS   As with the OPEN command, optional implementation and device-specific parameters may be allowed with the USE command. These parameters may change functional characteristics associated with the device such as right margins, READ termination sequences (see READ command; Section 3.4.3), and so on. Again, check the system documentation for more information.

```
o|>Use 70:(speed="9600":parity="E")←                          |o
 |>                                                           |
```

EXAMPLE 3.59. USE command with parameters

This USE command could be used on some systems to alter the speed and parity of a terminal line. On those systems, it would also be possible to use the same parameters as arguments to an OPEN command to institute the same change.

3.4.3 READ Command

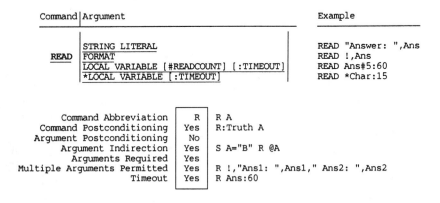

Command	Argument	Example
READ	STRING LITERAL	READ "Answer: ",Ans
	FORMAT	READ !,Ans
	LOCAL VARIABLE [#READCOUNT] [:TIMEOUT]	READ Ans#5:60
	*LOCAL VARIABLE [:TIMEOUT]	READ *Char:15

Command Abbreviation	R	R A
Command Postconditioning	Yes	R:Truth A
Argument Postconditioning	No	
Argument Indirection	Yes	S A="B" R @A
Arguments Required	Yes	
Multiple Arguments Permitted	Yes	R !,"Ans1: ",Ans1," Ans2: ",Ans2
Timeout	Yes	R Ans:60

The READ command is used to input character-oriented data from devices; data read from the device are used to create or modify local variables. The READ command is not the primary method for accessing databases on disk; these data elements (the *global* variables) are created and modified with the SET command. The READ command is used to input strings of characters from byte-oriented devices such as terminals, magnetic tapes, or sequential disk files.

For convenience, the READ also has some of the functionality of the WRITE command, allowing the programmer to output text or format control characters as part of the READ command.

The target of the READ (the device from which characters will be read) is the current device (identified by the system variable $IO), which is established with the USE command. A complete discussion of devices under MUMPS is given in Chapter 12. For the time being we will examine the READ command in the context of the MUMPS environment a programmer encounters after first signing onto MUMPS. In this case, the current device is the terminal used to sign onto the system, and all READ and WRITE commands will be directed to that device.

3.4.3.1 Argument = STRING LITERAL
This form of the argument (as well as Argument = FORMAT discussed next) are extensions to the READ command

that allow it to perform like a WRITE command. These features are included to improve the programming environment and facilitate the development of interactive programs. Consider the following examples.

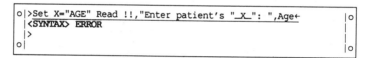

EXAMPLE 3.60. READ command with STRING LITERAL

Example 3.60 actually demonstrates the first three argument formats permitted. The READ initiates two carriage-return line-feed operations (!!, using the FORMAT form of the argument), writes out the prompt "Enter patient's AGE: " (using the STRING LITERAL form of the argument), and then performs a READ into the LOCAL VARIABLE **Age**. Note that the STRING LITERAL must be just that: a string of characters surrounded by quotation marks. *No* variables are allowed in a STRING LITERAL and the following example would be illegal.

```
o|>Set X="AGE" Read !!,"Enter patient's "_X_": ",Age←        |o
 |<SYNTAX> ERROR                                             |
 |>                                                          |
o|                                                           |o
```

EXAMPLE 3.61. Illegal use of output strings in READ command

While Example 3.61 may work on some systems, it does *not* conform to the standard and its use is *not* recommended.

3.4.3.2 Argument = FORMAT This form of the argument is identical to the FORMAT form described under the WRITE command (Section 3.4.4.2). Review that section for more details. Basically, three formatting arguments can be used with the READ command: the **#** character is used to initiate a new-page sequence; the **!** character is used to initiate a new-line sequence; and the **?nn** format control sequence is used to TAB to the **nn**th column.

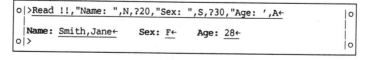

EXAMPLE 3.62. READ command with FORMAT control

3.4.3.3 Argument = LOCAL VARIABLE [#READCOUNT] [:TIMEOUT] The basic format for this form of the argument is **LOCAL VARIABLE** with two optional extensions: [#READCOUNT] is the number of characters to be read, and [:TIMEOUT], the number of seconds an unfinished READ can be pending before it is automatically terminated.

Normal read operations from a terminal read ASCII characters from the keyboard and place them into the specified LOCAL VARIABLE. Each implementor determines what the normal terminating sequence is and whether or not the terminating sequence is returned with the other characters at the end of the READ. In practice, at least for terminals, all implementors provide a standard read terminator, which is initiated from the keyboard by pressing the <ENTER> key. Additionally, only the characters read before the <ENTER> key is pressed are placed in the LOCAL VARIABLE on completion of the read.

Many implementors also permit the programmer to establish other terminating sequences, usually through special parameters included in the OPEN or USE command. You must check your documentation to see if this option is possible with your implementation and, if so, how to activate these other terminating sequences. The terminating character becomes particularly important when trying to read function key values from some terminal types. Pressing a function key at a VT-100 type of terminal causes the transmission of an ESCape character (decimal code 27) followed by one or more characters that define which of the function keys was pressed. Unfortunately, no <RETURN> character (decimal 13) is sent at the end of the string and, consequently, the READ is not terminated. Approaches for reading such sequences are presented in Chapter 12.

A number of special characters are usually processed in a different fashion than graphic (displayable) characters input from the terminal. They act as control codes to the READ operation and are not generally included in the variable into which the characters are being accumulated. Table 3.1 represents some of the more common control characters and the effect they have on the READ operation. It must be noted that these sequences are nonstandard and may be interpreted by different implementations (or even different devices in the same implementation) in different fashions.

As characters are input from the device, the system variables $X and $Y, representing the current position of the cursor or print-head, are automatically updated by MUMPS in much the same manner as in the WRITE command.

The optional parameter [#READCOUNT] changes the conditions on which the READ terminates. READCOUNT is evaluated as an integer number representing the maximum number of characters that will be read before the READ is terminated. The READ will be terminated as soon as the specified number of characters (READCOUNT) have been input or when the terminating sequence (again, usually the <ENTER> key) is encountered.

```
o|>Read "Enter up to 4 characters: ",Ans#4 Write " Ans=",Ans←|o
 |Enter up to 4 characters: 12← Ans=12                        |
 |                                                            |
o|>Read "Enter up to 4 characters: ",Ans#4 Write " Ans=",Ans←|o
 |Enter up to 4 characters: 4321 Ans=4321                     |
 |>                                                           |
```

EXAMPLE 3.63. Fixed-length READ command

TABLE 3.1 Input/Output control characters

Char	Key	ASCII Code	Function
ETX	<CTRL>C	3	This character can be generated from the keyboard by holding down the <**CTRL**> key and pressing C, that is, <**CTRL**>**C**>. If BREAKS are enabled (see description of the BREAK command, Section 3.5.1), receipt of this character interrupts program execution and causes an ERROR condition. See Chapter 13 for details on error processing.
FF	<CTRL>L	12	The form feed character is sometimes considered a READ terminator (often effective only when the device is magnetic tape).
CR	<ENTER>	13	The carriage return character (usually labeled <**ENTER**> or <RETURN> on the keyboard) normally terminates a READ.
SI	<CTRL>O	15	This code causes characters being sent to the device to be discarded (that is, *no* output), but the MUMPS process continues execution (the characters are "lost"). Normal character output resumes on receipt of the next <CTRL>O or when an OPEN, USE, or READ command is encountered.
DC1	<CTRL>Q	17	This character is often referred to as XON. It has the effect of resuming output that has been suspended with a <CTRL>S (XOFF).
DC3	<CTRL>S	19	This character is often called XOFF and suspends output to the device until a XON character is received. Many implementations will resume output on receipt of *any* character after the XOFF.
NAK	<CTRL>U	21	This character causes the deletion of all characters input since the beginning of the current READ. Some systems use <CTRL>X for this function.
DEL	<DEL>	127	Deletes the last character read from the keyboard. Repeated DELs remove successive characters from the input stream up to the beginning of the current READ.

Note that in the second READ we did not have to press the <ENTER> key (←). Instead, after entering the 4th character, the READ automatically terminated.

The standard specifies that READCOUNT must be a positive integer; a READCOUNT of zero or less is considered an error. It does *not* define what happens to the additional characters if *more* than READCOUNT characters are available. When a normal READ is issued (that is, READ ans), characters that have been entered since the last READ was completed may be lost (see the discussion concerning keyboard buffering later in this section). Whether a system should truncate longer input strings or use them as input for future READ commands is implementation specific.

The fixed-length read is especially useful when reading data records from other computer systems. Consider reading the data from a magnetic tape that consists of a series of *records*, each of which has five fixed-length *fields* in the following format:

Record	Field1..	Field2.......	Field3	Field4..	Field5.........
Field width	8	13	6	8	15

If we assume that device number 47 is used to designate the magnetic tape drive, the code in Example 3.64 could be used to input a record, parse it into five individual variables (F1,F2,...,F5), and then process the data.

```
o|GetRec ;Read one RECORD from magtape, parse into 5 FIELDS  |o
 |        Use 47 Read Rec                                     |
 |        Set F1=$E(Rec,1,8),F2=$E(Rec,9,21),F3=$E(Rec,22,27) |
o|        Set F4=$E(Rec,28,35),F5=$E(Rec,36,50)               |o
 |        Quit                                                |
```

EXAMPLE 3.64. Parsing a record from magnetic tape into fields

The $E function ($EXTRACT, Section 8.1.1) is used to extract character strings from a target string. The function $E(Rec,1,8) extracts the first through the eighth character from the string held in variable Rec. An alternative approach using fixed-length READs is demonstrated in the next example.

```
o|GetRec ;Read one RECORD from magtape, parse into 5 FIELDS  |o
 |        Use 47                                              |
 |        Read F1#8,F2#13,F3#6,F4#8,F5#15                     |
o|        Quit                                                |o
```

EXAMPLE 3.65. Parsing a record using fixed-length READ

The optional parameter [:TIMEOUT] also changes the conditions under which the read terminates. The value for TIMEOUT is evaluated as a positive integer representing the number of seconds to wait before automatically terminating the READ. On completion of a timed READ, the system variable $TEST is returned as a true/false value indicating whether or not the READ was successful; it is TRUE if the READ was completed with a normal termination sequence before the optional READCOUNT was reached, or FALSE if the number of seconds represented by TIMEOUT elapsed before normal data entry termination. Refer to Section 6.1.5 for additional comments on TIMED commands.

```
o|>Read "Answer is: ",Ans:10 Write:'$T " No Response. ",Ans← |o
 |Answer is: 123 No Response. 123                             |
 |>                                                           |
```

EXAMPLE 3.66. Timed READ

Note in Example 3.66 that, even though the timed READ failed, the characters input before failure are still returned in the read argument. The *only* way to determine whether or not the read succeeded is to check the system variable $T.

The READ command with a TIMEOUT can also be used instead of a HANG command (Section 3.5.2). The HANG command suspends processing for a specified number of seconds and is often used after displaying a message and before clearing the screen to give the user time to read the message. Unfortunately, there is no way for users to override a HANG command; they must wait for the full duration before execution is resumed. If the HANG is replaced with a timed READ command, they can press the <ENTER> key and continue execution after they have read the message.

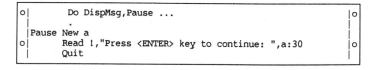

```
o|        Do DispMsg,Pause ...                                      |o
 |           .                                                      |
 |Pause New a                                                       |
o|        Read !,"Press <ENTER> key to continue: ",a:30             |o
 |        Quit                                                      |
```

EXAMPLE 3.67. Alternative to HANG command using Timed READ

In this example, the part Pause displays the message instructing the user how to resume execution (pressing <ENTER> key) and then pauses for up to 30 seconds. If the user presses <ENTER> before 30 seconds, execution resumes immediately. Otherwise, execution resumes automatically when the timed READ fails. *Note* that the Pause subroutine will alter the value of the system truth variable $TEST. To avoid this, Pause could have been made an extrinsic function (see Chapter 8); extrinsic functions preserve the value of $TEST and restore the original value before returning control to the calling code.

3.4.3.4 Argument = *LOCAL VARIABLE—Single-Character READ This form of the READ command returns a single ASCII character as an integer value.

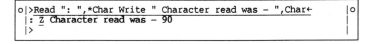

```
o|>Read ": ",*Char Write " Character read was - ",Char←              |o
 |: Z Character read was - 90                                       |
 |>                                                                 |
```

EXAMPLE 3.68. Single-character READ

In this example, the single character read from the keyboard was a "Z" whose decimal value (from the ASCII character set found in Appendix A) was **90**. Note that the standard does not state whether or not the character entered will also be echoed on the terminal; some implementations do while others do not. Additionally, the standard leaves it up to the implementor as to whether or not $X and $Y will be updated on the single-character READ. If your implementation does not automatically echo the characters on single-character READ, you might want to use the WRITE command coupled with the READ as shown in the next example.

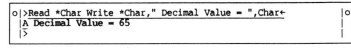

```
o|>Read *Char Write *Char," Decimal Value = ",Char←        |o
 |A Decimal Value = 65                                       |
 |>                                                          |
```

EXAMPLE 3.69. Displaying characters read with timed READ

During a normal read, MUMPS automatically handles many special characters from the keyboard, such as the <RUBOUT> or <DELETE> key. These are usually interpreted as, "If any characters have been input for this READ, delete the last character input and move the cursor to the left by one position." Normal processing of this type is *usually* bypassed for single-character READs and the value of the control character (for <DELETE> this would be decimal 127) is passed back into LOCAL VARIABLE. However, many implementations still handle some characters (such as <CTRL>C, <CTRL>S, and <CTRL>Q) as special cases and do *not* pass them through; instead, they process them in the normal manner (<CTRL>C usually interrupts a process, <CTRL>S usually "pauses" output to the device, and <CTRL>Q usually resumes "paused" output). You will have to experiment with your implementation to find out how it responds to these entries.

We should also examine the problem of buffering keyboard input and the potential for lost characters. Execution of a READ can be interpreted as reading all characters from the input device *since* the READ command was issued. Unfortunately, this interpretation can lead to characters being lost, especially with single-character READs. Consequently, most implementations provide for keyboard buffering, often referred to as *type-ahead* buffering.

In the type-ahead environment, MUMPS provides a buffer or temporary storage area for incoming characters. The READ command can be satisfied with characters from this buffer rather than directly reading from the keyboard. While this technique overcomes the potential loss of characters input before the READ command was initiated, it presents its own set of problems. Sometimes a process will determine, based on the characters input, the need to abort the process and start another. In these instances it is desirable to be able to flush the buffer (that is, delete any characters remaining in the buffer) before starting the new process. Most implementations that provide for keyboard buffering also provide a method for flushing the buffer, but, again, you will have to check your documentation. In addition, some of these implementations have special formats for the OPEN and USE commands that permit the programmer to activate or deactivate keyboard buffering under program control.

Finally, we should address the case of a single character READ with the optional TIMEOUT parameter. This format performs much the same as the READ LOCAL VARIABLE:TIMEOUT with one exception. If the TIMEOUT occurs before a character is read, then the LOCAL VARIABLE associated with the READ is assigned the value of -1. In the normal READ, if no characters are input before the TIMEOUT, the LOCAL VARIABLE is set to an empty string (""). In both cases, the system variable $TEST is set to reflect whether or not the TIMEOUT was reached before the normal read terminator is encountered.

```
o|>Read *A:0←                                              |o
 |
 |>Write A←
o|‾1                                                        |o
 |>
```

EXAMPLE 3.70. Single character timed READ command

In both forms of the READ with the optional TIMEOUT parameter, use of a TIMEOUT of *zero* (e.g., Read Ans:0) behaves differently depending on whether or not keyboard buffering is available. If no keyboard buffering is available, then the READ commands will likely fail with $T set to false. If keyboard buffering is available, the characters will be retrieved from the buffer and the READ *may* succeed.

3.4.4 WRITE Command

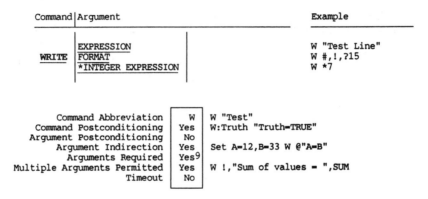

Command	Argument		Example
WRITE	EXPRESSION		W "Test Line"
	FORMAT		W #,!,?15
	*INTEGER EXPRESSION		W *7

Command Abbreviation	W	W "Test"
Command Postconditioning	Yes	W:Truth "Truth=TRUE"
Argument Postconditioning	No	
Argument Indirection	Yes	Set A=12,B=33 W @"A=B"
Arguments Required	Yes[9]	
Multiple Arguments Permitted	Yes	W !,"Sum of values = ",SUM
Timeout	No	

The WRITE command is used to output data to the current device. The current device is determined by previously executed OPEN and USE commands and is defined by the system variable $IO. $IO is initially defined in Section 3.4.2. A more detailed discussion of devices and device selection is given in Chapter 12. The format of the data written to the device, as well as the action on certain system variables ($X and $Y), depends on the argument type (EXPRESSION, FORMAT, or *INTEGER EXPRESSION).

As with the READ command, a number of special characters can be input from the device that affect the output of characters to the device. See Table 3.1 for a summary of these control codes.

3.4.4.1 Argument = EXPRESSION
The evaluated results of EXPRESSION are written out to the currently assigned device. Characters are output one at a

---

[9]Many MUMPS implementations provide a nonstandard, argumentless form of the WRITE command that causes all local variables to be output to the current device. Usually, both the variable names and the data values associated with the names are output.

time from the left to the right of the evaluated expression. As each character is output, the $X value for the current device is updated: $X is incremented by one for each printing character, is decremented by one for each backspace character (ASCII character whose decimal value is 8), and is left unchanged for all other characters (codes whose decimal values lie between 1 and 7, 9 and 31, and 127). *Note*: Some implementations keep track of the right margin of the device (usually established with the OPEN or USE command); in these implementations, the system may also perform an automatic new line sequence (carriage return and line feed) and then update both $X and $Y (that is, increment $Y by one and set $X to 0) when output to the device exceeds the right margin.

3.4.4.2 Argument = FORMAT CONTROL   There are three special format control arguments: the **!** to initiate a new line sequence, the **#** to initiate a new page sequence, and the format **?INTEGER EXPRESSION**, which initiates the tab to column sequence.

The new line sequence initiated by the **!** argument sends both a *carriage return* character (decimal 13) and a *line feed* character (decimal 10) to the device, and it increments the value of $Y by one while resetting the value of $X to 0. MUMPS also permits a *special* syntax of this argument where multiple exclamation points need not be considered separate arguments and separated by commas. The special argument format is demonstrated in the following example.

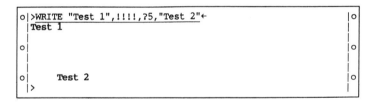

EXAMPLE 3.71.   WRITE Format, format = !

The new page sequence initiated by the **#** argument sends a *form feed* character (decimal 12) to the device and resets both $X and $Y to 0. Note that the form feed character does not necessarily perform a new page or clear screen function on all devices. See Chapter 12 for an in-depth discussion of input and output. Also, the **#** format character can be combined with the **!** character in a special syntax of the argument that requires no separating commas (for example, the command **W #!!!,"test"** would advance to a new page, move down three lines, and output the text **test**).

The tab to column (each column is one character wide) sequence initiated with an argument of **?INTEGER EXPRESSION** has the effect of moving to the $X position in the current line associated with INTEGER EXPRESSION. If the current $X position is greater than INTEGER EXPRESSION, the argument is ignored. If it is less than the current $X value, then the appropriate number of spaces are output to the device to bring $X equal to INTEGER EXPRESSION. The leftmost column (first $X position in a line) has a $X value of 0.

Efforts are currently underway in the MDC to define another broad type of FORMAT syntax to handle the bewildering array of mechanisms for performing device-specific functions, such as positioning the cursor on a video terminal or rewinding a magnetic tape drive. From early discussions it appears as if this form of the format syntax will be:

\mne[parameters] For example, Write \CUP(2,20) to move the cursor on a video terminal to location $X=2$, $Y=20$ or Write \rewind to rewind a magnetic tape.

where the special character "\" identifies the special format field and mne is the functional mnemonic to be performed (with an optional parameter list). If this syntax is adopted as part of the language standard, we will have gone a long way toward achieving device independence and will be able to transfer applications between systems with considerably more ease.

At the present, a number of MUMPS vendors already support this syntax, but the methods used for linking physical devices with the mnemonic list, as well as the mnemonics themselves, are usually incompatible between systems. For a more in-depth discussion of devices and device independence, refer to Chapter 12.

3.4.4.3 Argument = *INTEGER EXPRESSION In this format, the single character associated with INTEGER EXPRESSION is output to the device. The actual interpretation of the character and the effect of the WRITE are defined by the implementor. When sent to terminal-type devices, positive integers in the range of 0 to 127 are usually interpreted as ASCII characters with the equivalent decimal values (see Appendix A for a list of ASCII codes and their decimal equivalents). Consider the following examples.

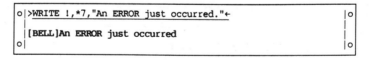

EXAMPLE 3.72. WRITE *var

In this example, the BELL (the ASCII character with decimal value of 7 is BEL) on the terminal would be activated and the error message would be displayed. Note that this method of outputing nonprinting characters is preferred over embedding those characters within a string literal where they cannot be seen.

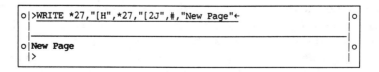

EXAMPLE 3.73. Clearing the screen

This second example shows a technique often used when trying to format output with different devices. We discussed earlier the use of the # FORMAT argument to start a new page. The # argument sends a form feed character (decimal 12) to the device and resets $X and $Y to 0. Unfortunately, many terminal types do *not* clear the screen on receipt of a form feed character. The preceding code shows the *ESCape* sequences that are needed to clear the screen on a VT-100 terminal.

Many terminals handle special functions, such as clearing the screen or positioning the cursor, with special ESCape sequences. These are usually initiated by first sending the ASCII ESCape character (decimal value 27), followed by one or more characters. The terminal interprets the characters that follow as control sequences and does not print them. In Example 3.73, the sequence *27,"[H" instructs a VT-100 terminal to "home" the cursor (move the cursor to the top-left corner of the screen), and the sequence *27,"[2J" instructs the VT-100 to erase all characters from the current cursor position to the end of the screen. We still need to send out the # argument to reset the system variables $X and $Y to 0 and synchronize the display and MUMPS. MUMPS does *not* know that the ESCape sequences have cleared the screen and homed the cursor to the top-left corner of the screen.

Another and more common approach to achieve the same results is to establish a defined set of terminal-specific variables at the beginning of an application and use these variables as indirect arguments to WRITE commands and thus provide a level of device independence for the application. Consider the following example:

```
o|>If DevType="VT100" Set ClrScrn="*27,""[H"",*27,""[2J"",#"←|o
 |>If DevType'="VT100" Set ClrScrn="#"←                        |
 |>                                                             |
o|>Write @ClrScrn,"New Page"←                                  |o
 |                                                             |
 |─────────────────────────────────────────────────────────────|
o|New Page                                                     |o
```

EXAMPLE 3.74. Indirect arguments to a WRITE command

In this example, we establish the variable ClrScrn to hold whatever arguments are required to perform the new page function on the current terminal type. We can then use this variable with argument indirection any time it is necessary to clear the screen in an application.

NOTE. The actual operation performed using the *INTEGER EXPRESSION form of a WRITE command is both device and implementor specific. Some implementors update $X and $Y with this format; others do not. The decimal values associated with INTEGER EXPRESSION are not necessarily limited to the ASCII character set. For example, some implementors use negative INTEGER EXPRESSIONs as special control arguments for some devices (for example, WRITE $*-5$ to rewind a magnetic tape). Check the reference manuals for your implementation for a complete description of the actions taken in these cases.

```
o|>Write !,?20,"One",*13,?10,"Two",*13,"Three"←          |o
|                                                        |
|Three      Two         One                              |
o|>                                                      |o
```

EXAMPLE 3.75.   Updating $X, $Y on WRITE *var commands

When executing commands in direct mode, MUMPS automatically initiates a new line sequence when the <ENTER> key is pressed at the end of the command line. However, when a routine is executing, all WRITE commands apply to the current location of the cursor or printhead; new lines are only generated by explicit command (for example, **Write !**) or, in some instances, when the right margin is exceeded. There is *not* an automatic new line sequence issued at the beginning of each WRITE command.

In Example 3.75, there is one explicit new line requested at the beginning of the WRITE command. The tab control is then used to move to the twentieth column and the characters "one" are output. The *13 argument causes a return to column zero, *without* sending a line feed character (*10). The tab function is then used to position to column 10 and "two" is output, and so forth. This example assumes that $X and $Y are being updated when the Write *Argument syntax is used. To guarantee the results shown using this syntax, you might have to use the following code:

```
o|>Write !,?20,"Line",*13 Set $X=0 Write ?10,"Test"←     |o
|              Test        Line                           |
o|>                                                       |
```

EXAMPLE 3.76.   Effect of $X on WRITE ?nn

The SET command is used in this example to explicitly set the value of $X to zero after the Write *13 forces the terminal to move the cursor to the first column of the current line.

3.4.5 CLOSE Command

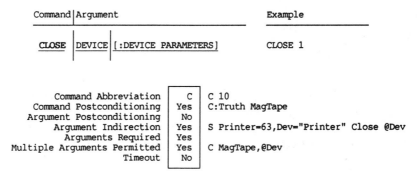

```
Command | Argument                              Example
─────────────────────────────────────────      ──────────────
 CLOSE  | DEVICE | [:DEVICE PARAMETERS]          CLOSE 1
```

Command Abbreviation	C	C 10
Command Postconditioning	Yes	C:Truth MagTape
Argument Postconditioning	No	
Argument Indirection	Yes	S Printer=63,Dev="Printer" Close @Dev
Arguments Required	Yes	
Multiple Arguments Permitted	Yes	C MagTape,@Dev
Timeout	No	

The CLOSE command is used to release ownership of one or more devices back to the pool of devices maintained by MUMPS. Ownership of a device is gained with the OPEN command, and the USE command makes an owned device active. There is a brief description of the general concepts of devices in Section 3.4 and a more detailed description of input/output operations in Chapter 12.

Basically, the CLOSE command is used to release a currently owned device back to the system. Once released, an attempt to USE that device before it has been OPENed again will result in an error. If the DEVICE being CLOSEd is the current device (established with the USE command), the device will be released and the principal I/O device (established at sign-on time) will become the current device (that is, as if a USE 0 command had been issued).

There is an implied CLOSE of all OPENed devices when a process terminates. For example, if a HALT command is executed, all DEVICES currently owned by the process are returned back to the system.

3.4.5.1 Argument = DEVICE If the device associated with the DEVICE designator is currently OPENed, then that device is released to the system and subsequent USE commands with that DEVICE designator result in an error. If the DEVICE being closed is the current device (established with the USE command), usually the principal I/O device is made current, but this is not specified by the language standard. The principal I/O device (usually established at sign-on time) can also be CLOSEd. However, that DEVICE is still considered the job's principal device and any output to it (such as error messages) will cause the process to hang until that device becomes available (that is, until ownership can be re-established).

It is legal to close a device that has not been opened or one that has already been closed. Unnecessary CLOSE commands are ignored.

3.4.6 PRINT Command[10]

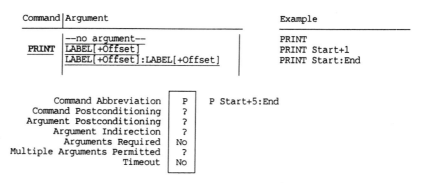

The PRINT command is not a part of the MUMPS standard, but it is included since almost all implementations support it. Even those systems that have implemented the PRINT command often implement a ZPRINT command as well.

The PRINT command is used to output lines from the routine currently loaded in the partition to the current device (as established with the USE command).

---

[10]The PRINT command is *not* part of the MUMPS standard.

Often the lines output are formatted to improve legibility (that is, the space separating a LABEL from the commands or preceding the commands on lines without LABELS is expanded to a TAB field).

Since this is a nonstandard command, you will have to refer to your reference manual for additional information concerning its use and syntax.

3.5 System and Miscellaneous Commands

This is a collection of commands that do not fall conveniently into any of the previous categories. Some, such as the LOCK command, are unique to the MUMPS environment, where the shared nature of global databases dictates the need for a mechanism for controlling access to data files. Others are used to spawn new MUMPS processes (JOB), to effect the timing of program execution (HANG), or to examine and change aspects of the operating system (VIEW).

Another category altogether includes those commands starting with the letter Z. Commands starting with this letter are reserved for implementors to include extensions to the language and to test new commands. However, by convention, most implementors use a standard set of commands to manipulate MUMPS routines (load, store, print, delete, and so on). In this section we will cover those Z commands available on most implementations.

The commands to be covered in this section are:

BREAK command	Used both to enable interrupts from the keyboard and also to insert breakpoints in a program for interactive debugging purposes.
HANG command	Used to pause program execution for a specified time interval.
JOB command	Used to spawn or start independent MUMPS processes in another partition.
LOCK command	Used to establish or relinquish ownership of one or more branches of a MUMPS global.
VIEW command	This command is specific to each implementation. In general, it permits the programmer to examine and change memory within the MUMPS operating system. To those familiar with BASIC, this command (and its companion function $VIEW) are similar to the POKE and PEEK operations, respectively.
ZLOAD command	Permits loading MUMPS routines from disk into a local work space (partition). Also permits (in some implementations) loading of programs from other devices such as magnetic tape.
ZINSERT command	Allows insertion of new program lines into the program currently loaded into the partition.
ZREMOVE command	Provides a means for deleting MUMPS programs from the local work space (partition) or from the disk. In some MUMPS implementations, the ZR command only removes lines of code from the partition. In these sys-

tems it is necessary to save an empty partition to disk to delete the program (that is, ZREMOVE ZSAVE ProgName).

ZPRINT command   This command allows the MUMPS routine (or parts of the routine) currently resident in the partition to be output to the currently active device. This command is closely related (often identical to) the PRINT command discussed in Section 3.4.6.

ZSAVE command   Allows the routine that is currently loaded into the partition to be saved to disk. This command can also be used (in some implementations) for saving routines to other devices such as magnetic tape.

3.5.1 BREAK Command

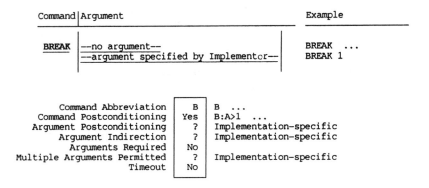

```
Command│Argument                                            Example
───────│────────────────────────────────────────────│    ──────────
 BREAK │──no argument──                              │    BREAK ...
       │──argument specified by Implementor──│            BREAK 1
```

```
        Command Abbreviation │ B   │ B ...
     Command Postconditioning │ Yes │ B:A>1 ...
    Argument Postconditioning │  ?  │ Implementation-specific
         Argument Indirection │  ?  │ Implementation-specific
           Arguments Required │ No  │
  Multiple Arguments Permitted │  ?  │ Implementation-specific
                      Timeout │ No  │
```

The BREAK command is not completely defined in the MUMPS standard, so its operation is dependent on the implementation being used. In general, it functions as a debugging tool to interrupt the execution of a program and enter direct mode. In direct mode, the programmer can examine or change the variable environment before restarting execution of the interrupted program. *No* method is specified by the language standard as to how program execution is restarted after a BREAK; most systems have implemented a **ZGO** command (without arguments) that resumes program execution after a BREAK. In addition, some systems permit an argumentless form of the GOTO command (refer to Section 3.3.1.4) as a non-standard method of resuming program execution.

How and where the BREAK command works is dependent on the implementation being used. Some versions will ignore BREAK commands encountered in programs that were *not* initiated from direct mode. That is, if a programmer first signs onto MUMPS in direct mode and initiates a program with a DO command, any BREAKS encountered in the program will cause the process to be interrupted; other methods of starting the program, such as a terminal being tied directly to an application program, will disable the BREAK command. Check your documentation for the specifics of how and when the BREAK command is interpreted and how to resume program execution from direct mode.

```
o|Test   ;Demonstrate use of BREAK command for debugging  |o
|         Write !,"LC=",LC Break                            |
|         For i=1:1:LC Write !,"Line ",i                    |
o|        Quit                                              |o
|_____|
|>Set LC=100 Do ^Test←                                      |
o|                                                          |o
|LC=100                                                     |
|<<BREAK>>                                                  |
o|>Set LC=2←                                                |o
|>Write "LC=",LC←                                           |
|LC=2                                                       |
o|ZGO←                                                      |o
|Line 1                                                     |
|Line 2                                                     |
o|>                                                         |o
```

EXAMPLE 3.77. Demonstration of the BREAK command

The Break command after the first Write interrupts program execution and puts the terminal back in direct mode. After changing the value of the variable LC, program execution is resumed with the ZGO command. Notice that altering the variable environment has a direct impact on program execution; the loop terminator LC is changed from 100 to a value of 2 while in direct mode. The use of the ZGO command to resume program execution is demonstrated since it is one of the more common methods used; the ZGO command may not work on all systems.

Many implementors also recognize a form of the BREAK command with arguments that may function in an entirely different manner than the argumentless form of the BREAK command. A common use of the BREAK with arguments is to enable or disable interrupts from the keyboard. In many implementations, program execution can be interrupted by pressing <CTRL>C (hold down the <CTRL> key and press C). While this can be an invaluable programmer aid, it may not be desirable to allow an end user to interrupt an application.

In implementations supporting this form of the BREAK, the argument is evaluated as a truth value; If TRUE (nonzero), keyboard breaks are enabled, if FALSE (zero), then keyboard breaks are disabled. Again, check your documentation for full specifications of the BREAK command under your MUMPS implementation.

3.5.2 HANG Command

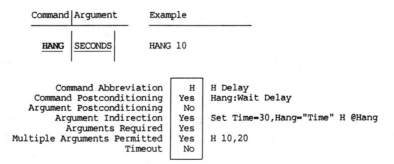

Command	Argument	Example
HANG	SECONDS	HANG 10

Command Abbreviation	H	H Delay
Command Postconditioning	Yes	Hang:Wait Delay
Argument Postconditioning	No	
Argument Indirection	Yes	Set Time=30,Hang="Time" H @Hang
Arguments Required	Yes	
Multiple Arguments Permitted	Yes	H 10,20
Timeout	No	

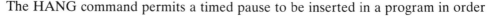

The HANG command permits a timed pause to be inserted in a program in order to temporarily suspend execution for SECONDS seconds. SECONDS is evaluated as an integer and represents the number of seconds to pause before resuming execution; if zero (0) or negative, the command has no effect. The period of time the hang pauses is not exact in that it relies on the system clock (as reflected by the system variable $H) and can be off by up to one second. For example, if a HANG 1 is issued immediately before the system clock advances by one second, the actual pause might be just a fraction of a second.

Both the HANG and the HALT command can be abbreviated to the single character **H**. MUMPS differentiates between these two commands based on the presence or absence of an argument; the HALT command has *no* argument while the HANG command does.

The HANG command is often used to pause a program to give the user a chance to read the messages on a screen before the screen is cleared and execution continues, as is demonstrated in the next example.

```
o|      Do DispTxt Hang 30 Do ClrScrn              |o
 |         .                                        |
 |         .                                        |
o|         .                                        |o
 |         .                                        |
```

EXAMPLE 3.78. HANG command

A problem with this approach is that the HANG duration is fixed and the user must wait the full time interval before execution continues. An alternative that allows the end user to prematurely terminate the pause during a timed READ command is shown in Example 3.67 under the READ command.

3.5.3 JOB Command

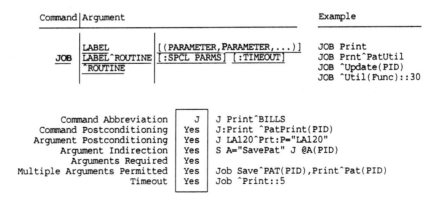

The JOB command permits the initiation of a MUMPS process to be run in another partition. MUMPS generally supports a multiuser environment (time-sharing) in which more than one application can be running at the same time. Each JOB is given its own partition, and each job running on the system has a unique job number (reflected by the system variable $JOB). Jobs run independently of each other but can communicate through global variables.

One process can spawn one or more other processes, which may run concurrently with the process that initiated them. The JOB command functions in a manner similar to signing onto the system and then starting a routine with a DO command, *except* that there may be no principal I/O device assigned to the started process.

Normally, when you sign onto the MUMPS terminal, that terminal becomes the job's principal device. MUMPS performs an implied OPEN and USE command with that device before execution begins, and all subsequent I/O is directed to that device until other OPEN and USE commands are issued. When a process is started with the JOB command, there may or may not be a principal I/O device associated with the process. The MUMPS standard does not specify what happens when a started job attempts to perform I/O without explicitly OPENing and USEing a device. In some implementations, the principal device for a started job is assumed to be the principal device for the process that initiated the job. Other implementations consider it to be an error condition if a started job attempts I/O without having specifically OPENed and USEd a device; usually, such systems permit an optional parameter to be included in the SPCL PARMS list to specify the new job's principal I/O device.

In implementations that assume the new job's principal I/O device to be the same as the starting job's principal I/O device, the started job may hang on I/O until the original process releases the principal device.

3.5.3.1 Argument Includes (PARAMETER,PARAMETER,...)[11]
This format is similar, but not identical, to the DO command with parameters (see Section 3.3.2.2). Each PARAMETER in the parenthesized list of actual arguments can be any valid MUMPS expression. The values for these expressions are then used to initialize the local symbol table in the started job according to the variable names in the formal list of arguments in the started process.

Values associated with local variables can only be passed in one direction, from the initiating process to the started process. The started process cannot pass back information, nor does it have access to the rest of the symbol table of the initiating process. Other communication between the two processes must be through global variables. Parameters in the actual list of parameter can *only* be passed by *value*, not by reference. See Section 3.3.2.2 and Chapter 9 for a more detailed discussion of parameters.

3.5.3.2 Argument Includes :SPCL PARMS
The optional parameter SPCL PARMS is used to specify certain operating considerations for the new process. Items included in SPCL PARMS might include the partition size, the new job's priority, principal I/O device, and so on. The SPCL PARMS list must start with a colon (:), but otherwise its syntax and structure are determined by each implementor.

[11]MDC Type A release, January 1987.

3.5.3.3 Argument Includes :TIMEOUT

The optional TIMEOUT parameter permits the initiating process to verify whether or not the requested job was initiated. In some instances, a job cannot be started (for example, there are no available partitions). The MUMPS standard does *not* specify what happens in such instances. Some implementations hang on these JOB commands until the process can be started; others ignore the request altogether. Neither alternative is desirable. If the TIMEOUT parameter is used, it is evaluated as an integer representing the number of seconds to attempt to initiate the background process before returning control to the program that issued the JOB command. If the requested JOB was successfully started, the system variable $TEST is set to TRUE; if the requested job could not be started, $TEST is set to FALSE. If the TIMEOUT parameter is not included in the JOB command, the value of $TEST is not changed.

In the example that follows we show how a report could be printed by a background process while the foreground process can continue with other activities (such as data collection). In this example, we assume that device number 15 is the system's line printer on which reports are to be printed. We do not show the code that actually does the printing, only the code needed to initiate the job. It is assumed that the background job will OPEN and USE device 15 before it starts outputing the report. The code used to initiate the background task will first check to see if the printer is available.

```
SPrint Set Status=0 O 15::0
        If '$T W *7,"Can't get Line Printer." Quit
        Job PRINT^REPORT(PID)::0 Close 15
        If  Write "Report Started." Set Status=1
        Else  Write "Can't start report now."
        Quit
────────────────────────────────────────────────
>Set PID=9913 Do SPrint←
Can't get Line Printer.
>D SPrint←
Can't start report now.
>D SPrint←
Report Started.
>
```

EXAMPLE 3.79.   JOB command

Notice the use of a TIMEOUT = 0 in both the OPEN and JOB command. In both cases, control is immediately returned to the program with $TEST set to TRUE or FALSE, depending on whether or not the requested action was successful. Also notice that we return the variable Status as either TRUE or FALSE depending on whether or not the requested job had been started. Finally, notice how we test to see if device 15 is available. The CLOSE 15 command is not issued until *after* the JOB command. If the requested job starts successfully and it starts off by trying to OPEN device 15, it will hang until the initiating routine CLOSEs that device. It is still possible for other jobs to gain ownership in the short lapse in time between when the foreground task releases the device and when the background task gains ownership, but the chances of that happening are small. Even if it does happen, the background task will simply hang (assuming it is not using a timed OPEN) until the printer is free and then output the report.

Remember that, if TIMEOUT is specified, but the optional SPCL PARMS are not, *two* colons (::) must separate the TIMEOUT parameter from the name of the routine being started.

Additional examples of the JOB command, including passing parameters, are presented in Section 9.5.

3.5.4 LOCK Command

Command	Argument		Example
LOCK	VARIABLE (VARIABLE,VARIABLE,VARIABLE,) --no argument-- +VARIABLE -VARIABLE	[:TIMEOUT]	LOCK XYZ LOCK (^A,^B(22)) LOCK ... LOCK +^XYZ(33) LOCK -^XYZ(33)

Command Abbreviation	L	L ^ABC
Command Postconditioning	Yes	LOCK:PID'="" ^Pat(PID)
Argument Postconditioning	No	
Argument Indirection	Yes	Set Gbl="^ZIP(14850)" L @Gbl
Arguments Required	No	
Multiple Arguments Permitted	Yes	L ^A,^XYZ(1,234)[12]
Timeout	Yes	L (^BC(23),^Addr):0

In Chapter 3 we discussed the concept of global variables. Unlike local variables that are unique to a given process, global variables reside on disk and are available to all processes running under the same directory. Many different processes can be accessing or changing data in the same global *simultaneously*. This powerful approach toward common, shared databases has some potential drawbacks. Consider the case where a program extracts a data node from a global in order to alter its contents. After the first program extracts the data for local processing, a second process also retrieves the same data node, modifies it, and stores the results back in the global. When the first process saves its version of the updated data, the changes incorporated by the second process are *lost* since the data node is overlaid by the first process. Clearly, there needs be a way to safeguard against conflicts of this type.

The LOCK command provides the mechanism to reserve databases or parts of databases for a particular process. While one process has a global or global branch locked, no other process can lock the same node(s). The LOCK command establishes ownership of a global or global branch *by convention*. A LOCKed node can still be accessed or even changed by another process that does not LOCK the

---

[12]**Warning:** The use of multiple arguments that are not included in parentheses will *only* leave the last argument in the list LOCKed on completion of the command. See Section 3.5.4.1 for more details.

node in question. To prevent the inadvertent loss of data resulting from multiple processes accessing the same data nodes, *all* such processes must use the LOCK command; the LOCK command is effective *only* if other programs also use the LOCK command.

> The LOCK command does not, in and of itself, prevent access to LOCKED variables by other processes.

LOCK commands are transient; that is, all global nodes that were LOCKed by a given process are automatically UNLOCKED when the process terminates (for example, with a HALT command). LOCKED nodes can also be explicitly UNLOCKED by the process that originally LOCKed them. The table of locked nodes applies to all processes on the system; a node locked by one process cannot be locked by another until the first has unlocked the node. On the other hand, a process that locked a node can lock the same node a second time without a conflict. The results of multiple LOCKs on the same node depend on the form of the LOCK. Incremental LOCK commands stack (count) LOCKs; each subsequent LOCK of the same node increments a lock counter for that node and should be matched with a subsequent decremental LOCK. Other forms of the LOCK clear previous LOCK commands before performing the requested LOCK(s).

Think back to our discussions on the hierarchical nature of globals. When a global node is LOCKed, that node *and all its descendants* are also locked. In addition, all *direct* parents of the locked node are also unavailable for locking by other processes. Consider the global structure shown in Figure 3.3.

If we lock the global node ^A(33,57), then that node as well as its two descendents [^A(33,57,17) and ^A(33,57,94)] cannot be locked by another process. In addition, the direct parent nodes [^A(33) and ^A] are also unavailable for locking by other processes. However, other nodes, even those siblings below direct parent nodes, *can* be locked by other processes. For example, given the lock command LOCK ^A(33,57), other processes can still lock ^A(1) and ^A(33,9).

Another interesting use of the LOCK command is when one or more of the arguments are not global variables, but rather local variable names. Normally, we consider the local variable environment of a given job (partition) to be independent of all other jobs on the system. However, it is possible to LOCK a local variable as well as a global variable. Local variables so locked are *unavailable* to all other jobs for locking, in the same fashion as are locked global variables. Locking local variables is a technique that could be used to communicate between independent jobs.

3.5.4.1 Argument = VARIABLE   This is the simplest form of the LOCK command. The argument VARIABLE is the name of local variable, a global variable, or an array node (name plus subscripts) to be locked. That variable or node, all

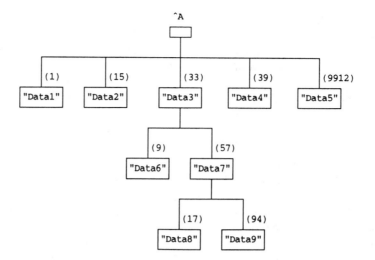

FIGURE 3.3. Demonstration global for the LOCK command

its descendants, and all its direct parent nodes in the case of arrays are then made unavailable for locking by other processes on the system.

This form of the LOCK command is *not* incremental; before attempting to LOCK any of VARIABLE references defined in the argument(s), the LOCK command first <u>UNLOCKS</u> all existing LOCKs for this process. It then proceeds by attempting to LOCK each of the specified arguments. If any argument is already LOCKed by another process, the current LOCK command will hang (that is, execution will be suspended for the processes requesting the LOCK) until the VARIABLE reference in contention is UNLOCKED by the other process. To maintain control of the locking mechanism, the optional TIMEOUT syntax (discussed later in this section) can be used. VARIABLES locked in this fashion can be UNLOCKED using the argumentless form of the LOCK command.

Remember, each time this form of the LOCK command is issued, all VARIABLE references previously LOCKed for this process are UNLOCKED before the new lock argument(s) is processed. To maintain previously LOCKed variables, they must also be in the current argument list. Also note that the nodes that are released at the time the new lock command is issued may be locked by other processes before the arguments to the current LOCK command are processed.

The fact that all existing locks are unlocked before locking the VARIABLEs in the argument list introduces an interesting problem when the argument string contains more than one variable name. Remember that multiple arguments are a shorthand form of *repeating the command* with new arguments. In other words, the command:

LOCK ^X,ABC,^TEST(3,4),ZZ←

is equivalent to issuing *four* separate LOCK commands:

LOCK ^X LOCK ABC LOCK ^TEST(3,4) LOCK ZZ←

If the lock command is issued with more than one VARIABLE in the argument string (for example, LOCK ^X,ABC,^TEST(3,4),ZZ←), each VARIABLE in the list is LOCKed in turn, but *only* the last argument in the list remains locked on completion of the command (each implied LOCK unlocks all previously locked variables). The next form of the LOCK command in which the arguments are enclosed in parentheses overcomes this limitation.

3.5.4.2 Argument = (VARIABLE,VARIABLE,...)   As in the previous form of the LOCK command, all VARIABLEs that were previously LOCKed are unlocked. The LOCK command then processes the VARIABLE arguments, one at a time and from left to right, trying to LOCK each. However, unlike the previous form, *all* the variables in the list are LOCKED without unlocking previous VARIABLEs in the same list that have been successfully locked. If the LOCK command encounters a VARIABLE that is already LOCKED by another process, execution is hung until the variable in contention is unlocked by the other process. Use of the TIMEOUT syntax with the LOCK command allows the program to maintain control over the locking function.

On completion of the command LOCK (^A,XYZ,^B(123,456))←, all three variables in the argument list will be locked.

If this form of the LOCK command FAILS and the :TIMEOUT parameter has been specified (Section 3.5.4.4), then *none* of the VARIABLEs in the argument list is locked on completion of the command. Execution of the LOCK is an all-or-nothing process; if all the variables cannot be locked, then none are.

3.5.4.3 Argument = —no argument—   The LOCK command with *no arguments* is used to UNLOCK all variables previously locked by a process. There is an implied LOCK command without arguments issued when a given process terminates (that is, HALTs), guaranteeing that all VARIABLEs LOCKED by that process are unlocked before the partition is released back to MUMPS.

3.5.4.4 Argument Includes :TIMEOUT   We indicated previously that the LOCK command will hang (that is, execution for the process will be suspended) if one or more of the variables to be locked are already locked by another process. Execution will resume only when the variables in question are unlocked by the other process. This means that a process might enter a suspended state for an indefinite period of time, clearly a situation to be avoided. The optional TIMEOUT parameter can be appended to any LOCK command to avoid losing control of a process.

TIMEOUT is evaluated as an integer representing the number of seconds during which the system attempts to gain ownership of the VARIABLE(s) in the argument list before returning control to the program. When used, the TIMEOUT parameter *must* be separated from the argument list with a colon (:). Upon completion of a LOCK command with a TIMEOUT, control is returned to the program with the system variable $TEST set to TRUE (1) if the LOCK command was successful, or to FALSE (0) if one or more of the variables could not be locked. If one or more of the variables could not be locked, then *none* of the variables in the argument list are locked. Consider the following example in which it is assumed that another process already has the global node PAT(1234) LOCKED:

```
o|GetPat Read !,"Enter Patient's ID Number: ",PID Q:PID=""    |o
 |        If PID'?1N.N Write *7," BAD Number." Goto GetPat     |
 |        Lock ^PAT(PID):5 If $T Write " got it." Quit         |
o|        W *7,!,"Patient ",PID," is being updated by someone" |o
 |        W " else,",!,?12,"please try this patient later."    |
 |        Goto GetPat                                          |
o|------------------------------------------------------------|o
 |>Do GetPat←                                                  |
 |Enter Patient's ID Number: 1234←                             |
o|Patient 1234 is being updated by someone else,               |o
 |              please try this patient later.                 |
 |Enter Patient's ID Number: 8765← got it                      |
o|>                                                            |o
```

EXAMPLE 3.80. Timed LOCK command

In this example, the LOCK command will try for up to 5 seconds to lock the global node PAT(PID). If the lock can be performed, control is immediately returned to the program with the requested node locked and $TEST set to TRUE. If another process already has the requested node locked, the LOCK command will continue trying to lock the node for 5 seconds. If it can lock the node within this time period, execution continues with the node locked and $TEST set to TRUE. If it cannot gain ownership within 5 seconds, control is returned to the program with the node unlocked and with $TEST set to FALSE.

If *no* TIMEOUT is specified in the LOCK command, the value of the system variable $TEST is *not* altered by the LOCK command.

Use of the optional TIMEOUT parameter is *strongly recommended* in application programs using the LOCK command. Otherwise, the program may "hang" for an indefinite period of time with no warning for the end user.

3.5.4.5 Argument = +VARIABLE or +(VARIABLE,VARIABLE,...)[13] This form of the LOCK command is similar to the two forms already described, but it is *incremental* in nature. Unlike the previous versions of the LOCK command, the incremental LOCK does *not* unlock previously locked references before locking the new arguments.

Each entry in the argument list is added to the system's lock table, and the same reference may be added more than one time. If the same reference is locked more than once by a given process, the lock table will have an entry for each time it was locked.

When the arguments are enclosed in parentheses, either *all* the arguments are locked or, if one or more cannot be locked, *none* of the arguments are locked. The use of the optional TIMEOUT parameter is identical to the previous description.

[13]MDC Type A release, January, 1987.

The LOCK command without arguments unlocks *all* locked variables, regardless of how they were locked (for example, with either the incremental or nonincremental form of the LOCK). Otherwise, the incremental unlocked form (LOCK -VARIABLE) can be used to incrementally unlock entries in the lock table.

The use of incremental LOCKs and unLOCKs is especially valuable when writing general-purpose subroutines in which the current status of the lock table may be unknown. If such a subroutine were to issue a nonincremental lock, then all previously locked variables would be released with potentially adverse effects. The use of the incremental form of the LOCK command permits such subroutines to lock and unlock variables without changing the status of the lock table entries that existed before it was invoked.

3.5.4.6 Argument = −VARIABLE or −(VARIABLE,VARIABLE,....)[14] This form of the LOCK command permits selective unlocking of variables, regardless of how they were locked. Because the incremental lock can be used to lock the same reference more than once, the incremental unlock must be applied once for each lock executed. For example, if the following commands were issued:

```
o|>Lock +^PAT(PID)←                                          |o
 |>Lock +^PAT(PID)←                                          |
 |>Lock -^PAT(PID)←                                          |
o|>                                                          |o
```

EXAMPLE 3.81. Incremental and decremental LOCK command

then ^PAT(PID) would still be locked; the reference was incrementally locked twice, yet only unlocked once. Alternatively, an argumentless LOCK command could have been issued to unlock *all* locked references.

3.5.5 VIEW Command

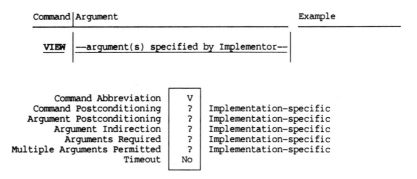

Command	Argument	Example
VIEW	—argument(s) specified by Implementor—	

Command Abbreviation	V	
Command Postconditioning	?	Implementation-specific
Argument Postconditioning	?	Implementation-specific
Argument Indirection	?	Implementation-specific
Arguments Required	?	Implementation-specific
Multiple Arguments Permitted	?	Implementation-specific
Timeout	No	

The VIEW command is implementation-specific. Each implementor can specify both the syntax and function of this command; consequently, code using the VIEW

---

[14]MDC Type A release, January 1987.

TABLE 3.2 VIEW command for UCD MicroMUMPS

VIEW Command	Results
View 0	Displays (to the current device) a list of the local variable names and their associated values. The names of arrays are displayed, but not their subscripted entries.
View 1	Displays the local variables names, subscripted array elements, and their associated values.
View 2	Displays a list of global variable names for the currently active global directory.
View 3	Displays a list of routine names for the currently active routine directory.
View 4	Displays a list of all file names (including the host operating system files) located under the disk and directory of the currently active routine directory.

command is unlikely to run on systems other than where it was originally developed. To repeat a well-worn phrase, check your documentation for specifics on the command.

Because the VIEW command is specific to the implementation under which it is running, programmers should not use this command in application packages designed to be used on more than one system. If they *must* be used, VIEW commands should not be spread throughout the application, and each should be well documented by defining the specific function(s) performed.

A relatively simple use of the VIEW command is shown in Table 3.2, which defines the valid arguments and results under UCD MicroMUMPS.

Other implementors use the VIEW command to alter memory locations, much like an extended version of the POKE command in BASIC. These systems typically have two different forms of the VIEW command: one to alter memory locations and the other to read and write specified disk blocks from or to memory. The $VIEW function (Section 8.3.3) in these systems usually complements the VIEW function and permits reading specified memory locations into MUMPS variables.

When using the VIEW command to access disk blocks, it is usually necessary to first establish ownership of a special device called the *view device* with the OPEN command; attempting to use the VIEW command without owning the view device results in an error. A typical summary of VIEW functions under this type of environment is shown in Table 3.3.

There are numerous variations on these commands that depend both on the hardware and MUMPS implementation being used. These are not commands that should be used by the novice programmer. For the most part, they are used by system utilities for patching the MUMPS operating system or for the repair of disk files.

WARNING. Improper use of the VIEW command can cause the system to crash and/or seriously degrade the structure of disk files! Do *not* use this command unless you are fully aware of the consequences.

TABLE 3.3 More advanced forms of VIEW command

VIEW Command	Results
View addr:value	Stores the numeric interpretation of <u>value</u> at the memory location specified by <u>addr</u>. NOTE that the size of <u>value</u> (byte, word, word size) is both machine and implementation specific, as is the evaluation of <u>addr</u>.
View block	Reads the disk block associated with the number in <u>block</u> into the buffer associated with the view device. There is usually an implementation-specific form of the $VIEW function that permits the programmer to retrieve the address of the view device buffer.
View −block	Writes the current contents of the view buffer back to the specified disk block.

3.5.6 ZLOAD Command

The ZLOAD command is used to load the source code of a routine from disk into the current partition. It is usually abbreviated to <u>ZL</u> and has the form

ZL ROUTINE

Before the indicated routine is loaded into the partition, MUMPS will erase any existing routine steps from the partition (it performs an implied ZREMOVE). It is not generally possible to join routines using the ZLOAD command.

Once a routine is loaded into the partition, lines can be inserted into or removed from the routine body with the ZINSERT and ZREMOVE commands, the routine (or parts of it) can be displayed with the ZPRINT command, and lines or parts can be executed with a local DO command (for example, DO LABEL).

Some implementors support an *argumentless* version of the ZLOAD command that loads the routine, not from disk, but rather from the currently assigned device (see the description of the OPEN and USE commands for more details on the current device).

3.5.7 ZINSERT Command

The ZINSERT command allows lines of code to be inserted into the routine body currently ZLOADed in the partition. It can usually be abbreviated to the characters <u>ZI</u> and has the basic form:

ZI "Line of Code":LABEL+OFFSET

where "Line of Code" is the line to be inserted and LABEL+OFFSET is the location within the routine body to insert the code. Note that some implementations will insert the line *before* the designated location, others *after* the location. In many cases LABEL and/or OFFSET are optional. Read the documentation that accompanies your implementation for more details.

3.5.8 ZREMOVE Command

The ZREMOVE command is used to delete lines of code from the routine currently loaded (ZLOAD) in the partition. It can usually be abbreviated to the characters ZR and has the general form

ZR LABEL + OFFSET or ZR LABEL + OFFSET:LABEL + OFFSET

where LABEL + OFFSET is the location of the lines to be deleted from the routine body (OFFSET is optional). If the argument contains two line references separated with a colon (:), then those two lines and all lines between them are deleted.

There is also usually an *argumentless* form of this command that deletes *all* lines in the current partition. The argumentless form does *not* usually delete the routine from disk. Deleting a routine from disk usually involves deleting it from the partition first and then saving the empty partition contents to disk with the ZSAVE command.

3.5.9 ZPRINT Command

The ZPRINT command is used to print lines of code from the routine currently ZLOADed in the partition to the current device (see the USE command for details on establishing the current device). It can usually be abbreviated to the characters ZP and has the general form

ZP LABEL + OFFSET or ZP LABEL + OFFSET:LABEL + OFFSET or ZP

where LABEL + OFFSET represents the line of code to be printed. In the form with two LABEL + OFFSET fields, those lines and all lines between them, will be printed. The argumentless form usually prints *all* lines.

Many implementors also provide a *PRINT* command that performs just like the ZPRINT command. The PRINT command is *not* part of the ANSI standard.

3.5.10 ZSAVE Command

The ZSAVE command is used to save the routine body currently loaded in the partition to disk. It can usually be abbreviated to ZS and has the general format

ZS ROUTINE

where ROUTINE is the name under which the routine will be filed. If the current partition is empty, many implementors will interpret the ZSAVE command as a request to delete the ROUTINE from disk.

In addition, many implementations support an *argumentless* form of the ZSAVE command to save the routine currently loaded into the partition to the current device. Routines saved in such a fashion can usually be reloaded into the partition using an argumentless form of the ZLOAD command. Other implementations reserve the argumentless form of the ZSAVE command to save the currently ZLOADed routine to disk, using the last referenced routine name as the default ROUTINE.

3.5.11 Miscellaneous Z Commands

All commands starting with the letter **Z** are defined by the standard as being implementor specific, although those presented in the previous sections are available on most systems. In this section we examine a few of the many command extensions supported by different implementations to provide the reader with a flavor of what some implementors are up to.

ZD(elete) Routine: Deletes the named routine from disk

ZE(dit): Used in some systems to invoke the routine editor.

ZO(ption) (routine directory:global directory): Used to change the current disk directories for routine or globals. The parameters *routine directory* and *global directory* contain both a disk drive specification and a directory specification (for example, **C:\MUMPS\APP**).

Z(space) "DIR": Used by some implementations to change the current routine and global directories (for example, switch to directory "DIR").

ZQ(uit): Similar to the QUIT command (Section 3.3.3), but in systems that do not clear the stacks when an error is encountered (see Chapter 13 for a discussion on error trapping), the ZQUIT command can be used to clear these stacks before quitting.

As mentioned, these are but a few of the many Z commands that are available on some systems; check your documentation. Do *not* plan on using these commands if you intend to move your programs between different implementations of MUMPS.

3.6 Summary

Commands form the heart of a MUMPS program and represent actions or directives to the computer. Most commands have arguments (explicit or implicit) that further define the action to be performed. The argument(s) to a command is separated from the command by a single-space character, and multiple arguments (where permitted) are separated from each other with commas.

Many commands and arguments can be modified by special syntactical constructs to determine, at the time of execution, whether or not they will actually be invoked (postconditioning). Some commands (READ, LOCK, JOB, and OPEN) can be further modified to indicate how long MUMPS should attempt their execution before returning control to the program (TIMEOUT). Both the postconditioning and TIMEOUT syntax are identified by a colon (:), which is associated with either the command or its argument(s). These special syntaxes are described in greater detail in Chapter 6.

An alphabetized list of the commands along with a brief description and examples can be found in Appendix C.

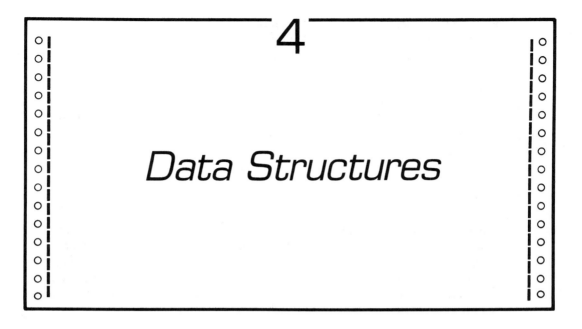

4

Data Structures

MUMPS handles all data internally as strings of characters. In contrast to most other languages, a MUMPS programmer does not have to declare the type of data (integer number, floating-point number, string of characters, or boolean value) that a given variable will hold. MUMPS interprets the contents of variables in context; they are evaluated as numbers for arithmetic operations, as strings of characters for string operations, and as TRUE or FALSE values for boolean operations. A given variable can represent, at different times in the same process, an integer, a floating-point number, a string of characters, or a boolean value. There are three type of MUMPS operators: numeric, string, and logical. The type or operator determines how MUMPS will evaluate the operand(s) (the arguments on which the operation is being performed), but the results of an operation are always represented internally as a string of characters.

There are strong arguments both for and against requiring strict definition and typing of variables. Proponents for formal declaration of variables and definition of data types associated with each variable argue that such steps force the programmer to seriously consider the use of the variable before writing an application. Individuals supporting this view argue that forcing this analysis and preventing mixed data operations (such as multiplying an integer value times a string value) will reduce programming errors. The computer language Pascal is a good example of this approach; it requires formal declaration of all variables and a strict definition of variable types, and it prohibits mixed-mode operations (such as multiplying an integer times a string). Opponents to formal variable definitions and typing argue that the overhead involved in such operations reduces programmer productivity. They also argue that such operations can be considered a matter of style, and even in a loosely typed language such as MUMPS, programmers can, by convention, rigorously define the variable environment. The MUMPS language allows dynamic variable creation at the time programs are executed, and does not support formal variable definitions or data typing.

4.1 Strings

The MUMPS language uses the seven-bit character code defined by the American Standard Code for Information Interchange (ASCII) as the basic character set for representing all data. This code consists of 128 unique characters and is reproduced in Appendix A. The MUMPS standard states that individual strings can be up to 255 characters in length, although many implementations permit longer strings (some permit string lengths of up to 20,000 characters).

Strings in MUMPS can be up to 255 characters in length.

String constants are referred to as *string literals* and are bounded on each side with quotation mark characters ("). Consider the following example:

```
o|>WRITE "This is a Test"←                                    |o
 |                                                            |
o|This is a Test                                              |o
 |>                                                           |
```

EXAMPLE 4.1.   String literals

The argument to the WRITE statement "This is a Test" represents a string literal. Empty string literals (often referred to as *null* strings in MUMPS) are also allowed (for example, SET A = ""). Care should be taken in distinguishing between a *null string* and the *NUL* character. A null string is an *empty* string (that is, a string with *no* characters, a string whose length is zero). The NUL character is the name of the ASCII character whose decimal equivalent is zero (0); it is a valid character and can be generated with the $CHAR function in MUMPS. A string consisting of a NUL character is *not* a null string.

> A *null string* is an empty string (one whose length is zero).
> The NUL character (decimal value of 0) is not the same as a
> null string. A string containing the NUL character is *not* empty.

Special attention must be paid to the quotation character (") since it is used in defining string literals, and yet MUMPS must also be able to process it as data. When two quotation marks appear together *within* the quotation marks defining a string literal, they are interpreted as a single quotation mark to be included in the string literal. Figure 4.1 illustrates a variety of string literals.

This Command (Input)	Results in (Output)
WRITE ""←	[nothing] ("" is an empty string)
WRITE "Test"←	Test
WRITE "A ""BIG"" Test"←	A "BIG" Test
WRITE """"←	"

FIGURE 4.1. String literals and quotation characters

According to the MUMPS standard, a string literal is bounded by quotes and contains any string of printable ASCII characters (decimal codes 32 to 126). This means that *control* codes (decimal values 0 to 31 and 127) and the extended ASCII characters used on many microcomputer systems (decimal codes 128 to 255) are *not* technically allowed as part of a string literal. In practice, most implementations permit inclusion of these other characters within a string literal.

While most of these control or extended characters can be generated from the keyboard (for example, the BEL character used to ring the bell on the terminal can be entered by holding down the <CTRL> key and then pressing the G key), it is *not* recommended that nonprinting characters be embedded in string literals. While it may be desirable to ring the bell when displaying an error message, the programmer will never know from a program listing that this is being done, since these characters do not appear on printed output. There are alternative methods to handle nonprinting characters; the $CHARACTER function discussed in Section 8.1.9 or the WRITE * syntax described in Section 3.4.4.3 makes the use of nonprinting characters more obvious.

4.2 Numbers

MUMPS makes no special distinction between integer or floating-point numbers when performing calculations and, unlike some languages, mixed calculations involving both types are permitted. Integers are defined as positive or negative whole numbers with no decimal fraction, while floating-point numbers do have a fractional part. Numbers may or may not be preceded by a positive or negative sign; if no sign is present, the number is assumed to be positive. The numeric equivalent to a string literal is the *numeric literal* (numeric constant). In the following example, the expressions 3.4, 2, and 1 all represent numeric literals.

```
o|>Write 3.4*2-1←                                           |o
 |5.8                                                        |
 |>                                                          |
```

EXAMPLE 4.2. Numeric literals

Many numbers, especially those involving repeating or endless fractional parts, are difficult to represent exactly on digital computers. Therefore, we must know how many significant digits in a number or calculation will be maintained. The MUMPS standard specifies that all numbers and calculations must be maintained to at least 12 digits of significance, although many implementors provide for even more digits of significance. This means that the 12 *most significant* digits (reading a number from left to right) will be maintained. Digits beyond the twelfth position cannot be guaranteed. Consider the following case:

```
o|>WRITE 22/7←                                              |o
 |                                                          |
o|3.142857142857142857                                      |o
 |>                                                         |
```

EXAMPLE 4.3. Significant digits

While the answer displayed shows 19 digits, only the first 12 (3.14285714285) can be considered as significant according to the standard. While a given implementation may support many more digits of precision, moving a program that makes use of this feature to a different MUMPS implementation may result in unacceptable inaccuracies.

4.2.1 Exponential Notation

MUMPS also provides a format for representing numbers in exponential notation. Exponential notation is a way of expressing both very large and very small numbers without the need for long strings of zeros. They are represented in MUMPS by entering the number followed by the letter E, then followed by a number representing the power of 10 to which the number is raised. For example, the notation **3.14E4** is equivalent to **31400** (the number 3.14 times 10 to the fourth power). Similarly, small numbers less than 0 can be represented using exponential notation with negative values to the right of the character E. The notation **4.56E−5** could be used to represent the number **0.0000456**.

Exponential notation can be used as input for any operation, but MUMPS converts such values to their numeric equivalent before the operation is performed, and the result is always returned in nonexponential form. Exponential notation is *never* used to return the results of an operation, regardless of the magnitude of the result.

```
o|>Write 1.32E3*2.6E-2←
|34.32
|>
```

EXAMPLE 4.4. Exponential notation

Exponential notation should not be confused with exponentiation. Exponentiation is an operation used to raise a number to a power and is often represented in other languages by the characters ** or ^ (for example, 3**4=81). Refer to Section 5.1 for a discussion of the exponentiation operator in MUMPS.

The MUMPS standard specifies that exponential notation include, as a minimum, the range of numbers falling between the limits **1E-25** and **1E25**. Despite this large range, only 12 decimal digits of precision are still specified by the standard.

4.2.2 Numeric Interpretation of Strings

We have indicated that MUMPS converts strings into appropriate values depending on the operation being performed. In most cases this conversion is fairly obvious.

```
o|>WRITE "+0.22"*4←
|
o|.88
|>
```

EXAMPLE 4.5. Numeric interpretation of strings

However, some cases are not this clear, and it is worthwhile reviewing the process by which MUMPS converts a string of characters into a number. MUMPS starts off scanning the string of characters from left to right, building a number as it proceeds. It stops the scan when the first nonvalid character is reached. Leading plus and minus signs (+ or −) are considered valid characters, as is the first decimal point (.) encountered; any other character will terminate the scan. Whatever valid numeric characters that have been built up to the time of the scan termination are used as the number for the operation. Figure 4.2 demonstrates, step by step, the internal conversion that MUMPS would initiate in evaluating the character string "+0.034ABC" as a number.

Note that a comma (,) is *not* specified as a valid character in the scan and would cause the scan to terminate. Conversion of the string value **10,000,000** to a number would evaluate to **10**.

When attempting to convert a string to a number and the string does *not* contain a valid numeric field, the evaluation of that string returns a zero (0). Consequently, the expression **3*"THREE"** results in 0 (3*0=0).

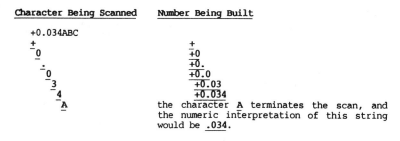

Character Being Scanned | Number Being Built

```
+0.034ABC
+                                       +
 0                                     +0
  .                                    +0.
   0                                   +0.0
    3                                  +0.03
     4                                 +0.034
      A         the character A terminates the scan, and
                the numeric interpretation of this string
                would be .034.
```

FIGURE 4.2. Evaluation of a character string as a number

4.3 Boolean (True/False)

There are several types of expressions in MUMPS that evaluate to true or false. Such examples are described in greater detail in Chapter 5, but consider the comparison of two numbers as in the next example.

```
o|>WRITE 7>2←                                              |o
 |                                                         |
o|1                                                        |o
 |>                                                        |
```

EXAMPLE 4.6. Boolean values

In the expression following the WRITE command, we are asking MUMPS to determine whether or not the numeric value of **7** is *greater* than the numeric value of **2**. Relational operations, such as that shown here, evaluate to TRUE or FALSE. The value returned by the expression is **1 if TRUE** and **0 if FALSE**. In general, any nonzero value (regardless of the sign) is considered TRUE, and any value that evaluates to a numeric 0 is FALSE.

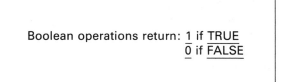

Boolean operations return: 1 if TRUE
0 if FALSE

4.4 Variables

This section presents a more rigorous definition of variables than earlier discussions. Variables are symbolic names that are used to reference data values; we can consider them as symbolic addresses that are associated with a data value. Variable names start with a single alphabetic character, followed by one or more alphabetic or numeric characters. While the length of a variable name can be any number of characters up to the string length limit (usually 255 characters), only the first eight characters are used to distinguish between variable names. Thus the variable names **DayOfTheWeek** and **DayOfThe** would both be interpreted by MUMPS to mean the same variable **DayOfThe**. Spaces are *not* allowed within a variable name.

Variable names start with a single alphabetic character optionally followed by additional alphabetic and numeric characters.

Variable names can be longer than eight characters, but only the first eight are used in resolving name conflicts.

Alphabetic characters in names can be either upper- or lowercase, and names are case sensitive. The variable name **Rate** is *different* from the variable name **RATE**.

Variable names are case sensitive.

We stated that variable names must start with a single alphabetic character, but there is an exception. They can also start with the percent character %. This character was included to permit the definition of variables that could be created and killed by library and utility routines and that would not likely conflict with the variable names within an application (remember the shared variable environment discussed in Chapters 1 and 2). The % character can *only* appear as the first character in a variable name; its occurrence anywhere else in the name is invalid.

All routines executed *within the same partition* share the same local variable storage area. Before the introduction of the NEW command and the concept of parameter passing, there was no way to ensure that variable names used in utility routines did not conflict with variable names used in an application program. By convention, most utility and library routines were written using locally defined variables starting with the % character. Also, by convention, application programs avoided using variables starting with this character except to pass information between an application and a utility subroutine. This convention was chosen to reduce variable name conflicts between routines. It was necessary for the programmer to know not only the function of a called subroutine, but also the variable names used by the subroutine. This was required to ensure that variables used within the called subroutine did not inadvertently alter the values of variables in the calling routine.

With features found in parameter passing, and with the NEW command (which permits selection of a new variable environment), the need for % variables has been largely eliminated. Unfortunately, many existing library and utility programs have not been rewritten to take advantage of these features and, consequently, % variables still appear in many MUMPS programs. It is recommended that application programs avoid the use of variable names starting with the percent sign unless they are needed to communicate with system utilities.

> Variable names can also start with the Percent (%) character, although its use is discouraged in application programs.

Finally, there is one more exception to the general rule that variable names must start with an alphabetic character. Any variable name can be changed from a local to a global variable (that is, one that resides on disk) by appending the up-arrow (^) to the front of the variable name.

> Variable names starting with the ^ character reside on disk and are referred to as GLOBAL variables.

4.4.1 Local Variables

To summarize previous discussions, local variables are those that reside in the local symbol table associated with a given process and partition. In contrast, global variables reside on disk. Local variables are transient; they are also not available to other MUMPS processes and they are killed when the current process is finished. All local variables start with a percent character % or with a single alphabetic character. Local variables can be either simple variables or arrays; array elements are defined by the presence of subscripts enclosed in parentheses after the variable name.

4.4.2 Arrays

Arrays are used to store related information both in local memory and also on disk. Local arrays are a special case of local variables and are subject to all the considerations that apply to local variables (Section 4.4.1). Global arrays in MUMPS replace traditional files used in other computer languages for storage of data on disk.

In most other languages, an array is declared as to type (integer, floating point, boolean) and size; space is then reserved for the defined number of elements. Usually, subscripts into these arrays are limited to numbers, and often only to integers.

The resulting array structure is often referred to as a *matrix* in which the number of subscripts defines the number of dimensions in the array. For example, $X(3)$ references a value in a one-dimensional array, while $Z(1,8)$ references a value in a two-dimensional array. Before using an array, it is usually necessary first to specify its *type* and *dimensions* so that space can be reserved for all possible elements. The array *type* defines how much space must be reserved for each cell in the array (for example, floating-point numbers typically take more space to store than integer numbers), and the *dimension* defines the number of cells that must be reserved. For example, dimensioning $X(3,5)$ could be used to reserve space for a three-row, five-column array (an array with 15 cells), as represented in Figure 4.3.

	Column 1	2	3	4	5
Row 1	17	35	21	11	71
2	94	76	14	49	53
3	5	31	68	19	51

FIGURE 4.3. Two-dimensional matrix

Based on this figure, the array element $X(2,4)$ would have the associated values of 49, $X(1,2) = 35$, etc.

In contrast, MUMPS arrays are *hierarchical* and *sparse*, and the subscripts pointing to array elements can be numbers (integer or floating point) or strings of ASCII characters. In the following discussion we examine how these characteristics affect the storage and retrieval of data.

4.4.2.1 Hierarchical Arrays Hierarchical arrays are often referred to as tree structured arrays and can be depicted as the roots of a tree. There is a branching structure as one moves down the levels; each branch point can have data associated with it and has only one parent, but it can have many descendants. Every descendant can, in turn, be the parent of another subbranch of the tree. The number of descendants under any given parent is arbitrary, as is the number of levels. Subtrees in the same array can contain different numbers of both descendants and levels.

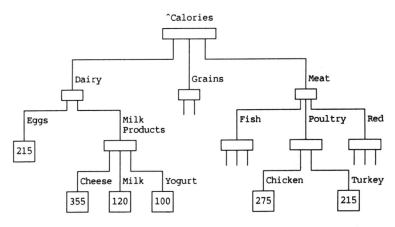

FIGURE 4.4. Hierarchical arrays

The branch points in an array are known as *nodes*, and the pathways (pointers) to nodes are referred to as *subscripts*; pathways are uniquely defined by their subscripts. There are three types of nodes: data nodes, pointer nodes with data, and pointer nodes without data. The type of a data node can change dynamically as the structure is altered (for example, a node that was a pointer without data can change to a node that is a pointer with data).

Figure 4.4 depicts the partial structure of a global array (^Calories) that could be used to categorize the nutritional value of foods. We will use this example to explore some of the basic aspects and implications of using hierarchical data structures to store information.

In this figure the boxes represent the nodes and the labels alongside the pathways represent the subscripts. Information in the boxes represents data associated with that node. Empty boxes are nodes that do not contain data and serve only as pointers to lower subtrees. For brevity, many of the subtrees have been omitted from the figure; these missing subtrees are represented by boxes with nonterminating lines descending from them [for example, ^Calories("Grains")].

Data in this array are held both in the values of the subscripts and within selected nodes. The subscripts define the food categories, while the data values held in some nodes contain the caloric value of the food type defined by the subscripts.

To access a particular data node, all the subscripts from the top of the tree to the desired node are specified, as shown in the next example.

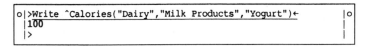

EXAMPLE 4.7. Subscripts of a hierarchical array

The subscripts used in this example represent one way in which the data could

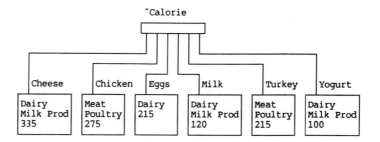

FIGURE 4.5. Alternative array structure

be organized. The use of subscripts to organize information permits rapid retrieval of related groups of data in MUMPS. For example, using the structure in Figure 4.4, it is possible to quickly retrieve all data filed as <u>Poultry</u> by looking only at the branches under ˆCalories("Meat","Poultry").

The same data could be reorganized and stored in the format shown in Figure 4.5.

Notice that, to represent the same amount of information held in the previous array design, we now have to store additional descriptive information concerning the type of food along with the caloric value of the food in each data node. Any searches for related data (for example, all "Meat" products) entails an exhaustive search of the entire database since the array is only organized by the food name.

Variable names can refer to single, unique data values and/or they can refer to an array of values. The same variable name can refer both to a single value as well as an array of values.

```
o|>Set A=1 Set A(1,2)="Test"←                                        |o
 |>Write A←
 |1
o|>Write A(1,2)←                                                     |o
 |Test
 |>                                                                  |
```

EXAMPLE 4.8. Simple and subscripted variable names

Here, variable **A** is both a simple variable name as well as the name of an array.

4.4.2.2 Sparse Arrays Consider another hierarchical data structure, one that could be used to store information on patient visits to a dentist's office. Assume that each patient has a unique identification number assigned on the first visit. We create a database in an array named <u>PatRec</u> that is organized by patient identification number and then by date of visit. In this database, we wish to record the patient's name, and for each visit, the chief complaint. We have arbitrarily defined two logical levels in the array defined by two subscript levels. The first subscript (**ID#**) is defined as an integer between 1 and 999999. The second level subscript

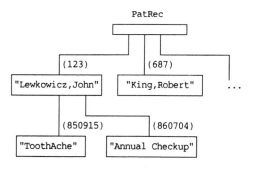

FIGURE 4.6. Sparse array

(**DATE**) is the date on which the patient is seen. To simplify the example, we define the date as a six digit number in the form YYMMDD (for example, Feb. 1, 1986, would be represented as **860201**). Figure 4.6 depicts the structure of array PatRec.

A number of interesting characteristics are demonstrated by this array structure. The first is that we are holding different types of data at different levels. The patient's name is held at the first level (for example, PatRec(123) = "Lewkowicz,John"); the reason for the visit is held at the second level (for example, PatRec(123,860704) = "Annual Checkup"). An organization such as this certainly makes sense, since the patient's name is likely to remain constant between visits, while the reason for specific visits is likely to change. Yet with this structure only one node is required to store the name, regardless of the number of visits recorded for that patient.

The second feature of this array is that we do not record the date of the visit as part of a data node. The visit date is encoded as a subscript of the array. The subscript contains data, and these data are available to the MUMPS program.

Finally, we should examine the consequences of the subscripts chosen for this example. We can ensure that the patient ID numbers used as subscripts are unique and assigned sequentially. As new patients are seen for their first visit, each would be given the next available number. Consequently, the first level of the array is well defined and packed. Unfortunately, the second-level subscript is based on the date of visit, and visits could be days or even years apart. If we had to reserve space for all possible visit days for each patient, we could rapidly approach a database whose size was so large that it could not be implemented even on the largest of computer systems. But MUMPS handles arrays and subscripts in a manner quite different from conventional matrices. Only those subscripts and data nodes actually defined take up space in the array. We do not reserve space for potential data nodes; MUMPS arrays are *sparse*.

In contrast, if we tried to save the same type of data in a more conventional matrix structure, we would first have to reserve enough space for the worst-case situation. It would be necessary to define the maximum number of patients that the array could accommodate and then the maximum number of visits allowed for each patient. If we assumed a maximum of 1,000 patients, 10 visits per patient, and a data size requirement of 100 bytes per patient, we would have to reserve 1,000,000 bytes of space for the patient array. This amount of space would be required, even if the average patient had only two visits. Additionally, we would probably encounter the inevitable problem of a patient with more than 10 visits. In this case, we would have to increase the dimensions of the array by one visit per patient *for the entire array*. For each additional patient visit dimensioned, it would be necessary to reserve an additional 100,000 bytes of data, even though this space would only be used for a limited number of patients.

4.4.2.3 Array Subscripts Subscripts into arrays can be any valid MUMPS expression. We discuss expressions in greater detail in Chapter 5, but can summarize the definition as follows. A MUMPS expression is a calculation that reduces to a single value. The result can be numeric (either integer or real), a string of ASCII characters (up to 255 characters in length), or a boolean (true/false) value. This means that a subscript can be any of these values, including a string of ASCII characters.

The only two exceptions to this general description are that a subscript *cannot* be an *empty string* (""), nor can it contain any of the ASCII control characters (decimal values 0 to 31 or 127). An empty string of characters is a special case and is used as a starting and terminating value when using the **$ORDER** function (Section 8.2.2) for searching sparse arrays.

Subscripts can be any nonnull string of characters that does *not* contain any of the ASCII control characters.

Multiple subscripts are separated from each other by commas, and an array reference consists of the array name followed by a list of subscript(s) enclosed in parentheses. Data nodes within an array are created using the SET command. For example, the following commands will add one new patient (Jane Doe, ID# = 4451) to the array PatRec and then add two visits (one on 5/1/1975, the other on 2/15/78) under the patient's name.

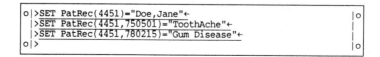

```
o|>SET PatRec(4451)="Doe,Jane"←                    |o
 |>SET PatRec(4451,750501)="ToothAche"←            |
 |>SET PatRec(4451,780215)="Gum Disease"←          |
o|>                                                |o
```

EXAMPLE 4.9. Setting array values

We can issue the following command to retrieve the stored information:

```
o|>WRITE PatRec(4451)←
 |Doe,Jane
o|>WRITE PatRec(4451,750501)←
 |ToothAche
o|>
```

EXAMPLE 4.10. Data retrieval from an array

Individual subscripts are defined as expressions; expressions can be as simple as a constant (string or numeric literal) or a single variable name. It follows, then, that variables can be used as subscripts. The use of variables as subscripts is demonstrated in the next example.

```
o|>SET PID=4451←
 |>SET DATE=750501←
 |>WRITE PatRec(PID,DATE)←
o|ToothAche
 |>
```

EXAMPLE 4.11. Variables as subscripts

Example 14.12 demonstrates the use of string subscripts to point to a data node in an array.

```
o|>SET Array("John Lewkowicz","Phone")="253-3606"←
 |>WRITE Array("John Lewkowicz","Phone")←
 |253-3606
o|>
```

EXAMPLE 4.12. Strings as subscripts

The use of strings as subscripts into arrays is unique to the MUMPS language and has many important ramifications. As mentioned earlier in this section, most other languages permit only numbers, usually integers, as subscripts into arrays. The use of strings as subscripts is a profound change from the traditional assignment of subscript values; subscripts in MUMPS can have meaning and need not be artificially mapped into a numeric value. A detailed discussion of subscripts will be deferred until Chapter 10.

It is important to realize that, while the *comma* character is used to separate individual subscripts, it can also be embedded within a string value used as a single subscript. Consider the following example:

```
o|>Kill Array←                                              |o
 |>Set Array("Doe,John")="Test Data 1"←                      |
 |>Set Array("Doe","John")="Test Data 2"←                    |
o|>Write Array("Doe,John")←                                 |o
 |Test Data 1                                                |
 |>Write Array("Doe","John")←                                |
o|Test Data 2                                               |o
 |>                                                          |
```

EXAMPLE 4.13.   Commas used within a subscript

The two SET commands in Example 4.13 have very different results; the first establishes a single node in the array pointed to by the subscript "Doe,John", while the second creates two nodes (a pointer node defined by the subscript "Doe" and a data node under it defined by the subscript "John"). The resulting array is depicted in Figure 4.7.

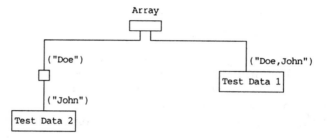

FIGURE 4.7.   Array created by Example 4.13

As previously discussed, array nodes can be data nodes, pointer nodes with data, or pointer nodes without data. A reference to a node with no data causes an error. Consider the following example:

```
o|>SET ABC(1,2,55)="Data"←                                  |o
 |>WRITE ABC(1,2,55)←                                        |
 |>Data                                                      |
o|>WRITE ABC(1)←                                            |o
 |<<UNDEFINED>> ERROR                                        |
 |>                                                          |
```

EXAMPLE 4.14.   Pointer nodes

While there is a node associated with ABC(1), it contains *no* data and is only a pointer to data at a lower level in the array. The status of any array node (that is, whether it is data, a pointer, or both) can be determined with the $DATA function, which is covered in Section 8.2.1. It is worth noting again that any node that was previously only a downward pointer can be assigned to a data value later *without* affecting the pointer. A node that is *both* a downward pointer and a data node cannot have the data deleted *without* also deleting all branches below that node. However, it can be set to an empty string ("") to indicate a lack of data. Setting a node to a null value results in a node with data; it is *not* the same as a node without data (that is, pointer only node).

```
o|>Set Test(1,2,3)="Data"↵                                    |o
 |>Write Test(1,2,3)↵                                         |
 |Data                                                        |
o|>Write Test(1)↵                                             |o
 |<<UNDEFINED>> ERROR                                         |
 |>Set Test(1)="Inserted data"↵                               |
o|>Write Test(1,2,3)↵                                         |o
 |Data                                                        |
 |>Write Test(1)↵                                             |
o|Inserted data                                               |o
 |>Kill Test(1)↵                                              |
 |>Write Test(1,2,3)↵                                         |
o|<<UNDEFINED>> ERROR                                         |o
 |>                                                           |
```

EXAMPLE 4.15.   Pointer nodes with data

When an array node is *deleted* (using the KILL command; Section 3.1.2), that node, all its descendants, and all its immediate predecessors that contain only pointer information are also removed from the array. Deletion continues up the tree until a node containing data or a node containing another downward pointer is encountered. If there was only one data node in the array, deleting that node will cause deletion of the entire array.

Another important charactersitic of subscripts is that they are always inserted into an array in collating sequence, regardless of the order in which the data nodes are created. In general, new subscripts are inserted in alphabetic order, but differentiate between numbers and nonnumeric strings (see the discussion of the MUMPS collating order in Sections 8.2.2 and 10.2.2). Subscripts are retrieved from the array using the $ORDER function; they are returned by $ORDER in the same collating sequence as they are stored internally.

4.4.3 Globals

We previously described the difference between local and global variables. Local variables are transient and reside in the partition's symbol table. As soon as the process is completed and the partition is released back to MUMPS, the local variables disappear. Global variables, on the other hand, are automatically mapped to disk where they remain until explicitly killed. In Example 4.15, all the arrays were local. To make them global arrays, and consequently permanent, requires only adding the up-arrow character (^) to the front of the array name. Changing all references from **PatRec** to **^PatRec** in the preceding examples will create global arrays that reside on disk rather than local memory.

4.4.4 System Variables

In addition to the variable types already described, another type of variable is available to the MUMPS programmer. The system variables contain important information about a given process or job running in MUMPS. All system variables start with a dollar sign ($) followed by one or more alphabetic characters.

> System variables all start with the dollar sign character ($).

The MUMPS standard does *not* allow special variables (that is, system variables starting with $) to be altered with the SET command. However, almost all implementations permit setting the variables $X and $Y to synchronize the cursor location on input/output devices and the MUMPS interpretation of this location. A summary list of system variables is presented in Appendix F.

4.4.4.1 $HOROLOG: Date and Time

Abbreviation **$H**

The word horolog is derived from the Greek *horologion* and means a timekeeping device. $H contains the current date and time in the format

$$\$H = DATE,TIME$$

where **DATE** is the number of days that have elapsed since December 31, 1840 (that is, DATE is 1 for January 1, 1841), and **TIME** is the number of seconds that have elapsed since midnight for the current day. As an example, a value of "**53312,11811**" for $H represents 12/18/86, 3:16 AM. The choice of January 1, 1841, as day number 1 has no special significance other than the fact that MUMPS was originally designed for medical applications in the early 1960s, and it was assumed that no current patients would have been born before 1/1/1841. The choice of this starting date may impose limitations on some applications (for example, those needing to record dates before January 1, 1841), resulting in the need to use alternative date formats (such as YYMMDD).

Representing the date and time as sequential intervals facilitates interval calculations. For example, it is easy to calculate the elapsed days between two dates so recorded by simply subtracting the earlier date from the later one. If the date is recorded in a different format (for example, YYMMDD), then calculations for elapsed days become considerably more difficult.

Most systems provide utility subroutines for converting the date and time from $H format to a more readable form.

4.4.4.2 $IO: Current Device Number

Abbreviation **$I**

$I contains a value that identifies the curently active device. While this is often an integer device number, in many layered implementations it may be the operating system's name for the current device. See Section 3.4 and Chapter 12 for a discussion of MUMPS devices.

4.4.4.3 $JOB: Job or Partition Number

Abbreviation **$J**

$J is an integer number that uniquely identifies a job or process in the MUMPS environment. It is often used as a first-level index into scratch globals to ensure data independence between jobs.

It should be noted that $J is unique *only to a single computer*; in networked MUMPS environments with jobs running on different computers, more than one process can have the same value for $J.

4.4.4.4 $STORAGE: Partition's Free Space

Abbreviation **$S**

$S is an integer value that indicates the amount of free space (in bytes) left in the partition. Partitions and how they are managed are discussed in Section 2.2.1 and you might wish to review that section. $S returns the number of characters left in the partition but, since partitions are handled differently under different implementations, the true meaning of this variable may be implementation specific. Check the documentation for the system you are using.

4.4.4.5 $TEST: Test Switch

Abbreviation **$T**

$T contains the boolean truth value (1 = true, 0 = false) of the most recently executed IF command containing an argument or an OPEN, LOCK, READ, or JOB command with a timeout specified. Refer to Chapters 3 and 6 for general information on syntax and timeouts and for these commands.

While command and argument postconditioning (Section 5.4) provides some of the functionality of an IF command with arguments, neither of these syntactical structures alters the value of $TEST.

4.4.4.6 $X: X Coordinate of the Current Device

Abbreviation **$X**

MUMPS keeps track of the current X and Y coordinates of the cursor or print-head of each device used in a process. The X coordinate refers to the column, the Y coordinate to the row. Both $X and $Y are returned as nonnegative integers. The starting position (upper-left corner of a screen or page) has the coordinates $X=0, $Y=0.

The variables $X and $Y are typically used with page-oriented devices such as video terminals or printers. These variables are not meaningful in the same way when associated with devices such as magnetic tape or sequential disk files.

$X is reset to 0 each time MUMPS outputs a form-feed (Write #) or carriage-return line-feed (Write !) sequence to the device. In addition, MUMPS increments $X by one for each printing character that is input or output to or from the device. See the description of the READ and WRITE commands in Sections 3.4.3 and 3.4.4 as well as Chapter 12 for more details.

While both $X and $Y are used to keep track of the current cursor or printhead position, they *cannot* be used to *set* the physical location of either. They are used by MUMPS, to the best of its ability, to reflect the current cursor position and are updated as characters are either input or output. On the other hand, terminals that permit direct cursor positioning do so in a bewildering variety of ways. MUMPS cannot be expected to know what character sequences are required to directly position the cursor on a given terminal type. Consequently, moving the cursor on a terminal usually involves sending an escape sequence to the terminal directing it to move the cursor, and then updating $X and $Y to reflect the new position. Cursor positioning and management of $X and $Y are covered in greater detail in Chapter 12.

4.4.4.7 $Y: Y Coordinate of the Current Device

Abbreviation **$Y**

$Y is similar to $X but keeps track of the Y coordinate (row) of the current device. It is reset to 0 each time MUMPS outputs a form-feed sequence (Write #) and is incremented by 1 each time MUMPS outputs a carriage-return line-feed sequence (Write !). Again, refer to the description of the READ and WRITE commands in Sections 3.4.3 and 3.4.4 as well as Chapter 12 for more details.

4.4.4.8 $Z...: System Variables All variables starting with the characters $Z are implementation specific and are defined only for a given MUMPS implementation. You should check the documentation for your system to see what $Z system variables are available.

Care should be exercised when using $Z variables as they are not likely to be the same (or even available) on different MUMPS systems. In this section we examine *some* of these variables found on *some* MUMPS systems to provide you with a general idea concerning their use.

$ZA   Used in some systems to hold status information concerning the "current" active device (such as a magnetic tape drive status register). See Section 12.4.3 for a discussion concerning the use of a status register for a magnetic tape drive.

$ZC(ount)   Used to return the number of available free blocks on disk for global storage. Note that the number returned reflects *blocks*, not *bytes* of free space; the size of a block is implementation-specific.

$ZE(rror)   A system variable that contains the error code and location of the most recently encountered error. Some systems also use $ZE to establish the address (LABEL^ROUTINE) to which control will be transferred on encountering an error (others use a variable named $ZT(rap) to establish the trap address). See Chapter 13 for additional discussion on error trapping.

$ZIOS   Returns a value indicating how the last READ command was terminated.

Value	Meaning
0	Normal termination
1	Length limit exceeded
2	Timeout occurred
3	End of file or end of medium
4	I/O error occurred

$ZNAKED: Holds full global definition (name and subscripts) of the most recently referenced global node. Useful in establishing what the current global naked reference is.

Again, these are just a few of the many possible $Z variables that may be available on your system. Use them with discretion, as they likely exist on only one system.

4.5 Chapter Highlights

- Strings in MUMPS can be up to 255 characters in length (4.1).
- A *null string* is an empty string (one whose length is zero) (4.1). The *NUL* character (decimal value of 0) is *not* the same as a null string. A string containing the NUL character is *not* empty (4.1).
- Variable names start with a single alphabetic character optionally followed by additional alphabetic and numeric characters (4.4).
- Variable names can be longer than eight characters, but only the first eight are used in resolving name conflicts (4.4).

- Variable names are case sensitive (4.4).
- Variable names can also start with the percent (%) character although its use is discouraged in application programs (4.4).
- Variable names starting with the ˆ character reside on disk and are referred to as GLOBAL variables (4.4).
- Subscripts can be any nonnull string of characters that does *not* contain any of the ASCII control characters (4.4.2.3).
- System variables all start with the dollar sign character ($) (4.4.4).

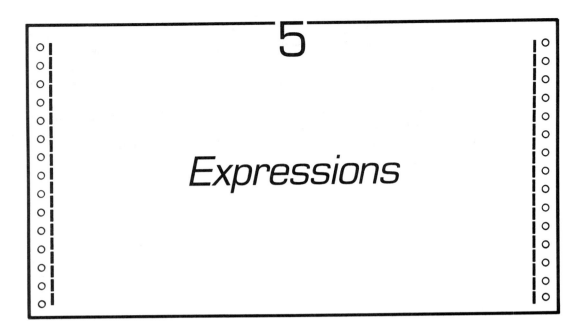

5

Expressions

MUMPS performs calculations, whether they be numeric or string oriented, by evaluating expressions. Stated another way, an expression is a formula involving one or more values that are reduced to a single value. Consider the following MUMPS command:

```
o|>Write 4*12/6←
 |8
 |>
```

EXAMPLE 5.1. Expressions

This is equivalent to the English statement "Write out the results of the arithmetic calculation *four times twelve divided by six*." The COMMAND in this example is WRITE (it acts like a verb and instructs MUMPS to perform a specific operation), while the expression 4*12/6 is an ARGUMENT to the command. Within the expression shown, the * and / characters are called operators (* designating multiplication and / division); the numbers 4, 12, and 6 are the values on which the operations are performed (the *operands*).

In Example 5.1, it makes no difference in which order MUMPS performs the calculations, as the values calculated in different orders yield the same results [both (4*12)/6 and 4*(12/6) yield an answer of 8]. Other calculations can be ambiguous without a defined rule for the order of evaluation. Consider the following examples:

```
o|>Write 4*12-6←
 |42
 |>Write (4*12)-6←
o|42
 |>Write 4*(12-6)←
 |24
o|>
```

EXAMPLE 5.2. Order of evaluation

In these examples, the order in which the operations are performed has an impact on the results of the calculation. If the subtraction is performed *after* the multiplication, the result is **42**; if the subtraction is performed *before* the multiplication, the result is **24**. MUMPS evaluates expressions from left to right unlike some languages (FORTRAN, for example) in which multiplication and division operations take precedence over addition and subtraction.

> MUMPS evaluates expressions from *left* to *right*, assigning no hierarchical precedence to numeric or other operators.

Example 5.2 also demonstrates how the strict left to right evaluation of expressions in MUMPS can be altered with the use of parentheses; those parts of an expression enclosed in parentheses are evaluated as a single value before the rest of the expression is evaluated. For example, the following expression would yield a result of 3:

```
o|>Write (4+8)/(34-30)←
 |3
 |>
```

EXAMPLE 5.3. Order of evaluation modified by parentheses

Evaluation of this expression proceeds in three steps:

  1. (4 + 8) = 12
  2. (34 − 30) = 4
  3. 12/4 = 3

> The use of *parentheses* can alter the strict Left to Right order of expression evaluation.

Expressions need not involve arithmetic calculations at all. Indeed, constants and variable names are valid expressions. In the following list of SET commands, the expressions have all been underlined.

$$SET\ A = \underline{1}$$
$$SET\ A = \underline{\text{"Test"}}$$
$$SET\ A = \underline{SUM}$$
$$SET\ A = \underline{4*B}$$

Expressions in MUMPS can evaluate to either a number or a string of characters, depending on the operations and order in which the operations are performed. An example of an expression that resulted in a string result was given in Chapter 1 using the **concatenate** operator ("500 Miles"_"25 Gallons" = "500 Miles25 Gallons"). In MUMPS there are three broad categories of operators: those that produce numeric results, those that produce string results, and those that produce boolean (true/false) results. A summary of the MUMPS operators can be found in Appendix E.

5.1 Numeric Operators: +, −, *, **, /, \, and

When a numeric operator is used, MUMPS evaluates the value(s) being operated on as number(s) and produces a numeric result. There are two categories of numeric operators: unary operators used to force numeric interpretation of an expression and binary operators, which specify a calculation between two operands.

5.1.1 Unary Operators: + and −   The unary operators are used to force MUMPS to evaluate the expression following the operator as a number rather than a string of characters. There are two unary operators: the plus sign (+) forces conversion of the operand to a number whose sign is dependent on the sign of the evaluated expression (for example, + "1.00" = 1, + " − 1.30" = -1.3) and the negative sign (−), which also forces conversion of the operand and then inverts its sign (for example, − "1.00" = -1, − " − 1.30" = 1.3).

It may be valuable to review the rules used to interpret a string of characters as a number presented in Section 4.2.2. In short, the string is evaluated from left to right, building a number from the characters in the string. The first character inconsistent with a numeric entry terminates the scan. Strings that cannot be converted to a number (for example, "ABC") are evaluated as zero (0)

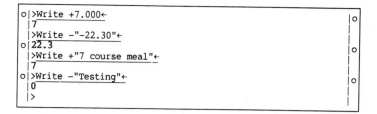

```
o|>Write +7.000←
 |7
 |>Write -"-22.30"←
o|22.3
 |>Write +"7 course meal"←
 |7
o|>Write -"Testing"←
 |0
 |>
```

EXAMPLE 5.4. Unary operators

5.1.2 Binary Numeric Operators

Binary numeric operators are used to instruct MUMPS to evaluate the two operands on either side of the operator as a single numeric result. The term binary is used to indicate that *two* operands are associated with the operator, *not* that the operations are being performed in base-2 arithmetic. The following is a list of the binary numeric operators recognized by MUMPS:

+   The ADDITION operator ($4 + 36 = 40$).

−   The SUBTRACTION operator ($7.8 - 4.4 = 3.4$).

*   The MULTIPLICATION operator ($8*1.2 = 9.6$).

**   The EXPONENTIATION operator ($3**4 = 81$)[1]

/   The DIVISION operator ($14/2 = 7$).

\\   The INTEGER DIVISION operator ($22\backslash7 = 3$). The remainder of a normal division operation is always *dropped* (no rounding) to form an integer result.

\#   The MODULO (remainder) operator ($6\#4 = 2$). This operation returns the remainder of a division operation as an integer. Thus 6 divided by 4 results in a quotient of 1 and a remainder of 2. The result of the calculation **0#nn** (zero#nn), where nn represents any number, is always zero (0).

A more formal definition of the modulo operator should be presented since the results obtained by this operator when evaluating negative values are not always clear.

$$\text{ABC\#XYZ} = \text{ABC} - (\text{XYZ*FLOOR(ABC/XYZ)})$$

where FLOOR(NUMBER) is defined as the largest integer *less than or equal to* NUMBER. If we expand the expressions $7\#4$ and $7\#(-4)$ we obtain:

$$
\begin{aligned}
7\#4 &= 7 - (4*\text{FLOOR}(7/4)) \\
&= 7 - (4*\text{FLOOR}(1.75)) \\
&= 7 - (4*(\underline{1})) \\
&= 7 - (4) \\
&= 3
\end{aligned}
\qquad
\begin{aligned}
7\#(-4) &= 7 - (-4*\text{FLOOR}(7/-4)) \\
&= 7 - (-4*\text{FLOOR}(-1.75)) \\
&= 7 - (-4*(\underline{-2})) \\
&= 7 - (+8) \\
&= -1
\end{aligned}
$$

[1] MDC Type A release, January 1987.

The absolute value of the (-1.75) is *not* the same as the absolute value of the FLOOR(1.75). The results of modulo calculations are not necessarily symmetrical around 0. The sign of the result of a modulo operation always takes the sign of the expression *following* the modulo operator (#).

```
o|Odd    Write !,"Check for ODD or EVEN numbers"        |o
 |Getn   Read !,"Number: ",n If n="" Quit                |
 |       If n#2 Write " is ODD"                           |
o|       Else  Write " is EVEN"                          |o
 |       Goto Getn                                        |
 |_____|
o|>Do Odd←                                               |o
 |Check for ODD or EVEN numbers                           |
 |Number: 10← is EVEN                                     |
o|Number: 3← is ODD                                      |o
 |Number: 2← is EVEN                                      |
 |Number: ←                                               |
o|>                                                      |o
```

EXAMPLE 5.5.   Modulo Operator

Note, also, that in any operation involving division, division by zero is illegal and will result in an error. This applies to normal division (/), integer division (\) and to the modulo (#) operators.

> Division by 0 is illegal and will cause an error.

Another, slightly more meaningful use of the modulo operator is presented in the next example, which calculates and displays the current day-of-the-week based on the contents of the system variable $H. These calculations are based on the fact that day one of the $H date scheme was on <u>Friday</u> January 1, 1841.

```
o|Day     ;Display the Day-of-the-week based on $H       |o
 |        Set day=$H#7                                    |
 |        If day=1 Write "Friday"                         |
o|        If day=2 Write "Saturday"                      |o
 |        If day=3 Write "Sunday"                         |
 |        If day=4 Write "Monday"                         |
o|        If day=5 Write "Tuesday"                       |o
 |        If day=6 Write "Wednesday"                      |
 |        If day=0 Write "Thursday"                       |
o|        Quit                                           |o
 |_____|
 |>Do Day Write " - ",$H←                                |
o|Monday - 53601,24735                                   |o
 |>                                                       |
```

EXAMPLE 5.6.   Use of modulo operator for day-of-the-week

The modulo operator is also used extensively in conjunction with the $DATA function (Section 10.2.2) and in bit-oriented manipulations (Examples 12.17 and 12.18).

5.2 String Operators: Concatenate, _(Underscore)

When evaluating a string operator, MUMPS always interprets the values being operated on as strings and produces a string result. There is one MUMPS operator that falls into this category:

— The CONCATENATE operator (represented by the underline character) is used to append one string to the end of another (for example, "NICE"_ ""_ "DAY" = "NICE DAY"). The result of a concatenate operation is a string.

EXAMPLE 5.7   CONCATENATE operator

5.3 Logical and Relational Operators: >, <, =, [,], ?, &, !, and '

Logical and relational operators evaluate expressions as strings or numbers (depending on the operation) but the result is always a truth value (boolean true or false). An expression using these operators that proves to be TRUE provides a result of **1**, while an expression that evaluates to FALSE provides a result of **0**. Relational operators are used to compare values, whereas logical operators are used to test combinations of truth values. As mentioned earlier in this chapter, MUMPS interprets values in the context of the operation being performed. Consequently, it is important to distinguish those operators that compare numeric values from those that are used to compare string values. If the values **"2"** and **"2.0"** are compared numerically, they are *equal*; if compared as strings of characters, they are *not equal*. Relational operators are subdivided into two categories: those that compare numeric values and those that compare string values.

5.3.1 Numeric Relational Operators

For numeric relational operators, MUMPS interprets both values being operated on as numbers before performing the comparison. Two numeric relational operators are defined in MUMPS: GREATER THAN and LESS THAN.

5.3.1.1 GREATER THAN Operator: > The GREATER THAN operator compares the numeric interpretation of two expressions and results in TRUE (1) if the first value is greater than the second or in FALSE (0) if the first value is not greater than the second.

```
o|>Write "Two>One = ",2>1←
 |Two>One = 1
 |>Write "Four>Five = ",4>5←
o|Four>Five = 0
 |>Write "Five>Five = ",5>5←
 |Five>Five = 0
```

EXAMPLE 5.8.   GREATER THAN operator

5.3.1.2 LESS THAN Operator: <   The LESS THAN operator compares the numeric interpretation of two expressions and results in TRUE (1) if the first value is less than the second or in FALSE (0) if the first value is not less than the second.

```
o|>Write "6<22 = ",6<22←
 |6<22 = 1
 |>Write "22<6 = ",22<6←
o|22<6 = 0
 |>Write "22<22 = ",22<22←
 |22<22 = 0
```

EXAMPLE 5.9.   LESS THAN operator

5.3.2 String Relational Operators

For string relational operators, MUMPS interprets the expressions being compared as strings before it performs the comparison. Four string relational operators are recognized by MUMPS: EQUALITY, CONTAINS, FOLLOWS, and PATTERN MATCH.

5.3.2.1 EQUALS Operator: =   The EQUALS operator compares the EQUALITY of two strings ("AbC" = "AbC" is TRUE, but "2.2" = "2.20" is FALSE). To determine the equality of two numbers, one could use a unary operator (see Section 5.1.1) to force the evaluation of the operands as numbers (for example, +"2" = +"2.0" would be TRUE). Note that the use of an equals sign as an operator between two values performs a different function altogether than the equals sign in the SET command. The basic form of the SET command is demonstrated by

SET A = 22

which translates to "Set the contents of the memory location associated with the variable named **A** to the value of 22." On the other hand, the MUMPS command

SET A = 22 = 3

translates to "Set the contents of the memory location associated with the variable **A** to the results of the comparison between the values 22 and 3 (FALSE or zero)."

```
o|>Write "abc"="abc"←
 |1
 |>Write 234="+234"←
o|0
 |>Write 234=+"+234"←
 |1
o|>
```

EXAMPLE 5.10. EQUALS as a relational operator

The difference in results between the second and third comparisons in the previous example is due to the use of the *unary* plus operator (Section 5.1.1). The leading **+** character in the expression +"+234" forces the string "+234" to be evaluated as a number, and the leading + in the string is dropped (234).

5.3.2.2 CONTAINS Operator: [

The CONTAINS operator is used to compare two strings of characters. If the string on the right side of the operator is contained *exactly* (letter for letter including spaces and the correct case) in the string on the left side of the operator, the result of the comparison is TRUE (1). Otherwise, the result is FALSE (0).

```
o|>Write "Nice day."["ce d"←
 |1
 |>Write "Nice day"["Nc"←
o|0
```

EXAMPLE 5.11. CONTAINS operator

5.3.2.3 FOLLOWS Operator:]

The FOLLOWS operator is used to compare two ASCII strings to see if one *FOLLOWS* the other in the ASCII collating order. For example, the string "Z" follows the string "ABC", while the string "AB" does *not* follow the string "ABC". The ASCII collating sequence is defined by the relative position of characters within the ASCII character set (see Appendix A). Characters whose numeric representation (that is, decimal value) are larger *follow* those whose numeric representations are smaller. For example, the character "a" (decimal value of 97) follows "A" (decimal value of 65) in the ASCII collating sequence. The string "Bz" (decimal values 66,122) follows the string "B1" (decimal values 66,49).

```
o|>Write "ABC"]"A"←
 |1
 |>Write "ABC"]"a"←
o|0
```

EXAMPLE 5.12. FOLLOWS operator

Note especially that the expressions being compared are evaluated as *strings of characters*, not their numeric equivalents. To compare numbers, the GREATER THAN or LESS THAN operators are used, as demonstrated in the next example.

```
o|>Write 123]4←
 |0
 |>Write 123>4←
o|1
 |>
```

EXAMPLE 5.13. FOLLOWS operator, nonnumeric

MUMPS uses two different collating sequences for character strings; the ASCII collating sequence used for comparing strings with the FOLLOWS operator, and the MUMPS collating sequence used for organizing array subscripts. The MUMPS collating sequence is similar to the ASCII collating sequence with the exception of how it orders numbers. The MUMPS collating sequence is described in more detail in the chapter on globals (Chapter 10).

Another interesting use of the FOLLOWS operator is to check for the occurrence of a null (empty) string. Since *any* character follows an empty string, checking for a nonempty string can be accomplished with the FOLLOWS operator using the code

If ans]"" ;succeeds if ans is NOT an empty string

This is equivalent to If ans' = "" (the NOT operator ' is covered in Section 5.3.3.3). I personally like the second form (If ans' = "") since it more clearly states the condition being checked, but you are likely to encounter the first form in many existing programs.

5.3.2.4 PATTERN MATCH Operator: ? The PATTERN MATCH operator is similar to the CONTAINS operator except that it checks a target string to see if it consists of a particular sequence of characters. Unlike the CONTAINS operator, the pattern match can be used to check the string for categories or types of character strings. The types (pattern codes) of character strings that can be checked in MUMPS are:

TABLE 5.1 Pattern Match Codes

A	The 52 upper- and lowercase Alphabetic characters such as A, B, C, m, z (decimal range 65 to 122).
C	The 33 ASCII Control characters (decimal values 0 to 31 and 127). These are all nonprinting characters.
E	The Entire ASCII character set (decimal range 0 to 127).
L	The 26 Lowercase alphabetic character set (a to z) (decimal range 97 to 122).
N	The ten Numeric digits (0 to 9) (decimal range 48 to 57).
P	The 33 Punctuation characters (decimal range 32 to 47, 58 to 64, 91 to 96, and 123 to 126). These include all printing characters not falling in the A or N categories.
U	The 26 Uppercase alphabetic characters (A to Z) (decimal range 65 to 90).

Pattern codes are *not* case sensitive (e.g., Ans?1N is the same as Ans?1n).

In addition to these categories, we can also use STRING LITERALS (strings of characters enclosed in quotation marks) as patterns. We can specify the number of occurrences of each pattern type or string literal we wish to check for and the order in which they must appear in the target string for the evaluation to be TRUE. A pattern expression has the general format

Variable?nnPATTERN

where Variable contains the string to be checked and PATTERN is the pattern match specification to be checked. The characters nn represent an integer count defining the number of PATTERN code characters or string literal sequences that must be present, and PATTERN code is either one of the pattern types listed previously or a string literal. For example, the pattern **?2N** could be used to check a string to see if it contained exactly two numeric digits.

The value of nn can also contain a period (.), which has the special meaning of **"any number"** of occurrences, including zero (0). The decimal point can be interpreted to mean "a range of values." The number before the decimal point is the minimum number of required pattern matches, and the number after the period is the maximum number of matches. The default minimum number is zero (0), and the default maximum number is "any number of occurrences."

For example, the pattern code of **1N.A** could be used to check for a string that contains one numeric digit followed by any number (including none) of alphabetic characters (either upper- or lowercase). Any other type of character (punctuation, control or numeric digit after the first character) would cause the pattern match to fail. A pattern match code of **?1.4N** could be used to check a string to see if it contained 1, 2, 3, or 4 numeric digits.

The pattern types listed previously can be made into composite PATTERN CODEs so that, for example, a PATTERN CODE of AN could be used to check for either Alphabetic characters or for Numeric characters. The following examples demonstrate the use of pattern match codes:

ZIP?5N	Checks to see if the variable ZIP contains exactly 5 Numeric digits (14853 would be TRUE, 14853-2602 would be FALSE).
DATE?2N1"/"2N1"/"2N	Checks the variable DATE for a valid date in the format 2 numeric digits, the character /, 2 numeric digits, the character /, and 2 more numeric digits (for example, 12/01/86 would be TRUE; 1/10/86 would be FALSE).
PATID?1N.N or PATID?1.N	Checks a patient ID number to ensure that it contains at least 1 numeric digit followed by any number of other Numeric digits (4 would be TRUE, 91134 would be TRUE, and 23Ab and 23.4 would be FALSE).
ENTRY?.E1C.E	Checks the variable ENTRY to see if it contains any (at least 1) occurrence of a Control character. The .E pattern codes in this example check for

the occurrence of *any* ASCII character, including nothing. For example, a pattern expression of ?1E.E will evaluate to TRUE if the string being checked contains one character followed by any number (including *zero*) of other characters.

PATID?1.6N

Checks the variable PATID to see if it contains from 1 to 6 Numeric digits (123 is TRUE, 999999 is TRUE, 1.23 is FALSE, and 1456729 is FALSE).

DATE?1.2N1"/"1.2N1"/"2N

A more complete check on a DATE field verifying that it contains from 1–2 numeric digits followed by a /, followed by from 1–2 numeric digits, then a /, and finally exactly 2 numeric digits (1/12/86 is TRUE, 5/1/49 is TRUE, and 12/14/1981 is FALSE). Note that this pattern check does *not* check ranges for validity, just for the correct pattern. Consequently the DATE string 87/14/86 would evaluate TRUE in this example, but clearly a value of 87 for a month is illegal.

5.3.3 Logical Operators

Logical operators are used to combine the results of relational operations, and result in a truth value (true or false). There are three logical operators: AND, OR, and NOT.

5.3.3.1 AND Operator: & The AND operator (the ampersand character &) is used to combine the results of two or more boolean comparisons in a manner consistent with the Table 5.2.

TABLE 5.2 AND Truth Table

Operation	Results in:
True&True	True
True&False	False
False&False	False

```
o|>Write (1=+"1.0")&("abcd"["bc")←          |o
 |1                                          |
 |>Write 4]1023&1←                           |
o|1                                          |o
 |>Write 122>121&("aBc"["b")←                |
 |0                                          |
```

EXAMPLE 5.14. AND operator

Remember that there is *no* implied order of precedence when evaluating expressions. They are evaluated in a strict left to right sequence unless the expression is modified with parentheses.

5.3.3.2 OR Operator: !

The OR operator (the exclamation point character) is used to combine the results of two or more boolean comparisons in a manner consistent with Table 5.3.

TABLE 5.3 OR Truth Table

Operation	Results in:
True!True	True
True!False	True
False!False	False

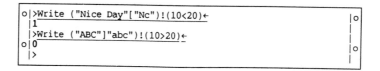

EXAMPLE 5.15. OR operator

5.3.3.3 NOT Operator: '

The NOT operator (apostrophe character, ') is used to reverse the truth value of an expression ['(1 = "1.0") is TRUE as the expression 1 = "1.0" is FALSE and the NOT operator reverses the FALSE to TRUE]. In general, the NOT operator can also be placed directly in front of a relational operator to reverse the results of the comparison. For example, the expression '(1.2 = 1.3) could also be represented as 1.2' = 1.3 (both expressions result in a value of TRUE).

EXAMPLE 5.16. NOT operator

Use of the NOT operator with the GREATER THAN or LESS THAN operators permits the construction of operator sequences to perform the functions *GREATER THAN OR EQUAL* and *LESS THAN OR EQUAL* as shown in the following table.

Operators	Explanation
'<	Translates to NOT LESS THAN and is equivalent to GREATER THAN OR EQUAL TO.
'>	Translates to NOT GREATER THAN and is equivalent to LESS THAN OR EQUAL TO.

5.4 Combined Operator Types

MUMPS can handle, in the same expression, multiple operations of a mixed nature (numeric, string, relational, and logical). The result of the expression is dependent on the operators used and the order in which they are evaluated. Consider the following example:

```
o|>WRITE 2*4=8_" TEXT"←                                        |o
|                                                              |
o|1 TEXT                                                       |o
|>                                                             |
```

EXAMPLE 5.17.   Combined Operators

As usual, MUMPS processes the expression from left to right, and the individual steps for evaluating this expression can be broken down as follows:

Step 1	2*4 = 8_" TEXT"	;Evaluate **2*4** (8)
Step 2	8 = 8_" TEXT"	;Evaluate **8 = 8** (1, True)
Step 3	1_" TEXT"	;Evaluate **1_" Text"** *("1 TEXT")*
Results	*"1 TEXT"*	

> Mixed operator types can be used in an expression, with the resulting type determined by the last operation being performed.

Remember that the results of logical operations evaluate to either one or zero (true or false). The results of logical operations can be combined with nonlogical operators in many useful ways. Consider the following example used to check the contents of a variable.

```
o|    If "YyNn"[ans=$Length(ans) ...                           |o
```

EXAMPLE 5.18.   Answer check with combined operators

This code is used to check the variable <u>ans</u> for a <u>single</u> character from the list "Y", "y", "N", or "N". The first part of the expression ("YyNn"[ans) checks if the

TABLE 5.4 Evaluation of "YyNn"[ans = $Length(ans)

Value of **ans**	"YyNn"[ans	$Length(ans)	"YyNn"[ans = $Length(ans)	Results
"Y"	1 (True)	1	1 = 1	1 (True)
"n"	1 (True)	1	1 = 1	1 (True)
"X"	0 (False)	1	0 = 1	0 (False)
""	1 (True)	0	1 = 0	0 (False)
"Yy"	1 (True)	2	1 = 2	0 (False)

value of ans is contained in the test string. This subexpression evaluates to TRUE (1) if ans is a "Y", "y", "N", "n", empty string (""), or a multicharacter string such as "Yy", "yN", "YyN"; otherwise, it evaluates to FALSE (0).

The logical result of the first operation (0 or 1) is then compared against the length of the answer [the $LENGTH function (Section 8.1.3) returns the number of characters in the argument to the function]. If ans contains one of the target characters *and* is exactly one character long, the If command succeeds. The second check eliminates a number of possibilities that are passed by the first (such as an empty string or multicharacter sequences). See Table 5.4.

While there are cases in which mixing operator types within a single expression adds programming flexibility, this technique can obscure the purpose of the code. The following code fragment was found in a date conversion utility supplied by one MUMPS vendor.

```
If Date<1E6*Date = Date*Date<1 Quit
```

This code is designed to check the contents of the variable Date for correct format (that is, the same format as $H, a nonnegative number of six or less digits). If the format check FAILS, the QUIT command is executed. Does it actually perform these checks and, if so, how? After experimenting, you will discover that the code evaluates to TRUE under two conditions: if Date is less than one or if Date is greater than 999,999. In that case, it could be rewritten as

```
If Date<1E6*Date<1 Quit
```

or even more explicitly as

```
If Date>999999!(Date<1) Quit
```

Did the original author intend the code to perform additional checks (such as for noninteger values) and then incorrectly code those checks? It is difficult to guess the intent from the code.

Don't get too clever, you might wind up maintaining your own code.

5.5 Chapter Highlights

- MUMPS evaluates expressions from left to right, assigning no hierarchical precedence to numeric or other operators (5).
- The use of parentheses can alter the strict left to right order of expression evaluation (5).
- Division by 0 is illegal and will cause an error (5.1.2).
- Mixed operator types can be used in an expression, with the resulting type determined by the last operation being performed (5.4).

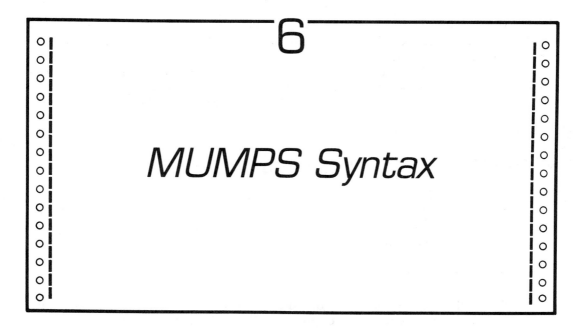

6

MUMPS Syntax

In this chapter, we examine the structure and syntax of MUMPS commands in lines and programs. The examples that accompany the text make extensive use of the commands described in the previous chapters; if you encounter difficulty with either command syntax or function, refer back to the appropriate section in Chapter 3 for help.

There is an inherent hierarchy in the structure of MUMPS syntactical elements, starting with individual commands and proceeding up to a program. The smallest executable element in the MUMPS language consists of a *command* and its arguments. Individual commands can be grouped together on a single *line* of code; lines of code can be grouped into executable *subroutines* (*parts*); and the subroutines can be organized and filed on disk as a *routine*. Additionally, routines can be linked together to form a complete *program*. For our purposes, we will differentiate between the definitions for a routine and a program; a program consists of the collection of all routines necessary to perform a particular process or function.

Before we investigate the basic structure of commands, we should briefly examine an important concept. MUMPS is a *line-oriented* language; each line of MUMPS code can consist of many MUMPS commands. Each command and its argument(s) are separated from other commands on the line with one or more space characters. The scope of many commands (such as IF, ELSE, and FOR) consists of the rest of the line following the command and, consequently, these commands must be examined in the broader context of lines of commands. In normal program flow (that is, in the absence of flow control commands such as DO or GOTO), MUMPS processes command lines within a routine from top to bottom and individual commands within a line from left to right.

6.1 Commands

A command is the smallest executable element in the MUMPS language and forms the basis from which all other structures in the language are built. A command consists of a directive to the interpreter (a verb) and a list of arguments used as objects of the directive (nouns).

6.1.1 Command Arguments

Generally speaking, two forms of syntax apply to MUMPS commands: those with and those without arguments. Consider the **IF** and the **ELSE** command. The general form of the **IF** command is

IF EXPRESSION ; then execute the rest of the line.

When EXPRESSION evaluates to TRUE (nonzero), the rest of the commands on the line will be executed; when EXPRESSION evaluates to FALSE (zero), the rest of the line is ignored. The **ELSE** command is closely related to the IF command, but checks the opposite truth value (FALSE) and has the general form

ELSE ; then execute the rest of the line. (*Note*: Two spaces separate

the ELSE command from the next command on the line.)

We briefly discussed the $TEST system variable earlier (Section 4.4.4), and it is discussed in even more detail in later chapters. $TEST contains the TRUTH value (TRUE or FALSE) of the most recently executed test (such as an IF command with arguments). The ELSE command relies on this variable and is a shorthand method of saying

IF '$TEST ; then execute the rest of the line.

If the TRUTH value associated with $TEST is FALSE (zero), then the rest of the line following the ELSE command is executed. If $TEST is TRUE (nonzero), the remainder of the line after the ELSE command is ignored. A section of MUMPS code using IF and ELSE might look something like this:

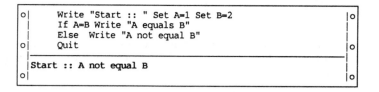

```
o|      Write "Start :: " Set A=1 Set B=2           |o
 |      If A=B Write "A equals B"                   |
 |      Else  Write "A not equal B"                 |
o|      Quit                                        |o
 |_____ |
 |Start :: A not equal B                            |
o|                                                  |o
```

EXAMPLE 6.1. Commands with and without arguments

The IF command in this example has an argument (the expression $A = B$), while the ELSE command has no argument (its actions are based on the implied argument $TEST whose value was established by the previously executed If command).

Commands (Write, Set, If, and the like) are separated from their arguments ("Start :: ", $A = 1$, $B = 2$, and so on) by a single space (Set_A = 1). The space character is used to separate commands from their arguments and multiple commands on the same line.

In commands with arguments, the arguments must be separated from the command by exactly one space.

When more than one command appears on a line, succeeding commands are separated from the argument(s) of the previous command by one or more spaces (Set $A = 1$_Write A).

In the case of commands *with* associated arguments, the next command on the line is separated from the last argument of previous command by at least one space.

To maintain syntactical consistency, argumentless commands such as ELSE must be separated from succeeding command elements on the same line by *two or more spaces* (Else_ _Write...). Omitting the second, required space after the ELSE command will result in a SYNTAX error. Argumentless commands (like the QUIT command shown previously) that end a logical line need no spaces to the right of the command.

Some commands (including IF) have two permissible forms: one with an
argument and one without.

```
1   o|      Write "Start --> " Set A=1 Set B=2 Set C=A      |o
2    |      If A'=B Set C=B                                  |
3    |      If  Write "A was not equal to B, C set to B"     |
4   o|      Quit                                            |o
     |----------------------------------------------------- |
     |Start --> A was not equal to B, C set to B             |
    o|                                                      |o
```

EXAMPLE 6.2.   IF command, with and without arguments

In this example, the second IF command (line 3) has no arguments and must
be separated from the rest of the commands on the line by at least two spaces.
Like the ELSE command, the argumentless IF command relies on the TRUTH
value of $TEST, which was established by the most recently executed test (in this
example, the IF with arguments on the previous line). When $TEST is TRUE, the
rest of this line is executed; when FALSE, the remainder of the line is ignored.
The argumentless IF command is equivalent to

IF $TEST (then execute the rest of the commands on the line).

6.1.2 Implied Commands

In the previous section we examined three commands with arguments (IF, SET,
and WRITE). In some instances, we repeat identical commands with different
arguments one after another (for example, Set A = 1 Set B = 2 Set C = A). MUMPS
offers a shorthand method for achieving the same effect. Multiple arguments for
a given command can be appended to a single command; multiple arguments are
separated from each other with commas. For example:

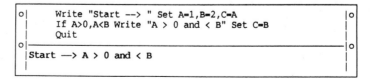

```
o|      Write "Start --> " Set A=1,B=2,C=A               |o
 |      If A>0,A<B Write "A > 0 and < B" Set C=B          |
 |      Quit                                              |
o|----------------------------------------------------- |o
 |Start --> A > 0 and < B                                 |
 |                                                       |
```

EXAMPLE 6.3.   Implied commands

In Example 6.3, the SET command on the first line has three separate sets of arguments ($A=1$, $B=2$, and $C=A$) and the IF command in the second line has two separate sets of arguments ($A>0$ and $A<B$). The shorthand form allows the programmer to extend the scope of a given command without having to retype the actual command.

If A>0,A<B Write ...

is equivalent to:

If A>0 If A<B Write ...

or

If A>0&(A<B) Write ...

> Multiple arguments to a single command are separated from each other with a comma.

As with many MUMPS language elements, the history of multiple command arguments can be traced back to the early, purely interpreted versions of MUMPS. When scanning a line of code during execution, it was desirable to keep the number of characters being scanned to a minimum, both to reduce storage space and to increase the speed of execution. In Example 6.3, the three Sets require only 15 characters, while three separate SET commands require 23 characters to perform the same function. The same general reasoning leads us to our next topic of discussion, the abbreviation of commands.

6.1.3 Command Abbreviation and Command Case

To reduce the number of characters that have to be typed and then scanned at execution time, all MUMPS commands can be abbreviated to the first letter of the command. Example 6.3 could also be rewritten as:

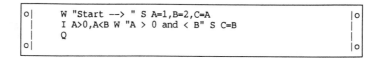

```
o|     W "Start --> " S A=1,B=2,C=A                |o
 |     I A>0,A<B W "A > 0 and < B" S C=B           |
 |     Q                                           |
o|                                                 |o
```

EXAMPLE 6.4. Command abbreviation

While this syntax reduces the total number of characters in a line or routine, it also detracts from the legibility of the code. In the more recent implementations of MUMPS, the source code is usually compiled before it is executed to reduce the overhead involved in scanning and interpreting the code at run time. Compilation converts each command, whether spelled out or abbreviated, to a common, internal, representation. Why then do programmers continue to write code in this somewhat cryptic shorthand form? Part of the answer lies in the fact that it is quicker to enter a program using abbreviations and implied commands than it is to spell out each command. Another, more subtle reason lies in MUMPS's line-oriented nature.

Some MUMPS commands, such as the IF, ELSE, and FOR, apply only to the remainder of the commands following them in the same line. Command lines in MUMPS are generally limited in length; the portability requirements defined by the MUMPS Development Committee (MDC) specify a maximum line length of 255 characters, although most implementations permit more. There are always cases (even if they are bad form) when programmers will try to make a full subroutine out of a single command line. MUMPS is sometimes referred to as the language of the "one-liners"; programmers often pride themselves on the amount of computing that can be built into a single line of code. While such techniques and shortcuts often reduce the time required to write a program, most good programmers recognize the potential for decreased legibility and the resulting increase in difficulty of maintaining such programs.

Commands, then, can either be spelled out in their entirety or abbreviated to the first letter of the command name. Other forms of a partial command name are not allowed. In addition, the CASE (that is, upper- or lowercase characters) of the command is ignored. Ignoring the CASE of *commands* is in direct contrast to how CASE is handled for variable names.

SET A = 1	Valid
Set A = 1	Valid
set A = 1	Valid
S A = 1	Valid
s A = 1	Valid
Se A = 1	Invalid; command must be either the entire command name or just the first character of the name.

Commands may either be spelled out in their entirety or they can be abbreviated to the first character of the command name. The *CASE* of a command (upper- or lowercase characters) does not matter.

The ability to use either upper- or lowercase characters also applies to a variety of other language elements, including pattern codes and the names of intrinsic functions.

6.1.4 Conditional Execution of Commands

As we have seen in the previous examples, the IF and ELSE commands can be used to determine whether or not the remaining commands on the line are executed or ignored. MUMPS also provides a number of alternative methods to enable or disable the execution of individual commands. These are called *postconditionals*, which can be applied either to the command or its arguments.

6.1.4.1 Command Postconditionals Individual commands can be defined in such a way that their execution is dependent on the evaluation of a MUMPS expression. The general format for conditioning a command is as follows:

Command:expression [argument,argument, . . .]

The term expression is evaluated before the command is executed; if it evaluates to TRUE, the command is executed; otherwise, the entire command is ignored. If the command contains more than one argument (for example, **Set:expression** $A=1,B=2,C=3$) then *all* the arguments are ignored if expression evaluates to FALSE. Consider the following example of code in which we examine an array of 10 numbers looking for both the largest and smallest numbers in the array:

```
o|  For j=1:1:10 Set Ary(j)=j                                    |o
|   Set Hi=0,Lo=9999999                                          |
|   For j=1:1:10 S:Ary(j)<Lo Lo=Ary(j) S:Ary(j)>Hi Hi=Ary(j)    |
o|  Write !,"High = ",Hi,!,"Low = ",Lo                          |o
|_____|
|High = 10                                                       |
o|Low = 0                                                        |o
|                                                                |
```

EXAMPLE 6.5. Command postconditionals

The FOR command provides the basic loop function in MUMPS; the FOR loops in Example 6.5 translate to "starting with $j = 1$ and then incrementing j by 1 for each iteration of the FOR command until j exceeds the value of 10, execute the remainder of the line." Note the use of the colon (:) in the examples both to separate values in the FOR command (1:1:10) and to function as part of the postconditional syntax in the Set command. The purpose of the FOR loop in line 3 is to go through the array elements one at a time, checking to see if the individual values represent either a new High or Low value. If we tried to duplicate this loop using only the IF command, we could encounter unexpected problems.

```
o|>For I=1:1:10 If Ary(I)<Lo Set Lo=Ary(I) If Ary(I)>Hi Set Hi=Ary(I)  |o
|>Write "High=",Hi," Low=",Lo↵                                          |
|High=0   Low=0                                                         |
o|>                                                                     |o
```

EXAMPLE 6.6. Incorrect use of IF command

We would successfully get the lowest value in the array (since the first IF command would be executed on every iteration of the FOR loop), but we would almost never get the correct High value (only if it were the first element in the array). When the argument of the IF command evaluates to FALSE, then the rest of the line is ignored and the next iteration of the FOR loop is processed. In our particular example, the first IF command would evaluate to TRUE *only* on the first iteration of the FOR loop since the smallest data value is the first data node processed. In all other iterations the Array element being checked would *not* be smaller than the current value of Low and consequently the rest of the line would be ignored; the second IF would not be executed after the first iteration of the loop. The value for High in this case would be erroneously reported as 0.

The conditional SET commands shown in Example 6.5 overcome this problem. The colon (:) following each SET command indicates that the command has been conditioned by the expression following the colon. Each time MUMPS encounters such a syntax, it suspends the execution of the command and first evaluates the postconditional expression. If this expression evaluates to TRUE (nonzero), the command is executed. If it evaluates to FALSE (zero), then *this* command is ignored, and execution begins again at the next command in the line. Thus, in Example 6.5, we always check both the Low and High conditions each pass through the FOR loop, but only change the values for Low and High when they meet the criteria of the postconditionals for their respective SET commands.

Commands can be *postconditioned* by appending a colon (:) and a *true/false* expression to the end of the command.

Postconditionals can be added to all MUMPS commands except IF, ELSE, and FOR.

Consider the previous example, but a new case in which you are only interested in finding the High value in the array *and* you wish to abort the FOR loop if you encounter an array element equal to 5. The third line of the example might be written as follows:

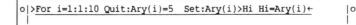

```
o|>For i=1:1:10 Quit:Ary(i)=5  Set:Ary(i)>Hi Hi=Ary(i)←        |o
 |                                                              |
```

EXAMPLE 6.7. Termination of FOR loop with postconditioned QUIT

Here we have postconditioned the QUIT command to stop the FOR loop as soon as an array element with a value of 5 is encountered. This is an extremely useful method of terminating loops and one that we will encounter in many future examples. Note, especially, that the QUIT command still has no arguments and *two spaces* are required after its postconditioned expression and the next command on the line.

> Postconditionals are *not* arguments to a command.

Another feature demonstrated in Example 6.5 is the use of compound WRITE commands. There are a number of special arguments to the WRITE command, one of which is the exclamation point (!). Whenever an exclamation point is given as an argument to a READ or WRITE command, MUMPS will output a carriage return and line feed to start a new line. In Example 6.5, the line

```
o|>Write !,"High = ",Hi,!,"Low = ",Lo←                          |o
 |                                                               |
```

is equivalent to:

```
o|>Write ! Write "High = " Write Hi←                            |o
 |>Write ! Write "Low = " Write Lo←                             |
```

EXAMPLE 6.8.   Expansion of compound WRITE command

As you can see, use of multiple arguments can significantly reduce the amount of code required to perform a given set of operations.

6.1.4.2 Argument Postconditionals   There is another method, called argument postconditioning, by which *some* commands can be conditionalized. In these instances, not only the command, but each argument can also be conditioned.

> Only three commands are defined as allowing argument postconditionals: DO, GOTO, and XECUTE.

Of the three commands permitting argument postconditioning, only the GOTO command will be examined in this section; the DO and XECUTE commands function in much the same manner when using argument postconditionals. The GOTO command is used to transfer control to another LABELed line of MUMPS code and has a basic form of

GOTO LABEL   or   G LABEL

Consider the case where we wish to transfer control of execution to different parts of a program depending on the contents of a variable. In the following example, if the integer value of the variable Var is less than 1 or greater than 3, we will continue normal execution. If its value is from 1 to 3, we wish to change program flow by dispatching control to one of three different parts (ONE, TWO, or THREE), depending on the value of Var.

```
o|          If Var<1!(Var>3) Goto CONT                    |o
 |          If Var=1 Goto ONE                             |
 |          If Var=2 Goto TWO                             |
o|          If Var=3 Goto THREE                           |o
 |CONT      Write !,"Variable = ",Var                     |o
 |          Quit                                          |
o|ONE       Set Var=97 Goto CONT                          |
 |TWO       Set Var=98 Goto CONT                          |o
 |THREE     Set Var=99 Goto CONT                          |
```

EXAMPLE 6.9. Explicit branching with GOTO

The code in Example 6.9 could be rewritten using *command postconditioning* as follows:

```
o|          Goto:Var<1!(Var>3) CONT                                  |o
 |          Goto:Var=1 ONE Goto:Var=2 TWO Goto:Var=3 THREE           |
 |CONT      Write !,"Variable = ",Var                                |
o|          Quit                                                     |o
 |ONE       Set Var=97 Goto CONT                                     |
 |TWO       Set Var=98 Goto CONT                                     |
o|THREE     Set Var=99 Goto CONT                                     |o
```

EXAMPLE 6.10. Command postconditioning

In this example, the individual Goto commands are postconditioned to form the branching logic. Using *both* command and argument postconditioning, Example 6.9 could more efficiently coded as follows:

```
o|          Goto:Var>0&(Var<4) ONE:Var=1,TWO:Var=2,THREE:Var=3   |o
 |CONT      Write !,"Variable = ",Var                            |o
 |          Quit                                                 |
o|ONE       Set Var=97 Goto CONT                                 |
 |TWO       Set Var=98 Goto CONT                                 |o
 |THREE     Set Var=99 Goto CONT                                 |
```

EXAMPLE 6.11. Command and argument postconditioning

In Example 6.11, the *entire* GOTO command is conditioned by the expression Var>0&(Var<4); if Var is not greater than 0 and less than 4, the *entire* GOTO command (including all implied GOTOs defined by the multiple arguments) is ignored, and control drops through to the next command line (label CONT). If the command postconditional evaluates to TRUE (for example, Var was 1, 2, or 3), then each argument is processed in order, with the argument postconditional determining which of the three possible GOTOs is actually executed. Use of argument postconditioning provides some of the functionality of the computed GOTO command found in some other languages.

> Postconditioning of a command takes precedence over postconditioning of an argument.

Note that a command line of **G ONE:Var = 1,TWO,THREE:Var = 3** does not make sense. Control would be transferred to label ONE if Var = 1; otherwise, it would always be transferred to label TWO; the third possible condition (Var = 3) would *never* be checked since the second argument to the GOTO would force transfer of control to label TWO (no argument postconditioning).

6.1.5 Timed Commands

Another special syntax is associated with commands that may "hang" the process until they are completed, or for which the success or failure of the initiated operation must be evaluated (for example, did the request to start another job succeed or fail?). For example, consider the READ command with a basic format of

Read Variable

This command will issue a READ to the current device. The results of the read are returned in Variable for subsequent processing by the program. Normally, READs of this type are considered to be finished when the <ENTER> key is pressed; all characters read from the keyboard except the <ENTER> key are placed in the variable name used as the argument to the READ command.

During the read, the program relinquishes control to the MUMPS operating system until the user presses the <ENTER> key. If the user goes off to lunch, the program and the terminal will simply hang in the READ state until someone finally gets around to pressing <ENTER>. For cases such as this, MUMPS provides a command syntax that allows time limits to be set on the operation and will return a status flag indicating whether or not the requested operation was successful.

The basic syntax of the timeout field in one of these commands is similar to the syntax of argument postconditionals, although the results are quite different. To add a timeout field to a command argument, a colon (:) and a numeric expression (seconds to wait) are appended to the end of an argument, as in

Read A:20

In this example, a READ is issued and, if completed *before* 20 seconds have elapsed, all subsequent actions are identical to a READ command with no timeout. If the READ goes beyond 20 seconds without being satisfied, then control is returned to the program with the following conditions:

- Whatever characters have been successfully read are returned in the variable A.

- The special system variable $TEST is set to FALSE (the READ was unsuccessful). If the READ had been completed successfully before the timeout occurred, $TEST would have been set to TRUE.

Timed commands affect the value of $TEST.

Consider the following code used to read a patient's ID number:

```
GETID   Write !,"Enter Patient ID Number: "
        Read PATID:600 Goto:$T GETNAM
        Write " Please answer the question..." Goto GETID
GETNAM  Write !,"Enter Patient Name: "
        .
        .
        .
```

EXAMPLE 6.12. Timed READ command

In this example the program displays a question and then requests a keyboard entry from the user. If the user completes the response within 10 minutes (600 seconds), then $T is returned as TRUE and control is transferred to label GET-NAM. Otherwise, the program writes out a message to the user and reissues the question. It is easy to see how this concept could be expanded to, say, Quit the program if the question is repeated five times, and so on.

Since both the ELSE command and the argumentless IF command test the condition of $TEST, Example 6.12 could also be written as:

```
o|GETID   Read !,"Enter Patient ID Number: ",PATID:600      |o
 |         Else  Write "Please answer the question..." G GETID |
 |            .                                               |
o|            .                                               |o
```

EXAMPLE 6.13. Testing timed READ overrun

Notice the use of command abbreviation in this example (G GETID instead of Goto GETID). The commands in this book will normally be spelled out in full, but in cases where a line is full, some commands may be abbreviated.

While the timeout parameter can be any valid number, the resolution of the system clock (as represented by the system variable $H) is only 1 second; some implementations allow fractional parts of a second to be expressed. Negative time-outs are converted to 0 before the command is executed.

The use of zero (0) as a timeout argument has special significance, especially when coupled with the READ command. A zero timeout argument generally means "try to execute the command, but return immediately with $TEST set to FALSE if unable to do so." This works well with the JOB, LOCK, and OPEN commands, but only makes sense with the READ command if keyboard READs are buffered. When keyboard reads are not buffered (that is, type-ahead is disabled), most implementations ignore any characters recieved from the keyboard *before* the READ command is issued. Consequently, a timed READ with a timeout argument of zero will almost never succeed. Systems that buffer keyboard input (usually called type-ahead, are enabled or disabled with parameters to the OPEN or USE command) do not clear the buffer when the READ command is issued, and any characters input since the last READ will be used to satisfy the current READ. A timeout of zero with the READ command is most often used in tight loops reading single characters (Read *a:0) from the keyboard.

More detailed information on timed READs, as well as on timed JOB, LOCK, and OPEN commands, is found in Chapter 3 under the respective command descriptions.

6.1.6 Comments

Comments can be inserted in lines of MUMPS code for documentation purposes. Comments are preceded by a *semicolon* (;) appearing in a location MUMPS would expect to find a command. All the remaining characters on the line are considered to be part of the comment and are ignored by the interpreter. The semicolon *must* be in the position of a MUMPS command; in a sense, it is another command, instructing MUMPS to ignore the rest of the line. For example, the line

If Answer = "YES" Do SAVE ;Save results when user affirms readiness

would be valid, whereas the following command line would generate a SYNTAX error, since the interpreter expects a space after the argument to the <u>Do</u> command and the next command on the line.

<u>If Answer = "YES" Do SAVE; Save the results when user affirms readiness</u>

Comments can be inserted in a line by inserting a semicolon (;) wherever MUMPS is expecting a command. The remainder of the line will be ignored.

6.2 Lines

As mentioned in the introduction to this chapter, MUMPS is a line-oriented language. Individual commands can be grouped together on the same physical line. In many instances this is simply a matter of convenience; it permits the logical grouping of related commands and reduces the number of physical lines in a routine.

```
Sqrt     ;Calculate Square Root of IN, return result in OUT
         Set OUT=0
         Quit:IN'>0
         Set OUT=IN+1/2
Loop     Set x=OUT
         Set OUT=IN/x+x/2
         Goto Loop:OUT<x
         Quit
_____
>Set IN=16←
>Do Sqrt←
>Write OUT←
4
>
```

EXAMPLE 6.14. MUMPS commands, one per line

If we include more than one command on a line, each command, including its argument(s), must be separated from the next command on the line by at least one space. If the command lacks arguments, then it must be separated from the next command on the line by at least two spaces (one for separating the command from its nonexistent argument, and one separating the command from the next command on the line). Beyond these considerations, it is possible to include *additional* spaces between commands (command separators) to improve the readability of a line.

Each line of MUMPS code can have an optional <u>LABEL</u>. Labels are used to reference lines from other parts of the program (that is, <u>DO</u> or GOTO a labeled line). Lines only need to be labeled if they are referenced; most lines in a MUMPS program lack labels.

Line labels can start with an alphabetic character (upper- or lowercase), a numeric digit (0 to 9), or the percent character (%). The first character in a label can be followed by an arbitrary number of alpha or numeric characters. However, if the first character is a digit (0 to 9), then *all* remaining characters in the label must also be digits.

Labels are *case sensitive*; that is, the label Start is different from the label START. While labels can be of any arbitrary length, only the first eight characters are used in evaluating a label address. Thus, as far as MUMPS is concerned, the labels LETSGONOW and LETSGONO are identical. Labels may *not* include embedded spaces.

Labels are separated from the commands in a line by a *linestart* character. The MUMPS standard does not define which character (or characters) is to be used as the linestart; this is left to the implementor. The linestart character may differ between implementations and even within the same implementation under different conditions. The most frequently used linestart characters are the space (decimal 32) and the TAB (decimal 9).

Some implementations use different linestart characters in direct mode versus program execute mode. When commands are read in direct mode, the <TAB> key is often used to determine if the command should be executed immediately or included within the routine currently loaded in the work area (partition). Using this convention, lines entered in direct mode that contain a TAB character as a linestart are inserted in the work area and are *not* executed. Lines that do not contain a TAB as a linestart are executed as a direct command; they are not inserted into the work area. Commands entered for immediate execution do *not* have a linestart character; those entered for inclusion in the work area do. When using routine editors, this distinction is usually ignored, and either the SPACE or TAB character can be used as a linestart. Check the documentation for the routine editor on your system to determine line-entry conventions.

Lines that begin with a LABEL must have at least one linestart character separating the label from the first command on the line. Additional linestart characters can be used to indicate the *level of the line* (see Section 6.6 for a description of line levels and *block structuring*). After the last linestart character on a line, additional space characters (command separators) can be used to improve line clarity.

If a line within a routine does not have an associated label, it must begin with at least one linestart character.

When passing parameters to a subroutine or extrinsic function, the parenthesized parameter list (*formal* parameter list; see Chapter 9) is a part of the label. This initial label consists, then, of the label name followed by an open parenthesis, the list of parameters, a closing parenthesis, one or more linestart characters, and then the remainder of the line.

To reiterate, a distinction must be made between lines entered for immediate execution at the keyboard (that is, in direct mode) and those entered as part of a routine. For direct mode commands, labels are *not used* and the linestart character is not used. For lines that are part of a routine, the linestart character is required. It is the first character in the line for those lines without labels; for lines with labels, the linestart character is used to separate the label from the commands on the line.

```
o|Sqrt   ;Calculate Square Root of IN, return results in OUT |o
 |        Set OUT=0 Quit:IN'>0                                 |
 |        Set OUT=IN+1/2                                        |
o|Loop    Set x=OUT,OUT=IN/x+x/2 Goto Loop:OUT<x              |o
 |        Quit                                                  |
 |_____|
o|>Set IN=16 Do Sqrt Write OUT←                               |o
 |4                                                            |
 |>                                                            |
```

EXAMPLE 6.15. MUMPS commands, many per line

In these examples, the choice of putting more than one command on a physical line is at the discretion of the programmer and is mostly a matter of style. However, in other cases, the semantics of a command necessitates placing multiple commands on a single line. In particular, the commands IF, ELSE, and FOR apply only to subsequent commands on the same line.

```
o|Sqrt ;Calculate Square Root of IN, return results in OUT   |o
 |       Set OUT=0 If IN'>0 Quit                               |
 |       Set OUT=IN+1/2 For  Set x=OUT,OUT=IN/x+x/2 Quit:OUT'<x|
o|       Quit                                                 |o
 |_____|
 |>Set IN=16 Do ^Sqrt Write OUT←                              |
o|4                                                           |o
 |>                                                           |
```

EXAMPLE 6.16.   Line-oriented commands

In this example, the IF command (line Sqrt + 1) and the FOR command (line Sqrt + 2) make sense only if there are additional commands on the same line. About the only logical example of a stand-alone conditional command is shown in the following example:

```
o|Pause ;Delay execution for DLY loop iterations             |o
 |        For i=1:1:DLY                                        |
 |        Quit                                                 |
```

EXAMPLE 6.17.   Conditional command without subsequent commands

The code in Example 6.17 could be used to pause program execution for a the time that would be required to execute DLY FOR loop iterations. While this code may make functional sense, it is not particularly good programming practice. The delay actually experienced would depend on a variety of factors, such as the version of MUMPS being used, the hardware (CPU) speed, and the system load.

6.3 Subroutines (Parts)

In MUMPS, *subroutines* are groups of lines that start with a label, perform a defined operation, and end with a QUIT command. They can consist of one or more lines and are typically invoked by a DO (or sometimes a GOTO) command. Due to earlier language structures, subroutines used to be termed *parts*, and you may hear them referred to as such by old-timers.

Subroutines can contain code that performs a variety of functions, but good programming practice would be to keep their functionality to a single, specific action. Clean, modular programming with subroutines that perform single, well-defined functions can greatly improve the clarity, reliability, and subsequent maintainability of a program. Threaded code, in which the functionality of the code is spread throughout the program, will have just the opposite effect. The creation of reusable subroutines can also speed up program development. Subroutines within one routine can be invoked from other routines.

```
Sqrt    ;Calculate Square Root of IN, return results in OUT
        Set OUT=0 Quit:IN'>0
        Set OUT=IN+1/2
Loop    Set x=OUT,OUT=IN/x+x/2 Goto Loop:OUT<x
        Quit
─────────────────────────────────────────────────────
>Set IN=16 Do Sqrt Write OUT←
4
>
```

EXAMPLE 6.18. MUMPS subroutines

In this example the lines from Sqrt to Loop + 1 represent a single subroutine that is invoked with the command Do Sqrt.

6.4 Routines

Routines are collections of MUMPS lines, often subdivided into subroutines. As discussed in Chapter 2, the *MUMPS Portability Standard* specifies that individual routines should be less than 5,000 bytes in length to ensure that they can run on all implementations adhering to the portability standard. It is because of this fact that we usually make a distinction in the MUMPS environment between a *routine* and a *program*; most languages treat these two terms synonymously. It would be extremely difficult to write most application programs, no matter how powerful the language, if one were limited to a total of 5,000 bytes of code. MUMPS routines provide a method for subdividing an application into individual pieces that are saved on disk and can be loaded into the partition for execution.

By *convention*, the first line of a routine contains a label, and the label is identical to the routine name. Routine names have a similar format to line labels: they start with an alphabetic character (upper- or lowercase), followed by one or more alpha or numeric characters. As with labels, only the first eight characters of the routine name are used in evaluating the name. Routine names are *case sensitive*; the routine GetPat is different from the routine GETPAT. Like labels, routine names can start with the special character %. Use of routine names starting with the % character is usually reserved for *library* routines that can be invoked from any directory.

Also, by *convention*, the first two lines of a routine are comment lines; the first identifies the programmer and the date and time the routine was last saved to disk, and the second is a single line of comment summarizing the function of the routine. While the first-lines convention is not required, it is strongly recommended that the programmer follow these conventions. The following is an example of the beginning of a routine:

```
o|PATDEM   ;JML-NYSCVM; 10/8/86-14:55                           |o
 |          ;Collect Patient Demographic Data                    |
 |PATID     Read !,"Patient ID number: ",PID                     |
o|             .                                                 |o
 |             .                                                 |
 |             .                                                 |
```

EXAMPLE 6.19. Routine first-line conventions

The first line of the routine has, as a label, the name of the routine. In addition, it identifies the programmer (JML-NYSCVM stands for John Meigs Lewkowicz, New York State College of Veterinary Medicine), and it contains the date and time the routine was last modified. Most routine editors automatically insert the date and time each time the routine is edited and filed. The second line of the routine is a comment line that states, in simple terms, the function of the routine.

6.5 Programs

A program in MUMPS is the collection of all routines necessary to perform a defined function. Again, the distinction between a routine and a program in the MUMPS environment is somewhat artificial. Since the *Portability Standard* (current type B proposal) limits the maximum size of a routine to 5,000 bytes or less, it is often necessary (and advisable) to break an application into a number of discrete parts (routines). A program is simply the collection of these routines.

Another common and useful convention concerns the naming of individual routines (and data files) within an application package. Most programmers reserve the first letter of a routine to identify the application (for example, all routines starting with the letter I might refer to an Inventory package). Additionally, some reserve the second and third characters of the name to further subdivide the application (for example, all routines starting with the characters IE are related to data Entry/Edit options, those starting with IS relate to Search options, and so on).

6.6 Block Structuring[1]

Block structuring (also referred to as the argumentless Do command) is an enhancement that is designed to encourage the writing of structured programs in MUMPS. Because of the line-oriented nature of the MUMPS language and the line length limitations (255 characters), it is often necessary to write numerous, small subroutines that are referenced only once. Consider the following example, which is used to check a string of characters and convert it to a number (a task that is actually handled automatically by MUMPS; see Section 4.2.2).

```
Ncnv    ;Interpret string "STR" as a number
        New char,i,flag,num Set num="",flag=0
        For i=1:1:$L(STR) Do Chkchar Quit:flag
        Set:num="" num=0 Set:num?1P.E num=$E(num,2,99)
        Set STR=num Quit
Chkchar ;check each character, set "flag"=TRUE if done
        Set char=$E(STR,i) If char?1N Set num=num_char Quit
        If "+-"[char Do PMtest Quit
        If char="." Do Dtest Quit
        Set flag=1
        Quit
PMtest  If num[char Set flag=1 Quit
        Set num=char_num Quit
Dtest   If num["." Set flag=1 Quit
        Set num=num_"." Quit
```

EXAMPLE 6.20. Subroutine to interpret a string as a number

This subroutine loops through the input string (STR) one character at a time, and terminates whenever a character that is inconsistent with the numeric conversion is encountered. The following conditions will terminate the process:

- A character other than a digit (0 to 9) or the special character +, −, or . is encountered.
- If the character being checked is a +, −, or . *and* the number being built already has that character.

The function $L returns the *length* of the input string (see Section 8.1.3), and the function $E is used to *extract* characters from a target string (see Section 8.1.1).

The subroutines Chkchar, PMtest, and Dtest are temporary and are needed, primarily, to overcome the limitations imposed by the scope of some commands such as For and If. It might be possible to perform the entire check on a single line with extensive use of postconditioning, but the resulting code would be difficult to understand and maintain.

---

[1]MDC Type A release, January 1987. Note that, while this is a MDC Type A release, there is still a good deal of controversy concerning how to achieve a more structured syntax in MUMPS. Block structuring and the argumentless DO command presented here may *not* be included in the upcoming MUMPS standard.

Using block structuring, Example 6.20 could be rewritten as follows:

```
o|Ncnv   ;Interpret string "STR" as a number          |o
 |       New char,i,flag,num Set num="",flag=0         |
 |       For i=1:1:$L(STR) Do    Quit:flag             |
o|       . Set char=$E(STR,i)                          |o
 |       . If char?1N Set num=num_char Quit            |
 |       . If "+-"[char Do    Quit                     |
o|       . . If num'[char Set num=char_num Quit        |o
 |       . . Set flag=1                                |
 |       . If char="." Do    Quit                      |
o|       . . If num'[" . " Set num=num_"." Quit        |o
 |       . . Set flag=1                                |
 |       . Set flag=1                                  |
o|       Set:num="" num=0 Set:num?1P.E num=$E(num,2,99)|o
 |       Set STR=num Quit                              |
```

EXAMPLE 6.21. Example 6.20 rewritten with Block Structuring

The argumentless <u>Do</u> command is used to initiate execution of *inner blocks* of lines (designated with leading periods). To understand the construction of blocks of lines, we must return to the definition of a *line* (see the initial discussion of line structure in Section 6.2).

Each *line* starts with an optional *label* and *formal list* of parameters, which are followed by one or more *linestart* characters. Following the last linestart character are zero or more spaces (*command separators*, used to improve line legibility), followed by zero or more commands. Notice the extra spaces between the argumentless <u>Do</u> commands and the <u>Quit</u> commands that follow them in the previous example. Only two spaces are required between these commands; the additional spaces are only used to make the <u>Do</u> commands stand out.

Subroutines are executed in a sequence of *blocks* which consist of a set of lines, all having the same *level* as the label referenced by the <u>Do</u>, the *extrinsic function*, or the *extrinsic variable* used to invoke the subroutine. The *level* of the subroutine is defined by the number of linestart characters in the line; the greater the number of linestart characters, the higher (more deeply nested) is the line level. After the first linestart character, subsequent linestart characters must be preceded with a period (used to provide a visual indicator of the line level).

The <u>Do</u> command without arguments initiates execution of an inner block of lines (lines with a higher level). The current line location (that is, the location at which execution will resume after the subroutine is done) is saved, the line level is increased by one, and execution continues at the line following the <u>Do</u> command. On encountering an implicit or explicit QUIT command at the same line level, the line level is decremented by one and execution resumes at the command following the argumentless <u>Do</u>.

The argumentless <u>Do</u> command can be postconditioned. If the command is postconditioned and the postcondition expression evaluates to FALSE, execution continues at the current level (that is, the execution level remains the same and the inner block of lines is skipped).

Upon entry to a block of lines, the current line level is incremented by one. Lines that have a higher line level than the new level (greater number of linestarts)

are ignored (that is, *not* executed) unless they are explicitly invoked with an argumentless <u>Do</u> at the new current level. When a line with a lower level (smaller number of linestarts) is encountered, an implicit QUIT command is executed; the new line level is decremented by one; and the block is terminated.

The <u>Do</u> command with arguments and references to *extrinsic functions* or *variables* provide for a generalized call to a subroutine. The subroutine name is specified by the argument to the <u>Do</u> or the name of the *extrinsic function or variable*. The line specified by such references *must* have a level of *one* (that is, one linestart character); reference to a line whose level is not one is erroneous.

Any line, regardless of its level, can have an associated label. The <u>Goto</u> command can be used to branch to labeled lines, provided that both the following conditions are satisfied.

1. The destination line must have the same line level as the line containing the <u>Goto</u> command.

2. The destination line must be within the same block as the invoking line (that is, there are no lines of a lower execution level between the line specified by the <u>Goto</u> command and the line containing the <u>Goto</u> command).

Whew! As a colleague once remarked about an unrelated topic, "If it wasn't so confusing, it would be simple." However, look back at Example 6.21 and compare it to Example 6.20. The periods at the beginning of lines are used to designate the line level. The argumentless <u>Do</u> commands are used to initiate the next higher line level (those subsequent lines containing more periods). These higher-level blocks are terminated, either when an explicit QUIT command is executed or when a line with fewer periods is encountered. Blocks of indented commands are automatically skipped after the completion of the argumentless <u>Do</u> command. It only sounds confusing.

6.7 Chapter Highlights

- In commands with arguments, the arguments must be separated from the command by *exactly one space* (6.1.1).

- In the case of commands *with* associated arguments, the next command on the line is separated from the last argument of the previous command by at least *one space* (6.1.1).

- In commands *without* arguments, the command must be separated from the next command on the line by *two or more spaces* (6.1.1).

- Multiple arguments to a single command are separated from each other with *commas* (6.1.2).

- Commands may either be spelled out in their *entirety* or they can be *abbreviated to the first character* of the command name (6.1.3).

- The case of a command (upper- or lowercase characters) does *not* matter (6.1.3).

- Commands can be *postconditioned* by appending a *colon* (:) and a true/false expression to the end of the command (6.1.4.1).

- Postconditionals can be added to all MUMPS commands except IF, ELSE, and FOR (6.1.4.1).
- Postconditionals are *not* arguments to a command (6.1.4.1).
- Only three commands are defined as allowing argument postconditionals: DO, GOTO, and XECUTE (6.1.4.2).
- Postconditioning of a command takes precedence over postconditioning of an argument (6.1.4.2).
- Timeout syntax is permitted in four commands: JOB, LOCK, OPEN, and READ (6.1.5).
- Timed commands affect the value of $TEST (6.1.5).
- Comments can be inserted in a line by inserting a semicolon (;) wherever MUMPS is expecting a command. The rest of the line will be ignored by MUMPS (6.1.6).

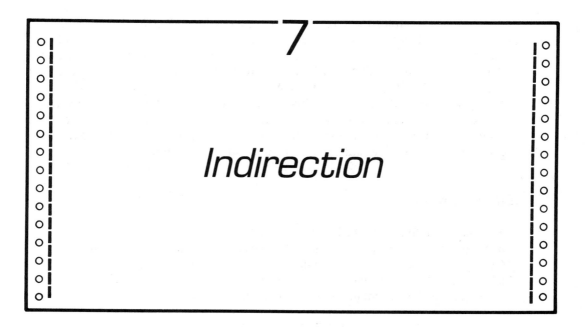

7

Indirection

Most computer systems in use today process two types of information; the first type consists of the commands or instructions used to control the execution of an application, and the second consists of the data being processed. While the basic operation of MUMPS usually conforms to this traditional dichotomy, there are also constructs supported by MUMPS in which information stored as data can be executed. Execution of instructions held in data fields is called *indirection* and is not generally supported in high-level computer languages.

This chapter is devoted to an examination of indirection. While the use of indirection is an important tool in the MUMPS environment, it is not essential for an understanding of the language and is a potential source of confusion for the beginning programmer. It is recommended that the beginning programmer either skim this chapter or skip it altogether, and then come back and study it in detail after gaining some experience with the language.

Indirection is a technique that permits part or all of a command line, a command, or a command argument to be replaced with information from data fields before execution of the command. Consider the following example:

```
o|>Kill  Set Var="XYZ",@Var=1 Write "Var=",Var," XYZ=",XYZ←  |o
 |Var=XYZ XYZ=1                                                |
 |>                                                            |
```

EXAMPLE 7.1. Introduction to indirection

In this example, the character @ is called the *indirection operator*, and it instructs MUMPS to use the *contents* of the variable Var in the SET command; the location set to a value of 1 is *not* Var but rather XYZ. MUMPS replaces the characters "@Var" with "XYZ" (the contents of the variable Var) before that argument of the SET command is executed.

Two broad categories of indirection are found in the MUMPS language: (1) the XECUTE command in which the argument to the command is a data field containing MUMPS instructions to be executed, and (2) the use of the indirection operator (@) in which data values are substituted for command arguments.

7.1 XECUTE Command

You may wish to review the basic description of the XECUTE command described in Section 3.5 before proceeding with the rest of this section. Basically, the XE-CUTE command takes as an argument a string of characters that is interpreted as a line of MUMPS code and then executes that code. The commands being executed are stored as data elements, not as command lines in a routine.

```
o|>Set data="For i=1:1:5 Write !,i*i"←          |o
 |>Write data←                                   |
 |For i=1:1:5 Write !,i*i                         |
o|>Xecute data←                                  |o
 |1                                               |
 |4                                               |
o|9                                              |o
 |16                                              |
 |25                                              |
o|>                                              |o
 |                                                |
```

EXAMPLE 7.2. XECUTE command

The actual command string being executed is held in the variable data and can be dependent on run-time conditions. Indeed, we can carry this process a step further and read, from within a general-purpose program, a string of characters from the keyboard and execute them just as if they had been entered as a direct-mode command. These high-level control programs are often referred to as shell programs or just shells.

```
o|Shell  Read !,": ",xeq Quit:xeq="" Xecute xeq Goto Shell |o
 |                                                          |
 |>Do Shell←                                                |
o|                                                         |o
 |: Set a=22,b=3 Write "a*b=",a*b←                          |
 |a*b=66                                                    |
o|: If a>b Write "a greater than b"←                       |o
 |a greater than b                                          |
 |: ←                                                       |
o|>                                                        |o
```

EXAMPLE 7.3. XECUTing commands from the keyboard

All valid MUMPS commands (including additional XECUTE or DO commands) can be executed out of the argument string. Expanding this approach, one can write a MUMPS program that provides a direct mode shell that operates under the control of a MUMPS program. Some MUMPS implementations do just this; direct mode operations are controlled by a shell written in MUMPS that XECUTEs the data read from the keyboard. This permits a more user friendly direct mode environment that can offer on-line help text, keyboard history, and so on.

The XECUTE command operates in a fashion similar to the DO command. The DO command transfers control to a routine line, while the XECUTE command temporarily transfers program execution to a line of data. Both return control to the command following that which initiated the control transfer and continue execution from that point.

Some reservations should be exercised when using the XECUTE command in a program. Because this code may be dependent on the contents of variables established at run time, it must be interpreted each time the code is executed. This means, especially in implementations that compile routine source code, that code executed with the XECUTE command can be significantly slower than execution of the same code held in routines. Additionally, and possibly more important, routines making extensive use of the XECUTE command are often more difficult to maintain. It is often impossible to look at routine listings and determine program flow, since the code being executed may be built during program execution and not appear on a static listing.

7.2 Indirection Operator @

The indirection operator is the "at-sign" (@) and is used to indicate that a command argument (or part of the argument) is to be modified before execution of the command. Four general forms of indirection are possible:

1. Name indirection
2. Pattern indirection
3. Argument indirection
4. Subscript indirection

All are similar in that the command is modified at the time of execution by the contents of variables (or string literals). The modification of commands by data is the general pattern for the indirection, and breaking it into four separate categories is done to help clarify where such syntax is permitted and where it is not. All four forms are identified by the presence of the indirection operator @.

7.2.1 Name Indirection

Name indirection is permitted in the MUMPS language wherever a variable, label, or routine name is expected as part of a command argument. In these cases, the contents of the variable following the indirection operator (@) are substituted for the indirection operator and variable name before the command is executed. Consider the following example of name indirection:

```
o|Label  Set A="B",C="ONE",B=1                                        |o
 |       Set @A=C If B'=1 Goto @C                                      |
 |       Quit                                                          |
o|ONE     Write !,"B = ",B                                            |o
 |        Quit                                                         |
 |                                                                     |
o|----------------------------------------------------------------------|o
 |>Do Label←                                                          |
 |B = ONE                                                             |
```

EXAMPLE 7.4. Name indirection

In this example, all the indirection is handled in the second line of code. At execution time, the contents of variable A replace the @A part of the SET command to yield

Set B=C

The @C in the GOTO command is replaced with the contents of variable C to yield an effective command of

Goto ONE

> Name indirection can be used anywhere MUMPS is expecting
> a valid name (variable, label, or routine).

There is an extended form of the syntax of the GOTO command that was not covered in the previous examples:

Goto LABEL^ROUTINE

In the earlier examples we used the simpler syntax of the GOTO command (Goto LABEL) in which the routine name was assumed to be the same as the routine in which the GOTO was found. The extended form of the GOTO command permits control to be transferred to a specified label in another routine. Both the LABEL and ROUTINE are valid MUMPS names, and the use of name indirection permits the following code:

```
o|      Set Label="TEST",Routine="GETANS"                             |o
 |      Goto @Label^@Routine                                          |
 |                                                                     |
o|                                                                     |o
```

EXAMPLE 7.5. Name indirection

It is also possible to combine both names into a single variable (for example, **Address** = "TEST^GETANS") and issue a **Goto @Address**. This is not a form of name indirection, but rather argument indirection [**Address** consists of *two* separate names (one a label name, the other a routine name) separated by the ^ character]. Argument indirection is discussed later.

Another common use of name indirection illustrates additional versatility that would be difficult to achieve without this syntax. Let's assume that we have picked up a data node from a global that contains general information on a person's address in the form

Data = "Doe,Jane;55 State St.;Any Town;NY;14850;(607) 253-3333"

Data represents a compound record that we wish to use to initialize a number of local variables (Name, Street, City, State, ZIP, and Phone) for subsequent processing. We could initialize the individual variables with the following code:

```
o|    Set Name=$P(Data,";",1),Street=$P(Data,";",2)     |o
 |    Set City=$P(Data,";",3),State=$P(Data,";",4)      |
 |    Set ZIP=$P(Data,";",5),Phone=$P(Data,";",6)       |
o|                                                      |o
```

EXAMPLE 7.6. Setting variables directly

In this example, **$P** represents the **$PIECE** function, which is used to extract pieces of information from a string of characters. The command **S Street = $P(Data,";",2)** is roughly equivalent to saying "Extract the substring of characters in Data that lies between the second and third semicolon and place those characters in the variable Street."

Another method for achieving the same results would be the following code:

```
o|    S X="Name;Street;City;State;ZIP;Phone"           |o
 |    F I=1:1:6 S @$P(X,";",I)=$P(Data,";",I)          |
 |    .                                                 |
o|    .                                                 |o
```

EXAMPLE 7.7. Setting variables using name indirection

With the explanation of the $PIECE function just given, you should be able to work out the FOR loop in line 2 and see how the variables Name, Street, City, State, ZIP, and Phone will be initialized to the corresponding pieces from the variable Data.

7.2.2 Argument Indirection

In the two previous examples we examined how indirection can be used with parts of an argument. In this section we deal with indirection of entire arguments.

Argument indirection refers to those cases where the entire argument to a command is replaced by the contents of a variable. We have already seen one example of argument indirection (**Goto @Address** - where **Address** = "TEST^GETANS"); other examples include:

```
o|      Set A="ZIP=14850",B="Age=22"                        |o
 |      Set @A,@B Write !,"ZIP Code = ",ZIP,!,"Age = ",Age  |
 |      Quit                                                 |
o|----------------------------------------------------------|o
|ZIP Code = 14850                                            |
|Age = 22                                                    |
o|                                                          |o
```

EXAMPLE 7.8. Argument indirection

It is often difficult for some beginners to see the difference between name and argument indirection. In both cases the results are similar: the variable following the indirection operator @ is replaced by the contents of the variable before the command is executed. The two different forms are defined to show exactly where indirection can and cannot be used. Consider the following three examples:

```
o|ONE    Set @"Var1"=1+2       |o
 |TWO    Set @"Var1=1+2"       |
 |THREE  Set Var1=@"1+2"       |
o|                            |o
```

EXAMPLE 7.9. Illegal use of name/argument indirection

The first two examples (ONE and TWO) work correctly. The first is an example of name indirection (Var1 is a variable name) and the second is an example of argument indirection (Var1 = 1 + 2 is the argument to a Set command). Example THREE is *not a valid syntax*; the string of characters 1 + 2 is neither a name nor is it an argument (it is only a portion of the argument).

In commands that permit *both* argument indirection *and* multiple arguments, more than one argument can be defined by indirection. Consider the following example in which three separate arguments are used in a WRITE command:

```
o|>Write @"!,""4 squared is "",4*4"←        |o
 |                                           |
 |4 squared is 16                            |
o|>Write "!,""4 squared is "",4*4"←          |o
 |                                           |
 |!, "4 squared is ",4*4                     |
o|>                                         |o
```

EXAMPLE 7.10. Argument indirection with multiple arguments

Another common use of argument indirection involves option dispatch with the DO or GOTO, command as demonstrated in the next example.

```
o|Opts    ;Main Option Dispatch                                          |o
 |        Set o="Enter data/Search/Print/Utilities/QUIT"                  |
 |        For i=1:1:5 Write !,$P(o,"/",i)                                 |
o|Gopt    Read !,"Option NUMBER: ",opt Quit:"5"[opt                       |o
 |        If opt'?1N!(opt>4)!'opt Write *7," ??" Goto Gopt                |
 |        Do @$P("EDIT,SRCH,PRNT,UTIL",",",opt) Goto Opts                 |
o|          .                                                             |o
 |          .                                                             |
 |          .                                                             |
```

EXAMPLE 7.11.   Option dispatch using argument indirection

There is one exception to the use of argument indirection; it *cannot* be used when specifying the argument to a FOR command. Consider the valid use of name indirection in the following example:

```
o|>Set A="I" For @A=1:1:3 Write !,I←                                     |o
 |1                                                                       |
 |2                                                                       |
o|3                                                                       |o
 |>                                                                       |
```

EXAMPLE 7.12.   Name indirection with the FOR command

While this form of indirection is allowed, attempting to make the entire argument to the FOR command an indirect reference is illegal.

```
o|>Set A="I=1:1:5" For @A Write I←                                       |o
 |<SYNTAX> ERROR                                                          |
 |>                                                                       |
```

EXAMPLE 7.13.   Illegal use of argument indirection with the FOR command

> Argument indirection is permitted for all commands that accept arguments with the exception of the FOR command.

7.2.3 Pattern Indirection

The pattern match operator (?) is used to check a string for a particular pattern of characters (Section 5.3.2.4). The result of a pattern check is TRUE or FALSE depending on whether or not the pattern was found. For example, to check and see if the variable ZIP contains a valid ZIP code, we can use the following code:

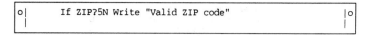

```
o|        If ZIP?5N Write "Valid ZIP code"                    |o
 |                                                            |
```

EXAMPLE 7.14. Pattern matching

This translates into the statement "If the contents of the variable ZIP contains exactly five numeric digits, then set $TEST to TRUE; otherwise, set $TEST to FALSE." As you can imagine, pattern matching arguments can be quite complex. The actual pattern specification (<u>5N</u>) is neither a valid name (which would indicate a variable, label, or routine), nor is it an argument (the argument to the IF command in Example 7.14 is the entire string <u>ZIP?5N</u>); yet it would be desirable to permit indirection in pattern matching. The following example demonstrates pattern indirection:

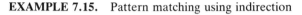

```
o|        Set Pattern="5N"                                    |o
 |        If ZIP?@Pattern Write "Valid ZIP code."             |
 |         .                                                  |
```

EXAMPLE 7.15. Pattern matching using indirection

Pattern indirection is frequently used in high-level applications in which question descriptions are held as data in a global (often referred to as a data dictionary), and a general-purpose *question driver* subroutine is used to ask and verify the answer. Consider the data depicted in Figure 7.1, which shows a simple data dictionary used to define question text and the pattern that must be matched before the answer is accepted. The subscript ("<u>Name</u>") is used both as a pointer to the question description and as the local variable name in which a successful data entry will be stored.

```
                              ^Cdict
                               ┌┬┐
                               │││

                            ("Name")

    Client name (Last,First): \1A.A1","1A.E
```

FIGURE 7.1. Simple data dictionary defining questions

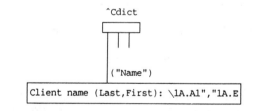

```
o|Getdata ;Get client data from user                         |o
 |        Set mne="Name" Do Getans Quit:Name=""               |
 |         .                                                  |
o|         .                                                  |o
 |Getans  ;Display question associated with "mne", read an    |
 |        ;answer from the keyboard, verify, and return the   |
o|        ;answer in @mne. NULL entries are always accepted.  |o
 |        Set q=^Cdict(mne),p=$P(q,"\",2),q=$P(q,"\",1)        |
 |Read    Write !,q Read ans Goto GetX:ans=""                 |
o|        If ans?@p Goto GetX                                 |o
 |        Write " ??, please try again." Goto Read            |
 |GetX    Set @mne=ans                                        |
o|        Quit                                                |o
```

EXAMPLE 7.16. Use of pattern indirection to verify a keyboard entry

Keyboard entries are checked in line <u>Read+1</u> using pattern indirection; if the pattern match fails, the question is reasked.

7.2.4 Subscript Indirection

Subscript indirection is a special case that does not follow the simpler substitution rule described previously. This form of indirection is used in manipulating local arrays and globals in an indirect fashion.

The syntax of subscript indirection consists of two parts: an array or global reference and a subscript extension. Both parts are preceded with the indirection operator (@) with *no* spaces between any of the four elements. Consider the following:

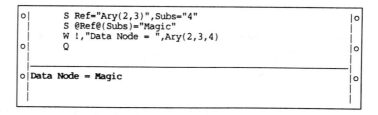

```
    S Ref="Ary(2,3)",Subs="4"
    S @Ref@(Subs)="Magic"
    W !,"Data Node = ",Ary(2,3,4)
    Q


Data Node = Magic
```

EXAMPLE 7.17. Subscript indirection

The expression **@Ref@(Subs)** is expanded before execution using the contents of variables **Ref** and **Subs** to <u>Ary(2,3,4)</u>. Note that this is not a simple substitution as we have seen in the previous examples of indirection, but one based on the context of a subscripted data element. The closing parenthesis in REF [Ary(2,3)] is dropped, the opening parenthesis in Subs [(4)] is dropped, and a comma (,) is substituted in place of the closing and opening parentheses that were dropped. Consider the following examples of subscript indirection and how the code is expanded before the command is executed:

Given: **Ref1 = "A", Ref2 = "A(1)", Ref3 = "A(1,2,3)"**
and: **Sub1 = "7", Sub2 = "7,8,9"**

Then:	Subscript Indirection	Expands to
	@Ref1@(Sub1)	A(7)
	@Ref2@(Sub1)	A(1,7)
	@Ref3@(Sub2)	A(1,2,3,"7,8,9")
	@Ref2@(Ref1,Sub1)	A(1,"A",7)

If you use subscript indirection for the first level of an array or global, then the array or global reference (<u>Ref</u>) does *not* include an opening or closing parenthesis.

Also, carefully note the third example [@Ref3@(Sub2)]. The results of evaluating this reference point to the *fourth* level of the array, *not* to the *sixth* level. The variable Sub2 is evaluated to a single subscript, a string that happens to contain commas.

Only *one* occurrence of subscript indirection is permitted within an array reference. Consider the next example.

```
o|>Set Ary(1,2,3)=1,ref="Ary(1)",sub2=2,sub3=3←          |o
 |>Write @ref@(sub2,sub3)←                               |
 |1                                                      |
o|>Write @ref@(sub2)@(sub3)←                             |o
 |<<SYNTAX>> ERROR                                       |
 |>                                                      |
```

EXAMPLE 7.18.   Illegal multiple subscript indirection

In the second part of this example, the attempt to append multiple subscript indirections to the initial reference is illegal and results in an error.

> It is *illegal* to use more than one subscript indirection argument in an array reference [e.g., @Ref@(Sub1) @(Sub2)]

7.3 Dynamic Routine Linking

Another powerful feature of the MUMPS language is the manner in which routines and subroutines are linked together to form an application. In Section 2.2.1, we described the general concept of subroutines as being a natural extension of the calling routine, sharing a common local symbol table. Because of indirection, it is impossible to know accurately what subroutine might be called within a given application; linking of subroutines is dynamic and determined at execution time.

```
o|Option ;Option Dispatch Routine                             |o
 |        Read !,"Option Number (1-9): ",opt Quit:opt=""       |
 |        If opt'?1N!'opt Write " ??, try again." Goto Option  |
o|        Do @("^Opt"_opt)                                     |o
 |        Goto Option                                          |
```

EXAMPLE 7.19.   Dynamic linking of routines

In this example, the name of the routine invoked by the DO command is not known until the user enters a choice from the keyboard; the name of the routine is built at the time of execution (see, also, Example 7.11).

7.4 Indirection: Cautions and Caveats

Indirection can be a powerful and positive tool in MUMPS programs, but it also represents one of the two most frequently abused syntaxes in the language (the other being the naked global references discussed in Chapter 10). One main problem with use of such syntax comes in trying to maintain the MUMPS programs after they are written. In most cases, a programmer can examine code months or years after it was written to correct bugs or add enhancements with little or no difficulty; the code is apparent and any experienced MUMPS programmer can usually derive the functionality of the code, even if it is not documented. The use of indirection increases the difficulty of understanding the code, because the actual commands or arguments may be derived at execution time and may not be clear from a listing of the programs.

When indirection is used, the variables used for indirection should be clearly documented to show how and where they are derived and the limits of their permissible values.

To further confuse the issue, indirection can also be nested. Try to figure out what really happens in the following two examples. Remember, these are relatively straightforward; all the variables used in the examples are defined just prior to the indirection.

```
o|      S A="B",B="C",@@A=B                         |o
 |      W !,A,", ",B,", ",C                          |
 |  _____ |
o|B, C, C                                            |o
 |                                                   |
```

EXAMPLE 7.20. Double indirection

```
o|      S A="X(@E)",B=1,C=2,D="B",E="C"              |o
 |      S @A@(@D)=@E                                  |
o|                                                   |o
```

EXAMPLE 7.21. Indirection carried to absurdity

Were you able to figure out the second example? The second line results in the setting of the array element $X(2,1)=2$. Now that you have the answer, can you work out the indirection? Tough, isn't it? It is also poor programming style!

Now consider maintaining a complex package using such code, where the variables used for indirection could have been set anywhere in the program, and the values of the variables depend on conditions established during execution of the program. How comfortable would you feel making changes to such commands?

> Use indirection only where necessary, and document it well.

7.5 Chapter Highlights

- Name indirection can be used anywhere MUMPS is expecting a valid name (variable, label, or routine) (7.2.1).
- Argument indirection is permitted for all commands that accept arguments, with the exception of the FOR command (7.2.2).
- It is *illegal* to use more than one subscript indirection argument in an array reference [for example, @Ref@(Sub1)@(Sub2)] (7.2.4).
- Use indirection only where necessary, and document it well (7.4).

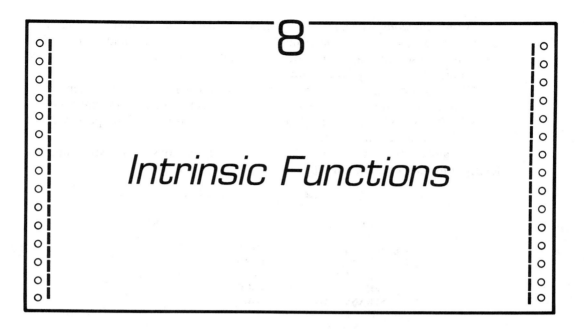

8

Intrinsic Functions

In addition to the commands and operators described in Chapters 3 and 4, the MUMPS language provides a variety of built-in (intrinsic) functions used to perform special actions. These functions are defined as part of the language standard, as contrasted to the extrinsic functions (described in Chapter 9), which can be defined by the programmer. A function is evaluated as an expression and returns a single value that is interpreted in context.

Each function begins with a dollar sign ($) followed by the name of the function, and then followed by a list of parameters enclosed in parentheses. The function name is case insensitive (lowercase characters are converted to uppercase for interpretation), and most can be abbreviated to the first character of the name (for example, the $EXTRACT function can be abbreviated to $E). Function parameters are enclosed in parentheses and are separated from each other with commas. Many functions have multiple forms denoted by the number of parameters supplied to the function.

Functions can be grouped into three main categories determined by the types of data they process:

- String functions
- Data functions
- Other (miscellaneous) functions

String functions typically process strings of data (for example, extract characters form a target string, determine the length of a string, and so on), *data functions* are used to search and check on database elements, and all others are lumped into the category "other" functions.

There is also a special category of functions starting with the characters **$Z....** These are intrinsic functions designed by the implementors and are *not* standard across MUMPS implementations. Use of these functions may inhibit portability of applications to different systems.

An alphabetized list of the MUMPS intrinsic functions, along with summary descriptions, can be found in Appendix D.

String Functions	Data Functions	Other Functions
8.1.1 **$EXTRACT**	8.2.1 **$DATA**	8.3.1 **$SELECT**
8.1.2 **$PIECE**	8.2.2 **$ORDER**	8.3.2 **$RANDOM**
8.1.3 **$LENGTH**	8.2.3 **$NEXT**	8.3.3 **$VIEW**
8.1.4 **$FIND**	8.2.4 **$QUERY**	
8.1.5 **$TRANSLATE**	8.2.5 **$GET**	
8.1.6 **$JUSTIFY**		
8.1.7 **$FNUMBER**		
8.1.8 **$ASCII**		
8.1.9 **$CHAR**		
8.1.10 **$TEXT**		

8.1 String Functions

String functions are used to perform operations on strings. They return either string or numeric values, depending on the specific function and how it is used.

8.1.1 $EXTRACT

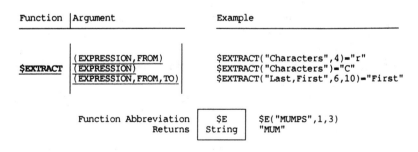

Function	Argument	Example
$EXTRACT	(EXPRESSION,FROM) (EXPRESSION) (EXPRESSION,FROM,TO)	$EXTRACT("Characters",4)="r" $EXTRACT("Characters")="C" $EXTRACT("Last,First",6,10)="First"

Function Abbreviation	$E	$E("MUMPS",1,3)
Returns	String	"MUM"

The $EXTRACT function is used to extract a substring from a target string by character position(s). The result of the $EXTRACT function is a string of characters, which can be an empty string (that is, *no* characters). There are three forms of the $EXTRACT function that relate to the range of characters to be extracted.

8.1.1.1 Argument = (EXPRESSION,FROM) EXPRESSION is the target string from which a single character is to be extracted and is evaluated as a string. FROM is an integer expression that denotes the position within the target string from which the character is to be extracted. While FROM can assume any integer value, only positive integers return a character from the target string. If FROM is less than one or greater than the length of the target string EXPRESSION, an empty string (no characters) is returned.

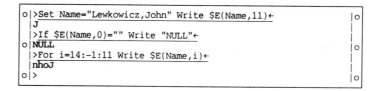

EXAMPLE 8.1. $EXTRACT(EXPRESSION,FROM)

Notice that the $EXTRACT function has been abbreviated to $E in Example 8.1. For the most part, this is the convention that will be followed whenever functions are encountered in the examples; spelling them out takes too much space.

8.1.1.2 Argument = (EXPRESSION) This is a shorthand form of the previous format in which FROM is implied to be **1** [$E(EXPRESSION,1)]. It returns a single character (or empty string if the target string is also an empty string) corresponding to the first character in the target string.

EXAMPLE 8.2. $EXTRACT(EXPRESSION)

Pay particular attention to the different results generated in the second and third lines in Example 8.2. In the first case the argument is treated as an expression (22/7) and evaluated *before* the $EXTRACT function is executed; in the second case the argument is considered to be a string (due to the enclosing quote characters).

8.1.1.3 Argument = (EXPRESSION,FROM,TO) This form of the $EXTRACT function returns the substring of characters within the target string EXPRESSION, from the integer position specified by FROM to the integer position specified by TO. If TO is less than FROM or FROM is greater than the length of the target string EXPRESSION, an empty string (no characters) is returned. If the FROM and TO are the same, the function returns a single character (or empty string).

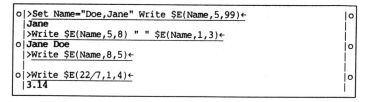

```
o|>Set Name="Doe,Jane" Write $E(Name,5,99)←
 |Jane
 |>Write $E(Name,5,8) " " $E(Name,1,3)←
o|Jane Doe
 |>Write $E(Name,8,5)←
 |
o|>Write $E(22/7,1,4)←
 |3.14
```

EXAMPLE 8.3. $EXTRACT(EXPRESSION,FROM,TO)

8.1.2 $PIECE Function

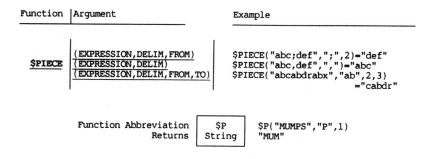

Function	Argument	Example
$PIECE	(EXPRESSION,DELIM,FROM) (EXPRESSION,DELIM) (EXPRESSION,DELIM,FROM,TO)	$PIECE("abc;def",";",2)="def" $PIECE("abc,def",",")="abc" $PIECE("abcabdrabx","ab",2,3) ="cabdr"

Function Abbreviation	$P	$P("MUMPS","P",1)
Returns	String	"MUM"

The $PIECE function is similar to the $EXTRACT function in that it returns specified substrings from the target string EXPRESSION. Unlike $EXTRACT, which parses characters out of the target string by absolute character position, $PIECE extracts groups of characters relative to a specific delimiting character or string of characters. Consider the following target string:

Doe,Jane;55 State Street;Any Place;State;99999

When we defined this string, we arbitrarily chose the semicolon (;) character to separate the address fields. We could have just as easily used any other character or group of characters to separate the fields. The *third* piece of this string, using a semicolon as a delimiting character, is the string of characters "Any Place". The third piece of this string, using a *space* character as a delimiter, is the string "Street;Any". How a string is parsed depends both on the character or character sequence used as delimiters and the specified position(s) of the pieces within the target string.

8.1.2.1 Argument = (EXPRESSION,DELIM,FROM) EXPRESSION is a MUMPS expression evaluated as a string of characters. DELIM is a second expression, also evaluated as a string of characters and defining the delimiting characters. FROM is an integer expression defining which piece of the target string is to be extracted using the character(s) in DELIM as field separators. If FROM is zero, negative, or greater than the number of fields as defined by the character(s) in DELIM, then the results of the $PIECE function are an empty string (no characters). Otherwise, the returned substring is the FROMth piece of the target string using DELIM as a field separator. Even if the FROMth field is defined in the target string, the results of the $PIECE function can return an empty string (for example, the field between two adjacent DELIM character sequences).

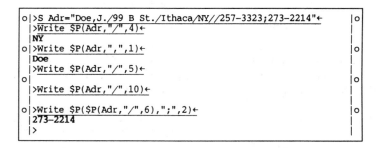

```
o|>S Adr="Doe,J./99 B St./Ithaca/NY//257-3323;273-2214"←      |o
 |>Write $P(Adr,"/",4)←                                       |
 |NY                                                          |
o|>Write $P(Adr,",",1)←                                       |o
 |Doe                                                         |
 |>Write $P(Adr,"/",5)←                                       |
o|                                                            |o
 |>Write $P(Adr,"/",10)←                                      |
 |                                                            |
o|>Write $P($P(Adr,"/",6),";",2)←                             |o
 |273-2214                                                    |
 |>                                                           |
```

EXAMPLE 8.4. $PIECE(EXPRESSION,DELIM,FROM)

Note the interesting use of nested $PIECE functions demonstrated in Example 8.4. Since functions return values, they can be used as arguments to other functions. Also note the use of subfields within the phone field using a different delimiting character.

The demarcation characters specified by DELIM represent *nonoverlapping* occurrences of that character string in the target string. For example, if we piece the string "10$$$20$$$30" using a delimiter of "$$", there are three pieces:

10$$$20$$$30

The next example is one frequently encountered in MUMPS and is used to initialize a variable list from a data record. Two related lists are pieced: the first contains a list of variable names; the second is the data record containing individual data fields.

```
o|>Set Vars="Sex,DOB,Height,Weight,HairClr",com=","←          |o
 |>Set Data="Male;7/15/52;6-3;195;Black"←                     |
 |>For i=1:1:5 Set @$P(Vars,com,i)=$P(Data,";",i)←            |
o|>For i=1:1:5 Write !,$P(Vars,com,i),"=",@$P(Vars,com,i)←    |o
 |Sex=Male                                                    |
 |DOB=7/15/52                                                 |
o|Height=6-3                                                  |o
 |Weight=195                                                  |
 |HairClr=Black                                               |
o|>                                                           |o
```

EXAMPLE 8.5. $PIECE(EXPRESSION,DELIM,FROM) with indirection

This example makes extensive use of indirection (Chapter 7), and the reader is advised to examine it carefully. This technique is also commonly used to dispatch program control with the DO and GOTO commands, as is demonstrated in the following example:

```
o|Opt    Read !,("Option Number (1-3): ",opt                    |o
 |       Quit:opt<1!(opt>3)                                      |
 |       Do @$P("Edit,Search^Pat,Print",",",opt) Goto Opt        |
```

EXAMPLE 8.6. Option dispatch using $PIECE and indirection

8.1.2.2 Argument = (EXPRESSION,DELIM) The two-argument form represents a shorthand case where Argument is (EXPRESSION,DELIM,FROM) and FROM is not given but assumed to have the value of $\underline{1}$.

```
o|>Set Days="Monday,Tuesday,Wednesday,Thursday,Friday"←         |o
 |>Write $P(Days,",")←                                          |
 |Monday                                                        |
o|>Write $P(Days,",Th")←                                        |o
 |Monday,Tuesday,Wednesday                                      |
 |>Write $P(Days,"XX")←                                         |
o|Monday,Tuesday,Wednesday,Thursday,Friday                      |o
 |>                                                             |
```

EXAMPLE 8.7. $PIECE(EXPRESSION,DELIM)

In the last line of the previous example, Write $P(Days,"XX"), the target string does *not* contain the specified delimiter string. In such instances, the returned string consists of the entire target string.

8.1.2.3 Argument = (EXPRESSION,DELIM,FROM,TO) This form is similar to the first form but returns the fields within the target string delimited by the character(s) in DELIM from field position FROM to field position TO. Both FROM and TO are evaluated as integer expressions. If TO is less than FROM, an empty string is returned. The returned substrings will include any DELIM character(s) that separate fields.

```
o|>S Mnths="Jan,Feb,Mar,Apr,May,Jun,Jul,Aug,Sep,Oct,Nov,Dec"←|o
 |>Set Spring=$P(Mnths,",",4,6) Write !,"Spring=",Spring←      |
 |Spring=Apr,May,Jun                                          |
o|>Set Winter=$P(Mnths,",",11,99) "," $P(Mnths,",",0,3)←       |o
 |>Write "Winter=",Winter," (at least in Ithaca, NY)."←        |
 |Winter=Nov,Dec,Jan,Feb,Mar (at least in Ithaca, NY).        |
o|>Write $P(Mnths,",",4,3)←                                    |o
 |                                                            |
 |>Write $P(Mnths,",",-10,1)←                                  |
o|Jan                                                          |o
 |>                                                           |
```

EXAMPLE 8.8. $PIECE(EXPRESSION,DELIM,FROM,TO)

8.1.2.4 SET $PIECE At present, $PIECE is unique among the functions in that it is allowed to replace the VARIABLE name on the left side of an equals sign when using the SET command. The use of this form permits the direct SETting of pieces of a variable without having to concatenate fields together. In many respects, this form of the $PIECE function does not behave like normal functions; functions generally return a value and do *not* modify their arguments. However, for the sake of convenience and completeness, the SET $PIECE syntax will be described here. It is also covered under the SET command in Section 3.1.1.3.

```
o|>Set Var="",$P(Var,";",5)="insert" Write Var←        |o
|;;;;insert                                            |
|>                                                     |
```

EXAMPLE 8.9.   Set $PIECE

A second example of the SET $PIECE function (and an alternative method for accomplishing the same goal) is shown in the next examples.

```
o|>Set Nmbrs="10-20-30-40-50-60-70-80-90"←               |o
|>Set $P(Nmbrs,"-",4)="forty" Write Nmbrs←               |
|10-20-30-forty-50-60-70-80-90                           |
o|>Set Nmbrs=$P(Nmbrs,"-",1,2)_"-thirty-"_$P(Nmbrs,"-",4,9)← |o
|>Write Nmbrs←                                           |
|10-20-thirty-forty-50-60-70-80-90                       |
o|>Set $P(Nmbrs,"-",5,6)="fifty-sixty"←                  |o
|10-20-thirty-forty-fifty-sixty-70-80-90                 |
|>                                                       |
```

EXAMPLE 8.10.   Set $PIECE, multiple fields

When replacing multiple fields within a string, it is necessary to supply the internal delimiters (the hyphen in the string "fifty-sixty"). When the $PIECE function is used on the left side of an equals sign in a SET command, its first argument must evaluate to a valid VARIABLE name (refer to Section 3.4), *not* to a general expression.

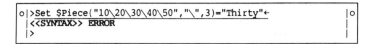

```
o|>Set $Piece("10\20\30\40\50","\",3)="Thirty"←          |o
|<<SYNTAX>> ERROR                                        |
|>                                                       |
```

EXAMPLE 8.11.   Set $PIECE, evaluated as variable Name

The <<SYNTAX>> ERROR in Example 8.11 is generated because the $Piece function on the left of the equals sign does *not* evaluate to a legal variable name; the Set command requires an expression on the left of the equals sign that evaluates to a variable name.

Aside from being used to insert data fields within a record, the SET $PIECE... syntax is also useful in initializing a variable to a particular character pattern.

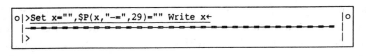

```
o|>Set x="",$P(x,"-=",29)="" Write x←                              |o
|                                                                  |
|>                                                                 |
```

EXAMPLE 8.12. SET $PIECE to initialize strings

This form of the $PIECE is covered in more detail under the SET command in Section 3.1.1.3. There is currently active discussion within the MUMPS Development Committee to extend a similar capability to the $EXTRACT function, but this proposal has not yet been accepted as part of the standard.

8.1.3 $LENGTH Function

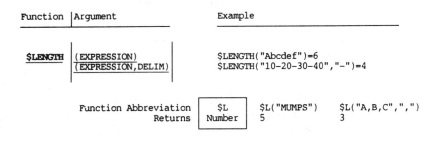

Function	Argument	Example
$LENGTH	(EXPRESSION) (EXPRESSION,DELIM)	$LENGTH("Abcdef")=6 $LENGTH("10-20-30-40","-")=4

Function Abbreviation	$L	$L("MUMPS")	$L("A,B,C",",")
Returns	Number	5	3

The $LENGTH function returns the integer length, in characters, of a specified target string (EXPRESSION) or an integer defining the number of fields within a target string using the character(s) in DELIM as field separators. Both EXPRESSION and DELIM are evaluated as strings.

8.1.3.1 Argument = (EXPRESSION) This form of the $LENGTH function returns the number of characters found in EXPRESSION as an integer value. The number of characters can range from zero (the length of an empty string) to the maximum number of characters permitted in a string. Nonprinting characters that may be in the string are also counted.

```
o|>Set Test="The ""Complete"" MUMPS"←                              |o
|>Write $L(Test)," *",Test,"*"←                                    |
|20 *The "Complete" MUMPS*                                         |
o|>Set X=""←                                                       |o
|>For i=1:1:$L(Test) Set Y=$E(Test,i) Set:Y'=" " X=X_Y←            |
|>Write X," = ",$L(X)," bytes."←                                   |
o|The"Complete"MUMPS = 18 bytes                                    |o
|>                                                                 |
```

EXAMPLE 8.13. $LENGTH(EXPRESSION)

Another example using the $LENGTH function is demonstrated in the next example, which is used to check an answer for exactly *one* of the characters in a specified string.

```
o|Save    ;Save edited data                                         |o
 |GetYN Read !<"Ready to SAVE (Y or N): Yes  :: ",ans               |
 |         If "YyNn?"[ans'=$L(ans) Write *7," ??" Goto GetYN         |
o|         Set:ans="" ans="Y" If ans="?" Do Help Goto GetYN          |o
 |         If "Yy"[ans Do FILE                                       |
 |         Quit                                                      |
```

EXAMPLE 8.14. Single-character check using $LENGTH

The <u>If</u> command in the third line checks to see if the keyboard entry was *exactly* one of the characters "<u>Y</u>", "<u>y</u>", "<u>N</u>", "<u>n</u>", or "<u>?</u>". The first part of the <u>If</u> expression evaluates to TRUE (1) only if <u>ans</u> is contained in the string "YyNn?"; however, the keyboard entries "Yy", "yN", or "" (<ENTER> only) all satisfy this requirement. The second part of the <u>If</u> expression guarantees that the answer was exactly one character in length.

8.1.3.2 Argument = (EXPRESSION,DELIM)   This form of the $LENGTH function is used to determine the number of *nonoverlapping* fields that are found in EXPRESSION using the character(s) in DELIM as field separators. This equates to the number of non-overlapping occurrences of the character(s) in DELIM plus one. If DELIM evaluates to an empty string, the result of the $LENGTH function is zero, regardless of the contents of EXPRESSION.

```
o|>Set Str="Jones,John;55 State Street;Davis,CA"←                   |o
 |>Write $L(Str,";")←                                               |
 |3                                                                 |
o|>Write $L(Str," ")←                                               |o
 |3                                                                 |
 |>Write $L(Str,"CA")←                                              |
o|2                                                                 |o
 |>Write $L(Str,"?")←                                               |
 |1                                                                 |
o|>Write $L(Str,"")←                                                |o
 |0                                                                 |
```

EXAMPLE 8.15. $LENGTH(EXPRESSION,DELIM)

If there are *no* occurrences of the *DELIM* string in the target string, $LENGTH returns a **1** (one) as the number of fields [for example, $L(Str,"#") = 1].

The preceding definition contains the term *nonoverlapping* occurrences of the character(s) in DELIM. Consider the following examples to see the impact of this definition.

```
o|>Set X="abababab" Write $L(X,"ab")←                               |o
 |5                                                                 |
 |>Write $L(X,"aba")←                                               |
o|3                                                                 |o
```

EXAMPLE 8.16. $LENGTH(EXPRESSION,DELIM), nonoverlapping search

If we had not included the caveat of *nonoverlapping occurrences* in the definition, the second example would have resulted in a value of 4 rather than 3. In some instances (see the third sample in Example 9.19), this can have a significant impact on programming techniques. See the related discussion of nonoverlapping delimiters for $PIECE in Section 8.1.2.1.

8.1.4 $FIND Function

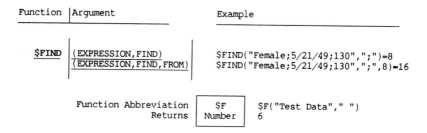

Function	Argument	Example
$FIND	(EXPRESSION,FIND) (EXPRESSION,FIND,FROM)	$FIND("Female;5/21/49;130",";")=8 $FIND("Female;5/21/49;130",";",8)=16

	Function Abbreviation	$F	$F("Test Data"," ")
	Returns	Number	6

The $FIND function searches a target string (EXPRESSION) for the character(s) in FIND and returns an integer corresponding to the *next* character position in the target string *after* the found string. If *no* match is found, $FIND returns a value of zero (0). FROM is an optional parameter that defines the character position within the target string at which the search is to begin. If absent or less than one, scanning of the target string begins at the first character. If FROM is greater than the length of the target string, no search is performed and the result of the $FIND is zero (0). Both EXPRESSION and FIND are evaluated as strings, and FROM is evaluated as an integer.

8.1.4.1 Argument = (EXPRESSION,FIND) This form of the $FIND command searches the target string EXPRESSION for the first occurrence of the character(s) in the string FIND. If FIND is *not* contained in EXPRESSION, the function returns a value of zero (0). If a match is found, the function returns an integer representing the character position of the first character *after* FIND in the target string.

```
o|>Set Target="abc.de,fg.h,ij.kl,mn.op"←
 |>Write $Find(Target,".")←
 |5
o|>Write $Extract(Target,1,$F(Target,","))←
 |abc.de,f
 |>Write $F(Target,"$"),",",$F(Target,"")←
o|0,1
```

EXAMPLE 8.17. $FIND(EXPRESSION,FIND)

Notice in Example 8.17, what happens when we search for an empty string (""). The $FIND function returns a result of one (1) since there is an implied empty string in front of the target string. Remember, too, that the result of this function is *not* the position of the first character of the search string (FIND) within the target string (EXPRESSION), but, instead, the character position in the target string *after* the search string.

```
o|>Set X="Let's   remove   multiple      spaces."←                   |o
 |>F i=0:0 S F=$F(X," ") Q:'F  S X=$E(X,0,F-2)_$E(X,F,255)←           |
 |>Write X←                                                          |
o|Let's remove multiple spaces.                                      |o
 |>                                                                  |
```

EXAMPLE 8.18.   Searching for more than one character

In Example 8.18, we continue executing the FOR loop until there are no longer occurrences of multiple spaces; each time the loop is executed, one space character from a pair of space characters is removed. Work out the $EXTRACT functions to make sure you understand the Set command in the FOR loop.

8.1.4.2 Argument = (EXPRESSION,FIND,FROM)   The three-argument form of the $FIND command is similar to the two-argument form except the search in the target string begins at the character position specified by FROM. In the two-argument form, FROM is assumed to be **1** (start the search at the first character). FROM is evaluated as an integer; if FROM is less than 1, the search starts at the first character. If FROM is greater than the length of the target string, $FIND fails and returns a value of zero (0).

```
o|>Set Tar=",Monday,Tuesday,Wednesday,Thursday,Friday"←             |o
 |>S F=0 F i=0:0 S F=$F(Tar,",") Q:F=""  W !,$E(Tar,F,F+2)←          |
 |Mon                                                                |
o|Tue                                                                |o
 |Wed                                                                |
 |Thu                                                                |
o|Fri                                                                |o
 |>                                                                  |
```

EXAMPLE 8.19. $FIND(EXPRESSION,FIND,FROM)

8.1.5 $TRANSLATE Function[1]

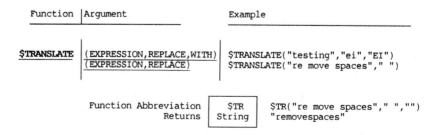

Function	Argument	Example
$TRANSLATE	(EXPRESSION,REPLACE,WITH)	$TRANSLATE("testing","ei","EI")
	(EXPRESSION,REPLACE)	$TRANSLATE("re move spaces"," ")

	Function Abbreviation	$TR	$TR("re move spaces"," ","")
	Returns	String	"removespaces"

[1]MDC Type A release, January 1987.

The $TRANSLATE function performs a character-by-character substitution of characters in the target string (EXPRESSION) that are found in the REPLACE string with characters from the WITH string. The string in EXPRESSION is evaluated character by character. Each character examined that is *also* in the REPLACE string is replaced in the original string by the character in the WITH string having the same relative position as in the REPLACE string. The WITH string is optional and is assumed to be an empty string ("") if not specified.

8.1.5.1 Argument = (EXPRESSION,REPLACE,WITH)
Characters found in EXPRESSION that are also found in REPLACE are replaced in the original string with the character in WITH that corresponds to the first occurrence of the character in the REPLACE string.

```
o|>Set Test="How now, brown cow?"←              |o
 |>Write $TR(Test,"H","h")←                      |
 |how now, brown cow?                            |
o|>Write $TR(Test," ,?","*-!")←                  |o
 |How*now-*brown*cow!                            |
 |>Write $TR(Test," ,?","-")←                    |
o|How-now-brown-cow                              |o
 |>                                              |
```

EXAMPLE 8.20. $TRANSLATE(EXPRESSION,REPLACE,WITH)

This is a character-by-character replacement, *not* a string replacement. If the REPLACE is longer than WITH, all characters in REPLACE with no corresponding characters in the WITH string will be *deleted* from the EXPRESSION string. If WITH is an empty string, *all* characters in the REPLACE string will be deleted from the EXPRESSION string. If a character appears more than once in the REPLACE string, $TRANSLATE uses only the *first* occurrence. Consequently, $TRANSLATE cannot be used to remove double occurrences of the same character from a string, as is demonstrated in the next example.

```
o|>Set X="Can't  Remove  Double  Spaces"←        |o
 |>Write $TR(X," "," ")←                          |
 |Can't  Remove  Double  Spaces                   |
o|>                                              |o
```

EXAMPLE 8.21. $TRANSLATE, single-character replacement

For those who do not enjoy brain teasers, skip to the next paragraph. For those who do, try to solve the next problem using the $TRANSLATE function.

PROBLEM. Invert the characters in any arbitrary string of up to 15 characters in length. That is, if the string to be inverted is "Nice Day", then the inverted string would be "yaD eciN". Use only a single $TRANSLATE function for this inversion.

A solution to this problem is found in Section 8.1.5.3.

One useful application of the $TRANSLATE function is to convert strings to upper- or lowercase. Consider the following examples:

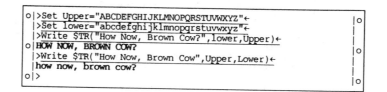

```
o|>Set Upper="ABCDEFGHIJKLMNOPQRSTUVWXYZ"←                    |o
 |>Set lower="abcdefghijklmnopqrstuvwxyz"←                    |
 |>Write $TR("How Now, Brown Cow?",lower,Upper)←              |
o|HOW NOW, BROWN COW?                                         |o
 |>Write $TR("How Now, Brown Cow",Upper,Lower)←               |
 |how now, brown cow?                                         |
o|>                                                           |o
```

EXAMPLE 8.22. Case conversion using $TRANSLATE

The code for converting a string to either upper- or lowercase can be made an extrinsic function (see Chapter 9) and used whenever case conversion is necessary. The following code defines two extrinsic functions; $$UPPER is used to convert a string to uppercase and $$LOWER is used to convert a string to lowercase. Also included is an example demonstrating how to convert a person's name in the general form "LAST,FIRST" to a form where the first characters of the first and last names are capitalized while all the remaining characters are forced into lowercase.

```
o|START Read !,"Name (Last,First): ",Name Q:Name=""          |o
 |      Set Name=$TR(Name," ","")                             |
 |      Set First=$P(Name,",",2),Last=$P(Name,",")            |
o|      Set First=$$UPPER($E(First)) $$LOWER($E(First,2,99))  |o
 |      Set Last=$$UPPER($E(Last)) $$LOWER($E(Last,2,99))     |
 |      Write " --> ",Last_"," First GOTO START               |
o|UPPER(X) ;Convert X to UPPER case                           |o
 |      Quit $TR(X,"abcdefghijklmnopqrstuvwxyz","ABCDEFGHIJKL |
 |           MNOPQRSTUVWXYZ")                                 |
o|LOWER(X) ;Convert X to LOWER case                           |o
 |      Quit $TR(X,"ABCDEFGHIJKLMNOPQRSTUVWXYZ","abcdefghijkl |
 |           mnopqrstuvwxyz")                                 |
o|---------------------------------------------------------- |o
 |>Do START←                                                  |
 |Name (Last,First): smith,JOHN← --> Smith,John               |
o|Name (Last,First): DUCK, donald← --> Duck,Donald            |o
 |Name (Last,First): ←                                        |
 |>                                                           |
```

EXAMPLE 8.23. Name conversion using $TRANSLATE

8.1.5.2 Argument = (EXPRESSION,REPLACE) This form is identical to the preceding form, except WITH is not specified and is assumed to be an empty string. Any characters in REPLACE are *deleted* from the string EXPRESSION.

8.1.5.3 Solution to the Brain Teaser *Problem:* Invert the characters in any arbitrary string of up to 15 characters in length. That is, if the string to be inverted is "Nice Day", then the inverted string would be "yaD eciN". Use only a single $TRANSLATE function for this inversion.

Solution

```
o|Start  Read !,"Test String: ",Str Quit:Str=""
 |       Write " --> ",$$Invert(Str) GOTO Start
 |Invert(X) ;Invert (reverse) characters in X
o|       Quit $TR("abcdefghijklmno","onmlkjihgfedcba",X)
 |_____
 |>Do Start←
o|Test String: Have a nice day←  --> yad ecin a evaH
 |Test String: ←
 |>
```

EXAMPLE 8.24. String inversion using $TRANSLATE

The only two tricks in this solution are that EXPRESSION must contain a string of unique characters as long or longer than the maximum length of the string to be inverted, and REPLACE is the same string as EXPRESSION, but in reverse order.

8.1.6 $JUSTIFY Function

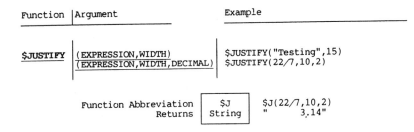

Function	Argument	Example
$JUSTIFY	(EXPRESSION,WIDTH) (EXPRESSION,WIDTH,DECIMAL)	$JUSTIFY("Testing",15) $JUSTIFY(22/7,10,2)

Function Abbreviation	$J	$J(22/7,10,2)
Returns	String	" 3.14"

The $JUSTIFY function is used to *right-justify* a string or number (EXPRESSION) in a field of WIDTH characters. EXPRESSION is padded with spaces on the left, if necessary. This function is especially useful in formatting data for output.

8.1.6.1 Argument = (EXPRESSION,WIDTH) In this form of $JUSTIFY, EXPRESSION is evaluated as a string, and WIDTH is evaluated as an integer representing the width of the field (in characters) within which EXPRESSION is to be right-justified. If the length of the EXPRESSION is equal to or greater than the width specified by WIDTH, the result of the $JUSTIFY is the original EXPRESSION, as there is no truncation of EXPRESSION. If EXPRESSION is shorter than WIDTH, space characters (" ") are padded to the left of EXPRESSION until it is WIDTH characters long.

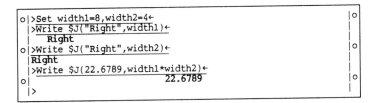

```
o|>Set width1=8,width2=4←
 |>Write $J("Right",width1)←
 |      Right
o|>Write $J("Right",width2)←
 |Right
 |>Write $J(22.6789,width1*width2)←
o|                        22.6789
 |>
```

EXAMPLE 8.25. $JUSTIFY(EXPRESSION,WIDTH)

8.1.6.2 Argument = (EXPRESSION,WIDTH,DECIMAL) This form of the $JUS-TIFY function is quite different from the previous form. In the first place, EXPRESSION is evaluated as a *number*, rather than a string of characters. The resulting number will be right-justified within a field of WIDTH characters with the number of decimal places to the right of the decimal point determined by DECIMAL. The decimal point (.) *is* included in the calculation of width. In addition, the numeric value for EXPRESSION is *rounded* to DECIMAL digits. If the integer part of the number being justified is zero (0), then a zero *is* included to the left of the decimal point. The fractional part of the number is padded with zeros on the right, if necessary. Finally, the number is padded with space characters on the left side to bring the entire expression to WIDTH characters wide.

```
o|>Set X=1234.5678←
 |>Write $J(X,10,2)←
 |    1234.57
o|>Write $J(X,10,0)←
 |       1235
 |>Write $J(X,12,6)←
o| 1234.567800
 |>Write $J(X-1234,8,1)←
 |     0.6
o|>Write $J(-X,10,2)←
 |  -1234.57
 |>
```

EXAMPLE 8.26. $JUSTIFY(EXPRESSION,WIDTH,DECIMAL)

Note that, when justifying negative numbers, the leading minus sign (−) is also counted as part of the WIDTH.

8.1.7 $FNUMBER Function[2]

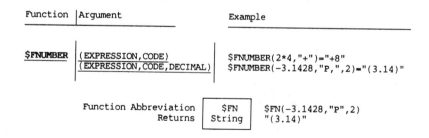

Function	Argument	Example
$FNUMBER	(EXPRESSION,CODE)	$FNUMBER(2*4,"+")="+8"
	(EXPRESSION,CODE,DECIMAL)	$FNUMBER(-3.1428,"P,",2)="(3.14)"

Function Abbreviation	$FN	$FN(-3.1428,"P",2)
Returns	String	"(3.14)"

The $FNUMBER function is used to format numbers in a variety of ways. EXPRESSION is evaluated as a number and then formatted using the codes specified by CODE. The optional DECIMAL field represents the number of fractional digits to be displayed to the right of a decimal point.

[2]MDC Type A release, January 1987.

8.1.7.1 Argument = (EXPRESSION,CODE) After EXPRESSION has been evaluated as a number, the transformations defined by CODE are applied to that number to change its format. The values of CODE can contain the following:

CODE = " + "   If the number is <u>POSITIVE</u>, then it will be displayed with a leading plus sign (" + "). Normally, the plus sign is omitted when WRITEing positive numbers.

CODE = " − "   This code suppresses the minus sign (−) on negative numbers. Normally, negative values are displayed (WRITE command) with a leading minus sign.

CODE = ","   When a comma is included in the CODE field, a comma will be inserted in every third position to the left of where the decimal point would occur in the number. Leading commas are not inserted.

CODE = "T"   Causes the sign of the number to be inserted at the end of the number (trailing, right end) rather than the front of the number. Note that this code does *not* force a trailing sign. If a + code is not also specified, no trailing + sign will be inserted at the end of the string. If the CODE contains a − character, no trailing minus sign will be included for negative numbers. If no sign is appended to the end of the number, a space is appended to the end of the string in the place of the missing sign.

CODE = "P"   Formats the number such that all negative values are included in parentheses, rather than having a minus sign (−) displayed.

CODE can contain more than one of the characters just listed and the alphabetic codes are case insensitive (t is the same as T). CODE can also be an empty string, which, in the case of the two-argument form of $FNUMBER, has no effect on the format of EXPRESSION.

```
o|>Set Pos=31428.34,Neg=-Pos←                    |o
 |>Write $FN(Pos,"+,")←                            |
 |+31,428.34                                        |
o|>Write $FN(Pos,"t")                             |o
 |31428.34                                          |
 |>Write $FN(Pos,"t+,")←                            |
o|31,428.34+                                       |o
 |>Write $FN(Neg,",P")←                             |
 |(31,428.34)                                        |
o|>Write $FN(Neg,"-,")←                            |o
 |31,428.34                                          |
 |>                                                 |
```

EXAMPLE 8.27. $FNUMBER(EXPRESSION,CODE)

Note that some combinations of CODE do not make sense and may result in an error. If we specify a format using trailing signs ("T") *and* representing negative numbers in parentheses ("P"), the formats conflict and an error results. Common sense dictates that some CODEs cannot be combined (that is, the code P cannot be combined with either +, −, or T)

An interesting use of the $Fnumber function is for calculating the *absolute value* of a number. The expression

$$\text{Set abs} = + \text{\$FN(number,''T'')}$$

results in evaluating <u>number</u> as a positive number. The $FN function with the "T" code moves the minus sign (if present) to the end of the number, and the unary + forces numeric interpretation of the results (see Section 4.2.2 for a discussion of numeric interpretation of strings), dropping any trailing signs.

8.1.7.2 Argument = (EXPRESSION,CODE,DECIMAL)

In this form, DECIMAL is evaluated as an integer and represents the number of fractional digits to be displayed to the right of the decimal point *after* rounding the number. It is similar to the DECIMAL value in the $JUSTIFY function. Trailing zeros are added to the right of the decimal point as needed. Additionally, if the number being formatted is less than one, a leading zero (0) is inserted to the left of the decimal point. If DECIMAL evaluates to zero (0), the number is formatted as an integer with no decimal point.

```
o|>Set Numbr=-3.1428 Write $FN(Numbr,"P",3)←                o
 |(3.143)                                                    
 |>Write $FN(3+Numbr,"",2)←                                  
o|0.14                                                       o
 |>Write $FN(Numbr*1000,",T",0)←                             
 |3,143-                                                     
o|>                                                          o
```

EXAMPLE 8.28. $FNUMBER(EXPRESSION,CODE,DECIMAL)

The $FNUMBER function performs some, but not all, of the same functions performed by $JUSTIFY. Often the two functions are combined to produce a final, right-justified result. However, some care should be taken, especially when using *both* functions to round decimal digits.

```
o|>Set Value=1234.547 Write $J($FN(Value,"+,"),12,2)←        o
 |    +1,234.55                                              
 |>Write $FN(Value,"",1),?15,$J($FN(Value,"",2),10,1)←       
o|1234.5                   1234.6                            o
 |>                                                          
```

EXAMPLE 8.29. Potential Rounding Errors With $JUSTIFY and $FNUMBER

Note the difference in results in the two examples on the third line. The correct *rounded* result should be **1234.5**, but nesting the $JUSTIFY within the $FNUMBER formats causes *two* roundings and an erroneous result.

8.1.8 $ASCII Function

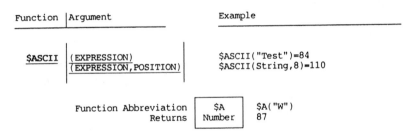

The $ASCII function returns the decimal value for the ASCII character in EXPRESSION, whose position within the EXPRESSION is determined by the integer evaluation of POSITION. If POSITION is absent, its value is assumed to be one (the first character in EXPRESSION). If POSITION is greater than the number of characters in EXPRESSION or less than 1, $ASCII returns a value of −1. See Appendix A for the full ASCII character set and the decimal equivalents for each character.

The $CHAR function (next section) is used to convert a decimal value to an ASCII character.

```
>Set X="AbCd1-?"
>For i=1:1  Write !,$E(X,i),?5,$A(X,i) Quit:$A(X,i)=-1
A    65
b    98
C    67
d    100
1    49
-    45
?    63
     -1
>Write $E(X),"-",$A(X)
A-65
>Write $A(X,0)
-1
>Write $A(X,3.99)
67
>
```

EXAMPLE 8.30. $ASCII

8.1.9 $CHAR Function

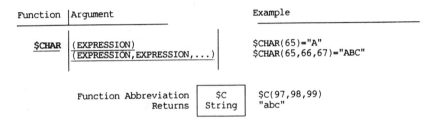

The $CHAR function is the logical opposite of the $ASCII function described in the previous section. Each EXPRESSION in the argument list is evaluated as an integer number, which is then converted to its equivalent ASCII character (see Appendix A for the ASCII character set and decimal equivalents). Negative expressions result in an empty string ("").

The MUMPS Standard states that each integer EXPRESSION in the range from 0 to 127 maps into the standard seven-bit ASCII table. It does *not* state what is returned for EXPRESSIONS greater than 127. The value of 127 is the largest number that can be represented in seven bits, but characters are stored internally as eight bits. This increases the range of possible ASCII values from 127 to 255, and many I/O devices can, and do, respond to characters whose decimal equivalent lies in the range from 128 to 255. Various implementations handle these extra characters in different fashions. Some adhere strictly to a seven-bit character set and wrap-around when the decimal value exceeds 127 (for example, 128 is converted to 0, 129 to 1, and so on). Other implementations (especially those found on microcomputers) map the characters in the range from 128 to 255 into an extended ASCII character set. You will have to check your documentation to see how these characters are handled.

It is also worth noting that characters output with a WRITE command using the $CHAR function affect the values of the system variables $X and $Y just as if they had been output as part of a string literal. This is in contrast to using the WRITE *CHAR syntax where the MUMPS standard does not specify whether or not $X and $Y are updated.

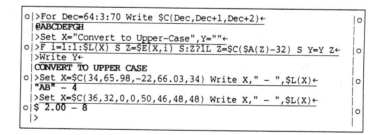

```
o|>For Dec=64:3:70 Write $C(Dec,Dec+1,Dec+2)←
 |@ABCDEFGH
 |>Set X="Convert to Upper-Case",Y=""←
o|>F i=1:1:$L(X) S Z=$E(X,i) S:Z?1L Z=$C($A(Z)-32) S Y=Y_Z←
 |>Write Y←
 |CONVERT TO UPPER CASE
o|>Set X=$C(34,65.98,-22,66.03,34) Write X," - ",$L(X)←
 |"AB" - 4
 |>Set X=$C(36,32,0,0,50,46,48,48) Write X," - ",$L(X)←
o|$ 2.00 - 8
 |>
```

EXAMPLE 8.31. $CHAR

In Example 8.31 we included two zeros (0) in the string of decimal values to be converted to ASCII characters. Decimal 0 represents the <u>NUL</u> character, but it is *not* the same as an empty string (""). The NUL character (as with all characters whose decimal value is less than 32) is nonprinting, but still takes up space in the string. Since the NUL character does not print, it is not displayed, but it still takes up space in the final string. Many control characters (decimal range from 0 to 31) have special meaning to MUMPS, to devices to which they are written out, or both. For example, the <u>CR</u> character (carriage return: decimal 13) will cause the cursor on many terminals to be returned to the leftmost column of the current line and MUMPS to reset $X to zero. Use care when including nonprinting characters within a string; they may produce unpredictable results when output to some devices. The same is true for the characters whose decimal equivalents lie in the range from 128 to 255.

8.1.10 $TEXT Function

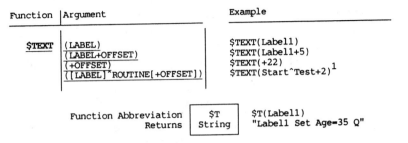

The $TEXT function is used to return command lines within the routine body for manipulation by the routine. In those forms using a LABEL as the argument (or part of the argument), LABEL represents one of the labels in the routine body; it is *not* a variable containing the desired label. If the desired label is held in a variable, then indirection must be used in referencing that label. The examples that follow should help clarify this syntax.

8.1.10.1 Argument = (LABEL) In this form, $TEXT returns the line of source code associated with the line whose label is LABEL. The labeled line must be the current routine (that is, the one currently loaded in the partition). The string returned is the full line of source code, including the LABEL. In lines returned with the $TEXT function, all *linestart* characters (Section 6.2) are replaced with SPACE characters (decimal 32), regardless of the actual linestart character used when entering the routine line. Thus, the label is separated from the remainder of the line by one or more spaces. If LABEL is *not* defined in the current routine, the function returns an empty string ("").

```
o|Start  Set L="Start" Write !,$T(Start)                          |o
 |L        Write !,$T(L)                                          |
 |         Write $T(@L),!,"Now $T("""Start""")",$T("Start")       |
o|         Quit                                                   |o
 |_____|
 |>Do Start↵                                                      |
o|Start Set L="Start" Write !,$T(Start)                           |o
 |L Write !,$T(L)                                                 |
 |Start Set L="Start" Write !,$T(Start)                           |
o|Now $T("Start")                                                 |o
 |<SYNTAX> ERROR                                                  |
```

EXAMPLE 8.32. $TEXT(LABEL)

Note the difference between the argument LABEL and EXPRESSIONs that have been used as arguments in the past. LABEL is *not* a general expression but

³MDC Type A release, January 1987.

must resolve to a valid label name. The statement Write $T(L) instructs MUMPS to search for the label **L** and write the line associated with that label. Label L and the variable L are handled quite differently. Similarly, the example Write $T("Start") fails with a syntax error since quotation marks are *not* valid in a label.

8.1.10.2 Argument = (LABEL + OFFSET) This form is similar to the previous one except that an integer offset to the label can also be supplied. OFFSET is evaluated as a nonnegative integer and is added to the line number of the LABEL to calculate the line to be returned. If the LABEL is undefined in the partition, then, regardless of the OFFSET, the value returned by the $TEXT function is an empty string ("").

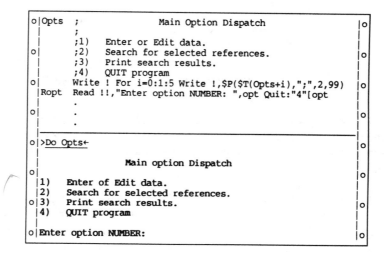

```
o|Opts  ;                    Main Option Dispatch                    |o
 |      ;
 |      ;1)   Enter or Edit data.
o|      ;2)   Search for selected references.                        |o
 |      ;3)   Print search results.
 |      ;4)   QUIT program
o|      Write ! For i=0:1:5 Write !,$P($T(Opts+i),";",2,99)          |o
 |Ropt  Read !!,"Enter option NUMBER: ",opt Quit:"4"[opt
 |         .
o|         .                                                          |o
 |         .
 |_____
o|>Do Opts←                                                           |o
 |
 |                    Main option Dispatch
o|                                                                    |o
 |1)   Enter of Edit data.
 |2)   Search for selected references.
o|3)   Print search results.                                         |o
 |4)   QUIT program
 |
o|Enter option NUMBER:                                                |o
```

EXAMPLE 8.33. $TEXT(LABEL + OFFSET)

Example 8.33 demonstrates a fairly common use of the $TEXT function to display a program header or other relatively fixed data fields. It eliminates the need to repeat a number of WRITE commands. Another use is for displaying HELP text associated with a question. Text lines being displayed could also be held as global nodes; in some versions of MUMPS (especially compiled versions) there may be a speed cost associated with references to routine lines with $TEXT. In these instances, it may be necessary to retrieve the source code of the routine from disk to get the text. See the related discussion in Section 8.1.10.5.

8.1.10.3 Argument = (+OFFSET) This form is similar to the previous form except the LABEL reference is omitted. OFFSET is evaluated as an integer and represents the LINE NUMBER to be returned. A (+1) returns the first line in the routine, (+2) the second line, and so on. A value for OFFSET for which there is no corresponding line number returns an empty string.

An OFFSET of (+0) is handled as a special case and returns the *routine name*, not a line of code. In Chapter 6 we discussed a number of conventions, including the one indicating that the first line of a routine should start with a LABEL and that LABEL should be the same as the name of the routine filed on disk. However, this is only a convention, and the routine name, as filed on disk, does not even have to appear as a LABEL in the routine body. Using a $TEXT(+0) always returns the name of the current routine *as filed on disk*. In all cases, $TEXT(+0) will be different from $TEXT(+1), since a routine name is *not* a valid line of MUMPS code.

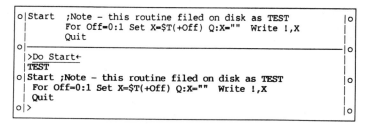

EXAMPLE 8.34. $TEXT(+OFFSET)

8.1.10.4 Argument = ([LABEL]^ROUTINE[+OFFSET][4]
This recent addition to the language permits reference to routine lines outside the current routine. In other respects it is similar in function to the first two forms of $TEXT described previously.

8.1.10.5 $TEXT in Compiled Versions of MUMPS
Versions of MUMPS that are compiled offer some interesting problems for routines using the $TEXT function. $TEXT returns the line of source code associated with the argument. In most compiled versions of MUMPS, the source code and the compiled code are maintained by the system as separate files. The fact that there are two versions of the program is normally transparent to the programmer. When editing or printing routines, MUMPS automatically uses the source code; when executing routines, MUMPS automatically uses the compiled version. However, when executing the $TEXT function, MUMPS must refer back to the source code, even if the compiled version is loaded and running in the partition. This look-up can slow the performance of a program, often significantly.

A greater problem exists when the source code is deleted from the system and only the compiled code is available. Erasing the source code is often done in commercial packages when software developers do not wish to distribute source code. In these cases, the $TEXT function can become meaningless, since there is no source code to serve as input for this function. Some vendors have resolved this problem by creating special syntaxes for lines of source code that are to be included within the body of a compiled routine. One convention adopted by a number of MUMPS vendors is the use of double semicolons; text or comments following two adjacent semicolons are automatically included with the compiled

[4]MDC Type A release, January 1987.

code, eliminating the overhead of retrieving the text from the source code and permitting the program to be distributed without the source.

8.2 Data Functions

In this section we consider a number of functions specific to data retrieval in the MUMPS environment. In earlier chapters we examined a number of features that make MUMPS unique among computer languages, including the hierarchical and sparse nature of data arrays and the absence of the need to define variables before they are used in a program. While these features contribute significantly to the ease of developing an application, they also require a major conceptual break from traditional techniques used for processing sequential data files.

8.2.1 $DATA Function

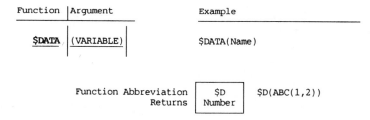

The $DATA function returns a number defining the status of the argument VARIABLE. VARIABLE is any valid variable name and can be a simple local variable name, the name of an array (local or global), or a subscripted array element (local or global). The value returned by this function describes whether or not the variable exists and, if it does, whether or not there are data associated with the variable. The possible results of the $DATA function and their meanings are described as follows:

$DATA = 0 If $DATA returns a zero (0), the variable name or array element used as the argument is *undefined*.

$DATA = 1 The variable name or array node specified by the argument *was defined* and contains data.

$DATA = 10 The argument is an array name (with or without subscripts), and the referenced node is defined but consists only of a downward pointer to other array elements. Use of such a variable name in a general EXPRESSION will result in an ERROR since there are no data directly associated with this array node.

$DATA = 11 The argument is an array name (with or without subscripts), and the referenced node is *both* a downward pointer *and* a data element. The reference used for the argument can be used in a general expression since there is a data value associated with it.

Notice that $DATA does not return the type of data held by a given variable or array node (that is, string, integer, and so on), only a status flag indicating whether or not data is contained at the specified reference. It is important to be able to distinguish between those array nodes that are defined but only contain a pointer to lower array elements and those that also have data associated with them.

```
Start  K  Set X=0,Y="",^X(1,2,3,4)=10
          Write $D(X)," ",$D(Y)," ",$D(Z)
          Write !,$D(^X),",",$D(^X(1,2)),",",$D(^X(1,2,3,4))
          Set ^X(1,2)="test"
          Write !,$D(^X(1,2))," ",$D(^X(1,2,3))
          Quit
       _____
       >Do Start←
       1 1 0
       10,10,1
       11 10
       >
```

EXAMPLE 8.35 $DATA

Chapter 10 (especially Section 10.2.2) contains additional examples using the $DATA function.

8.2.2 $ORDER Function

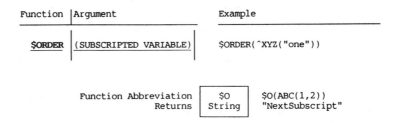

Function	Argument	Example
$ORDER	(SUBSCRIPTED VARIABLE)	$ORDER(^XYZ("one"))

Function Abbreviation	$O	$O(ABC(1,2))
Returns	String	"NextSubscript"

Given the sparse and hierarchical nature of data storage using globals, it is necessary to provide a means by which a program can search through such arrays for data. The $ORDER function provides this utility. The reader is also referred to the descriptions of the $GET and $QUERY functions for retrieving data from globals.

The argument to the $ORDER function is a subscripted array or global reference, and the function returns the next defined subscript *at the level of the reference*. Subscripts can be any valid expression (including numbers or strings of characters); the only invalid subscript is an empty string (""). The empty string as a subscript is reserved as both the starting point and the end point for searches of an array using $ORDER or $QUERY; an empty string cannot be used as an actual array subscript.

When new data are entered into an array or global, MUMPS automatically inserts the subscripts in sequential order, with numbers first and then alphabetized strings. The actual collating sequence (referred to as the MUMPS collating order) used to organize array subscripts is similar to the ASCII collating sequence described under the follows operator (], Section 5.3.2.3), except for the manner in which it treats numbers. A complete definition of the MUMPS collating order is deferred until Section 10.2.1; as a capsule summary, numbers collate first (in ascending numeric order), followed by character strings (alphabetized by their relative character code positions within the ASCII table).

For example, if a global already has two nodes defined [^X("ABC") and ^X("GHI")] and we issue the command **Set ^X("DOG") = "Canine"**←, the new data node is inserted *between* the two existing nodes. The string "DOG" follows the string "ABC" but precedes the string "GHI".

In the examples used to demonstrate the $ORDER function, we will use the global depicted in Figure 8.1. The boxes with text represent nodes that contain data, while those that are empty represent *pointer* nodes (that is, nodes that do not contain data, but are only pointers to lower array nodes).

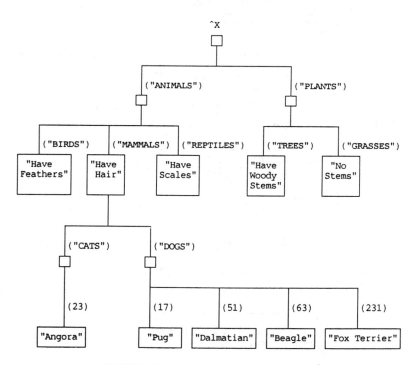

FIGURE 8.1. Structure of Test Global ^X

The following example demonstrates how we can use the $ORDER function to find all the first-level nodes in ^X.

```
o|>Set Sub=""←                                                        |o
 |>For i=0:0 Set Sub=$O(^X(Sub)) Quit:Sub=""  Write !,Sub←             |
 |ANIMALS                                                              |
o|PLANTS                                                               |o
 |>                                                                    |
```

EXAMPLE 8.36 $ORDER

We start off with the target subscript equal to an empty string (Sub = ""). The first time the FOR loop is executed, the $ORDER function returns the next higher (MUMPS collating order) subscript following null (ANIMALS). This value is placed in the variable Sub; on the next pass of the FOR loop, we look for the subscript following "ANIMALS" ("PLANTS"). On the third pass through the FOR loop, there is *no* higher subscript than "PLANTS", and the $ORDER function returns an empty string (""), which is the condition on which we terminate the FOR loop.

The next question we could pose is how to pick up all the subscripts on the second level of the global *under* the heading "ANIMALS"?

```
o|>Set S1="ANIMALS",S2=""←                                          |o
 |>F i=0:0 S S2=$O(^X(S1,S2)) Q:S2=""  W !,S2,?10,^X(S1,S2)←         |
 |BIRDS      Have Feathers                                          |
o|MAMMALS    Have Hair                                              |o
 |REPTILES   Have Scales                                            |
 |>                                                                 |
```

EXAMPLE 8.37 $ORDER search at lower global levels

We can expand on Example 8.37 with a small routine that dumps all the defined subscripts in a database as follows:

```
o|Start  Set (S1,S2,S3,S4)=""                                      |o
 |        F i=0:0 Set S1=$O(^X(S1)) Q:S1="" Do Level1              |
 |        Write !,"All Done."                                       |
o|        Quit                                                      |o
 |Level1 W !," ",S1                                                 |
 |        F i=0:0 S S2=$O(^X(S1,S2)) Q:S2="" Do Level2             |
o|        Quit                                                      |o
 |Level2 W " ",S2                                                   |
 |        F i=0:0 S S3=$O(^X(S1,S2,S3)) Q:S3="" Do Level3          |
o|        Quit                                                      |o
 |Level3 W " ",S3                                                   |
 |        F i=0:0 S S4=$O(^X(S1,S2,S3,S4)) Q:S4="" Do Level4       |
o|        Quit                                                      |o
 |Level4 Write " ",S4                                               |
 |        Quit                                                      |
o|------------------------------------------------------------------|o
 |>Do Start←                                                        |
 |ANIMALS BIRDS MAMMALS CATS 23 DOGS 17 51 63 231 REPTILES         |
o|PLANTS TREES GRASSES                                              |o
 |All Done                                                          |
 |>                                                                 |
o|                                                                  |o
```

EXAMPLE 8.38. $ORDER multiple-level search

The $ORDER function returns *all* defined subscripts at the specified level, but how do we know if there are data or only a downward pointer at any given node? The most common method is to check the global documentation that should be developed for each global data file used in an application. This documentation should describe the basic global structure in terms of the subscripts used at each level (for example, what the subscript represents, how it is calculated, and what are the legal values), and whether or not the node holds data. If the node is to hold data, then the documentation should describe the data at the same level of detail that the subscripts were defined. However, in some instances the nodes at any given level may or may not contain data. In these cases, the $DATA function (Section 8.2.1) can be used to determine whether or not data exist and whether or not there are lower levels in the global. Usually, such information is known from the documentation. Unfortunately, the documentation is often incomplete!

8.2.3 $NEXT Function (OBSOLETE)

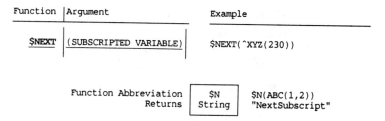

The $NEXT function was the precursor to the $ORDER function and should *not* be used in new code. The $ORDER function provides all the features available in $NEXT. The only differences between the two functions are the starting and ending conditions. The definition of $NEXT is included only to provide a reference for those older programs that have not been converted to the $ORDER function.

The $NEXT function uses a starting value of -1 (negative one) to return the first subscript at a given level of an array or global, and returns a -1 as a result if there are no higher subscript values at that level. Since 1983, the MUMPS standard permits the use of negative subscripts (including -1), and $NEXT cannot be used to unambiguously define the end of a subscript level. Nor can -1 be used to find the first subscript at a given level since other subscripts can precede it (-2, -200, ...).

> Use the $ORDER function instead of the $NEXT function.

8.2.4 $QUERY Function[5]

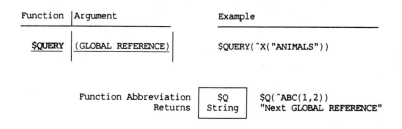

[5]MDC Type A proposal, January 1987.

The $QUERY is used to traverse a global and return the *next* global reference that has an associated data value as a full global reference. The global is traversed from the specified GLOBAL REFERENCE down and to the right. All references *below* the specified starting point are returned before advancing to the right at any given level. The best way to demonstrate this function is with an example. The test global defined in Figure 8.1 is used to demonstrate the $QUERY function.

```
o|>Set Ref="^X" F i=0:0 S Ref=$Q(@Ref) Q:Ref=""  W !,Ref←            |o
 |
 | ^X("ANIMALS","BIRDS")                                             |
o| ^X("ANIMALS","MAMMALS")                                          |o
 | ^X("ANIMALS","MAMMALS","CATS",23)                                |
 | ^X("ANIMALS","MAMMALS","DOGS",17)                                |
o| ^X("ANIMALS","MAMMALS","DOGS",51)                               |o
 | ^X("ANIMALS","MAMMALS","DOGS",63)                                |
 | ^X("ANIMALS","MAMMALS","DOGS",231)                               |
o| ^X("PLANTS","TREES")                                             |o
 | ^X("PLANTS","GRASSES")                                           |
 |>                                                                 |
```

EXAMPLE 8.39. $QUERY

Unlike the $ORDER function, $QUERY returns not just the next subscript at a given level, but rather the entire global reference. The $QUERY function expects an actual GLOBAL REFERENCE as an argument, and hence the indirection shown in the command line. Also, $QUERY traverses the global *vertically* as well as *horizontally*. Finally, $QUERY returns only those nodes with valid data in them; it ignores (except for internal needs) data nodes that are only downward pointers.

We can retrieve the data associated with the global reference returned by the $QUERY function using argument indirection with the returned reference. Consider the following example in which we traverse the "PLANT" branch of the test global and display both the global references returned by $QUERY and the data associated with each reference.

```
o|>Set Ref="^X(""PLANTS"")"←                                        |o
 |>F i=0:0 S Ref=$Q(@Ref) Q:Ref=""  W !,Ref," = ",@Ref←             |
 |
o| ^X("PLANTS","TREES") = Have Woody Stems                         |o
 | ^X("PLANTS","GRASSES") = No Stems                               |
 |>                                                                 |
```

EXAMPLE 8.40. $QUERY dump of global branch

Notice that, like the $ORDER function, $QUERY returns an empty string ("") if there are no further globals references below or to the right of the requested reference.

8.2.5 $GET Function[6]

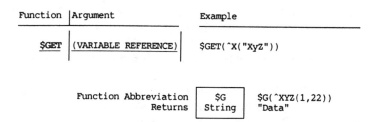

Function	Argument	Example
<u>$GET</u>	(VARIABLE REFERENCE)	$GET(^X("XyZ"))

| Function Abbreviation | $G | $G(^XYZ(1,22)) |
| Returns | String | "Data" |

The $GET function evaluates the argument as a variable reference (simple or subscripted, local or global) and returns the value associated with that reference. If the reference is *undefined* or a pointer-only node in an array, the $GET function returns an *empty string* ("").

The $GET function is especially useful in retrieving information from globals or local arrays without having to perform a $DATA check on the referenced node first. If the referenced node is undefined or if it is a downward pointer only, the function returns an empty string and does not generate an <UNDEFINED> error. See the related discussion of the $DATA function used to determine whether or not there are data associated with a particular array node (Section 8.2.1).

```
GetPat Set Pdata=$GET(^Pat(PatID))
       If Pdata="" Write *7," --> Patient NOT found."
       Quit

>Set PatID=1234 Do GetPat←
 --> Patient NOT found.
>
```

EXAMPLE 8.41. $GET

Example 8.42 demonstrates a common technique used before the availability of the $GET function to retrieve data from globals when not sure of the status of the referenced node. It is the functional equivalent of Example 8.41.

```
GetPat If $DATA(^Pat(PatID)) Set Pdata=^Pat(PatID)
       Else  Set Pdata=""
       If Pdata="" Write *7," --> Patient NOT found."
       Quit

            -or-

GetPat Set Pdata=$S($D(^PAT(PatID)):^(PatID),1:"")
       If Pdata="" Write *7," --> Patient NOT found."
       Quit

>Set PatID=1234 Do GetPat←
 --> Patient NOT found.
>
```

EXAMPLE 8.42. Alternative code for $GET

[6]MDC Type A release, January 1987.

8.3 Other Functions

A number of other intrinsic functions defined by the MUMPS standard do not fit conveniently into either the *string function* or the *data function* categories. These are presented here. They include the $SELECT function used as a conditioned expression, the $RANDOM function that returns a random number, and the $VIEW function.

The $VIEW function and all functions starting with the characters **$Z...** are implementation specific. However, the $VIEW function is part of the standard and must be recognized by each implementation, regardless of its interpretation or its arguments. The **$Z...** functions may be unique to each implementation and may not be recognized across implementations. Both forms of intrinsic functions are likely to produce errors when run on systems other than the one on which they were written. The **$Z...** functions are covered in Section 8.4.

8.3.1 $SELECT Function

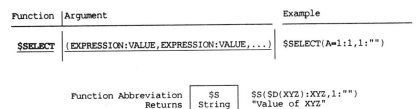

Function	Argument	Example
$SELECT	(EXPRESSION:VALUE,EXPRESSION:VALUE,...)	$SELECT(A=1:1,1:"")

Function Abbreviation	$S	$S($D(XYZ):XYZ,1:"")
Returns	String	"Value of XYZ"

The arguments of the $SELECT function are pairs of the form EXPRESSION:VALUE with pairs separated from each other with commas. The $SELECT function considers arguments from left to right, evaluating the EXPRESSION parts as TRUE or FALSE. When it first encounters a TRUE EXPRESSION, it evaluates the corresponding VALUE (which may be any MUMPS expression) and returns the result as the value of the $SELECT function.

There may be any arbitrary number of pairs within the argument list, but at least one must have an EXPRESSION that evaluates to TRUE (nonzero). If all list elements are processed without encountering a TRUE EXPRESSION, then an error results.

As the argument list is being processed from left to right, only the EXPRESSIONs are evaluated until one evaluates to TRUE. Only at that time is the expression associated with VALUE evaluated. Consequently, *global references* within the $SELECT function may (or may not) affect the *naked reference indicator*. Special care should be exercised when using naked reference within, and immediately after, the evaluation of a $SELECT function.

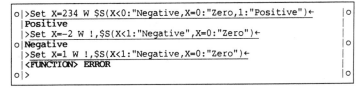

```
o|>Set X=234 W $S(X<0:"Negative,X=0:"Zero,1:"Positive")←    |o
 |Positive                                                    |
 |>Set X=-2 W !,$S(X<1:"Negative",X=0:"Zero")←               |
o|Negative                                                    |o
 |>Set X=1 W !,$S(X<1:"Negative",X=0:"Zero")←                |
 |<FUNCTION> ERROR                                            |
o|>                                                           |o
```

EXAMPLE 8.43. $SELECT

The second example succeeds while the third example does not. In the second example there is a TRUE value for one of the EXPRESSIONs before the argument list has been exhausted, while in the third, *none* of the EXPRESSIONs evaluate to TRUE before the list of paired elements is finished. The first TRUE EXPRESSION encountered terminates execution of the $SELECT function.

```
o|>Set A=24,B=2 W $S(B:A/B,1:"Divide by ZERO")←
 |12
 |>Set B=0 Write $S(B:A/B,1:"Divide by ZERO")←
o|Divide by ZERO
 |>
```

EXAMPLE 8.44. Additional Examples of $SELECT

Note in these examples that the EXPRESSION in the last pair of list elements is a ONE (<u>1</u>:"Divide by ZERO") and, consequently, TRUE (nonzero). This is a good method to ensure that the $SELECT function will not fail during execution. Remember, if none of the EXPRESSIONs evaluates to TRUE, the $SELECT function will generate an error condition.

The final example shows an alternative method of providing the same functionality as the $GET function (Section 8.2.4).

```
o|GetPat S Pdata=$S($D(^Pat(PatID)):^(PatID),1:"")
 |        If Pdata="" Write " --> NEW Patient."
 |        Quit
o|
 |>Set PatID=1234 Do getPat←
 | --> NEW Patient.
o|>
```

EXAMPLE 8.45. Alternative code for $GET using $SELECT

Notice the use of the naked global reference in the $SELECT command. In this case, the reference is unambiguous and is unlikely to be changed by inserted code, since the full global reference immediately precedes it as a paired list element.

8.3.2 $RANDOM Function

Function	Argument		Example
<u>$RANDOM</u>	(RANGE)		$RANDOM(100)

Function Abbreviation	$R	$R(33)
Returns	Number	20

The $RANDOM function evaluates the argument RANGE as a positive integer and returns a uniformly distributed integer value in the range of 0 through RANGE-1. Some implementations permit negative values for RANGE; this feature should not be used since the standard specifies that if RANGE evaluates to less than one an error occurs. If negative random numbers are needed, precede the $RANDOM function with a unary minus sign [for example, Set X = −$R(100)].

The integer value returned by this function does *not* include the value of RANGE. For example, invoking the function with RANGE = 100 returns random integers in the range from 0 to 99, *not* 1 to 100.

To generate random numbers in the range from −99.99 through +99.99 with up to two decimal digits, the following code could be used.

```
o|Drnd   ;Return R as random number -99.99 through 99.99         |o
 |          S R=$S($R(2):"-",1:"")                                |
 |          S R=+(R_$R(100)_"."_$R(100))                          |
o|          Quit                                                  |o
 |_____    |
 |>For i=1:1:10 D Drnd W R," "←                                   |
o|-83.24 68.16 77.63 7.99 1.5 87.72 -6.92 90.19 -72.06 5.4        |o
 |>                                                               |
```

EXAMPLE 8.46. $RANDOM

Note the use of $R(2); this expression will return a value of either zero (0) or one (1) so the sign of the results will be uniformly distributed between "-" and "" (implied positive number). The plus sign in the last line of the subroutine forces the results into the form of a canonic number (no leading or trailing nonsignificant zeros).

Another approach, using an extrinsic variable (similar to an extrinsic function; see Section 9.3) to generate the random number, is shown in the next example.

```
o|Drnd() ;Return random number from 0.00 through 99.99           |o
 |          Quit $R(10000)/100                                    |
 |_____    |
o|>For i=1:1:10 Write $S(i=1:"",1:", "),$$Drnd←                   |o
 |27.38, 30.65, 1.09, 42.81, 1.97, 50.23, 7.6, .42, 92.4, .06     |
 |>                                                               |
```

EXAMPLE 8.47.   Using $RANDOM in an extrinsic variable

Extrinsic variables and functions have been briefly discussed in previous sections and will be covered in greater detail in Chapter 9.

8.3.3 $VIEW Function

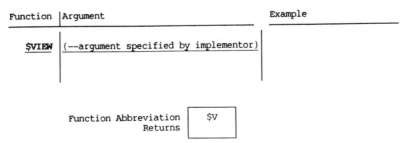

Function	Argument	Example
$VIEW	(--argument specified by implementor)	

Function Abbreviation	$V
Returns	

The $VIEW function is implementation specific; each implementor can define both the syntax and results of this function. You will need to read your documentation to discover just what $VIEW will do under your version of MUMPS.

WARNING. The $VIEW function is not likely to be portable between different implementations of MUMPS. Try to avoid its use in applications unless absolutely necessary. If it is needed, be sure to isolate the code that uses it, and carefully document the function(s) being performed.

Often the $VIEW function is used to read system-specific information (similar to the BASIC PEEK command); it is used extensively by system utilities for patching the operating system or disk structures and is often used in connection with the *VIEW* command (Section 3.5.5). It should *not*, in general, be used by application programs.

8.4 $Z... FUNCTIONS

All functions starting with the characters **$Z...** are *implementor specified* and are *not* likely to be available on other versions of MUMPS. Care should be exercised when using these functions to ensure portability of programs between different MUMPS implementations.

The following is a sampler of some $Z functions that are available on some implementations. It is designed to provide you with a general idea of the kinds of special functions handled by various implementors.

$ZCONVERT(string,mode)	Used to convert the characters in *string* to uppercase (mode = "U") or lower-case (mode = "L"). For the most part, this function can now be handled in a standard fashion using the $TRANSLATE function (Section 8.1.5).
$ZDATE(expr)	Evaluates expr as a $HOROLOG date value and returns an external (i.e., "readable") form of that date (e.g., $ZDATE(53312) = "12/18/86").

Math Functions:

$ZCOS	Trigonometric cosine function
$ZLOG	Base 10 logarithm
$ZLN	Natural logarithm (base e)
$ZSIN	Trigonometric sine function
$ZSQR	Square root function
$ZTAN	Trigonometric tangent function

For the most part, these functions were created before extrinsic functions were part of the language (see Chapter 9 for a discussion of extrinsic functions); they would probably be accomplished today through use of extrinsic function libraries.

8.5 Summary

In this chapter we have examined each of the intrinsic functions available to the MUMPS programmer. These form a powerful library of primitives for string and data manipulations for developing applications.

When functions are evaluated at run time, they return an expression that can be used as part of a larger expression; functions can be *nested*. Consider the next example, which is used to extract the first letter of an individual's FIRST name from a complex string.

```
o|>Set str="123;Smith,Jane;44 West Road;Ithaca;NY;14850"←      |o
 |>Write $E($P($P(str,";",2),",",2),1)←                         |
 |J                                                             |
o|>                                                            |o
```

EXAMPLE 8.48. Nested functions

Nested functions are evaluated from the innermost function out, and the code demonstrated in the previous example would be processed as:

1. $P(str,";",2) = "Smith,Jane"
2. $P("Smith,Jane",",",2) = "Jane"
3. $E("Jane",1) = "J"

While these functions provide a powerful mechanism for processing data, they do not provide all the basic primitives that may be desirable within the application environment. For instance, while the $TRANSLATE function permits easy replacement of individual characters within a string, it does not allow the replacement of multicharacter strings with new characters. In the next chapter we will discuss subroutines and ways in which programmers can develop their own functions called *extrinsic functions*.

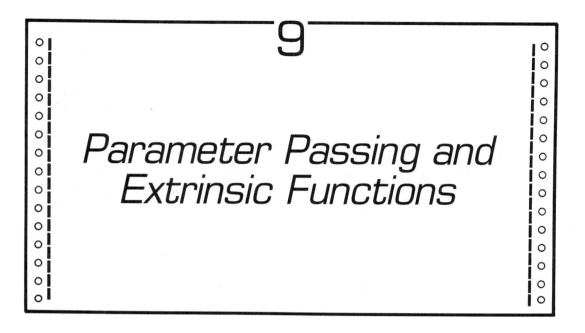

9

Parameter Passing and Extrinsic Functions

We have already discussed the local variable environment (Section 2.2.3) and some exceptions to the general rule that local variables are *shared* by all routines within a common partition (DO command with parameters, Section 3.3.2.2; QUIT command terminating an extrinsic function, Section 3.3.3.2; the NEW command, Section 3.1.3; and the JOB command, Section 3.5.3). In this chapter, we examine the specifics concerning the management of the local symbol table in more detail.

The NEW command and parameter passing are techniques by which information can be passed to a subroutine, and the subroutine can use locally defined variables without conflicting with the variable name space of the calling routine. There are three ways to invoke ancilliary subroutines: the JOB command, the DO command, and as an extrinsic function. While the specific syntax used for each case may differ, all three share many common traits.

9.1 Parameter Passing with the DO Command

The basic format for invoking a subroutine with the DO Command is

DO SUBROUTINE(PARAMETERs)

where SUBROUTINE is the name of the code being called (LABEL, ˆROUTINE, or LABELˆROUTINE), and PARAMETERs is an optional list of parameters to be passed to the subroutine. Parameters need not be passed to the subroutine. In general, the called subroutine has available to it all the variables that existed when it was invoked. In addition, any variables altered within the subroutine remain in their altered state after control is returned to the calling routine; variables SET or KILLED within the subroutine are permanently changed. Exceptions to these general rules occur when parameters are passed or when the NEW command is used.

When calling a subroutine and passing parameters, the list of parameters associated with the DO command is known as the *actual parameter list* while the corresponding parameter list associated with the LABEL of the subroutine being invoked is referred to as the *formal parameter list*.

DO SUBROUTINE(Actual1,Actual2,Actual3,...,Actualn)

SUBROUTINE(Formal1,Formal2,Formal3,...,Formaln) ; Subroutine Entry

> The parameter list associated with the DO command is known as the *actual parameter list* while the list associated with the label being called is known as the *formal parameter list*.

The entry point of the subroutine being called must start with a valid MUMPS LABEL followed by an opening parenthesis, a list of formal parameters (individual parameters within the list are separated by commas), a closing parenthesis, and finally one or more linestart characters preceding the code associated with that line. Each formal parameter *must* be a valid *local* variable name or a *nonsubscripted* array name.

> A parameter in the formal list must be the name of a local variable without subscripts.

The names of the local variables in the formal list do *not* need to be the same as those in the actual list. Each variable name in the formal list takes on the *value* associated by position of the corresponding value in the actual list.

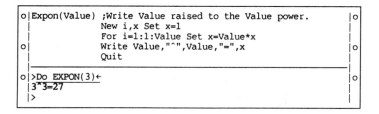

```
o|Expon(Value) ;Write Value raised to the Value power.      |o
 |              New i,x Set x=1                              |
 |              For i=1:1:Value Set x=Value*x               |
o|              Write Value,"^",Value,"=",x                 |o
 |              Quit                                         |
 |_____|
o|>Do EXPON(3)←                                             |o
 |3^3=27                                                    |
 |>                                                         |
```

EXAMPLE 9.1.   Subroutine with parameters

Before executing the designated subroutine, MUMPS performs an implicit NEW command on all variables in the formal list. It then initializes each parameter in the formal list with the value of the corresponding parameter in the actual list.

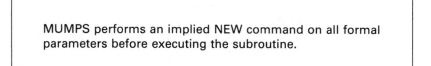

MUMPS performs an implied NEW command on all formal parameters before executing the subroutine.

The *actual* list of parameters can be *shorter* than the *formal* list. In such cases, those parameters in the formal list that do not have an associated entry in the actual list are initialized to *undefined*. While the actual list can be shorter than the formal list, it *cannot* have gaps. For example, an actual list of Actual1,, Actual3 would be *illegal*. No unnecessary commas can be included in the actual list.

The *actual* list of parameters can be shorter than the *formal* list of parameters.

In cases where the actual list is shorter than the formal list, those parameter names in the formal list without associated parameters in the actual list will be *undefined* in the subroutine. These are usually optional parameters that may be passed to the subroutine to override internal default values. In cases where parameters are optional, the subroutine must explicitly check to ensure that they have been passed.

```
o|Pwr(N,P) ;Write N raised to the P power. Default P=2        |o
 |         New i,x Set x=N Set:'$D(P) P=2                      |
 |         For i=1:1:P-1 Set x=x*N                             |
o|         Write N, to the ",P," power = ",x                   |o
 |         Quit                                                |
 |_____|
o|>Do Pwr(3,3)←                                                |o
 |3 to the 3 power = 27                                        |
 |>Do Pwr(5)←                                                  |
o|5 to the 2 power = 25                                        |o
 |>                                                            |
```

EXAMPLE 9.2.   Optional parameters

If the actual list of parameters is empty but there are formal parameters, the DO command must still have parentheses, even though they enclose an empty list [for example, **DO TEST**()].

Additional NEW commands can be issued within the subroutine body to ensure that other variables created and used within the subroutine do not alter the symbol table of the calling routines. Do *not* issue a NEW command on any of the variable names in the *formal* list or these variables will be undefined within the subroutine. The NEW commands, both implied and explicit, save the old contents (if any) of the named variables and provide a fresh copy of that variable for use in the subroutine. When a QUIT command is encountered that terminates the subroutine, all variables that have been NEWed within the subroutine are restored back to their original state before the subroutine was called. If the variable was defined before the subroutine call, it will be restored to its old value; if undefined before the call, it will be undefined when control is returned to the calling program.

```
o|Pwr(N,P) ;Write N raised to the P power.                     |o
 |         New i,x Set x=N                                      |
 |         For i=1:1:P-1 Set x=x*N                              |
o|         Write N," to the ",P," power = ",x                   |o
 |         Quit                                                 |
 |_____|
o|>Set i=10,x=2 Do Pwr(i,x) Write !,"i=",i,?10,"x=";x←         |o
 |10 to the 2 power = 100                                       |
 |i=10       x=2                                                |
o|>                                                             |o
```

EXAMPLE 9.3.   Actual and formal parameter lists

There are two forms that parameters in the actual list may assume: parameters defined by **value** and parameters defined by **reference**. The two forms are different, both in syntax and in their impact on the calling routine.

9.1.1 Passing Parameters by VALUE

Parameters in the actual list that are passed *by value* are evaluated as MUMPS expressions, and it is the results of those expressions that are used to initialize the corresponding parameters in the formal list. If the actual parameter is a variable name, there is *no* linkage between that name and the variable name in the formal list of parameters. Since there is an implied NEW command for each variable name in the formal list, the subroutine can alter the contents of variables in the formal list without changing the values of the calling routine's variables. Indeed, passing parameters by value is one-directional: the calling routine can pass information to the subroutine, but the subroutine *cannot* pass back results through the parameter list.

Data passed by VALUE is one-directional; the data are accessible to the subroutine, but the subroutine cannot use the parameter to pass results back to the calling routine.

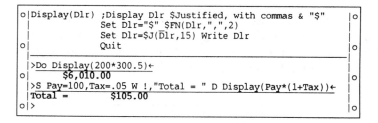

```
o|Display(Dlr) ;Display Dlr $Justified, with commas & "$"    |o
 |             Set Dlr="$"_$FN(Dlr,",",2)                     |
 |             Set Dlr=$J(Dlr,15) Write Dlr                   |
o|             Quit                                           |o
 |
 |>Do Display(200*300.5)←
o|        $6,010.00                                           |o
 |>S Pay=100,Tax=.05 W !,"Total = " D Display(Pay*(1+Tax))←
 |Total =         $105.00                                     |
o|>                                                           |o
```

EXAMPLE 9.4. Parameters passed by value

9.1.2 Parameter Passing by REFERENCE

Passing parameters *by reference* is significantly different from passing by value. Parameters passed by reference *must* be valid local variable names or the names of local arrays. They *cannot* be the names of global variables nor subscripted array elements. Parameters passed by reference are distinguished from parameters passed by value by the addition of a period (.) immediately preceding the variable name.

A parameter passed by REFERENCE in the actual list must be the name of a local variable or array. It is preceded in the actual list with a period (.).

In a call by reference, the variable or array name passed in the actual list is linked *directly* to the symbolic name associated with that parameter in the formal list. Any change made to the formal variable in the subroutine, *regardless of the name used in the subroutine*, is also reflected in the original variable. This, then, provides two-way communication between the calling routine and the subroutine. Note that KILLing a parameter passed to a subroutine by reference also KILLs the original variable in the calling routine's environment. You can visualize variable names passed by reference as a form of indirection. The variable name assumes an *alias* in the subroutine but any references to this alternative name are actually referred back to the contents of the *original* variable name.

When passing a parameter by REFERENCE, the variable name in the actual list is linked to the variable name in the formal list; any changes to the variable in the formal list also change the value of the variable in the actual list.

Since the period (.) is used to identify parameters passed by reference, it cannot be used as the first character in a numeric literal when that literal is passed by value or an error may result. To avoid this situation, the numeric literal can be padded with a leading zero or sign (+ or −) character.

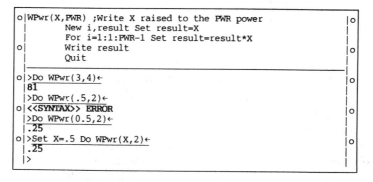

```
WPwr(X,PWR) ;Write X raised to the PWR power
        New i,result Set result=X
        For i=1:1:PWR-1 Set result=result*X
        Write result
        Quit

>Do WPwr(3,4)←
81
>Do WPwr(.5,2)←
<<SYNTAX>> ERROR
>Do WPwr(0.5,2)←
.25
>Set X=.5 Do WPwr(X,2)←
.25
>
```

EXAMPLE 9.5. Parameters with leading periods

When we pass the value .5 to the subroutine, it is interpreted as a parameter being passed by reference (because of the leading period). Yet all parameters passed by reference must evaluate to a legal variable name; 5 is *not* a legal variable name.

While the period (.) is *required* in the actual list of parameters to flag a parameter as being passed by reference, *no* periods are permitted in the formal list of arguments. The called subroutine is not aware (except by convention) of how the actual list of parameters is being passed.

```
o|Avg(X,R) ;Average the nodes in array X and pass back the   |o
 |            ;results in R as "Number of Values,Total,Average"  |
 |            New i,n,s,t Set (n,t)=0,s=""                       |
o|            F i=0:0 S s=$O(X(s)) Q:s=""  S n=n+1,t=t+X(s)     |o
 |            Set R=n_","_t_","_(t/n)                            |
 |            Quit                                               |
o|------------------------------------------------------------|o
 |>Kill  F i=1:1:10 Set Ary(i)=i*10←                            |
 |>Do Avg(.Ary,.Ans) Write "Result string = ",Ans←             |
o|Result string = 10,550,55                                    |o
 |>                                                             |
```

EXAMPLE 9.6.   Arrays passed to a subroutine by reference

An array name can be passed to the subroutine *only* by reference. If we had left off the period in front of ".Ary" we would have gotten an <UNDEFINED> error since the simple variable Ary was not defined. All actual parameters, when passed by value, *must* be defined before the DO command is executed. In this case, we are passing Ary by reference only as a means of making the array available to the subroutine, not to pass data back to the calling routine.

Since arrays are passed *by reference*, any changes made to the array in the subroutine will be reflected in the array name found in the actual parameter list when control is returned to the calling routine.

> Entire arrays can be passed to a subroutine if the array name is passed by REFERENCE.

Also note that the variable **Ans** is *not* defined before being passed to the subroutine by reference. Variables passed by reference do *not* have to be defined before the DO command is executed. They will be undefined in the subroutine until the corresponding variable in the formal list of parameters is defined (SET, READ), at which time it is also set (under the name of the actual parameter) in the calling routine's variable environment.

> Variable names in the actual list that are passed by REFERENCE do not have to be defined before the call to the subroutine.

While we cannot pass an array address into a subroutine *by value*, we can pass an expression containing the array reference and then use subscript indirection to achieve the same results shown in the previous example. Consider the next example in which we pass the array reference to the subroutine <u>Avg</u> by value rather than by reference.

```
o|Avg(X,R) ;Average nodes in array passed by X and pass back |o
 |          ;results in R.                                    |
 |          New i,n,s,t Set (n,t)=0,s=""                      |
 o|         F  S s=$O(@X@(s)) Q:s=""  S n=n+1,t=t+@X@(s)       |o
 |          Set R=n_","_t_","_(t/n)                           |
 |          Quit                                              |
 o|----------------------------------------------------------|o
 |>Kill  For i=1:1:10 Set Ary(i)=i*10←                        |
 |>Do Avg("Ary",.Ans) Write !,Ans←                            |
 o|10,550,55                                                  |o
 |>                                                           |
```

EXAMPLE 9.7.   Arrays passed to a subroutine by value

The array named <u>Ary</u> is passed to the subroutine in the actual parameter list as a string literal and used with subscript indirection in the subroutine. Refer to Section 7.2.4 for a description of subscript indirection.

9.2 Extrinsic Functions

Extrinsic functions are similar to a DO command with parameter passing except that, when they are executed, the call to the extrinsic function is logically replaced by the results of that function. From a logical standpoint, an extrinsic function translates to a VALUE, much the same as an intrinsic function (Chapter 8).

> Extrinsic functions are evaluated as *expressions* and the results of the function replace the call to the function when the code is executed.

Extrinsic functions are not formal language elements; they may be supplied by the MUMPS vendor or written by a programmer (as contrasted to intrinsic functions, which are part of the language and available on all systems). Extrinsic functions are identified in MUMPS code by the syntax

$$FUNCTION(PARAMETERS)

Each reference to an extrinsic function starts with two dollar signs ($$) followed by the name of the FUNCTION and a list of PARAMETERS enclosed in parentheses. As with the DO command, the FUNCTION name can be a <u>LABEL</u>, a <u>^ROUTINE</u>, or a <u>LABEL^ROUTINE</u> that identifies the code to be executed when the function is evaluated. The two dollar signs in the extrinsic function name *do not* appear on the label associated with the name. Also like the DO command, the parameters in the PARAMETER string are known as the *actual parameter list*. The list of parameters associated with the LABEL of the invoked code is referred to as the *formal parameter list*; individual parameters are separated from each other with commas.

Set A = $$FUNCTION(Actual1,Actual2,...Actualn)

FUNCTION(Formal1,Formal2,...,Formaln) ;

.
___
.
___

Quit EXPRESSION

As with subroutines initiated with the DO command, an extrinsic function *must* begin with a labeled line. The label must be followed by an opening parenthesis, the list of formal parameters (if any), a closing parenthesis, and one or more linestart characters that precede the code associated with that command line.

Unlike subroutines invoked with the DO command, the QUIT command associated with the termination of the extrinsic function must have an argument. The argument to the QUIT is in the general form of a MUMPS expression. It is the value of this expression that is substituted for the call to the extrinsic function in the code invoking the function. Consider the following example:

```
o|%ZZM      ;JML–NYSCVM                                              |o
 |           ;Utility containing Extrinsic Math Functions            |
 |Abs(X)     ;Return Absolute Value of X (If X<0 then X=–X)          |
o|           Quit $S(X<0:–X,1:X)                                     |o
 |
 |_____
o|>For i=10,–23.4,17.6,–.34 Write !,i,?5,$$Abs^%ZZM(i)←             |o
 |
 |10         10                                                      |
o|–23.4      23.4                                                    |o
 |17.6       17.6                                                    |
 |–.34       .34                                                     |
o|>                                                                  |o
```

EXAMPLE 9.8. Extrinsic functions

The extrinsic function is similar to the subroutine invoked by a DO command with parameters except that:

1. It returns a value that replaces the call to the extrinsic function. The value returned is the value of the expression used as the argument to the QUIT command that terminates the function. Any QUIT command that terminates an extrinsic function *must* have an argument; it is an *error* to terminate an extrinsic function with an argumentless QUIT command.

2. The value of the system variable $TEST is saved before the code associated with the extrinsic function is executed and is restored to its original state when control

is transferred back to the code invoking the function. This is an important difference between the DO command and extrinsic functions. When DOing a subroutine, an IF command or a timed LOCK, READ, JOB, or OPEN command can change the value of the system variable $TEST. With an extrinsic function, $TEST is automatically saved at the beginning of the function and restored before returning control to the calling routine.

The Value that replaces the call to an extrinsic function is the value of the argument to the QUIT command that terminates the extrinsic function.

The value of $TEST is saved before an extrinsic function is called and restored upon return from the extrinsic function.

As in the DO command, parameters can be passed to the extrinsic function either by *value* or by *reference*. All the definitions described in Sections 9.1.1 and 9.1.2 apply to parameters passed to the extrinsic function. So does the use of the NEW command to preserve the calling routine's variable space. While extrinsic functions usually pass results back as a value, they can be used to perform any MUMPS function, including I/O, global references, and so on. Results can also be passed back through the parameter list passed as in the DO command. Consider the following extrinsic function that calculates the average of the absolute values of the elements in an array. In addition to calculating the average, all negative elements in the array are converted to positive values in the original (calling) array.

```
AvgAry(A)  ;return the average of absolute values in A.
           ;Also, convert neg. array element to positive.
           New i,n,s,t,x Set (n,t)=0,s=""
           F i=1:1 Set s=$O(A(s)) Q:s=""  S x=A(s) D AddX
           Quit t/n
AddX       If x<0 Set x=-x,A(s)=x
           Set n=n+1,t=t+x
           Quit

>Kill  F i=1:1:25 Set Ary(i)=$S($R(2):"-",1:"") i←
>Set Neg=0 F i=1:1:25 If Ary(i)<0 Set Neg=Neg+1←
>Write Neg←
12
>Write $$AvgAry(.Ary)←
13
>Set Neg=0 F i=1:1:25 i Ary(i)<0 Set Neg=Neg+1←
>Write Neg←
0
>
```

EXAMPLE 9.9.   Passing parameters to extrinsic functions

In this example, note the use of the NEW command to guard against the subroutine altering the symbol table of the calling routine. Also note that Ary is passed to AvgAry *by reference* both because it is an array, and because the array contents are to be changed by the subroutine. The code associated with the label AddX is also a subroutine. The real function exit point is the QUIT command preceding the line labeled AddX.

9.3 Extrinsic Variables

The extrinsic variable is a variation of the extrinsic function. In this form, no parameters are passed to the subroutine and the function call does *not* have parentheses. The subroutine being referenced, however, still requires opening and closing parentheses after the LABEL. Consider the following example of an extrinsic variable used to translate the value of the system clock from the number of seconds that have elapsed since midnight to a more readable format.

```
o|Time()  ;Convert $H to HH:MM with HH being 0-24 hours       |o
 |         New minutes,hours,seconds Set seconds=$P($H,",",2)  |
 |         Set hours=seconds\3600                              |
o|         Set minutes=seconds-(hours*3600)\60                 |o
 |         Set:Minutes<10 minutes="0"_minutes                  |
 |         Quit hours_":"_minutes                              |
o|_____            |o
 |>Write $$Time←                                              |
 |12:59                                                        |
o|>Write $$Time←                                              |o
 |13:01                                                        |
 |>                                                            |
```

EXAMPLE 9.10. Extrinsic variables

9.4 Subroutine Libraries

With the introduction of parameter passing and the NEW command to the MUMPS language, it has become possible to develop a standard library of reusable routines that are independent of the calling environment. Such libraries of commonly used functions can significantly reduce the time required to develop an application.

In this section we examine a number of subroutines, extrinsic functions, and extrinsic variables that could be incorporated into a library and made available for program development. The primary purpose of this section is to demonstrate features of the language discussed in this and previous chapters and to provide the reader with a variety of examples using these features.

9.4.1 Conversion of $H Time and Date to Readable Format

In the previous section we covered the conversion of the current time as held in the system variable $H from its internal representation (the number of seconds elapsed since midnight) to a more readable format.

In expanding on the previous example to make it more general purpose, we will consider the need to:

- Allow for conversion of any expression in $H time format to a more readable form. If *no* expression is passed, we will assume that the calling program wants the current value of $H to be converted.
- Allow the calling program to specify the format of the results (that is, 24-hour time or 12-hour time with AM or PM indicators). If *no* format is specified by the calling program, the subroutine will use the 24-hour format as a default.
- Provide a means to pass back error information in cases where the expression to be converted is illegal.

```
1    TimeFH(Secs,Format) ;Convert Secs since midnight to Time
2            New ampm,hours,minutes
3            Set:$S('$D(Secs):1,Secs="$H":1,1:0) Secs=$P($H,",",2)
4            Set Format=$S('$D(Format):24,Format=12:12,1:24)
5            Set:Secs="0" Secs=86400
6            If Secs<1!(Secs>86400 Set Time="" Goto TimeFHX
7            Set hours=Secs\3600,minutes=Secs-(hours*3600)\60
8            Set ampm=$S(Format=24:"",hours<12:" AM",1:" PM")
9            If Format=24 Set hours=$S(hours<10:"0",1:"")_hours
10           Else  Set hours=hours-$S(hours>12:12,1:0)
11           Else  Set hours=$S(hours<10:" ",1:"")_hours
12           Set minutes=$S(minutes<10:"0",1:"")_minutes
13           Set Time=hours_":"_minutes_ampm
14   TimeFHX Quit Time

     >Write $$TimeFH()←
     13:22
     >Write $$TimeFH("$H",12)←
     1:22 PM
     >Write $$TimeFH(81000)←
     22:30
     >
```

EXAMPLE 9.11. Extrinsic function to convert time from $H format; see Appendix G for documentation

A number of features are demonstrated in this example, one of which is the *variable number of actual parameters* that can be passed to the subroutine. We mentioned earlier that the number of *actual parameters* did not have to agree with the number of *formal parameters*. If the actual list of arguments is shorter than the formal list, all variables in the formal list *without* a corresponding element in the actual list will be *undefined* at the start of the subroutine. Lines 3 and 4 in the example check to see whether or not the parameters Secs and Format were passed to the extrinsic function. If not, they are initialized to *default* values.

Good documentation of subroutines is critical if they are to be effectively used in building applications. A programmer must know what type of subroutine it is (that is, whether it is invoked as an extrinsic function, as an extrinsic variable, or with a DO command), what parameters can be passed, which parameters are optional (and what defaults are used for parameters that are not passed), and how the results are returned.

The documentation for this example (and many of the others that follow in this chapter) is presented in Appendix G. This documentation provides the programmer with a concise description of what the function does and how it is invoked. Additional documentation on a subroutine including algorithms, variables used, and so on, is also required, and the descriptions presented in Appendix G represent only one aspect of the necessary subroutine documentation.

As mentioned earlier, the number of actual parameters can be less than the number of formal parameters, but gaps are *not* allowed in the actual list. The following example is illegal and results in an error.

```
o|>Write $$TimeFH(,12)←                                              |o
 |<PARAMETER> ERROR                                                  |
 |>                                                                  |
```

EXAMPLE 9.12.   Missing parameters

Since all the parameters for this extrinsic function are *optional*, the function can also be invoked as an extrinsic variable to return the current time in 24-hour format.

```
o|>Write $$TimeFH←                                                   |o
 |16:07                                                              |
 |>                                                                  |
```

EXAMPLE 9.13.   Use of $$TimeFH with optional parameters

Next we examine the somewhat more complex process of converting the date from its $H format (days since December 31, 1840) to a more readable format (Month/Day/Year). The conversion is made more difficult due to the varying number of days in any given month and is further complicated by the addition of an extra day every leap year. Leap years are all those that are evenly divisible by 4 with the exception of century years; century years must be evenly divisible by 400 to be considered a leap year. Example 9.14 shows an extrinsic function that will convert a date in $H format to the form Month/Day/Year (for example, 5/22/87).

```
o|DateFH(Date) ;Convert Date from $H to "MM/DD/YY" format.      |o
 |     New Days,i,Ldays,leap,mon,Year,Years                     |
 |     Set Date=+$S('$D(Date):$H,Date="":$H,1:Date)             |
o|     If Date'?1.5N!'Date Set results="" Goto DateX            |o
 |     Set Ldays=Date\365\4-(Date>21608) ;Number of LeapDays|
 |     Set Years=Date-Ldays-1\365 ;        Years since 1841     |
o|     Set Days=Date-(Years*365)-Ldays ;    Days in this year|o
 |     Set Year=Year+1841,leap='(Year#4)*(Year'=1900),mon=1    |
 |     For i=31,28+leap,31,30,31,30,31,31,30,31,30,31 Quit:i'<D|
o|  ---ays  Set mon=mon+1,Days=Days-i                           |o
 |     Set result=mon_"/"_Days_"/"_Year                         |
 |DateX Quit result                                             |
```

EXAMPLE 9.14.   Conversion of $H date to MM/DD/YY; see Appendix G for documentation

Notice the two checks for the century year 1900 in calculating leap days (Ldays) and whether or not the year being checked is a leap year. The value 21608 corresponds to 2/28/1900, which was *not* a leap year (not evenly divisible by 400). Also examine the mixed-operator calculation in line DateFH + 7 used to determine whether or not the year is a leap year.

9.4.2 Check and Conversion of Numbers

Next we turn our attention to a different type of subroutine, one that is used to check a data value for validity. Consider the general problem of reading data from the keyboard and verifying them. When collecting entries from an end user, the programmer is faced with conflicting needs. There is the need to ensure that the entry is valid, both in format and range, but there is also the need to make the data collection program user-friendly. Programs should allow the end user to enter data in a variety of formats, yet convert the entry to a common format for internal use and storage.

Example 9.15 demonstrates some variations and uses of previously discussed commands and operators to validate a numeric entry. After removing extraneous characters with the $TRANSLATE function, the subroutine makes a basic test to see if the data field is in a valid number format. To be so, it *must* contain at least 1 numeric digit (?.E1N.E) and can contain a negative sign or decimal point or numeric digits, but not any other character types (?."−".N.".".N). Neither the negative sign nor the decimal point are required. Checks after this point are for the number falling in the correct range, and having no more than the specified number of decimal digits.

```
 1  o|NumChk(Data,Range,Dec) ;Check for valid NUMBER              |o
 2   |        Set Data=$TR(Data,"+ $,")                           |
 3   |        Goto NumChkE:Data'?.E1N.E,NumChkE:Data'?."−".N.".".N |
 4  o|        If $D(Dec),Dec?1N.N G NumChkE:$L($P(Data,".",2))>Dec |o
 5   |        Set:'$D(Range) Range="" Set:Range="" Range="−1E25:1E25" |
 6   |        If $P(Range,":")'="" Goto NumChkE:Data<$P(Range,":") |
 7  o|        If $P(Range,":",2)'="" Goto NumChkE:Data>$P(Range,":",2) |o
 8   |        Set Data=+Data Goto NumChkX                          |
 9   |NumChkE Set Data=""                                         |
10  o|NumChkX Quit Data                                           |o
```

EXAMPLE 9.15. Extrinsic function to verify numeric values; see Appendix G for documentation

The parameters Range and Dec are both optional. If Range is passed, an additional check is made to ensure that the number falls within the range (for example, Range = "1:100"). If the optional parameter Dec is passed, it is used to further check the value of Data for a maximum number of Decimal digits to the right of the decimal point.

9.4.3 Numeric Conversion between Bases

While MUMPS uses base 10 arithmetic for all calculations, it is sometimes desirable to convert numeric values to or from other bases [such as octal (base 8) or hexadecimal (base 16)]. Example 9.16 demonstrates one method by which this can be accomplished. This subroutine has *two* possible entry points: if invoked with a Do ^%Convert, it prompts the user for the number to be converted, its base, and the base to which it is to be converted; the second entry point is an extrinsic function (Cnvrt^%Convert), which can be called by other routines with parameters specifying the number and bases.

```
o|%Convert ;JML-NYSCVM                                                |o
 |        ;Convert NUMBERS between BASES                               |
 |        New num,from,to,result                                      |
o|Read    Read !,"Number to be converted: ",num Quit:num=""           |o
 |        Read ?30,"FROM Base: ",from Goto Read:from=""                |
 |        Read ?45,"TO Base: ",to Goto Read:to=""                      |
o|        Set result=$$Cnvrt(num,from,to)                              |o
 |        Write " = ",$S(result'="":result,1:"input ERROR")           |
 |        Goto Read                                                    |
o|        ;                                                            |o
 |Convrt(n,f,t) ;Convert POSITIVE INTEGER "n" from base "f"            |
 |        ;to base "t". Errors return null ("").                       |
o|        New ans,x Set ans=""                                         |o
 |        If n<0!(f<2)!(f>16)!(t<2)!(t>16)!(+n["." ) Goto ConX         |
 |        Set n=$$Dec(n,f) If t=10 Set ans=n Goto ConX                 |
o|        For  Set x=n#t,n=n\t,ans=$S(x>9:$E("ABCDEF",x-9),1:x)|o
 |   --- ans Quit:'n                                                   |
 |ConX    Quit ans                                                     |
o|Dec(n,f) ;Convert "n" base "f" to base-10                            |o
 |        New ans,i Set ans=0 If f=10 Set ans=n Goto DecX              |
 |        For i=1:1:$L(n) Set ans=ans*f+($F("0123456789ABCDEF",       |
o|   ---$E(n,i))-2)                                                    |o
 |DecX    Quit ans                                                     |
```

EXAMPLE 9.16.   Converting numbers between different bases; see Appendix G for documentation

This subroutine can be used to convert any positive integer from one base to another. The bases must be in the range 2 (binary) through 16 (hexadecimal). Note the use of $+n[$"." in line Convrt+3 to check for integer numbers. This check could also have been performed with the code $n\1'=n$.

9.4.4 Simple Statistics

Next we examine one more example of a library subroutine that is more complex in function and in structure. The following subroutine could be used to calculate simple statistics on a list of numbers held in an array or global.

```
 1  o|Stats(Ref,Results) ;Calculate simple Statistics on Array nodes  |o
 2   |        New High,i,Low,Mean,Num,StdDev,StdErr,s,Sum,SumSQ,Var    |
 3   |        Set High=-1E25,Low=1E25,(Sum,SumSQ,Num)=0,s=""           |
 4  o|        For i=0:0 Set s=$O(@Ref@(s)) Q:s="" Do StatsV(@Ref@(s))  |o
 5   |        If 'Num Set Results="" Goto StatsX                       |
 6   |        Set Mean=Sum/Num,StdErr=Mean/$$SQroot(Mean)             |
 7  o|        Set (StdDev,Var)=""                                      |o
 8   |        If Num>1 Set Var=-Num*Mean*Mean+SumSQ/(Num-1)           |
 9   |        If  Set StdDev=$$SQroot(Var)                            |
10  o|        Set Results=Num_";"_Low_";"_High_";"_Mean               |o
11   |        Set Results=Results_";"_Var_";"_StdDev_";"_StdErr        |
12   |        Goto StatsX                                              |
13  o|StatsV(Val) ;Process an individual VALue                        |o
14   |        Set Val=$$NumChk^%Zu(Val) Quit:Val=""                   |
15   |        Set Num=Num+1,Sum=Sum+Val,SumSQ=Val*Val+SumSQ           |
16  o|        Set:Val<Low Low=Val Set:Val>High High=Val               |o
17   |        Quit                                                     |
18   |StatsX Quit                                                     |
```

EXAMPLE 9.17. Simple statistics; see Appendix G for documentation

This subroutine can be invoked with the following code:

$$\text{Do } \hat{} \text{Stats(}"\hat{} \text{Data(1)}",.\text{Results)}$$

The data values to be analyzed are held in an array [in this case, $\hat{}$Data ($\hat{}$Data(1,1), $\hat{}$Data (1,2),...)], and the results of the analysis are returned in the variable defined as the second parameter (that is, Results). The input data array name is passed by value, and the location for the returned results is passed by reference. But didn't we say earlier in this section that arrays (local or global) could *not* be passed by value and that, even if passed by reference, array references with subscripts are illegal? Both statements are true. In this case we pass a subscripted array reference by value *as a string literal* that is used with *argument indirection* in the subroutine.

The subscript indirection is used in line 4 of the subroutine Stats. This form of indirection allows the program to use almost any array structure for the input of data values. The subscripts below the reference node can be in any format such as strings, sequential numbers, or nonsequential numbers. Subscript indirection is used both to get the next data value to be processed [$Order(@Ref@(s))] and to retrieve the data node.

The only constraint on the array structure is that the data values associated with each array node be simple numbers rather than multiple-field strings. We could even avoid this limitation by including optional parameters in the formal list that would specify the delimiting character(s) of the data fields and which piece(s) of the data field should be used in the calculations. It is left up to the reader to experiment with these extensions.

Also observe the use of exponential notation (line 2 of Stats) in establishing the High and Low data values in the array being processed. This code is used to initialize the low and high values to the largest and smallest numbers specified by the language standard.

The main body of the subroutine Stats calls two other subroutines: StatsV to process a single data value and SQroot to calculate the square root of a number.

In addition, the subroutine StatsV invokes the extrinsic function NumChk (Example 9.15) to verify a number. To complete the statistical subroutine, we still need a SQroot function.

```
1  o|SQroot(Num)  ;Return the SQUARE ROOT of abs(Num)            |o
2   |             New prec,Root Set Root=0 Goto SQrootX:Num=0     |
3   |             Set:Num<0 Num=-Num Set Root=$S(Num>1:Num\1,1:1/Num) |
4  o|             Set Root=$E(Root,1,$L(Root)+1\2) Set:Num'>1 Root=1/Root |o
5   |             For prec=1:1:6 Set Root=Num/Root+Root*.5        |
6   |SQrootX Quit Root                                            |
```

EXAMPLE 9.18. Extrinsic function to calculate square root; see Appendix G for documentation

The subroutine SQroot uses a technique of successive approximations to converge on the square root of a number. Line 4 in this example is used to initialize the root to a best guess or starting point for the calculation. The accuracy of the calculation is determined by the number of times the loop in line 5 is executed.

For those readers who are not familiar with calculations of this type, it is recommended that you work out the logic of the square root calculation by hand. Keep track of the variables Num and Root throughout the calculation and see how Root converges on the square root. Use 16 as the number whose square root is to be calculated. It might also be instructive to try different algorithms for calculating the starting value and different numbers of loop iterations to see how they affect the accuracy of the calculation and how rapidly the results converge on the desired results.

A number of other techniques could have been used to terminate the loop, rather than executing it a fixed number of times. We could have initiated an endless loop and QUIT under the following condition:

Quit:Root*Root=Num

Unfortunately, there are many numbers whose exact square root is indeterminate, and such a loop could, indeed, be endless. Another approach is to save the calculation from the previous loop iteration and compare it with the results of the current iteration; if they are the same to 12 significant digits, then the loop can be terminated. However, both of these techniques add considerable code to a relatively short loop that is only executed six times. The amount of time saved by reducing the number of iterations would probably be offset by the additional computations required to end the loop.

9.4.5 An Extrinsic Function to Replace Strings

As a final illustrative example of functions for a subroutine library, we consider an extrinsic function to replace strings of characters within a target string. The intrinsic function $TRANSLATE is useful in replacing individual characters, but cannot be used to replace multiple-character strings. However, the need to replace strings or even patterns of characters with other strings occurs regularly. For example, consider the desirability of removing double spaces (that is, occurrences of adjacent space characters) from a string.

```
o|Rep(T,F,W) ;Replace From str with With str in Target str    |o
 |      For  Quit:T'[F  Set T=$P(T,F)_W_$P(T,F,2,999)           |
 |      Quit T                                                  |
o|                                                             |o
 |    --or--                                                    |
 |                                                              |
o|Rep(T,F,W) ;Replace From str with With str in Target str    |o
 |Repl  If T[F Set T=$P(T,F)_W_$P(T,F,2,999) Goto Repl          |
 |      Quit T                                                  |
o|                                                             |o
 |    --but NOT--                                               |
 |                                                              |
o|Rep(T,F,W) ;Replace From str with With str in Target str    |o
 |      New i For i=1:1:$L(T,F) Set T=$P(T,F)_W_$P(T,F,2,999)|
 |      Quit T                                                  |
o|                                                             |o
```

EXAMPLE 9.19. String replace function; see Appendix G for documentation

The first two forms of the extrinsic function perform the same task but use different techniques; the first example uses a FOR loop and the second a GOTO loop. There has been considerable argument in the past between experienced MUMPS programmers as to which is the fastest technique. In purely interpreted versions of MUMPS, the FOR loop usually has been, since the GOTO command requires a linear search of the routine for the specified label. In compiled versions, the GOTO seems to have the advantage, since the address has already been calculated and the FOR loop overhead (especially when using a counting FOR loop) was eliminated. In point of fact, when using the argumentless form of the FOR command, the compiled code generated for both these approaches is remarkably similar and differences in execution speed are negligible.

The third approach presented in Example 9.19 appears to have certain advantages over the first two. The terminating criteria are calculated once at the beginning of the loop, not during each pass of the loop. This reduces the number of MUMPS instructions that must be executed and should reduce the loop execution time. Indeed, it does reduce the execution time; unfortunately, the translation does not always work correctly. The problem can be demonstrated when we try to replace double occurrences of a character with a replacement string. Consider the following target string:

Targ = "This***is**a***test"

If we wish to remove occurrences of adjacent asterisks (that is, we want to convert the string to "This*is*a*test"), the third example would have returned "This*is*a**test"; it fails to replace the last set of double asterisks.

The failure is due to how the $LENGTH function works. The $LENGTH function returns the number of *nonoverlapping* occurrences of the delimiter string found in the target string. If we examine the use of $LENGTH to calculate the FOR loop terminating criteria, we find

$$\$L(\text{"This}***\text{is}**\text{a}***\text{test"},\text{"}*\text{"}) = \underline{4}$$

Because only nonoverlapping occurrences of the search string found in the target are counted, the number of occurrences of double asterisks (5) is *not* the same as the number of fields separated by the ** sequence (4). Consequently, the third example may work in 99.9% of the cases, but there are selected conditions under which it will fail.

9.5 Parameter Passing with the JOB Command

Passing parameters with the JOB command is similar to passing parameters with the DO command, with a few major differences. The JOB command starts a process in another partition and, consequently, the spawned job has its own variable environment. The purpose of parameters associated with the JOB command is to allow initialization of the variable environment of the second job. Parameter passing *cannot* be used to return parameters to the process initiating the started job.

The formal and actual lists of parameters are the same as the previous examples *except* that the actual list can *only* pass parameters *by value*. No linkage is established between the variables in the two partitions since they have separate local symbol tables, and there is no guarantee that the initiating job will continue execution after the second job has started.

Parameters can only be passed to a started job by VALUE.

One consequence of this is that arrays *cannot* be passed to started jobs. Arrays can only be passed as a parameter *by reference*.

Since parameters can only be passed to a started job by VALUE, arrays cannot be passed as parameters with the JOB command.

In other respects, the spawned job behaves like a subroutine started with a DO command except that the local symbol table is empty at the start of the process. All variables in the formal list of arguments that have corresponding parameters in the actual list are initialized to the value of the parameter in the actual list. No other variables are defined at the beginning of the spawned process.

9.6 Technique and Style

We introduce two additional factors at this time: programming *technique* and programming *style*. Programming techniques are general rules that should, by convention, be followed when writing programs. Programming style, on the other hand, is more a matter of personal preference.

Good programming technique dictates that variable names within the scope of the current process always refer to a common data meaning. In Example 9.11, we could have saved one variable name by using the variable **Seconds** in place of the temporary variable **Time** (in lines 6, 13, and 14). However, the variable **Seconds** would then mean different things at different times. This makes documentation of the variable difficult, and also means that a programmer examining the code at a later time will have difficulty recognizing the meaning of the current variable state.

> Variable names within the scope of a given process should always refer to a common data meaning.

Additionally, although this borders somewhat on a question of style, variable names should be mnemonic for the data being processed. In Example 9.11, we could have used the variables **X** and **Y** above instead of **Secs** and **Format**, but the code would not have been as clear. One could argue that **Secs** should have been spelled out to **Seconds**, which would have made the code even more readable. This is a matter of judgment that reflects on programming style; both Secs and Seconds are reasonable names for this variable, although Secs is shorter and reduces the program entry time and the size of the source code.

> Variable names should be mnemonic for the data they represent.

Finally, it is good programming technique to have a *common exit point* for a subroutine. In Example 9.11 we could have modified the lines:

6	If Secs<1!(Secs>86400) Quit " "
13	--delete line altogether--
14	Quit hours_":"_minutes_ampm

In the process, we would also eliminate the need for the temporary variable **Time**. While in a small subroutine such as this it may seem that a single exit point is unnecessary, managing large or complex subroutines with multiple exit points can be very frustrating.

Subroutines should have a single, common exit point.

You have already been introduced to a style of programming in the examples given in this and previous chapters. Some of these reflect variable and label naming conventions, others the use of abbreviations for commands and functions.

I prefer a variable naming convention that goes beyond the scope of good programming technique discussed above. When using variables that are defined and used throughout a package (that is, defined once and assumed to be available to all routines within the program or package), I prefer using uppercase variable names. For variable names passed to or from a subroutine (that is, in either the actual or formal parameter lists), I prefer that the first character be uppercase and the remaining characters can be mixed case (although typically lowercase). And finally, I like all variables used locally within the scope of a given process to be lowercase. With such naming conventions, I can tell at a glance the scope of any particular variable. I stress the fact that these are *my* conventions and reflect *my* programming style.

We have seen numerous examples of command and function abbreviations in the previous chapters. For the most part, the examples have had the commands spelled out with the first character of the command in uppercase and the remaining characters in lowercase. I normally do not program in this fashion, but, since this text may be used by individuals just starting out in MUMPS, I did so to lend clarity to the examples. I prefer entering commands as single-letter abbreviations in lowercase. This makes them easy to identify in code and can reduce program entry time significantly.

9.7 Chapter Highlights

- The parameter list associated with the DO command is known as the *actual parameter list* while the list associated with the label being called is known as the *formal parameter list* (9.1).

- A parameter in the *formal* list must be the name of a local variable without subscripts (9.1).

- The *actual* list of parameters can be shorter than the *formal* list of parameters (9.1).

- MUMPS performs an implied NEW command on all formal parameters before executing the subroutine (9.1).

- Data passed by VALUE are one-directional; the data are accessible to the subroutine, but the subroutine cannot use the parameter to pass results back to the calling routine (9.1.1).

- A parameter passed by REFERENCE in the actual list must be the name of a local variable or array. It is preceded in the actual list with a period (.) (9.1.2).

- When passing a parameter by REFERENCE, the variable name in the actual list is linked to the variable name in the formal list; any changes to the variable in the formal list also change the value of the variable in the actual list (9.1.2).

- Entire arrays can be passed to a subroutine if the array name is passed by REFERENCE (9.1.2).

- Variable names in the actual list that are passed by REFERENCE do not have to be defined before the call to the subroutine (9.1.2).

- Extrinsic functions are evaluated and the results of the function replace the call to the function when the code is executed (9.2).

- The value that replaces the call to an extrinsic function is the value of the argument to the QUIT command that terminates the extrinsic function (9.2).

- The value of $TEST is saved before an extrinsic function is called and restored upon return from the extrinsic function (9.2).

- Parameters can only be passed to a started job by VALUE (9.5).

- Since parameters can only be passed to a started job by VALUE, arrays cannot be passed as parameters with the JOB command (9.5).

- Variable names within the scope of a given process should always refer to a common data meaning (9.6).

- Variable names should be mnemonic for the data they represent (9.6).

- Subroutines should have a single, common EXIT point (9.6).

10

Advanced Global Techniques

In Chapters 1 through 3 we discussed the general concepts involved in using global arrays in MUMPS as the primary method for managing databases. In this chapter, we expand on the earlier definitions and demonstrate the versatility of this approach to database management.

The structure of globals is unique to the MUMPS language. Global arrays are automatically mapped to disk and are hierarchical and sparse in nature. They can have an arbitrary number of levels (subscripts), data can be held at any level, and individual records are of variable length. They do not require any special job control language (JCL) to link global names to a process, they do not have to be OPENED or CLOSED, and any given process can have access to an unlimited number of global files during its execution. Subscripts into the global can be any valid MUMPS expression including strings of characters, and MUMPS automatically inserts new data nodes into the global in collating sequence based on the subscript contents. Finally, globals can be shared between multiple processes at the same time.

The nature of globals is so different from the traditional file-structured databases of other languages that many programmers have difficulty understanding how they work in an application environment. How does one go about designing a global? If data are not accessed with a READ command as in most languages, and if there are gaps in the records, how does one go about retrieving data? We examine these and other related questions in this chapter.

10.1 Introduction to Globals

Before we get into the specifics of global structures and use, let's examine a simple database application and see how it could be implemented in MUMPS.

Suppose we wish to establish a small personnel file containing employee's Name, Age, and Sex. The data file will be organized by employee name so that we can conveniently list the employees alphabetically and do name searches. The Name will be stored in the global as a subscript and the Age and Sex will be stored as a data node with the dollar sign character ($) used to delimit the two fields. Example 10.1 demonstrates a simple program that collects the desired information and files it on disk in the global named ^Employee.

```
Read    ;Read employee data from keyboard, file in ^Employee
        Read !,"Employee Name: ",nam Quit:nam=""
        Read ?25,"Age: ",age,?35,"Sex: ",sex
        Set ^Employee(nam)=age_"$"_sex
        Goto Read

>For   Do Read Quit:nam=""←

Employee Name: LEWIS,AL←       Age: 45←   Sex: M←
Employee Name: LARCH,MARY←     Age: 22←   Sex: F←
Employee Name: MILLER,RUTH←    Age: 37←   Sex: F←
Employee Name: ALLEN,ETHAN←    Age: 61←   Sex: M←
Employee Name: LOCKWOOD,JOE←   Age: 43←   Sex: M←
Employee Name: MORRIS,JANE←    Age: 28←   Sex: F←
Employee Name: KING,ROBERT←    Age: 48←   Sex: M←
Employee Name: KING,ALLICE←    Age: 46←   Sex: F←
Employee Name: ←
>
```

EXAMPLE 10.1.   Simple data collection subroutine

This simple demonstration program is all that is required to collect data from the keyboard and file it on disk; no other code is required. It does make a number of assumptions concerning the data being collected (for example, no identical names) and does not check data fields for logical errors (for example, no check is made for valid age entry). On the other hand, it does demonstrate the ease with which a database can be created in MUMPS.

Now that we have a small test database on file, what can we do with it? Example 10.2 demonstrates another simple subroutine that can be used to display the contents of the database that was just created.

The $Order function used in Example 10.2 is the primary means used to search sparse arrays in MUMPS. Notice a very important characteristic of the $ORDER function: it always returns subscripts in a collated order (that is, alphabetized) regardless of the order in which the entries were added to the global. Even though the names used as subscripts into ^Employee were entered in a random

```
o|Display  ;Display the contents of ^Employee                    |o
 |         Set sub="" For  Do Displ Quit:sub=""                   |
 |         Quit                                                   |
o|Displ    Set sub=$O(^Employee(sub)) Quit:sub=""                 |o
 |         Set data=^Employee(sub)                                |
 |         Set age=$P(data,"$",1),sex=$P(data,"$",2)              |
o|         Write !,sub,?20,"Age=",age," Sex=",sex                 |o
 |         Quit                                                   |
 |_____|
o|>Do ^Display←                                                   |o
 |                                                                |
 |ALLEN,ETHAN          Age=61 Sex=M                               |
o|KING,ALICE           Age=46 Sex=F                               |o
 |KING,ROBERT          Age=48 Sex=M                               |
 |LARCH,MARY           Age=22 Sex=F                               |
o|LEWIS,AL             Age=45 Sex=M                               |o
 |LOCKWOOD,JOE         Age=43 Sex=M                               |
 |MILLER,RUTH          Age=37 Sex=F                               |
o|MORRIS,JANE          Age=28 Sex=F                               |o
 |>                                                               |
```

EXAMPLE 10.2.   Display of a database

fashion in Example 10.1, MUMPS automatically inserted them into the database in order. Another important characteristic of globals demonstrated in these two examples is that the employee names are stored as subscripts in the database (not as part of a data node), yet they are still available to the program as data.

The $ORDER function returns array subscripts in collated order, regardless of the order in which the data were added to the array.

10.2 Subscripts

As we have just seen, subscripts are used to point to and uniquely identify nodes within an array. They are stored independently from the data they point to, but they can also be used by programs as data. They also impose an *order* on how the data are inserted into the array, which affects how the $ORDER function scans an array for retrieval purposes.

In the following sections we will examine the logical organization of globals (or arrays in general) and the tools used to process data held in globals (the $DATA and $ORDER functions).

10.2.1 Subscript Collating Sequence

When a new data node is added to a MUMPS array, it is *inserted* logically into the array based on the value of the subscript(s); it is *not* appended to the end of the file. The order or *collating sequence* used by MUMPS for insertion has a profound impact on data retrieval and programming techniques.

As seen in Example 10.2, the basic order applied to subscripts is *alphabetic*; the character A comes before B, B before C, the string AB before ABC, and so on. This collating sequence is defined by the ASCII character set (see Appendix A for the ASCII character set and Section 5.3.2.3) and is based on a character's relative position within the ASCII table. For example, the letter **A** follows the character **?** in the list, the character **a** follows **Z**, and so on. When using the ASCII character set to define the order, the *case* of the character (upper- or lowercase) will have an effect on how strings are ordered. For example, the string "abc" would *follow* the string "ZZ" using the ASCII collating sequence. Table 10.1 demonstrates the ASCII order of a variety of character strings.

TABLE 10.1 ASCII collating order with letters

Order	String
1	"A"
2	"AA"
3	"ABCD"
4	"AaB" The letter "a" follows "B"
5	"a"
6	"aa"

While this approach works well for alphabetizing strings of letters, the order of numeric subscripts assumes a less desirable sequence. Consider the results of sequencing the numbers 1, 2, 3, 10, 20, 30, 100, 200, and 300 using the ASCII collating sequence, as shown in Table 10.2.

TABLE 10.2 ASCII collating order with numbers

Order	Number	
1	"1"	
2	"10"	
3	"100"	
4	"2"	Character "2" follows "1"
5	"20"	
6	"200"	
7	"3"	
8	"30"	
9	"300"	

Clearly, it would be desirable to be able to order many types of data by numeric value rather than by the ASCII collating sequence. In fact, MUMPS uses a special internal collating sequence for subscripts usually referred to as the *MUMPS collating sequence*. This collating order differentiates between *canonic numbers* and strings of characters that are noncanonic.

Canonic numbers are defined as numbers (integer or real, positive or negative) that contain no nonsignificant leading zeros (or plus signs in the case of positive numbers) and no insignificant trailing zeros to the right of the decimal point. Additionally, if the number has no fractional part, it must have no decimal point. A simple check using the unary + operator can be used to determine whether or not a variable contains a canonic number:

If Var = + Var Write "Var contains a canonic number"

Canonic numbers are those with no insignificant characters (for example, Number = + Number).

Consider Table 10.3 in which a variety of numbers are represented in both their canonic and in various noncanonic forms. In all cases the noncanonic form of the number evaluates numerically (when used in the calculation of an expression) to the canonic form, yet each represents a different string of characters. When used as subscripts into an array or global, each would represent a different subscript. With an understanding of canonic numbers and noncanonic strings (any string that is not a canonic number), let us examine the rules used by MUMPS in ordering subscripts.

TABLE 10.3 Canonic numbers

Canonic Representation	Noncanonic Representation
1.01	+1.01, 01.01, 1.010
22	+22, 22., 0022, 22.0
−3.4	−3.40, −03.4
0.25	0.25, .250, +.25

10.2.1.1 MUMPS Collating Sequence

- An *empty string* ("") represents the first element in the MUMPS collating sequence. All other values follow an empty string. However, the empty string itself *cannot* be used as a subscript into an array (it is used as a starting and ending subscript value for the $ORDER and $QUERY functions).

- *Canonic numbers* follow the empty string and are ordered by numeric value. The number 147 follows 15, 212 follows 29, and so forth.

- All other strings follow the first two cases and are ordered in ASCII collating sequence.

> Canonic numbers collate before noncanonic strings when used
> as subscripts. Canonic numbers collate numerically, while
> noncanonic strings are ordered by the ASCII collating sequence.

It is important to remember that two different collating sequences are used in MUMPS. We have just covered the MUMPS collating sequence used for subscript ordering; the other is a pure ASCII collating sequence used by the FOLLOWS operator (see Section 5.3.2.3).

With a basic understanding of how MUMPS evaluates subscripts in the organization of arrays, let's examine why we should even care. In Example 10.1 we created a small database that was organized (subscripted) by employee name. Example 10.2 demonstrated how we could generate an alphabetized list of all employees. In Example 10.3 we will examine a subroutine to search for all employee names starting with a string of characters entered from the keyboard.

```
o|Search(Nam) ;Search ^Employee for names starting with Nam  |o
 |        New len,sub                                          |
 |        Set sub=Nam,len=$L(Nam) For  Do Srch1 Quit:sub=""    |
o|        Quit                                                 |o
 |Srch1 Set sub=$O(^Employee(sub)) Quit:sub=""                 |
 |        If $E(sub,1,len)'=$E(Nam,1,len) Set sub="" Quit      |
o|        Write !,?10,sub                                      |o
 |        Quit                                                 |
 |------------------------------------------------------------|
o|>For   Read !,"Employee: ",emp Quit:emp=""  Do Search(emp)← |o
 |                                                             |
 |Employee: L←                                                 |
o|            LARCH,MARY                                       |o
 |            LEWIS,AL                                         |
 |            LOCKWOOD,JOE                                     |
o|Employee: ←                                                 |o
 |>                                                            |
```

EXAMPLE 10.3. Partial global search

This example is similar to Example 10.2 except that only a small subsection of the global (those entries pointed to by subscripts starting with the character L) is searched. Note that, since the subscripts are returned in order, it is *not* necessary to perform an exhaustive search of the database for groups of related employee names; the $ORDER function begins its search for the first subscript following L and the search is terminated on the first returned subscript that does not start with L.

A slightly more complex example can be used to demonstrate how data are typically *sorted* in MUMPS. Using the same data, we sort all employees by sex and by age and then display the sorted list.

This example demonstrates a number of important techniques: it uses an

```
o|Sort    ;Sort ^Employee by Sex and then Age, Display results |o
 |        Kill ^Temp Set s="" For  Do srt Quit:s=""             |
 |        Do lst                                                |
o|        Quit                                                  |o
 |srt     Set s=$O(^Employee(s)) Quit:s=""                      |
 |        Set x=^Employee(s),age=$P(x,"$"),sex=$P(x,"$",2)      |
o|        Set ^Temp(sex,age)=s                                  |o
 |        Quit                                                  |
 |lst     Set (age,sex)=""                                      |
o|lst1    Set sex=$O(^Temp(sex)) Quit:sex=""  Write !,Sex       |o
 |lst2    Set age=$O(^Temp(sex,age)) Goto lst1:age=""           |
 |        Write !,?5,^Temp(sex,age),?25,"Age=",age              |
o|        Goto lst2                                             |o
 |_____|
 |>Do Sort←                                                     |
o|                                                              |o
 |F                                                             |
 |        LARCH,MARY          Age=22                            |
o|        MORRIS,JANE         Age=28                            |o
 |        KING,ALLICE         Age=46                            |
 |M                                                             |
o|        LOCKWOOD,JOE        Age=43                            |o
 |        LEWIS,AL            Age=45                            |
 |        KING,ROBERT         Age=48                            |
o|        ALLEN,ETHAN         Age=61                            |o
 |>                                                             |
```

EXAMPLE 10.4.   Sorting with globals

array (global) and automatic subscript ordering to perform sorts; it shows the use
of more than one subscript level, and one method for searching a multilevel array;
it also demonstrates the use of temporary scratch arrays (^Temp).

Sorting data in MUMPS is usually performed by creating temporary
arrays (local or global) using the fields to be sorted as keys
(subscripts) into the array.

In MUMPS, virtually all sorting applications are implemented using arrays
and the inherent collating sequence of subscripts. Sorts on multiple keys (sex and
age in this example) are achieved by using the sort keys as separate subscript levels,
with the primary key being the first-level subscript, the secondary key being the
second subscript level, and so on. Sorting data in this manner is both fast and easy
and simply requires a scratch global or array to hold the temporary results.

When sorting data on more than one key, the most significant key
is used as the first-level subscript; the least significant key
is used as the last subscript.

As a final topic in this section, we consider a relatively common situation in which the MUMPS collating order of subscripts must be carefully managed. For this example, we wish to order a number of addresses by their 5-digit ZIP codes. Consider the list of ZIP codes and their associated cities and states shown in Table 10.4.

TABLE 10.4 City and ZIP codes

City	ZIP Code
Albany, NY	12201
Bath, MI	48808
Forest, VA	24551
Ithaca, NY	14850
Plymouth, MA	02215
Sackets Harbor, NY	13685
Salinas, Puerto Rico	00751

If we attempt to sort these cities by ZIP code using the ZIP code as the primary subscript into a sorting array (for example, Set ˆsrt(ZIP) = adr), and then use the $ORDER function to retrieve the data, the subscripts will be returned in the order shown in Table 10.5.

TABLE 10.5 ZIP code ordering sequence

Subscript	City
12202	Albany, NY
13685	Sackets Harbor, NY
14850	Ithaca, NY
24551	Forest, VA
48808	Bath, MI
00751	Salinas, Puerto Rico
02215	Plymouth, MA

In this list the codes 12202-48808 are returned before the codes 00751 and 02215; 12202-48808 are handled as canonic numbers and collate *before* the non-canonic strings 00751 and 02215. Let's try another approach for creating the sorted index by forcing interpretation of the ZIP codes as canonic numbers. This could be achieved with the following code:

Set ˆsrt(+ ZIP) = adr

The plus sign (+) preceding the ZIP code forces evaluation of the field as numeric (that is, each ZIP code will be converted to a canonic number before it is used as a subscript). Retrieving data from the sorted array with $ORDER will return subscripts in the sequence shown in Table 10.6.

TABLE 10.6 ZIP codes order, numeric interpretation

Subscript	City
751	Salinas, Puerto Rico
2215	Plymouth, MA
12201	Albany, NY
13685	Sackets Harbor, NY
14850	Ithaca, NY
24551	Forest, VA
48808	Bath, MI

Notice that the ZIP codes returned as subscripts in this case are not all 5 digits in length; numeric conversion eliminates leading zeros. As the last example in this series, consider the effect of forcing a string interpretation of the ZIP code subscript with the following code:

Set ^srt("ZIP "_ZIP) = adr

Concatenating the string "ZIP " to the actual ZIP code forces all subscripts to be treated as noncanonic values and results in the sequence of subscripts returned by $ORDER as shown in Table 10.7.

TABLE 10.7 ZIP code order, string interpretation

Subscript	City
ZIP 00751	Salinas, Puerto Rico
ZIP 02215	Plymouth, MA
ZIP 12201	Albany, NY
ZIP 13685	Sackets Harbor, NY
ZIP 14850	Ithaca, NY
ZIP 24551	Forest, VA
ZIP 48808	Bath, MI

Forcing either pure numeric or pure string interpretation of the subscripts being entered into the global results in an identical retrieval order, but the actual subscript values are different. Remember that it is the method in which the data are originally *saved* in the array that determines the sequence with which it is retrieved using the $ORDER function.

10.2.2 $ORDER and $DATA Functions

Remember from our previous discussions that *nodes* in an array may or may not contain actual data. An array node (that is, a subscripted array reference) may contain data, may simply point to lower levels of data, or may contain data *and* point to lower levels of data. Consider the following array definition:

Ary(4) = "A"
Ary(4,10,3) = "B"
Ary(4,10,"xyz") = "C"
Ary(4,25) = "D"
Ary(5,10,3) = "E"

In this array, some nodes contain only data [for example, Ary(4,10,3), Ary(4,25), and so on], some are only pointers to data held at lower levels [for example, Ary(4,10), Ary(5), and so on], and some contain data and also point to data at a lower level [for example, Ary(4)]. Notice that, even though we did not explicitly assign values to some of the nodes [for example, Ary(5)], they do exist in the array; they are implicitly defined as pointer nodes when values are assigned to lower array nodes. The $ORDER function is used to retrieve the next highest subscript at a given level in the array, and the $DATA function can be used to test the type of node pointed to by the subscript.

> The $ORDER function is used to retrieve all subscripts at a given array level (local or global), regardless of whether or not a data value is associated with that array element.

The $ORDER function always returns the subscript of the next higher array node at a given level, regardless of the type of node it represents (that is, data, pointer, or data and pointer). However, attempting to retrieve data from a pointer node [for example, Set x = Ary(5)] results in an *error* since no data are associated with that node. The $DATA function can be used to interrogate the status of an array node prior to an attempt at retrieval. The possible values that can be returned by $DATA are indicated in Table 10.8.

TABLE 10.8 Results of $DATA function

$Data Value	Meaning	Example
0	Not defined	$D(Ary(50)) = 0
1	Data, no pointer	$D(Ary(4,25)) = 1
10	No data, pointer	$D(Ary(4,10)) = 10
11	Data and pointer	$D(Ary(4)) = 11

The $DATA function can be used to determine whether or not a given array node contains data and/or contains a pointer to data nodes at lower levels.

The value returned by the $DATA function is organized such that a simple numeric calculation can be used to determine whether or not the node contains data and/or whether or not it points to lower data structures.

```
o|>If $D(Ary(4))#2 Write "node contains data"↵            |o
 |node contains data                                      |
 |>If $D(Ary(4))\10 Write "node points to lower data"↵     |
o|node points to lower data                               |o
 |>                                                       |
```

EXAMPLE 10.5. Evaluation of $DATA function

Figure 10.1 displays the relationships between array references and the results of both the $ORDER and the $DATA functions for those references.

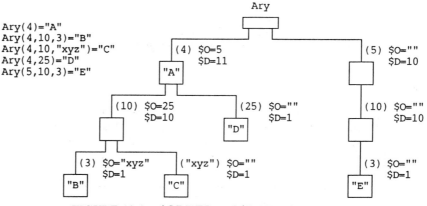

```
Ary(4)="A"
Ary(4,10,3)="B"
Ary(4,10,"xyz")="C"
Ary(4,25)="D"
Ary(5,10,3)="E"
```

FIGURE 10.1. $ORDER and $DATA functions

It is usually not necessary to check each data node before retrieving data from it; globals are usually searched in context, and the programmer knows whether or not data are located at a given level. Most arrays and globals are organized in a more orderly fashion than those used for these examples. Typically, each global level represents a logical level of organization for the data being saved, and the presence or absence of data associated with any particular level is by design convention. When examining data retrieval functions, the $GET function (Section 8.2.5) should also be considered.

10.3 Naked Global References

Naked syntax is a special syntax that can be used for global references as a shorthand form of notation. The basic format of naked syntax is similar to a full global reference without the global name. Consider the following example:

```
o|>SET ^XYZ(1,2,3,1)="Test"←
 |>SET ^(2)="New Test"←
 |>Write ^XYZ(1,2,3,2)←
o|New Test
 |>Write ^(1)←
 |Test
o|>
```

EXAMPLE 10.6. Naked global references

The first SET command uses the normal syntax for a global reference [^XYZ(1,2,3,1)], while the second SET uses naked syntax [^(2)]. Naked syntax is a shorthand form for referencing a global and is based on the *most recently executed global reference* (either full or naked syntax). MUMPS remembers the last global reference [for example, ^X(1,2,3,1)] for each process; this reference is saved as the internal naked indicator and is used to reconstruct the full global reference from the naked syntax.

> Naked syntax is a shorthand form of specifying the
> most recently referenced global node.

In a way, you can think of naked syntax somewhat like string substitution; in Example 10.6, the first naked reference is evaluated as ^XYZ(1,2,3,2). The name and level of the most recently executed global reference are substituted for the missing characters. Naked syntax can also reference data nodes at lower levels.

```
o|>SET ^XYZ(1,2,3,1)="Test"←
 |>SET ^(1,5)="New Test"←
 |>WRITE ^XYZ(1,2,3,1,5)←
o|New Test
```

EXAMPLE 10.7. Changing levels with naked syntax

In this example, the naked reference in the second SET command could be expanded to ^XYZ(1,2,3,1,5). If one is using naked reference, it is also important to note how MUMPS actually processes a command like SET. When MUMPS encounters a SET command, it *first* evaluates the expression to the right of the equal sign, and then it evaluates the reference on the left side of the equals sign. The internal naked indicator is set *at the time of evaluation*, not in a strict left to right precedence within the full command string. Consequently, some sequences of commands produce unexpected results.

```
o|>SET ^XYZ(22)=10←                              |o
 |>SET ^ABC(22)=250←                             |
 |>SET ^XYZ(22)=^(22)←                           |
o|>WRITE ^XYZ(22)←                               |o
 |250                                            |
```

EXAMPLE 10.8.   Effect of order of evaluation on naked syntax

The naked reference in the third line does *not* refer to ^XYZ, but rather to ^ABC, since the expression to the right of the equals sign is evaluated *before* the expression on the left side. When evaluating the right hand side, the most recently evaluated global reference is in the previous command line.

When using the SET command, expressions on the *right* side of the equals character are evaluated *before* the expression on the *left*.

The order of evaluation and its possible effect on naked syntax should also be explored for both conditional commands (or conditional arguments) and for the $SELECT function. In all cases where a command or argument is conditionalized, the TRUE/FALSE expression used to determine whether or not the command/argument is executed is evaluated *first*. If it FAILS, there is no further evaluation of the command or argument.

```
o|>Kill ^Test Set ^Test(1)=1←                                |o
 |>Set:^Test(1)="" ^Test(1,2)="Null" Set ^(2)=2←             |
 |>Write ^Test(1),!,^Test(2)←                                |
o|1                                                          |o
 |2                                                          |
 |>Write ^Test(1,2)←                                         |
o|<UNDEFINED> ERROR                                          |o
 |>                                                          |
```

EXAMPLE 10.9.   Effect of the order of evaluation on naked syntax

Since the conditioned SET command failed [^Test(1) did *not* equal an empty string], the expression ^Test(1,2) is never evaluated, and the naked syntax is left pointing to the first level of the global. The subsequent naked set command changes the value of ^Test(2), not ^Test(1,2).

Evaluation of the $SELECT command is similar. The basic format of $SELECT is:

$SELECT(EXPRESSION:VALUE,EXPRESSION:VALUE,...)

Each EXPRESSION in the argument string (from left to right) is evaluated until one is found that evaluates to TRUE (nonzero). Only at this time is the corresponding VALUE expression evaluated.

Naked reference, like command abbreviation, is designed to reduce the number of characters that have to be evaluated at execution time. With the more advanced compiled versions of MUMPS available today, there is usually little or no speed advantage in using naked syntax. Worse, many problems are associated with its use, especially when modifying existing routines and inadvertently inserting other global references before a naked reference. Insertion of any code using a global reference between the time the internal naked indicator was set and the time naked syntax is used will change the internal naked indicator and can have serious consequences. Naked references are *not* preserved before calling subroutines or extrinsic functions.

Programmers should exercise caution when using naked global references.

10.4 The LOCK Command

The <u>LOCK</u> command provides the MUMPS programmer with a mechanism to limit access by other processes to an entire global, a branch of a global, or to a single global node. The locking mechanism is not absolute, requiring programming *conventions* to work. A locked global node can still be retrieved or even changed by other processes; all the LOCK command does is to make that node unavailable for locking by other processes.

A LOCK command prevents other processes from being able to LOCK the same global branches; it does *not* prevent access to these branches by other processes that do not use the LOCK command.

Typically, the LOCK command is used to reserve one or more global references when records are being updated. It is used to prevent other processes from modifying the data between the time the original data are extracted from the global and when the updated information is refiled. When the nonincremental form of the LOCK command is used (for example, <u>LOCK ^X</u>) it first unLOCKS all previously locked references before locking the new reference(s).

> The nonincremental form of the LOCK command unLOCKS all previously LOCKed references before attempting to LOCK the current reference(s).

```
o|Edit   ;Edit the data associated with a patient.          |o
 |GetID  Set PID=$$GetPat Quit:PID=""                        |
 |       Lock +^PatRec(PID):0                                 |
o|       Else  Write *7,"Sorry, IN-USE" Goto GetID           |o
 |       Set OLD=$$GetRec(PID)                                |
 |       Do EDIT(OLD,.NEW) Goto Done:OLD=NEW                  |
o|       Do Save(PID,NEW)                                     |o
 |Done   Lock -^PatRec(PID)                                   |
 |       Goto GetID                                           |
```

EXAMPLE 10.10.   Incremental LOCK command

In Example 10.10, as soon as we identify the record to be edited and *before* we retrieve any existing data under that record, we first LOCK that branch of the global. As long as all processes that might alter the record also attempt to LOCK the record in a similar fashion, we can prevent update conflicts.

The incremental and decremental forms of the LOCK command have the advantage of not altering any existing lock elements for this process. They are particularly useful in general-purpose subroutines that may be called from a number of different routines.

> Incremental and decremental LOCK commands can be used without affecting previous LOCK commands for a given process.

Special attention should be paid when using the incremental form of the LOCK command to pair each incremental lock with an incremental unlock. Each time the incremental LOCK is performed the lock is stacked; each time an incremental unlock is performed, one lock argument is unstacked. If a global reference is inadvertently stacked more times than it is unstacked, it will remain locked to other processes. The coupling of incremental locks and unlocks can become especially important when handling errors in which the normal processing of commands may be aborted. Remember that a normal LOCK command without arguments will always unlock *all* locked references for a process, regardless of how they were initiated or how many are stacked.

In general, it is only necessary to lock global nodes when doing data entry or editing functions. Search programs that only retrieve data from the global usually do not have to attempt to lock nodes before accessing them.

10.5 Global Extensions

A number of implementor-specific techniques are used to increase access to databases (across directories or networked computers), ensure database integrity, and increase the throughput when processing global data. These techniques are described in general terms next, but you should consult your system manuals for the availability and specifics of these features.

10.5.1 Distributed Databases

In Section 2.2.3, we introduced the concept of global and routine directories. When a process is initiated, it is assigned a partition and a disk directory, which will be referenced when storing or retrieving data (either globals or routines). Each directory is unique and separate from other directories; different versions of the same routine or global can reside in different directories. Directories may share a common disk, be spread out over a number of disks, or, in networked systems, reside on separate computers. In many instances it is desirable, or even essential, to have access to data residing in directories other than the one currently associated with the process, and most implementors provide one or more techniques to support this need.

Within the constraints established by security codes (Section 10.5.4), systems supporting distributed databases permit a process to lock, read, or change global data in another directory or even another networked MUMPS system. To do this, the system must have additional information on each global so referenced. The directory to be accessed must be identified and, on networked systems, the system in which the directory resides must also be defined. Two basic approaches are used to supply this information: implicit definitions for each global and explicit distributed references.

Implicit definitions for individual globals are usually established with a system utility supplied by the implementor. Individual globals can be flagged such that each reference to that global, regardless of the computer or directory under which a process is running, will automatically be mapped to a specified computer and directory. No change in global syntax is required, and such mapping is system wide. In many respects, library globals are in the category of implicitly defined references. Library globals all start with the percent character (%) and usually reside in the library or manager directory for a given system. All references to globals starting with a percent character are automatically mapped to the appropriate directory on the system under which the process is running. Other implicitly defined references are similar to library references but may map outside of the current computer when in a networked environment.

The second form of distributed global reference is the explicit reference. These are cases in which the syntax of the global reference is modified to include specific system and/or directory information that can alter the location of the global. Usually, the syntactic changes in a global reference involve defining the desired computer and directory in square brackets ([]) after the up-arrow but before the global name.

^[System,Directory]Name(Subscripts)

Advanced Global Techniques   Chap. 10

Designations for both the <u>System</u> and <u>Directory</u> are implementation specific. Usually, a null value for the <u>System</u> will map the reference to the system on which the process is running, and a null value for the <u>Directory</u> will map to the default directory associated with the process. The use of square-bracket syntax for global references is *not* part of the MUMPS standard.

10.5.2 Replication

Replication is a process whereby additions or deletions to specified globals will automatically be duplicated in a global of the same name in a different directory; in a networked system the directory may reside on a different computer. A definition of which globals are to be replicated and where the duplicate copies will reside is usually established with a system utility supplied by the implementor.

Replication is most frequently used in a networked environment where multiple copies of the same global are maintained on more than one computer. Replicating primary databases to other systems or disks is one way of preventing loss of data due to hardware failures. In supporting multiple copies of the same database on different machines, processes can be distributed such that computer "hogs" (such as exhaustive searches) can be run on a different computer to minimize the impact on interactive data entry. The advantages of replicating the database rather than using implicit or explicit global references are many. The replicated database is a form of backup should anything go wrong with the primary copy. Usually, the changes to a database (SETs and KILLs) are relatively limited compared to the number of accesses performed during an exhaustive search; replicating changes to a database involves far fewer network accesses than frequent searching of a database across systems.

10.5.3 Journaling

Journaling global transactions is a technique used, in conjunction with periodic backup of globals, to ensure against the loss of data in the event of a hardware failure or other catastrophic loss of data. When journaling for a global is enabled, a separate record of each change to that global is recorded as a journal entry. The journal file usually contains change records from a variety of globals; the entries are inserted sequentially in the journal file depending on the actual order in which they were processed.

Usually the journal file consists of a series of sequential entries for each SET or KILL command affecting a journaled global. Each SET command results in two entries in the journal file: the first entry is a full reference of the global node being SET [for example, ^Test(1,"CBC",36445)] and the second is the data value used to set the node (for example, "36457\++\Rotochem"). Each KILL command results in a single entry in the journal file containing the full global reference of the node being KILLed. Note that *only* the specific node being killed is referenced in the journal file. Neither the data associated with that node nor any information on lower level nodes that may also be deleted as a result of the KILL command is recorded as part of the journal file. Each entry in the journal file contains information concerning the type of entry (SET or KILL), and many implementations also include additional information, such as the principal device and $JOB number associated with the process that made the change to the global.

Using both periodic backups of the entire database (often a time-consuming process) and incremental backups of the journal file (a much quicker process), databases can be conveniently protected from most catastrophic failures.

The journal file is typically used to recover the data entered since the last complete backup of a global was made. In this way, incremental changes made to the global since the last backup can be applied to the backed-up version of the global to restore its structure to that immediately preceding the failure. Journal files are *not* a complete representation of the global, but rather a list of the incremental changes made to that file; they are valuable *only* in restoring a global from a previously saved backup.

Journaling globals is *not* a substitute for a sound program of backing up databases.

There is overhead involved in journaling globals, since each SET or KILL command that changes the journaled globals also requires setting nodes in the journal file. It is probably wise to journal only primary data globals and perhaps those inverted indexes that may be difficult to rebuild from the primary files. Journaling of scratch globals should be avoided.

10.5.4 Global Security

MUMPS is notoriously lax about security of globals. Those implementations that do provide some form of security usually do so by establishing limits to accessing or changing a specified global from processes running outside the directory in which the global resides. In many implementations, for example, an *entire* global can be protected such that processes in other directories can READ only, READ and WRITE, READ WRITE and DELETE, or have NO ACCESS to it. In many layered MUMPS systems, it may be possible to employ the system security features of the host operating system to applications running in the MUMPS environment.

It is *not* generally possible to restrict access to specific parts or fields of data within a global. Indeed, individual programs can limit the access of users, but such restrictions have to be built into the program. A programmer in DIRECT mode generally has the ability to access any and all global nodes in the directory in which they are working.

10.6 Advanced Examples: Global Dumps and Copy Utilities

As a final topic for this chapter, we discuss some advanced techniques for scanning the contents of a global or selected branches of a global. The techniques employed in these examples make use of parameter passing, the NEW command, subscript indirection, and the $ORDER and $DATA functions.

Writing a general-purpose utility to scan globals or global branches is complicated by the fact that the target global can be of any arbitrary depth (that is, can have an arbitrary number of subscripts). Additionally, a global node at any given location may contain only data, may only be a pointer to data at a lower global level, or both. Code such as that demonstrated in Example 8.35 is fine if we know the maximum number of levels in the target global, but is potentially large and redundant for multiple-level globals.

In the examples that follow, we employ a programming technique referred to as *recursive programming* in which a subroutine calls itself in order to resolve ambiguities such as a variable number of subscript levels. While recursive subroutines were sometimes employed in the past, they were difficult to implement due to the shared variable environment; the programmer usually had to save all variables used within the subroutine as array elements, indexed by the nesting level of the subroutine. With the recent addition of parameter passing and the NEW command, and the automatic stacking and unstacking of the variable environment, recursive programming techniques are likely to become more prevalent.

As a first example, we develop a general-purpose utility program to dump the contents of a global or global branch to the terminal. The first step in creating this utility is to write the control section requesting a starting global reference from the user.

```
o|Gutil ;Global Utilities                                          |o
 |dump   ;Display global or global branch on terminal               |
 |       New %g                                                     |
o|       Write !!,$T(+0)," -- Dump a global subtree"                |o
 |GETgr  Write !,"Starting Reference: " Set %g=$$GR                 |
 |       Goto GETgr:%g="?" Quit:%g=""                               |
o|       Do Display(%g) Goto GETgr                                  |o
 |       ;                                                          |
 |GR()   ;Return valid global reference -or- "" -or- "?"            |
o|       New %rf                                                    |o
 |       Read %rf Goto GRend:"?"[%rf  Set:%rf'?1"^".E %rf="^" %rf   |
 |       If %rf'?1"^"1A.E Write *7,"??" Set %rf="?" Goto GRend      |
o|       If '$D(@%rf) Write *7," ?? undefined" Set %rf="?"          |o
 |GRend  Do:%rf="?" Help                                            |
 |       Quit %rf                                                   |
o|       ;                                                          |o
 |Help   Write !!,"Global reference like ""^XYZ"" or ""^x(1,2)"""   |
 |       Write !,"Variables used as subscripts must already exist",!|
o|       Quit                                                       |o
```

EXAMPLE 10.11. Control code for global dump; Routine continued in Example 10.12 and documented in Appendix G

Most of this code should be pretty much self-explanatory. The function $$GR is used to read a global reference from the keyboard. A null entry (<ENTER> only) is used to terminate the program. If a "?" is entered or an erroneous global reference is detected, a brief help message is displayed, the function returns a "?", and the question is repeated. Otherwise, the function returns a valid global reference. This subroutine is made a general-purpose function with the thought that it can also be shared with the global copy utility to be discussed next.

Notice that the main utility and the $$GR function both use internal variables beginning with the percent character (%g and %rf). Variables starting with a % are usually reserved for library routines and, even though we NEW both, we don't want to conflict with the local symbol table. The programmer may have already established the values for one or more local variables to be used as subscripts in the global reference entered from the keyboard. As long as they do not begin with a %, they will be available to all parts of the utility program and will not be altered. Now let's get down to the meat of the program.

```
  o|       ;                                                        |o
1 |Display(%gr) ;Display the subtree defined by %gr                 |
2 |       New %d,%s Set %s=""                                       |
3 o|      Set %d=$D(@%gr) Write:%d#10 !,%gr,"=",@%gr Quit:'(%d\10)  |o
4 |Dloop  Set %s=$O(@%gr@(%s)) Quit:%s=""                           |
5 |       If gr?.E1")" Do Display($E(%gr,1,$L(%gr)-1)_","""_%s_""")")|
6 o|      Else  Do Display(%g_"("""_%s_""")")                       |o
7 |       Goto Dloop                                                |
```

EXAMPLE 10.12.   Recursive subroutine to dump global branch

The subroutine Display is recursive (that is, it is called by itself), displaying all branches of the global reference specified by the calling parameter (%gr) containing data, regardless of the underlying global structure. Let us examine this code line by line to clarify the process.

Line	Description
1	This is the main entry point of the subroutine. The parameter being passed in (%gr) is the global reference being dumped and can assume two basic formats: ^Global with no subscripts if we are dumping the entire global, or ^Global(sub1,sub2,...) if we are dumping one of the branches of the global.
2	In this line, we first NEW the two locally used variables %d (used to hold the $DATA evaluation of the current global reference) and %s (used to find any subscripts held below the current global reference). We then initialize %s to an empty string used to check the lower subscript levels with the $ORDER function.
3	If the current global reference contains data (that is, %d=1 or %d=11), then WRITE out both the reference and the associated data value. Quit the subroutine if there are no lower data structures under the current reference (that is, %d<10 and %d'=11).
4	Dloop is the head of an internal loop used to pick up the next subscript below the current global reference. If none, QUIT the subroutine.
5	If the current global reference contains subscripts (the most frequent

Line	Description

case), recursively call the subroutine with a new global reference calculated from the current reference and the next level subscript. This involves stripping off the last) character and adding the new subscript. For example, if %gr = "^Test(1,2)" and the %s = 4, the actual parameter passed to <u>Display</u> would be "^Test(1,2,4)".

6   This is a special check for the case where the current global reference is not subscripted (that is, it is a global name such as "^Test"). The only time this case will occur is the first time <u>Display</u> is called and the user has specified a dump of the entire global. Each recursive call to <u>Display</u> will have subscripts associated with the global reference.

7   Loop back and check for the next subscript under the current global reference.

```
o|>Kill ^Test Set ^Test="Test Global"←          |o
 |>Set  ^Test(1,2,3)="one,two,three"←           |
 |>Set  ^Test(2)="two",^Test(2,3)="two,three"←  |
o|>Set  ^Test(2,4,1)="two,four,one"←            |o
 |>Set  ^(2)="two,four,two",^(3)="two,four,three"← |
 |>                                             |
```

EXAMPLE 10.13.   Initialize test database ^Test

After initializing the test database <u>^Test</u>, we can exercise the utility as shown in the next example.

```
o|>Kill Set S1=2,S2=4 Do dump^Gutil←            |o
 |                                              |
 |Gutil — Dump a global subtree                 |
o|Starting Reference: ^Test←                    |o
 |^Test=Test Global                             |
 |^Test(1,2,3)=one,two,three                    |
o|^Test(2)=two                                  |o
 |^Test(2,3)=two,three                          |
 |^Test(2,4,1)=two,four,one                     |
o|^Test(2,4,2)=two,four,two                     |o
 |^Test(2,4,3)=two,four,three                   |
 |                                              |
o|Starting Reference: ^Test(S1,S2)←             |o
 |^Test(2,4,1)=two,four,one                     |
 |^Test(2,4,2)=two,four,two                     |
o|^Test(2,4,3)=two,four,three                   |o
 |                                              |
 |Starting Reference: ←                         |
o|>                                             |o
```

EXAMPLE 10.14.   Dumping global subtrees

Much of the value of this utility subroutine could also be accomplished using the $QUERY function, but the next example, demonstrating copying one subtree to another, would be more difficult to achieve.

Example 10.15 incorporates many of the concepts developed in the previous example and is used to copy one global or global branch to another global. The starting points for the source and destination do *not* have to be at the same logical level for the target and destination globals. We will not show the control program (that is, the code that reads the source and destination references), but only the subroutine that performs the actual copy.

```
o|Copy(%f,%t) ;Copy global subtree %f to %t                        |o
 |        New %d,%s Set %s=""                                       |
 |        Set %d=$D(@%f) Set:%d#10 @%t=@%f Quit:'(%d\10)            |
o|Cloop   Set %s=$O(@%f@(%s)) Quit:%s=""                            |o
 |        Do Copy($$Cref(%f),$$Cref(%t))                            |
 |        Goto Cloop                                                |
o|Cref(%g) ;build a global reference from %g and %s                 |o
 |        Quit:%g?.E1")" $E(%g,1,$L(%g)-1)_",""" _%s_ """)"         |
 |        Quit %g_"("""_%s_ """)"                                   |
```

EXAMPLE 10.15. Copy a global subtree

Given the description of the dump subroutine presented in Example 10.12, you should not have trouble following the code given in this example. The control program that invokes the <u>Copy</u> utility will have to request both a source and a destination reference from the keyboard. Additionally, it should check to see if the destination global reference already exists. If so, it should ask the user if they want to merge the two (that is, add the source branch to the destination branch) or whether they wish to KILL the destination branch before starting the copy procedure.

10.7 Database Design

A database consists of a number of discrete pieces of information with each unique observation called a *data element*. Each observation can be logically organized into *records*, with each data element becoming a *field* within the record. Related records are organized together to form a *file* (or in MUMPS terms, a *global*), and all the files necessary for a particular application are referred to as a *database*.

> Data is usually categorized as:
> Field: a unique observation or data element.
> Record: one or more fields, often separated by delimiters.
> File: a collection of records (a global).
> Database: the collection of all files for an application.

Individual records are organized by *keys* or pointers to those records. In MUMPS the keys are defined as subscripts into the global. Individual globals can contain many different types of records, usually based on the values or sequences of the keys.

Keys into a file are data elements used to identify records. In MUMPS, keys take the form of subscripts into the global.

Consider a simple global design to hold information concerning patient visits to a hospital. In this global, we wish to record a number of data elements for each patient seen. Some elements are simple and nonrepeating (name, address, date of birth, and so on), while others might be repeated several times (date of admission and discharge, attending clinician, problems, diagnoses, prescriptions, and so on). An abbreviated list of the data elements that might be recorded for patients is shown in Table 10.9. These elements represent but a few of those that could be recorded, but even this short list demonstrates the structured nature of the data elements. We can organize these data elements into groups of related data to form data records as shown in Table 10.10.

TABLE 10.9. Data elements for a hospital record

Patient Identification Number (ID)
Patient Name
Patient Sex
Patient Date of Birth (DOB)
Patient Address (street, city, state, ZIP code)
Patient Phone Number
   Visit Date of Admission
   Visit Date of Discharge
   Visit Attending Physician
      Problems
      Procedures Performed
      Drugs Prescribed
      Diagnoses

If we examine the relationships that exist between these records, we can see that each patient has a single ID record, each ID record can be associated with one or more VISIT records, each VISIT record can be associated with one or more PROBLEM records, and so on. The task, then, is to organize these records in such a fashion that related records are kept together, and access to information concerning a particular patient is optimized.

The organization of records within a file is called *indexing* and is achieved in MUMPS by using subscripts. We need to define *keys* (subscripts) that point to the individual records. The keys or subscripts into a global must be unique at each

TABLE 10.10. Patient data elements organized into records

Patient ID Record:	ID | Name | Sex | DOB | Street | City | State | Zip | Phone
Visit Record:	Admission Date | Discharge Date | Attending Physician
Problem Record:	Problem 1 | Problem 2 | . . . | Problem n
Procedure Record:	Procedure 1 | Procedure 2 | . . . | Procedure n
Drug Record:	Drug 1 | Drug 2 | . . . | Drug n
Diagnoses Record:	Diagnosis 1 | Diagnosis 2 | . . . | Diagnosis n

subscript level, or we would not be able to identify logical records. Figure 10.2 represents one way of organizing the records in Table 10.10 into a keyed file.

The keys in this figure are represented by the subscripts enclosed in parentheses. Each subscript for a given level and under a given branch of the global must be unique (for example, each ID number must be unique, and each admission date for a given ID number must be unique) to avoid record conflicts.

Individual *records* in the database consist of one or more *fields* of data; each record is placed in a global node with individual fields separated from each other by a delimiting character. For example, the <u>Patient ID Record</u> might be recorded as

Patient ID Record = **"Name;Street;City;State;ZIP;Phone"**

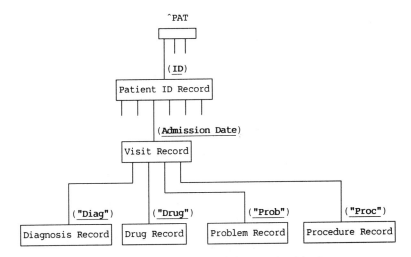

FIGURE 10.2. Patient records organized by keys

where the semicolon character is used internally as a field separator. The choice of the character(s) used to separate fields is up to the discretion of the programmer, but some care should be taken in its choice. Regardless of the delimiting character(s) chosen, the programmer must ensure that keyboard entries for the record fields do *not* contain that character. All programs accessing the record will undoubtedly use the $PIECE function to parse out individual fields, and delimiting characters appearing within a field will cause unpredictable results.

> Individual fields within a MUMPS record are usually of variable length with an arbitrary character sequence defined as field delimiters.

Some data entry and edit applications specifically check all answers to ensure that no control characters (decimal value of less than 32) have been entered inadvertently (for example, <u>If ans?.E1C.E Do Error</u>), and some programmers are tempted to use one of these control characters as field separators [for example, <u>Set rec = Name_$C(10)_Street_$C(10)_...</u>]. Care should be exercised when using this approach. In the first place, since most control characters are nonprinting, it may not be clear where the field separators are located when displaying the contents of a global.

A second consideration is that many control characters may affect the device to which a global is being dumped [for example, using $C(10) will usually cause line feeds between fields when dumping a global to a video terminal or printer]. In general, it is more desirable to use a special graphics character as a field separator and then ensure that *no* input for any of the fields can contain that character.

Globals in most applications will be accessed in different ways for different functions; stated another way, the optimum organization of a global depends on one's point of reference. In general, no single point of reference will satisfy all needs, and yet the choice of global design will have a significant impact on the speed with which a function executes. The global design presented in Figure 10.2 facilitates access to individual records, but a search for all patients prescribed a given drug would require an exhaustive search of the entire global. A good rule of thumb when designing a data file is to organize it by keys that reflect the most frequent use of the global; we can create other support globals to represent different points of reference.

> Files (globals) should generally be organized to reflect their most frequent use (that is, point of reference).

In addition to the primary data file, we can recognize the need for additional support data files. One type of support file is called an *inverted* or *key* file and is used to represent alternative points of reference to records within the primary file. Another type of support file is a *reference* index used to define coded data elements in the primary file.

10.7.1 Inverted or Key Indexes

The basic structure of ^PAT shown in Figure 10.2 reflects one of many possible organizations of patient records. It is well designed for retrieving information on a specific patient, given that the patient's ID number is known. But what if we only have the patient's name? With the defined global structure, we would have to perform an exhaustive search of the first level of the global for possible matches. A faster alternative to this common need is desirable.

One alternative is to create a second file organized by patient name and containing a pointer (patient ID number) back to the primary file. Such files are called inverted or key indexes and are designed to permit rapid access to individual records based on other points of reference. Using such an index, we can develop subroutines to look up patient ID numbers given their name (or a partial spelling of the name). Figure 10.3 depicts the structure of a key index to meet these needs.

> Key or inverted indexes are used to reflect other points of
> reference than those designated by the keys in the primary file.

Key indexes represent a trade-off between space and speed; they duplicate data in the primary database organized by different keys, and they can be used to reduce the time required to retrieve a record by a secondary key. If space and update time were not major concerns, we could create separate inverted indexes for each of the data fields in the primary index. Unfortunately, space is usually an important consideration in the design of an application. We usually try to reserve the use of key indexes for those fields in which rapid look-up is critical.

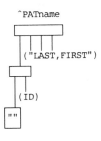

FIGURE 10.3. Key index organized by patient name

Notice that all the data in the global of Figure 10.3 are held as subscripts, and the only data node ['PATname("LAST,FIRST",ID) = ""] is an empty string used to define the subscripts. This structure is employed to ensure a unique key for each patient name; it is possible for different patients to have the same name. Example 10.16 demonstrates a subroutine that could be used to retrieve a patient ID number, given their name (or partial name). To avoid possible data entry ambiguities, the patient name used as the first-level subscript is the uppercase version of the name held in the primary file (^PAT).

```
GetPat() ;Return patient ID number (null if none chosen)
        New first,FIRST,ID,last,LAST,lf,ll,pat,sub,x
Read    Read !,"Patient ID (or NAME for search): ",pat
        Goto GPx:pat=""!(pat?1N.N) Set pat=$$UP^%Zu(pat)
        Set last=$P(pat,","),first=$P(pat,",",2)
        Set sub=last,ll=$L(last),lf=$L(first)
Loop1   Set sub=$O(^PATname(sub)) Goto Read:sub=""
        Set LAST=$P(^(sub),","),FIRST=$P(^(sub),",",2)
        Goto Read:$E(LAST,1,ll)'=last
        Goto Loop1:$E(FIRST,1,lf)'=first Set ID=""
Loop2   Set ID=$O(^PATname(sub,ID)) Goto Loop1:ID=""
        Set x=^PAT(ID) Write !,ID,?5,$P(x,";"),"  "
        Write $P(x,";",2),"  ",$P(x,";",3),"  ",$P(x,";",3)
        Goto Loop2
        Quit pat
```

EXAMPLE 10.16. Extrinsic function to find patient ID number from a name

This extrinsic function prompts the user for a patient ID number or name. A nonnumeric entry is assumed to be a name, and any possible matches to that name are displayed, along with auxiliary information from the main patient file to aid the user in identifying the patient. This example assumes that the patient ID record in the main file is of the following format:

$$^PAT(ID) = ``Name;Sreet;City;Sate;ZIP;Phone''$$

with the semicolon character used to delimit individual fields within the record. A sample session using this function is displayed in the next example.

```
Patient ID (or NAME for search): Smith,R←
32145   Smith,Rodger 55 State St., Kingston, NY
15469   Smith,Roy 1231 West King Rd, Syracuse, NY
Patient ID (or NAME for search): SM,←
72334   Small,Alice   15 West Way, New Bolton Center, PA
87910   Small,Alice   100 Highbush Rd., Boston, MA
19034   Smith,Allen   1291 West 57th St., New York, NY
32145   Smith,Rodger  55 State St., Kingston, NY
15469   Smith,Roy     1231 West King Rd., Syracuse, NY
10034   Smith,Tanya   100 Updike Rd., Dryden, NY
51034   Smythe,Alex   26 Garden Ave., Schenectady, NY
Patient ID (or NAME for search): 87910←
```

EXAMPLE 10.17. Sample using the name search function in Example 10.16

Another interesting variation of searching for names is the use of the *Soundex* coding system. Soundex codes are used to group English surnames into common groups based on phonetics. This technique is often used to store keys to the primary file in cases where spelling errors may make retrieval of the correct name difficult. The soundex coding scheme groups all similar names into a common code by converting each name into a code containing four or less characters. The code is created in the following manner:

- Save the first letter of the name.
- Assign the following digits to each characters in the name:
  - 0   letters A, E, H, I, O, U, W, or Y
  - 1   letters B, F, P or V
  - 2   letters C, G, J, K, Q, S, X, or Z
  - 3   letters D or T
  - 4   letter L
  - 5   letters M or N
  - 6   letter R
- In cases where two or more adjacent digits have the same value, drop all but the first occurrence.
- Eliminate all zeros (A, E, H, I, O, U, W, Y) from the code *after* the first digit (that is, retain the first digit even if it is a zero).
- Replace the first digit in the code with the first letter of the name saved in step 1.
- Truncate the final code to four characters (that is, letter, digit, digit, digit). Note that the original soundex coding scheme pads out codes of less than four characters with trailing zeros, but this is unnecessary in MUMPS.

```
o|SDX(Name) ;Extrinsic function to return SOUNDEX code        |o
 |     New c,i,fl,Last,lc,sdx,x                                 |
 |     Set Last=$$UP^%Z($P(Name,",")),fl=$E(Last)              |
o|       Set sdx=$TR(Last,"BFPVCGJKQSXZDTLMNRAEHIOUWY","11112|o
 |..22222233455600000000")                                      |
 |       Set (c,lc,x)=""                                        |
o|       For i=1:1:$L(sdx) Set c=$E(sdx,i) If c'=lc Set x=x_c|o
 |..,lc=c                                                       |
 |       Quit fc_$E($TR($E(x,2,99),"0",""),2,3)                |
```

EXAMPLE 10.18.   Extrinsic function to compute soundex code

The $TRANSLATE function converts the characters in the name to the appropriate digits, while the FOR loop is used to remove adjacent repeating digits. Using this algorithm, the name "**Lewkowicz**" results in a soundex code of "**L22**", as do the names LaCasse, Laczak, Lagoze, Laskowski, Lissick, Lucas, and Lyczkowski. A step by step analysis of converting "**Lewkowicz**" to its soundex equivalent follows:

- Save the first letter of the name, "L".
- Convert the name to digits → "400200022"
- Drop identical adjacent digits → "40202"

- Eliminate zeros *after* first character → "422"
- Replace first digit with first letter → "**L22**"

We could easily modify the global structure depicted in Figure 10.3 to use the soundex code rather than the name for the first-level subscript. Minor modifications to the subroutine presented in Example 10.16 would then permit searches on names by soundex code.

As mentioned earlier, inverted indexes represent a trade-off between disk space, update time, and execution speed. The number and types of inverted indexes used in a given application depend on the perceived needs of the user community. If it is essential to be able to look up records by data elements that are not used as the primary key in the main database, and the space for an inverted index can be accommodated, then the use of an inverted index may be desirable. Searches based on other data fields can still be performed, but will usually take longer since they may require an exhaustive search of the main data file.

10.7.2 Reference Files

Reference files are used to define data elements that are held in the main database as coded entities (such as the problem list and the diagnoses list).

> Reference files are used to hold descriptions of encoded data fields in the primary data file.

As an example, consider the data elements shown in Table 10.10. We could store the full name of the Attending Physician in the main patient file. Another approach is to assign each physician a unique *code number* and maintain a separate global indexed by the code and containing the physician's name; only the *code* would be stored in the main patient file.

Originally, the driving forces for encoding data were the poor string handling capabilities of most computer languages and the need to save space. When computers were first employed for database management applications, data storage was expensive, and saving a few bytes per record made substantial fiscal differences. In the early 1970s, for example, 1 megabyte (1 million characters) of disk storage cost approximately $10,000. By 1986 the cost for the same amount of disk storage had dropped to under $25. Thus the need to conserve space is no longer an overriding reason for encoding data. Indeed, the personnel costs associated with programming, encoding, and decoding data often outweigh any potential savings in storage costs.

A second reason frequently cited for encoding data is to standardize nomenclature. A standard nomenclature, however, does not require a coding system per se, but only a standardized, controlled vocabulary such as the key words used in many bibliographic retrieval systems. Many computer languages, including MUMPS, support sufficiently powerful string search capabilities that individual records could easily be located by key word searches (such as the NAME search in Example 10.16).

The most important reason for encoding data is in its potential to improve retrieval. The final worth of a recording system is its ability to faithfully retrieve data. Two concepts of data retrieval are important: the system's *precision* and *recall*. *Precision* is the ratio of the number of relevant records found in a search compared to the total number of records retrieved. In general, the more elaborate the coding system, the greater the precision. *Recall* is the number of cases found compared to the total number of relevant cases in the database. In general, there is an inverse relationship between recall and precision; efforts to enhance one often have the effect of reducing the other.

The most compelling reason to code data is to improve retrieval.

Adequate recall requires a standardized nomenclature. Each unique entity must have a single, standard representation (code or name). Unless all synonyms map to the same name, recall will be poor, since the entity may be filed under several different headings. Retrieval will require searching every conceivable synonym and, even so, it could be incomplete. Incomplete retrieval may introduce biases that lead to erroneous conclusions in retrospective analysis.

Conversely, a system must have sufficient precision to identify only those records that are relevant to the search. If a large number of the records found are irrelevant, inordinate time will be wasted separating the relevant records from others manually, and the records system will have failed an important task.

Most records systems are designed to support many different purposes, and the recording system must support retrospective analysis from differing points of view. A key word search cannot do this, even if a standard vocabulary were employed to resolve the problem of multiple synonyms for a single entity. While such a system could correctly retrieve records with a unique key or even all records containing a common key, it could *not* be used to retrieve *groups* of like cases. For example, it would be difficult to search an employee database for all technical personnel unless each engineer, laboratory technician, computer programmer, and the like, also had been cross-coded to "technical personnel". While such cross-coding might anticipate some common queries, it would be impossible to anticipate all the diverse reasons for which a database might be consulted, and it also would be difficult to ensure accuracy and consistency.

These considerations lead to the design of coding systems that attempt to maximize both precision and recall. Such systems need to be *hierarchical* so that each entity to be recorded can be identified as specifically as possible (to maximize

```
                    Domestic marketing
                        Northeastern U.S.
                            Maine
                                Portland
                            New York
                                New York
                                Albany
                                Buffalo
                            Pennsylvania
                                Philadelphia
                                Scranton
                            Massachusetts
                                Boston
                                .
                                .
                                .
                        Southwestern U.S.
                            .
                            .
                            .
                    Foreign marketing
                        Europe
                        Japan
                            .
                            .
                            .
```

FIGURE 10.4. One possible hierarchy for organizing a marketing department

precision) and yet be automatically grouped for retrieval at a higher level or gen-
erality (to increase recall). For example, a segment of a hierarchical scheme for
encoding a marketing department might be as shown in Figure 10.4.

In a hierarchical organization, each general category is considered to include
all more specific categories. Even this approach has limitations. Any given hierarchy
can only accommodate one point of reference; the marketing department could be
organized by location (as in Figure 10.4), or by function (advertising, retail outlets,
customer relations), but not by both. A particular question can be addressed more
advantageously from one viewpoint rather than the other, and the choice of the
hierarchy should be dependent on the most frequently used viewpoint. Other points
of view can be accommodated by additional cross-reference files or multiaxial
coding systems.

Multiaxial coding systems are often used in medical computing to encode
diagnoses or procedures to represent multiple viewpoints within the same code. A
diagnosis might consist of one field defining a body site (for example, the left
ventricular wall of the heart), another field defining the functional change at that
location (inflammation), and a third field defining the agent causing the problem
(due to trauma). Each field within the diagnosis code is hierarchical; the three
fields are combined to create a single diagnosis code representing three different
points of reference.

When choosing a coding system, carefully consider how it could be organized
to maximize subsequent retrievals.

10.8 Searching and Sorting

We have already seen numerous examples of searching a global based on subscript
values (for instance, Example 10.16); searches based on data elements stored in
global nodes are similar but usually require an exhaustive search of one or more

logical global levels. Sorting information in MUMPS is delightfully easy if we take advantage of the structure and automatic collating order of globals. Suppose, for example, that we wish to search the patient index depicted in Figure 10.2 for all patients seen by a particular attending physician in order to generate a report sorted alphabetically by state, then city, and then by the patient's name.

This will require a two-level search of ^PAT to identify the physician (the attending physician is held in the VISIT record indexed by the patient ID number and then the admitting date). We will assume the following structures for the patient ID record and the Visit record:

```
^PAT(ID)="Name;Street;City;State;ZIP;Phone"
^PAT(ID,VISIT)="Admission Data;Discharge Date;Physician Code"
```

Example 10.19 depicts a routine used to search and print all cases seen by a given clinician (clinician code 101). The printed results are sorted by state, city, and patient name.

```
Search Set (ID,VISIT)="",CLIN=101 Kill ^Srch($J)
GetID   Set ID=$O(^PAT(ID)) Goto Print:ID=""
        Set x=^PAT(ID)
        For i=1:1:5 Set @$P("Name;Street;City;State;ZIP;Phon
     ..e",";",i)=$P(x,";",i)
GetVIS  Set VISIT=$O(^PAT(ID,VISIT)) Goto GetID:VISIT=""
        Goto GetVIS:$P(^PAT(ID,VISIT),";",3)'=CLIN
Sort    Set ^Srch($J,State,City,Name,ID)=x Goto GetID
Print   .
        .
        .
```

EXAMPLE 10.19. Sample search and sort subroutine

As you can see from this example, sorting data in MUMPS is almost ridiculously easy. To sort the results we use a scratch global (^Srch) indexed first by the JOB number (so that multiple searches can be running simultaneously) and then by the keys to be sorted. The order of the sort keys is important; the most significant should be first, the least significant last. We arbitrarily add the patient ID number as the last subscript in the sort list to guarantee a unique entry for each patient (it might be possible to have two patients with the same name living in the same state and city).

The fields we are sorting on are all strings of characters that sort in ascending collating order. Numeric sort fields would also collate in ascending numeric order. To sort in descending numeric order, the sign of the sort key can be inverted. For example, to sort by AGE in descending order, the value of $-$AGE would be used as a subscript when saving the values to be sorted.

For a topic of such importance in database management systems, it seems almost criminal to devote such a small discussion to sorting data. Using structures inherent in the MUMPS language, sorting data is straightforward and uncomplicated. There is generally no need to write specialized sort subroutines, since globals automatically collate based on subscript value.

10.9 Chapter Highlights

- The $ORDER function returns array subscripts in collated order, regardless of the order in which the data were added to the array (10.1).
- Canonic numbers are those with *no* insignificant characters (for example, **Number = +Number**) (10.2.1).
- Canonic numbers collate before noncanonic strings when used as subscripts. Canonic numbers collate numerically, while noncanonic strings are ordered by the ASCII collating sequence (10.2.1).
- Sorting data in MUMPS is usually performed by creating temporary arrays (local or global), using the fields to be sorted as keys (subscripts) into the array (10.2.1).
- When sorting data on more than one key, the most significant key is used as the first-level subscript; the least significant key is used as the last subscript (10.2.1).
- The $ORDER function is used to retrieve all subscripts at a given array level (local or global), regardless of whether or not a data value is associated with that array element (10.2.2).
- The $DATA function can be used to determine whether or not a given array node contains data and/or contains a pointer to data nodes at a lower level (10.2.2).
- Naked syntax is a shorthand form of specifying the most recently referenced global node (10.3).
- When using the SET command, expressions on the *right* side of the equals character are evaluated *before* the expression on the *left* (10.3).
- Programmers should exercise caution when using naked global references (10.3).
- A LOCK command prevents other processes from being able to LOCK the same global branches; it does *not* prevent access to these branches by other processes that do not use the LOCK command (10.4).
- The nonincremental form of the LOCK command unLOCKS all previously LOCKed references before attempting to LOCK the current reference(s) (10.4).
- The incremental and decremental LOCK commands can be used without affecting previous LOCK commands for a given process (10.4).
- Journaling globals is *not* a substitute for a sound program of backing up databases (10.5.3).
- Data are usually categorized as:
    Field: a unique observation or data element.
  Record: one or more fields, often separated by delimiters.
    File: a collection of records (a global).
  Database: the collection of all files for an application. (10.7)
- Keys into a file are data elements used to identify records. In MUMPS, keys take the form of subscripts into the global (10.7).

- Individual fields within a MUMPS record are usually of variable length with an arbitrary character sequence defined as field delimiters (10.7).
- Files (globals) should generally be organized to reflect their most frequent use (that is, point of reference) (10.7).
- Key or inverted indexes are used to reflect points of reference other than those designated by the keys in the primary file (10.7.1).
- Reference files are used to hold descriptions of encoded data fields in the primary data file (10.7.2).
- The most compelling reason to code data is to improve retrieval (10.7.2).

11

MUMPS Internals

This chapter is intended for those readers wishing to gain a better insight into the internal operations of MUMPS and how they affect the general programming and application environment. The discussions are aimed at defining general concepts and implementation techniques employed by many vendors of MUMPS and cannot be used to accurately describe any given implementation. When possible, the topics are related to the real world by describing how various design criteria affect programming, especially as they relate to the speed of execution and the space required for an application. The chapter is divided into two main parts: the first section describes how data files (globals) are maintained on disk; the second covers the basics of program execution in MUMPS.

In examining the internal structure of disk files, we concentrate on defining the logical organization globals and how they relate to the physical file structure used in most MUMPS systems. We also explore some of the factors that affect the size of databases and the speed with which data can be saved or retrieved.

The sections on the MUMPS programming environment contrast purely interpreted versions of MUMPS with compiled versions. We examine a number of programming techniques that can be used to optimize program execution and explore a variety of other topics that directly affect program performance.

The subjects covered in this chapter fall outside of the realm of the MUMPS standard and are dependent on the implementation being used. The discussions involve a number of commonly used techniques, but the variations in implementing these techniques are endless. The concepts presented are accompanied by hypothetical models that should help in understanding the basic principles involved.

11.1 Global Disk Files

The logical structure of a database has little bearing on the physical structure that is used to maintain the file on a computer, although the physical structure has a bearing on performance. There are at least six important considerations when evaluating the performance of different file structures for database applications:

1. The time required to add a record to the file.
2. The time required to modify a record.
3. The time required to delete a record.
4. The time required to search the file for a particular record.
5. The time required to search the entire file.
6. The amount of space required for the file.

There are a large number of tradeoffs to be considered in deciding which of the many possible physical file structures to use for implementing a database. The choice of physical file structures is almost endless and includes piles, sequential files, indexed sequential files, indexed files, rings, hashed files, and trees, to mention but a few. There are numerous texts describing the structure and function of these file types; an excellent overview of the topic can be found in Walters' book on database principles.[1]

For a variety of reasons, most MUMPS implementors have chosen the *balanced tree* (more often referred to as a *B-tree*) for implementing a global structure. B-trees provide a powerful mechanism to manage sparse data that are organized by keys (subscripts). They also provide a very efficient method to store and retrieve specific data elements with a minimum number of disk accesses. In the following discussion, it is important to note that, while both the logical and physical appearances of both globals and balanced tree files have many of the same outward appearances, there is not a one to one correspondence between their physical and logical structures.

> Most MUMPS systems implement global file structure using balanced trees (B-trees), although globals could be maintained using other file structures.

---

[1]Richard F. Walters, *Database Principles for Personal Computers*, Prentice Hall Inc., Englewood Cliffs, N.J., 1987.

B-trees have two basic components: data blocks and pointer blocks. A *block* is a contiguous unit of disk storage that represents the minimum amount of information transferred between the disk and the computer memory for a requested operation. Most MUMPS implementations support block sizes of 1,024 or 2,048 bytes (characters). Each individual block of data can contain many global nodes (either pointer or data nodes).

> B-trees consist of *pointer* blocks and *data* blocks.

There are many variations on balanced trees. Differences in the variations usually involve what additional information (keys, pointers, and data) is stored at each of the physical levels of the tree and the use of optional block pointers (links) within the various levels. In the following discussion we do not concern ourselves with any specific type of B-tree. Instead, we concentrate on their general structure, on what happens to the structure as data are added or deleted from the tree, and on what implications the structure has with respect to modifying and searching globals. The balanced tree structure, as defined in this text, may not correspond exactly to any single implementation, but the basic principles for all B-tree structures are similar.

11.1.1 Adding Data to a B-Tree

For simplicity in the following examples, we will assume that only six pointer nodes or four data nodes will fit in a block. A *node*, for our purposes, is defined as a discrete set of related data. In reality, the number of nodes (data or pointer) that fits in a block is dependent on the block size, the length of the keys, and the length of the data field. Most MUMPS systems support block sizes that permit significantly more nodes than we use in these abbreviated examples, but keeping the numbers small allows us to observe what happens to the physical structure of the tree as data are added.

As we add data, both the pointer blocks and the data blocks will change, but in different ways. The discussions and figures that follow are based on the creation of a global using the code in Example 11.1.

```
o|>Set Subs="ZYXWVUTSRQPONMLKJIHGFEDCBA"←                                    |o
 |>Set Data="zyxwvutsrqponmlkjihgfedcba"←                                    |
 |>For i=1:1:26 Set sub=$E(Subs,i),dat=$E(Data,i),^X(sub)=dat←               |
o|>                                                                           |o
```

EXAMPLE 11.1. Creation of ^X in reverse collating sequence

In this example we create a global array (^X), adding subscripted data values in *reverse* MUMPS collating order [that is, ^X("Z") = "z", ^X("Y") = "y", and so on]. The order in which subscripted data nodes are inserted into the B-tree affects the physical distribution of data and blocks. The reasons for these differences and the resulting impact in terms of programming are expanded in the following discussions.

Figure 11.1 depicts the physical structure of the B-tree representation of ^X after the fourth iteration of the loop in Example 11.1. At the top of the figure is a special *global directory block* (block 103) that holds the names and block pointers for the globals currently defined in this directory. The entry under ^X points to the first pointer block for ^X (block 214).

Despite the fact that we have entered four data values into the global, there is only a *single* entry in the pointer block. A pointer node contains the key ("W") associated with the *first* data node in the data block it points to (block 171). Pointer nodes are added to pointer blocks *only* when it is necessary to assign a *new* data block. There is *not* a pointer node for each data node, rather a single pointer node for each data block. Pointer nodes are inserted into a pointer block in MUMPS collating order.

Pointer blocks contain pointer nodes with only *one* node for each lower-level pointer or data block.

Each data node (for example, "W":"w") contains *both* the key ("W") for that node *and* the data ("w") associated with the key. As data nodes are added to a data block, they are inserted in MUMPS collating order based on the key

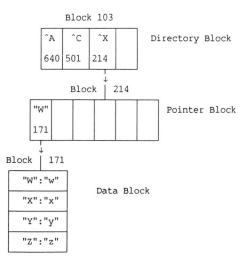

FIGURE 11.1. Physical structure of a B-tree

("W" comes first, then "X", "Y", and "Z", despite the fact that they were entered in the opposite order).

> Data blocks contain data nodes, one for each data record. Data nodes contain both the key (subscripts) and the data associated with the key.

The block numbers shown in Figure 11.1 were chosen arbitrarily, but they are used consistently throughout the examples. Every time a new disk block is needed, MUMPS assigns one from a list of available blocks maintained by the system.

Using the structure depicted, it is instructive to examine how MUMPS processes a command such as **Write X("Y")** or, at least, how it resolves the global reference.

1. The first step is to retrieve the global directory block (103) and search through it for ^**X**. This global is in the directory; the pointer associated with the name indicates that block 214 is the top-level pointer block associated with ^X.

2. Next, the top-level pointer block (214) is retrieved from disk and a search is initiated to see in which data block the key **"Y"** resides. The first (and only) key in the pointer block is **"W"**. This means that there are *no* keys into ^X preceding the subscript "W", and that all keys starting with or following the character **"W"** will be found in block 171.

3. The final step is to load the data block (171) and begin a sequential search through the nodes for a match on the requested key. The third data node has the desired key (**"Y"**), and the search returns the data value associated with that key.

Now let us examine what happens as we try to add more data to the global. In the next loop iteration (Example 11.1), setting ^X("V") = "v" will result in a data node that will *not* fit in the current data block. The data block must be split into two data blocks before the new node can be entered. The following steps are executed during the process of splitting a data block.

1. MUMPS finds the next unused or free disk block from its list of available blocks.

2. MUMPS then splits the data block (171) into two blocks and inserts the new node into one of these. There are two possible approaches to splitting the data block based on the value of the key being inserted and the current keys in the global.
   a. If the key for the data node to be inserted is the last key in the global, then the original data block is left unchanged and the new data node is inserted into the newly assigned block.
   b. If the key for the data node to be inserted is *not* the last key in the global, then the data nodes in the original data block are split evenly between the two blocks; those keys with lower collating sequences remain in the original block, and those

with higher collating sequences are moved to the new block. The new data node is then inserted into the appropriate location in one of these blocks, depending on the value of its key.

3. The pointer block is then updated to contain the key of the first data node in the new block along with a pointer to that block. In addition, the first key in the original data block is checked to make sure it has not changed since the split and insertion. If it has changed, the original pointer node is adjusted to reflect the new first key in the original data block. Both keys are inserted into the pointer block in MUMPS collating order.

After the split of the data block, the disk blocks will appear as in Figure 11.2.

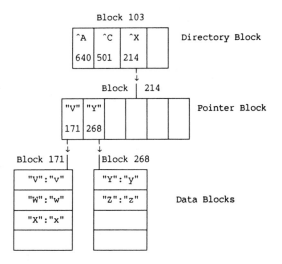

FIGURE 11.2. B-tree structure after splitting a data node

The key in the pointer block *always* reflects the key of the first entry in the corresponding data block. The keys in both the pointer and the data blocks are always maintained in MUMPS collating sequence.

When a data block fills, it is split into two data blocks, and a pointer node to the new block is inserted into the pointer block.

As we continue to fill the global using the FOR loop in Example 11.1, we will eventually reach the point where it is necessary to split a pointer block. The structure of the tree immediately *before* the pending split might be as shown in Figure 11.3.

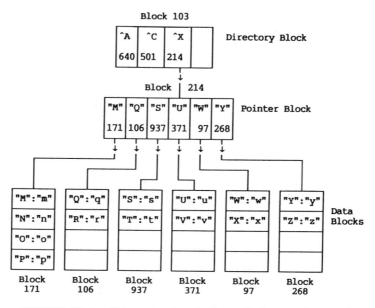

Block 103

^A	^C	^X	
640	501	214	

Directory Block

Block | 214

"M"	"Q"	"S"	"U"	"W"	"Y"
171	106	937	371	97	268

Pointer Block

"M":"m" "N":"n" "O":"o" "P":"p"	"Q":"q" "R":"r"	"S":"s" "T":"t"	"U":"u" "V":"v"	"W":"w" "X":"x"	"Y":"y" "Z":"z"

Data
Blocks

Block 171 Block 106 Block 937 Block 371 Block 97 Block 268

FIGURE 11.3. B-tree structure before splitting a pointer node

Before we examine what happens when we attempt to split a pointer node, let us look at the pointer node of Figure 11.3 and see what information we can glean from it. The first key in the pointer block is **"M"** and, since the keys are in MUMPS collating order, this indicates that there are *no* keys with a lower collating sequence in the global. All keys in the MUMPS collating sequence from the letter **"M"** and up to, but not including, the letter **"Q"** are defined in the data block numbered 171. Data associated with the keys from the letter **"Q"** to **"S"** are found in block 106, and so on.

When we attempt to set $^X("L") = "1"$, it is necessary to split the data block 171 in a manner similar to the way we split previous data blocks. However, the pointer block (214) is also full and it, too, has to be split. Splitting pointer blocks is handled differently from splitting data blocks. When pointer blocks are split, a new *physical level* is added to the structure which can be depicted as in Figure 11.4.

> When a pointer block fills, it, too, is split into two pointer blocks, and a *new* pointer level is created with pointer nodes to the pointer blocks.

The creation of new physical levels when splitting pointer blocks has interesting ramifications on the number of blocks that must be read when retrieving

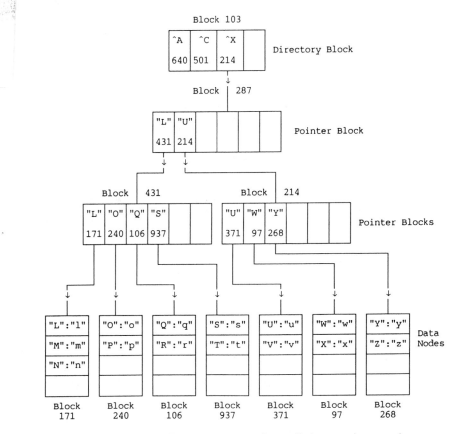

FIGURE 11.4. B-tree structure after splitting a pointer node

data nodes from disk. In a B-tree, the number of blocks that must be read to access a particular data node is the same, at any given instance, for every data node in that structure. Using more realistic values for the number of data and pointer nodes that fit in a block, we can demonstrate how the physical size of a B-tree grows with the addition of data. If we assume that we can fit, on average, 100 pointer nodes in a pointer block and 20 data nodes in a data block, then the number of disk accesses required to retrieve data for a global with increasing numbers of records is shown in Table 11.1.

TABLE 11.1 Number of blocks read to access a record

Number of Records	Number of Blocks Read
1–2,000	2
2,001–200,000	3
200,001–20,000,000	4
20,000,001–2,000,000,000	5

We can see from this table that B-trees are optimized for retrieval of individual records; the number of blocks required to access a given record is relatively small, regardless of the database size. Consider, for example, the average number of disk reads required to retrieve a record from a simple sequential file. If we assume a file of 200,000 records ordered by key(s) in which we can fit 20 records per block, then the resulting file would be 10,000 disk blocks in length. Using a binary search to retrieve a designated record from a sequential file would require reading an average of 12 to 13 disk blocks as compared to 3 for the same file stored as a B-tree.

> The number of disk blocks that must be read to access any data node in a balanced tree is always the same, regardless of the number of subscript levels.

However, since the data blocks in a B-tree are not packed as efficiently as sequential files, there is an increased overhead when performing an exhaustive search of the database. Storage efficiency and how it affects adding records and searching the database are covered in the following discussion and also in Section 11.1.2.

The physical structure of a B-tree is not only dependent on the key and data, but also on the order in which the data are entered into the tree. This is not necessarily a function of B-trees, but rather how they are implemented. In most MUMPS systems, when data are added to the tree in ascending sequential collating order, data are *not* divided between split blocks as shown in the preceding examples. Rather, the data from the original node are left intact. The new data node is entered as the first item in the newly allocated block, resulting in an efficiently packed global. If we changed the order in which data are inserted into ^X and then look at the resulting structure, we can see the effect the order of data entry has on the physical structure of the tree.

```
o|>Kill ^X←                                                               |o
 |>Set Subs="ABCDEFGHIJKLMNOPQRSTUVWXYZ"←                                 |
 |>Set Data="abcdefghijklmnopqrstuvwxyz"←                                 |
o|>For i=1:1:26 Set sub=$E(Subs,i),dat=$E(Data,i),^X(sub)=dat←            |o
 |>                                                                       |
```

EXAMPLE 11.2. Creating ^X in MUMPS collating sequence

Figure 11.5 demonstrates the physical structure of the B-tree created with this code after 15 loop iterations (the same as used in developing Figure 11.4).

Compare this figure with Figure 11.4, which shows the B-tree structure that results from creating the same number of data elements, but in reverse collating

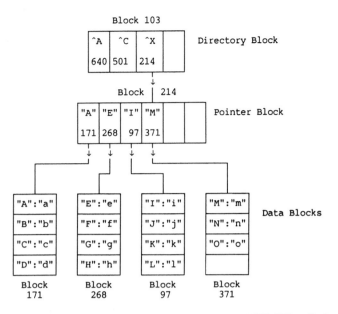

FIGURE 11.5. B-tree structure after adding data in MUMPS collating order

order. Creating a global in ascending MUMPS collating order results in more efficient utilization of the data blocks, which can, in turn, result in fewer physical levels.

> The order in which keys are added to a B-tree can affect the physical structure of the tree. Keys added in collating order generally result in more efficiently packed files (fewer physical levels) than when keys are added in random order.

11.1.2 B-Tree Variants

An interesting variation on the basic structure of the B-tree is when additional, redundant pointers are added to the data blocks. The only block pointers that are essential to the structure of a B-tree are those in the pointer nodes. However, additional pointers (links) can be added to each block, linking it to the other blocks in the structure.

Figure 11.6 demonstrates how block links can be added to the basic B-tree structure. This example shows forward links added to the blocks at the data level. Additional link information can be added to point back to the previous block in the chain, and links can also be added to the pointer blocks; the use of links varies between implementations.

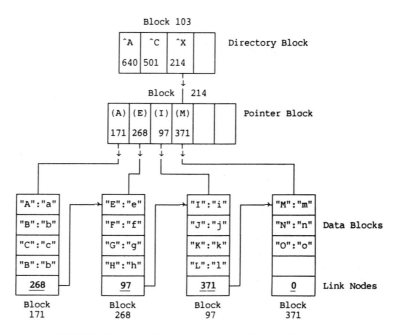

FIGURE 11.6. B-Tree showing additional block links

These links are redundant, since the same pointer information is held in the pointer blocks, but they can serve many useful purposes. They can be used, for instance, to traverse the entire data level without ever having to go back to a higher physical level (pointer block). Link pointers can be especially useful when performing exhaustive searches of a database. In addition, the links can be used in conjunction with the pointers to ensure the integrity of the B-tree. If an exhaustive search of the global is performed comparing the downward pointers with the horizontal links, potential inconsistencies can be identified and repaired.

> Redundant pointers are often included in a B-tree structure to facilitate movement within the file and ensure file integrity.

Additional links can be added to facilitate movement in all directions within the file (left, right, up, and down). Basically, there are four types of pointers that may be associated with data on disk.

1. *Downward pointer* (**DP**): This pointer is associated with a node in a pointer or directory block and contains the address of the block on the next lower physical level that is associated with the node. There is one downward pointer value for each directory or pointer node.

2. *Upward pointer* (**UP**): Often there is a single pointer value associated with each block of data on the disk that points to the parent block. The parent block is the block that contains the downward pointer to this block.

3. *Right-link pointer* (**RL**): When used, there is a single pointer for each block in the tree pointing to the next sequential block at that physical level of the tree. This pointer should agree with the downward pointer of the next node in the parent block.

4. *Left-link pointer* (**LL**): When used, there is a single pointer associated with each block in the tree that points to the previous block in the chain of blocks at a given physical level. This is similar to the right-link pointer, but pointing in the other direction. This pointer should agree with the downward pointer of the previous node in the parent block.

Figure 11.7 shows the block structure of a global using all four of these pointers. The basic structure is the same as Figure 11.6, but with the additional pointers appropriately inserted. The *downward pointers* are associated with each pointer node and are not labeled. There is one upward pointer (**UP**), right-link (**RL**), and left-link (**LL**) pointer per block.

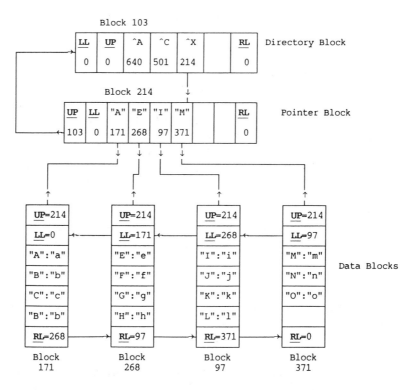

FIGURE 11.7. B-tree structure with ancillary pointers

11.1.3 Multiple Subscript Levels

Up to now, the global references used in the examples have been relatively simple, with only one subscript level. How does MUMPS map multiple-level global references into a B-tree structure with only one physical data level? The answer to this question lies in the definition of the *key* that is used to index the global. The key to a reference is the unique set of subscripts that points to the data node and is stored at both the pointer level(s) and at the bottom data level. For simplicity, the keys shown in the previous examples have consisted of the single-character subscript used in the global reference. In reality, the key used in most implementations consists of the *entire* global reference and often includes the global name. To maintain integrity and prevent possible key conflicts, we can picture the comma used to separate subscripts within a key as being replaced internally by a single character that cannot be used within a subscript and that collates before all other characters. In Figure 11.8 we represent this special delimiting mark with the asterisk (*) in the following example.

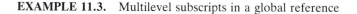

```
o|>Kill ^X Set ^X("A")="a",^X("AA")="aa",^X("AB")="ab"←          |o
 |>Set  ^X("A","B")="a comma b",^X("A,B")="A,B"←                  |
 |>Set  ^X("AB",1)="ab,1"←                                        |
```

EXAMPLE 11.3. Multilevel subscripts in a global reference

As you can see from Figure 11.8, multiple-level subscripts are handled in the same manner as single-level subscripts. While there is only a single level of data blocks, these blocks contain global references with more than one logical level.

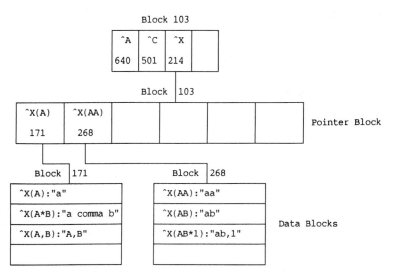

FIGURE 11.8. B-tree structure with multiple subscript levels

11.1.4 Key Compression

As can be imagined, there are numerous variations on the structure of both pointer and data nodes. One of the more common techniques employed is that of *key compression*, used to reduce the storage requirements of a database. Remember from our discussions that each data node contains both the key used to index the node and the data values associated with the key, and that the nodes are always maintained in MUMPS collating sequence within a data block.

Since keys used in indexing globals are often related, sequential nodes may contain many common characters in the key definition. Consider the global nodes shown in Table 11.2. These global nodes are listed in MUMPS collating sequence, just as they would appear within a data block. Each node in the block contains both the key for the node and the data associated with that key. Yet we can see that there is a substantial overlap in the key definitions, since each key starts out with the identical characters "Inventory,Bolts".

TABLE 11.2 Related keys

Global Reference	Data Value
^X("Inventory","Bolts","1/4")	1500
^X("Inventory","Bolts","3/8")	2500
^X("Inventory","Bolts","7/16")	750
^X("Inventory","Bolts","7/8")	2200

Using key compression, a count is maintained for each data node that defines the number of characters in the KEY that were common with the previous key. Consequently, each data node key needs to store only those characters that differ from the previous key in the block.

> Most MUMPS systems employ *key compression* to reduce the amount of space required to store related keys.

Each data block must start with a fully expanded key if any isolated block is to be successfully interpreted. Without a fully expanded first key, any loss of data integrity would be extremely difficult to detect and even more difficult to repair.

The amount of disk storage saved by key compression varies depending on the length and similarity of the keys being saved, but it can be substantial in many applications. There are also penalties associated with the use of key compression; it requires additional computer time to compress and reconstruct keys as nodes are inserted, retrieved, or deleted from a global.

11.1.5 Deleting Data from a B-Tree

We can see from the previous examples that, as data are added to the B-tree, pointer blocks are split and new levels are added as necessary to keep the tree balanced (that is, the same number of blocks must be read to access *any* data node in the tree). Under ideal conditions, the same should be true as data nodes are deleted.

However, the overhead for such reorganization is relatively high, and most implementors do not compress the structure of the B-tree as data are deleted. Any pointer or data blocks that become empty due to deletion of data are returned to the system for future allocation, but blocks still containing keys or data are generally not recombined, nor are the number of physical pointer levels compressed. A tree that has undergone many deletions may lose efficiency and have unnecessary pointer levels. Saving and restoring the global from/to disk will restore its more efficient structure.

> Most systems do *not* repack the B-tree as data are deleted from it. Optimum packing usually requires saving and restoring the global to/from an external device such as magnetic tape.

11.1.6 Buffering

Disk storage is logically divided into *blocks* of data defining the smallest packet of information transferred to or from the disk and the computer's memory. In most MUMPS implementations, a block of data holds from 1 to 2 Kbytes (thousands of bytes) of information, although many implementations support even larger blocks. The section of computer memory into which disk blocks are either read or written is referred to as a *buffer*.

It is usually much faster to retrieve a data node held in a memory buffer than retrieving the same node from disk. For this reason, most MUMPS systems maintain a pool of buffers to speed up the processing of disk data. The number of buffers available to a system depends on a number of factors, including the total amount of memory available and the number and size of the partitions. Most implementations assign all memory not dedicated to other needs to a buffer pool for processing data from disk.

> Buffering disk I/O in memory can significantly increase access to data files stored on disk.

When a block is needed for processing, MUMPS will first check to see if that block already resides in the buffer pool. If so, processing can continue immediately, with no need to retrieve the block from disk. If not, the required block will be read from disk into one of the memory buffers. If the contents of the memory buffer being replaced have been altered since that block was read from disk, they will be written out to disk before the new block is read in. The choice of which buffer to replace is implementation specific, but usually the oldest or least recently used block in the buffer pool is chosen.

The blocks held in the buffer pool are used for both reading and writing global data. When a global node is altered (SET or KILLed), the changes are made to the data held in the buffer. Usually, the block is not written out immediately after each individual change, but rather it is maintained in the buffer until such time as that buffer is required for another block of data. At that time, buffers with altered contents are written back to disk before the blocks are released for subsequent use.

While using buffers for processing disk data can dramatically improve global processing speeds, buffering does have potential drawbacks. Since changes to global structure are really made in memory, there is the potential for a crash before the disk has been updated to reflect changes, and this may result in the loss of data and/or integrity of the global structure. Lost data can be an inconvenience, but typically they involve only the most recently made changes and are usually easy to recover. Loss of global integrity, on the other hand, can be a serious problem that may result in the loss of substantial amounts of data on the disk.

A number of techniques are employed to reduce the likelihood of a loss of global integrity. Usually, a flag is associated with each buffer indicating whether or not the data in that block have been altered. Whenever it is necessary to write a modified block from the buffer pool to disk, *all* blocks in the pool that have been altered are written out (and the flags reset). As long as the system does not go down during these writes to disk, the structure of the disk files is guaranteed. Most implementations also employ a background process that flushes the buffer pool by periodically writing all altered blocks back to disk and resetting the buffer flags.

11.1.7 Storage Efficiency Considerations

Inserting data into a B-tree as outlined in Section 11.1.1, has some interesting consequences affecting the storage efficiency of globals. As data are added, the fixed-length blocks start out empty and slowly fill until they are 100% utilized. At that time, the addition of new data causes a split and results in two data blocks that are only 50% full. In a typical global file to which data are being added randomly, the storage efficiency (how full the blocks are) typically runs between 60% and 80%.

The storage efficiency can affect the time required to access global data. MUMPS always reads entire blocks of data from the disk, even if the blocks are only one-half full. A global that is only half full requires twice as many blocks as the same global packed to 100% efficiency; each read from the disk only brings in half the data it is capable of handling. This means that twice as many disk reads must be issued to process an entire global and that memory buffers are only being used to one-half of their capacity. On the other hand, when adding data to disk (for example, when setting a global node), there are definite advantages to having partially filled blocks. Each time a block has to be split to add data, there is the overhead of getting another (empty) block from disk, dividing the original in half, and writing the two blocks back to disk.

In general, it is best to aim for a storage efficiency of around 75% for globals in which data are being randomly added. This reflects a trade-off between the time required to read data from the global and the number of times that blocks must be split when adding data. For relatively fixed databases (such as reference files), it is desirable to have a more efficient global structure; in these files, new data are added infrequently (the ratio of the number of times the global is read compared to the number of times new data are added is high), and it is a good idea to optimize for disk reads.

> It is generally desirable to aim for efficiently packed static reference files and less efficiently packed active files to which data are constantly being added.

How can a programmer affect the efficiency with which data are stored on disk? As noted earlier, most MUMPS implementations handle the addition of data to a global differently when the nodes are entered sequentially (that is, in MUMPS collating order) as contrasted to when nodes are inserted randomly. When it is necessary to split a block and the node to be added falls *after* the last node in the block (in MUMPS collating order), the data in the original block are *not* divided between the original and the new block. Rather, the original block is left as it was, and the data node is placed as the first element in the new block. This allows globals created in sequential order to approach 100% storage efficiency.

The most common method employed by programmers to improve the storage efficiency of a global is to first save the global to a sequential device (such as magnetic tape) in MUMPS collating order, delete the global from disk (KILL ^GLOBAL), and then restore the global from the sequential device. Each MUMPS implementation supplies a set of utility routines to perform these functions. In addition, the global restore utility often allows the programmer to specify an efficiency factor to be used when restoring the global. This efficiency factor dictates whether or not data from the block being split will also be moved to the new block and, if so, how much will be moved. If a 75% efficiency factor is used, then one-quarter of the data from the original block will be moved to the new block before the data node is inserted into the new block. Global efficiencies of less than 100% are desirable if frequent updates are anticipated.

11.1.8 Database Errors

Database problems are usually the result of external factors interrupting the process of updating the disk from the memory buffers, such as a system crash, a disk hardware problem, or a loss of power. In these instances, it is possible that only part of the disk update has been completed, and this can result in loss of integrity of disk files. When system operation is restored, it is not always apparent that a loss of integrity has occurred; often these problems do not come to light for days or weeks after they occurred. Typically, a programmer is first aware of database problems when programs begin to return cryptic error messages such as "**Database Degradation ERROR**" or "**Block Number ERROR**".

The best way to protect against the loss of data on disk is through a sound operational procedure of backing up the databases to an external medium such as magnetic tape and by journaling critical globals. The need to directly patch disk files to correct inconsistencies generally reflects poor backup procedures. Usually, the best way to recover from database degradation errors is to restore the global from the most recent backup, and then to apply the changes made to that global as reflected in the journal file.

> The best way to protect against any type of database loss is through a sound and consistent backup procedure.

Backup procedures do not always find potential inconsistencies in the databases. There are two basic approaches to take in backing up globals: physical and logical saves. Physical saves involve writing the entire disk or the blocks in use to an external device. They pay no attention to the content of the data and, consequently, will only discover physical errors (for example, unable to read a block). Logical backups, on the other hand, perform an exhaustive search through the specified globals, saving both the global reference and the data associated with that reference to an external device. This type of save, while usually taking much longer to perform, will detect logical inconsistencies within the global, such as discrepancies between the various pointer blocks. If exhaustive searches are not routinely performed on a database, it is often wise to make periodic logical backups to ensure data integrity. Optionally, many implementors supply database integrity checkers that can be run periodically to spot potential problems.

The fact that a process, even one performing extensive disk writes, is interrupted by a system crash or loss of power does not necessarily mean that there will be a loss of global integrity. Most implementors go to great lengths to ensure the reliability of disk files. Whenever a block is written out to disk, all altered disk blocks held in memory buffers are also written. While data in buffers may be lost, the information on disk, at any time other than when the buffers are actually being written, should be accurate.

The first thing to be done on encountering an error that indicates a possible compromise of disk structures is to pause and reflect on the problem. *Do not panic* and immediately jump in to attempt a repair of the offending global; such unplanned efforts often result in greater data loss than the original problem. Before attempting any repair, follow these steps.

1. Suspend user operation of the system. Often the addition of new data can complicate the process of recovering the error. Remember that database degradation in one global does not mean that it is the only structure with problems.

2. If you are journaling changes to databases, save the journal file to an external media such as magnetic tape. This may be important in restoring changes made to globals since the last backup.

3. Attempt to back up all databases to an external medium such as magnetic tape. If you attempt a save of individual globals, you might encounter the same error that initiated the recovery process, which may thwart efforts to perform a logical save. If this occurs, it is usually possible to make a physical backup of the disk, especially if the problem concerns the logical structure of the disk files rather than a physical problem with the disk.

4. You should now examine the databases that reside on the system. Almost all MUMPS implementations supply some form of utility program to check on database integrity. When using this utility, it is best to check the integrity of all globals; the condition that caused the loss of data integrity may well have affected other databases as well. The integrity checker will usually display a variety of information about the problems discovered, such as the block(s) where inconsistencies were discovered along with the type of error encountered.

After performing these steps, you can attempt repair. The actual steps taken will depend on the nature of the error. The easiest (and probably safest) is to delete the globals in question, restore them from the last complete backup, and then apply the journal changes. Alternatively, you can try direct repair of the global using special utilities provided with your system. If, during the repair, you encounter unexpected problems, you can still go back to the data files saved in steps 2 and 3.

11.2 MUMPS Program Execution

In this section we examine some of the operating characteristics of MUMPS, both as an interpreted and a compiled language. As with the discussion concerning disk data structures, we concentrate on general approaches toward implementing MUMPS and do not discuss specific implementations.

All high-level computer languages face a common problem; each different computer type has its own internal instruction set (machine language), and the high-level language must be converted to these instructions before it can be executed. Two basic approaches are taken in reducing a high-level language to executable code. The first involves interpreting the source code as it is executed, and the second involves converting (compiling) the source code to machine language before it is executed.

When MUMPS was first developed, it was as an interpreted language; at execution time, each command in the *source* code is translated to a series of calls to machine language subroutines as execution takes place. Interpretation involves two rather distinct phases: (1) evaluating the code for correct *syntax* or structure and (2) evaluating the code for *semantics* or meaning. Since the source code is executed directly, interpreted languages generally provide an excellent program development environment. Source code can be entered and executed from the keyboard (direct mode), allowing the programmer direct access to the computer for developing and debugging applications.

Traditional compilers, on the other hand, evaluate and reduce the source code to machine language *before* it is executed. Since all syntactical and semantic checks have already been performed prior to execution, compiled languages tend to run faster than interpreted languages. On the other hand, compilation represents an intermediate step between writing or editing the program and its execution. In large applications, this multistep process can significantly increase the time required to develop and debug the application.

Due to the increased overhead involved in interpreting MUMPS commands each time they are executed, implementors explored methods to combine the advantages of interpreters with those of compilers. There are, however, a number of basic constructs in the language that hindered development of a MUMPS compiler:

- Since MUMPS variables are neither declared nor typed (integer numbers, floating point numbers, strings, and so on), it is difficult to reserve space and allocate absolute addresses for them.

- MUMPS permits indirection, whereby a command or command argument can be altered by the contents of data fields at execution time. Use of indirection means that the actual code to be executed may be altered by conditions that are not known until run time and cannot, therefore, be compiled ahead of time.

To circumvent these problems, MUMPS implementors have taken a compromise position. Source code is not reduced to machine language before execution but, rather, to a level intermediate between the two. MUMPS compilers perform all necessary syntax checks on the source code and produce, as output, a stream of *tokens* that can then be used as input to a much simpler (and faster) interpreter. Tokens can represent MUMPS commands (for example, a token for the <u>WRITE</u> command), a reference to a variable or literal, or internal commands for the interpreter.

> Most MUMPS implementations that compile the source code do
> so by creating a token stream from the source and using this
> stream as input to a simplified interpreter.

Compilation in MUMPS involves evaluating the routine, line by line, command by command, and creating an ordered token stream organized in a manner to optimize execution speed. By way of example, consider how we might create a token stream for the following command:

```
o|>Write 22+3←
 |25
 |>
```

EXAMPLE 11.4. MUMPS source code to be "tokenized"

In compiling this code, MUMPS must first check for valid syntax and then generate an output token stream organized by semantic content and suitable for input to the simplified interpreter. One of the more common techniques employed in today's compilers is to organize the code to be executed in such a way that sequential tokens can be pushed and popped on and off a stack during execution of the code. The use of a stack to hold intermediate results simplifies the execution of commands, but it requires a different organization of the command elements than is found in the source code. One approach used in managing stacks is called *postfix notation* or *reverse Polish notation* (RPN). A token stream that could be used to represent the command in Example 11.4 is shown in Figure 11.9. This stream is suitable for stack execution using RPN in the following fashion:

1. The first token (22) is pushed onto the stack.
2. The second token (3) is pushed onto the stack.
3. When the plus operator is encountered, the top two stack elements are popped off the stack and added together, and the result (25) is pushed back on the stack.
4. The WRITE token pops the top element of the stack and outputs it to the current device.

22	3	+	WRITE

FIGURE 11.9. Token stream generated from Example 11.4

By the time we are ready to execute a token stream, it is organized in such a fashion that all elements are in order for RPN stack evaluation. Each token in the stream is identified as to type (for example, variable, string or numeric literal, or MUMPS command), and the type determines how the stack processing proceeds. Consider the more complex code presented in the next example.

```
o|>Write:X=3 Y+Z
```

EXAMPLE 11.5. Conditional MUMPS command for tokenizing

In this example, a number of new language elements must be considered; the command is postconditioned, and a number of variables have to be evaluated. The

| X | 3 | = | pc | Y | Z | + | WRITE |

FIGURE 11.10. Token stream generated from Example 11.5

resulting token stream is shown in Figure 11.10. We can step through the evaluation of this token string using RPN as follows:

1. The first token (X) is a variable, so look up its value in the local symbol table and push that value on the stack.

2. Push the value 3 on the stack.

3. The third token is the string equal operator; pop the top two items off the stack and compare them. If they are equal, push a 1 on the stack; if they are not equal, push a 0 on the stack.

4. The next token (pc; postconditional token) is a new type; it represents an internal instruction to the interpreter and contains, as data, the address of the end of this MUMPS command in the token string. The top stack value is popped and, if it is 0, the interpreter uses pc to determine where to resume processing in the token stream (that is, it ignores the rest of the command). If the popped value was 1, token stream processing continues with the next token.

5. The remaining steps are similar to the previous example with the values for Y and Z being pushed onto the stack; then they are popped, added together, and the results pushed on the stack; finally, the results are popped from the stack and output to the current device.

Additional, often subtle, advantages can be achieved when tokenizing source code. One obvious technique is to calculate LABEL addresses as offsets within the token stream. In interpreted versions of MUMPS, it is necessary to scan the source code looking for labels when a branch command (DO or GOTO) is executed. In compiled versions, the label search can be performed when the token stream is created, and branching becomes much faster.

Another gain can be made in the conversion of numeric or string literals encountered in the source. We have emphasized that MUMPS maintains all data variables internally as strings of characters that are evaluated in context. Using interpreted versions of MUMPS, it is usually necessary to convert the internal string format to a number before a numeric operation is performed. In compiled versions, where we already know the operation to be performed, the literal can be converted to an appropriate form for inclusion in the token stream, reducing the time required for these conversions during execution.

Compiling the code also simplifies the process of skipping conditionalized code, such as the IF command or any of the commands that permit postconditioning. The actual addresses within the token stream that mark the *end of a line* or *end of a command* can be inserted within the stream. If the condition fails at execution time, the address used to resume processing is directly available in the token string, eliminating the need to scan the source code.

It is also possible to optimize the look-up of variables by employing look-up tables. For example, variables encountered in the source code can be assigned unique numeric values (a Variable Token or VT), which are placed in the token stream instead of the variable name. The variable token is also used to point into a Table of Variable Addresses (TVA), which, in turn, points into the local symbol table to the actual memory location(s) in which the data are stored.

When a variable token is encountered in the token stream, the interpreter uses it as an index into the TVA to obtain the address of the data. This address is then used to locate the data directly, without having to search through the local symbol table. Variable tokens lacking addresses in the TVA have to be linked with the variable entry in the local symbol table by performing a search of the local symbol table. This approach does not eliminate the need to manage a dynamic local symbol table, but it does allow a percentage of variable requests to be satisfied without a symbol table search. Borrowing from Example 11.5, we can depict the relationships between a variable token, the TVA, and the local symbol table as in Figure 11.11.

The use of a table of variable addresses can significantly improve the execution speed of an application, but it is also dependent on the structure of the program. To understand the limitations of this approach, we must examine how the TVA and the local symbol table are managed as an application is executed. Each *routine* has its own TVA, since routines are compiled individually, and the compiler does not know what routines might be linked together to form a complete package. Most systems implement sophisticated routine buffering schemes, which can dramatically reduce the overhead of calling external subroutines (those external to the routine being executed), especially routines that are frequently accessed. Despite this fact, there can be disadvantages to referencing external subroutines when compared to internal (within the same routine) subroutines.

When a routine is loaded for execution, the TVA associated with the routine

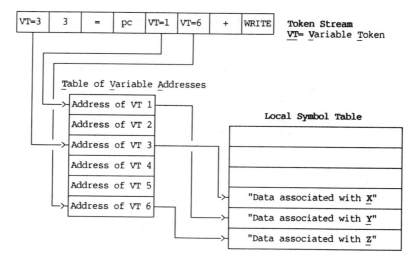

FIGURE 11.11. Variable look-up through table of variable addresses

is also loaded, and each entry in the table (a pointer into the local symbol table) is cleared. As variable tokens are encountered in the token stream, the run-time interpreter first checks the TVA to see if the variable has a defined pointer into the local symbol table. If so, it can be used to directly access the data associated with the variable. If not, the local symbol table must first be searched for the variable name before updating the TVA and returning the data.

The first time a variable is referenced in a routine, a search of the local symbol table is required; subsequent references to that variable in the same routine can be satisfied through the TVA. Local symbol tables are managed differently for almost all implementations, but, in all cases, searching the local symbol table takes considerably longer than an indexed look-up through the TVA.

When a subroutine is invoked that resides in *another routine*, the process outlined in the previous paragraphs is repeated. Moreover, when control is returned to the calling program, it is usually necessary to reinitialize all entries in the TVA of the calling routine and start the process over again. The called routine may have substantially changed the local symbol table, and the addresses stored in the calling routine's original TVA may no longer be correct. In routines with numerous calls to external subroutines, many of the advantages of using a table of variable addresses are lost. Subroutines that are part of the calling routine, on the other hand, do not clear the TVA, and it is not necessary to reinitialize this table.

Subroutines *external* to the calling routine increase execution overhead in that they necessitate clearing the Table of Variable Addresses of the calling routine when control is returned.

This discussion is *not* designed to discourage the use of external subroutine libraries. Indeed, the use of common, shared external libraries is desirable for both developing and maintaining applications. However, in cases where speed is of paramount importance, it might be desirable to limit or carefully control such external references.

The discussion does point to an area of optimization that is now being addressed by some MUMPS vendors: optimizing an entire application. Once an application has been written and debugged, it is possible to define a process whereby all the routines in the package are linked together using a common variable look-up table and automatically calculating routine and label address for the token streams of all the routines in the package. This process is analogous to *linking* object modules in other languages such as FORTRAN and can be expected to improve performance in many applications.

Unfortunately, we cannot completely divorce the compilation process from the execution phase. Because commands and arguments can be altered at the time of execution when indirection is used, not all source code can be converted into a tightly organized token stream.

```
o | Set X="A=22/7" Do test Set @X                                    | o
```

EXAMPLE 11.6. Effect of indirection on the token stream

In Example 11.6, MUMPS cannot evaluate the command "Set @X" until the command is actually encountered during execution. The value of X is variable and could be altered at any place in the program (for instance, by the subroutine test). Consequently, there must be special internal token commands that instruct the interpreter to invoke the compiler at run time to evaluate these cases of indirection. The fact that code using indirection (XECUTE command or "@" operator) requires a mini compilation at the time of execution has important programming implications; code that makes use of indirection will typically run slower than code that does not.

> Indirection is usually slower than executing the same code without indirection.

In evaluating the impact of indirection on program execution, a number of factors should be considered. Are there viable alternatives to indirection? In some instances (consider the global tree copy subroutine shown in Example 10.15), there are numerous alternative solutions, but they would require considerably more code and may not run faster even then. How much slower is indirection than an alternative without indirection? This is very much implementation specific. On a quick check of four MUMPS implementations, the command line Set a="b" For i=1:1:10000 Set @a=1 took from two to six times longer than a similar command without indirection (For i=1:1:10000 Set b=1). However, even if indirection takes much longer, it may not affect the total application performance. Usually, indirection accounts for only a very small percentage of the commands in an application, and its impact on the time required to execute the entire application would be difficult to measure.

Another important consideration when using compiled MUMPS is that the source code may not be available during execution. The absence of source code may be an advantage if you are developing commercial applications and wish to prevent examination or tampering of a program by outside sources. On the flip side, the $TEXT function may not work if the source is unavailable. Many implementors have adopted an informal convention that routine lines containing only a comment and beginning with *two* semicolons will be included with the compiled form of the routine as $TEXT literals. The lines may or may not have associated labels, and their relationship to other labeled lines in the routine (that is, offset from a labeled line) is maintained. This is only a convention and may not be available on all systems.

> The $TEXT function may not work as expected in compiled
> versions of MUMPS where the source code is unavailable.

One interesting side effect of using a compiled version of MUMPS is the problem encountered by the operating system in reporting errors. In purely interpreted versions of MUMPS, the system can determine and report exactly where errors occur during program execution. In compiled versions, where the source code may not be available and where the program steps have been tokenized and restructured for increased execution speed, it is often difficult to report exactly where in the source code the error occurred. Most implementations are able to resolve the problem to one or two lines within the source code, but error reporting and subsequent program debugging suffer when the precise location cannot be identified.

Finally, it should be noted that MUMPS object code generated on one implementation will *not* run under other implementations. Each implementor has developed its own compiler and definition of token strings. The only method to move routines between implementations is by transferring source code and then recompiling under the new system.

> Token streams generated under one MUMPS compiler will
> *not* run under other MUMPS implementations.

The process of compiling MUMPS source code is generally transparent to the programmer. The compilation phase is usually performed automatically when the source code is saved to disk. In most cases, this means that each routine exists in two forms: a source code version and a tokenized version. The source is used when making program changes, and the compiled code (often referred to as the *object* code) is invoked during execution. With the continuing drop in costs associated with disk storage, the additional disk space required for the two copies of the routine will probably not be a major consideration. The advantages of faster execution usually far outweigh the additional storage requirements.

11.3 Chapter Highlights

- Most MUMPS systems implement global file structure using balanced trees (B-trees), although globals could be maintained using other file structures (11.1).
- B-trees consist of *pointer* blocks and *data* blocks (11.1).

- Pointer blocks contain pointer nodes with only *one* node for each lower-level pointer or data block (11.1.1).
- Data blocks contain data nodes, one for each data record. Data nodes contain both the key (subscripts) and the data associated with the key (11.1.1).
- When a data block fills, it is split into two data blocks and a pointer node to the new block is inserted into the pointer block (11.1.1).
- When a pointer block fills, it, too, is split into two pointer blocks and a *new* pointer level is created with pointer nodes to the pointer blocks (11.1.1).
- The number of disk blocks that must be read to access any data node in a balanced tree is always the same, regardless of the number of subscript levels (11.1.1).
- The order in which keys are added to a B-tree can affect the physical structure of the tree. Keys added in collating order generally result in more efficiently packed files (fewer physical levels) than when keys are added in random order (11.1.1).
- Redundant pointers are often included in a B-tree structure to facilitate movement within the file and ensure file integrity (11.1.2).
- Most MUMPS systems employ *key compression* to reduce the amount of space required to store related keys (11.1.4).
- Most systems do *not* repack the B-tree as data are deleted from it. Optimum packing usually requires saving and restoring the global to/from an external device, such as a magnetic tape (11.1.5).
- Buffering disk I/O in memory can significantly increase access to data files stored on disk (11.1.6).
- It is generally desirable to aim for efficiently packed static reference files and less efficiently packed active files to which data are constantly being added (11.1.7).
- The best way to protect against any type of database loss is through a sound and consistent backup procedure (11.1.8).
- Most MUMPS implementations that compile the source code do so by creating a token stream from the source and using this stream as input to a simplified interpreter (11.2).
- Subroutines *external* to the calling routine increase execution overhead in that they necessitate clearing the Table of Variable Addresses of the calling routine when control is returned (11.2).
- Indirection is usually slower than executing the same code without indirection (11.2).
- The $TEXT function may not work as expected in compiled versions of MUMPS where the source code is unavailable (11.2).
- Token streams generated under one MUMPS compiler will *not* run under other MUMPS implementations (11.2).

12

Device Input/Output

This chapter examines the general MUMPS Input/Output (I/O) environment and some of the different types of devices often attached to a MUMPS system. It begins by defining the general I/O environment and how devices are managed by the system. This is followed by a section (12.4) describing the specifics associated with individual device types, such as video terminals, line printers, and magnetic tape drives. The remaining sections discuss advanced I/O techniques, especially as they apply to video terminals. Many of the concepts addressed in this chapter were introduced in earlier sections (Section 3.4 on I/O commands and Section 4.4.4 on device-related system variables); this chapter expands on those earlier discussions.

12.1 General I/O Environment

Like many other languages, MUMPS maintains a high degree of device independence by directing I/O operations to and from logical devices. MUMPS maintains an internal list of devices available to applications called the *device table*. Each device on the system is associated with a logical *name* or *number*. Dedicated MUMPS systems usually use device numbers, but when MUMPS is running under the control of another general-purpose operating system, the devices are often

TABLE 12.1 TYPICAL DEVICE TABLE
IN MUMPS

Device identifier	Description
1	Console terminal
2	Print spool device
3–5	Line printers
6–9	Magnetic tape drives
10–15	Sequential disk files
16–31	Terminals

designated by device mnemonics recognized by that operating system. The device table is both implementation and site specific (see Table 12.1); neither the device categories nor the device identifiers are necessarily the same between different systems.

The general method for using a device in the MUMPS environment involves gaining ownership of the device, performing the desired I/O operations (READs and WRITEs), and then relinquishing the device back to the system. Most devices can only be owned by one process at a time (the print spool device is usually an exception to this rule), but a single process can own more than one device. While a MUMPS process can own more than one device, only one is active at a time; all WRITE and READ operations are directed to and from the currently active device. There are five basic I/O commands in MUMPS: <u>OPEN</u>, <u>USE</u>, <u>WRITE</u>, <u>READ</u>, and <u>CLOSE</u>.

1. <u>OPEN</u>: The OPEN command is used to request device ownership. The argument(s) to the OPEN command specifies the device(s) being requested along with optional parameters to be used with that device. Attempting to OPEN a device that is currently owned by another process will suspend program execution until the device becomes available. Use of timeout syntax with the OPEN command permits the program to check on the availability of a device without being suspended for an indefinite period of time.

2. <u>USE</u>: The USE command establishes one of the owned devices as the current active device. The argument(s) to the USE command specifies the device being made current along with optional device parameters. A device cannot be made the current device unless it is already owned by the process; an attempt to USE an unowned device results in an error. All I/O operations (READS and WRITEs) are directed from or to the currently active device. The OPEN command establishes ownership of a device but does *not* make it the currently active device. The system variable $IO contains the device identifier of the current device; it is updated after each successful completion of a USE command.

3. <u>WRITE</u>: The WRITE command is used to output strings of characters or special format control characters (**#**, **!**, or **?nn**) to the currently active device. As characters are output, the system variables $X and $Y are updated to reflect the column and row position of the cursor.

4. <u>READ</u>: The READ command is used to input characters from the currently active

device into the contents of a local variable. As characters are read from the device, the system variables $X and $Y are updated to reflect the column and row position of the cursor. The manner in which the READ command is terminated [that is, the condition(s) under which a READ is satisfied] are both implementation and device specific. For example, most keyboard READs are finished when the <ENTER> key is pressed, but some implementations permit definition of other terminating characters. In addition, both the fixed-length and timed READ can return control to the program before a terminating character is input. For convenience, the READ command can also be used to output format control characters (#, !, or ?nn) or character strings in a manner similar to the WRITE command.

5. **CLOSE**: The CLOSE command is used to return ownership of a device to the MUMPS system. Once a device is closed, it becomes available for other MUMPS processes. There is an implicit CLOSE operation performed for each device owned by a process when that process terminates (that is, the process HALTs and the partition is returned to the system).

Figure 12.1 depicts the general process of establishing device ownership, using them for I/O operations, and finally returning them to the system for use by other processes.

Operation	Effect
Open 2	Establishes ownership of device 2.
Open 3	Establishes ownership of device 3.
Use 2	Makes device 2 the current active device.
Read ...	Reads are directed to device 2.
Write...	Writes are directed to device 2.
Use 3	Makes device 3 the current active device.
Read...	Reads are directed to device 3.
Write...	Writes are directed to device 3.
Use 2	Makes device 2 the current active device again.
Read,Write...	I/O operation directed to device 2.
Close 2	Relinquish ownership of device 2.
Close 3	Relinquish ownership of device 3.

FIGURE 12.1. Directing input/output operations

It is important to note that the OPEN command establishes device ownership, but does *not* make the device active; the USE command is required to direct I/O operations to a specific device.

12.2 The Principal Device

When an individual logs into MUMPS, the system automatically assigns a partition (Section 2.2.1) and designates the terminal being used as that job's *principal device*. MUMPS performs an implied OPEN and USE command for the principal device, and all I/O operations are directed to or from the principal device until another device is explicitly selected with a USE command.

Each job initiated from a terminal is assigned a *principal device* to which I/O is directed until another device is made active with a USE command.

A job's principal device has a special alias that can be used as an argument for subsequent OPEN, USE, or CLOSE commands. The device identifier **0** (zero) always refers to the job's principal device, regardless of the name or number associated with that device in the system's device table. Whenever a device identifier of 0 is encountered in one of these commands, it is automatically mapped to the appropriate device identifier from the device table. The principal device can be made the currently active device anywhere in a process with a **Use 0** command.

The principal device can be referenced with the special device identification code of 0 (zero). For example: Use 0.

There are a number of times that a job's principal device is made the current device through an implied Use 0 command.

- Whenever a user logs into MUMPS, the device used to log on becomes both the job's principal device and the current active device.
- Whenever the current device is CLOSEd, the principal device is made the current device.
- Whenever an error is encountered during program execution, the principal device is automatically made the current device. In addition, if a BREAK command is encountered when debugging a program, the principal device becomes the current device before entering direct mode.
- When a programmer is in direct mode, each time the execution of a direct-mode command line is finished, there is an implied Use 0 performed before MUMPS prompts for the next direct-mode command.

Processes started with the JOB command (Section 3.5.3) may or may not have a principal device. Some implementations automatically assign the started job the same principal device as the process that started it. Any I/O operations directed to the principal device will hang until the principal device is released (CLOSEd) by the starting process. Other implementations permit establishing a different principal device for a started job through the optional SPCL PARMS list associated with the JOB command. In any case, there is no clear-cut definition of the principal device for a started job, and you should check your system documentation. This

Sec. 12.2   The Principal Device

becomes especially important when an error is detected in the started process. Even if the started process performs no I/O, MUMPS performs an implied Use 0 before reporting the error. If there is no principal device associated with a started process, this condition may generate new errors when the system attempts to output the error information.

12.3 System Variables Associated with I/O Operations

We have already described three system variables ($IO, $X, and $Y) associated with I/O operations (Section 4.4.4), and this section examines the impact and use of these variables in the programming environment.

The system variable $IO contains the device identifier of the current device (that is, the device associated with the last Use command executed). If the current device is the principal device, $IO contains the actual device identifier, *not* the special alias 0. The variable $IO is often used by system utilities to perform special functions based on the device type as demonstrated in the next example.

```
o|Search ;Search database, output search results to DEV        |o
 |       New DEV,sub,rec                                        |
 |       Set DEV=$$GetDev Quit:DEV=""   ;Get output device      |
o|       Use DEV If $IO>5&($IO<10) Write *-5 ;Rewind MagTape    |o
 |       Set sub="" For  Do  Quit:sub=""                        |
 |       . Set rec=$$GetRec(.sub) Quit:sub=""                   |
o|       . Write rec,!                                          |o
 |       Use 0 Close:$IO'=DEV DEV                               |
 |       Write !,"All done with search."                        |
o|       Quit                                                   |o
```

EXAMPLE 12.1. Use of $IO

The use of $IO is demonstrated twice in Example 12.1: the first use is in line Search + 3 to check if the selected device is a magnetic tape drive; the second is in line Search + 7, where $IO is used to determine whether or not the selected device needs to be closed.

In the first example, we could use either the variable DEV or the system variable $IO as an argument to the IF command. Note that this use of device-dependent code does not represent a good programming practice. Checking for specific devices within an application lessens the portability of that application. If the program is moved to another implementation it may be necessary to search and change all device-specific references before the program can be run. It is desirable to move all device-specific checks to a single device selection utility. While it may still be necessary to rewrite this utility for each implementation, all the device-specific code is in one location and need be changed only once. In this example, the function $$GetDev should handle all special cases, such as rewinding tapes and the like.

The second example demonstrates a technique that is often employed to determine whether or not a device needs to be closed on completion of a process.

Often a programmer will specify output to the principal device when debugging programs. In this example, the search results could then be output to the screen, providing the programmer with a visual check of the program output. On completion, the device should be CLOSEd *only* if it was not the principal device. In Example 12.1, the conditioned CLOSE command will only be executed if DEV is *not* the principal device.

The system variables $X and $Y are used to reflect the system's "best guess" at the current line (row) and column position of the last character output to a device. These variables make most sense when considered in terms of output to a page-oriented device such as a video terminal or printer.

Each page consists of a number of lines (rows), and each row consists of a number of columns. The upper-left corner of a page is assigned the coordinates 0,0 [$Y (row)=0, $X (column)=0]. The row indicator ($Y) is set to zero each time a *new-page* sequence (# format control character) is output, and is incremented by one each time a *new-line* sequence (! format control character) is output. The column indicator ($X) is set to zero each time a new-page or new-line sequence is output. The value of $X is also incremented by one each time a graphics or printing character (decimal values 32 to 126) is output or input.

In addition, many implementations supply methods to synchronize the physical limits of a device with the internal updating of $X and $Y through the use of optional parameters to the OPEN and USE commands. For example, some implementations allow establishing the right margin of a device [for example, Use 10(RMAR = 132)] which is then used internally when updating $X and $Y. If this right margin is exceeded during an I/O operation, MUMPS automatically initiates a new-line sequence.

Thus, $X and $Y are used to keep track of the current position of the cursor within the page. The values of $X and $Y are used internally, as well as by MUMPS programs, and it is important that they accurately reflect the current page location. Internally, MUMPS uses the value of $X when using the format control sequences for tabbing to a column (that is, **?nn**). The tab control sequence is used to move the cursor from its current column position to the column position specified by nn by sending space characters to the device. If the starting value of $X is not less than the desired column position, no characters are output. At the end of the tab operation, $X is updated to reflect the new position. If the value of $X incorrectly reflects the column position, the actual effect of a tab format control sequence may be unpredictable.

While $X and $Y represent MUMPS best guess at the current page location, there are many instances in which MUMPS and the device lose synchronization. Consider what happens as lines are output to a video terminal. Most video terminals will display 24 lines with up to 80 characters on each line. On displaying the 25th line, the lines already on the screen are scrolled up; the first line is lost, and the new line is added at the bottom of the screen. Even though there are only 24 physical lines on the terminal, MUMPS still increments the value of $Y when the new line is displayed, and the value of $Y no longer reflects the actual screen line.

An even more dramatic difference occurs when special device functions such as cursor positioning are invoked. Most video terminals permit the cursor to be positioned at any screen location. Special character sequences are sent to the terminal, which are interpreted by the terminal as commands, not characters to be displayed. Unfortunately, terminal manufacturers have not settled on a uniform set of control sequences, and MUMPS does not generally recognize the effect of these character strings on the cursor position. When directly positioning the cursor on a device, it is usually necessary for the program to explicitly set $X and $Y to reflect to new location. The MUMPS standard does *not* allow altering the value of system variables with the SET command. However, most implementors recognize the need to synchronize the values of $X and $Y with the actual cursor position and permit these two system variables to be altered under program control.

The values of $X and $Y are saved and restored as devices are made current with the Use command. Each time the Use command is encountered, the values for $X and $Y are saved before the new device is made current. When a device is made current, the previous values for $X and $Y are reestablished; if this is the first time the device is used by the process, the values for $X and $Y are initialized to zero.

In addition to these three system variables, most implementations also support additional system variables used to track the status of the current device. These variables (like all implementation-specific variables) start with the characters $Z and are typically used to reflect device-specific information, such as the status of an I/O operation or the status of a device. See the discussion of magnetic tape drives (Section 12.4.3) for examples.

12.4 Devices

MUMPS supports a wide variety of device types, including video terminals, printers, magnetic tape drives, and others. These devices all have a single common trait when used within MUMPS; they are used to transfer strings of characters (usually from the ASCII character set) between the device and a MUMPS process. The READ and WRITE commands provide a rich choice of how the strings are processed (for example, fixed- or variable-length READs, timed READs, and a variety of formatting controls). The general I/O environment of MUMPS, coupled with its string-oriented functions, supports a level of device independence that exceeds what is typically found in other programming languages.

However, despite the overall functional similarity between devices, the physical differences between them often preclude a truly device-independent environment. Magnetic tape drives often have to be positioned (rewind, skip records, advance to tape mark, and so on), sequential disk files have to be opened, printers often lack keyboards, and so on. In addition, the physical characteristics of devices, even within the same general category, often cause major programming difficulties. For example, video terminals vary significantly in a number of basic characteristics, such as how the screen is cleared or how the cursor is positioned. In the next sections we examine some of the more common device categories and how they can be managed under control of MUMPS programs.

12.4.1 Video Terminals

Video terminals are the most commonly used devices for communicating with computers. They consist of a communications port, a video memory to hold characters sent by the computer, a display screen, and a keyboard to send data back to the computer. In many cases, simple video terminals are now being supplanted by microcomputers that emulate a terminal.

In the simplest mode of operation, characters sent by the computer are received by the terminal and stored in its video memory. Each character is displayed at the current cursor position and then the cursor position is advanced to the next location. If the character sent was the last on a line, the cursor is advanced to the first character position on the next line. If the next line is off the bottom of the screen, the entire screen scrolls up one line; the line originally at the top of the screen is lost, and the new line becomes the last line on the screen.

Characters are usually transmitted between the terminal and the computer over a twisted-pair cable using a standard hardware/software protocol referred to as **RS-232**. This standard defines the electrical and connection interface for transmitting digital information and is explained in some detail in Appendix H. Briefly, characters are transmitted between the terminal and computer as strings of bits (*serial* transmission). Interfaces internal to both the terminal and the computer are responsible for encoding and decoding the bit strings to and from their ASCII representation. Each character is serially divided into 10 bits of data before it is transmitted as a block. The speed at which the communications proceeds is referred to as the *baud* rate and reflects the number of *bits* that can be transmitted in one second; 9600 baud equates to 960 characters per second (960 characters times 10 bits per character equals 9,600 baud).

The RS-232 interface is described as *asynchronous*; that is, characters can be simultaneously transmitted and received over the same twisted-pair cable. RS-232 interfaces typically operate in one of two basic modes: *half-duplex* or *full-duplex*. As keys are pressed on the keyboard, the encoded character is sent through the communications port to the computer. When a terminal is running in *half-duplex* mode, each character sent to the computer is immediately displayed (by the terminal) on the terminal's screen. In *full-duplex* mode, the character is not automatically displayed on the terminal; instead, it is transmitted to the computer, which echoes it back to the terminal for display. The process of having the computer echo received characters is used to ensure that the character sent by the terminal is correctly received and interpreted by the computer; any transmission discrepancies will appear on the screen. Full-duplex operations can also affect programming in that the character echo can be suppressed for selected applications (such as reading a password or transmitting data between two MUMPS processes on different computers). MUMPS systems generally support both forms of protocol, although the full-duplex is the most commonly used.

12.4.1.1 Display Attributes In addition to the basic mode of operations, most video terminals are also capable of performing a wide variety of special functions that can significantly enhance interaction between the computer and the user. These include features such as erasing all or selected parts of the screen, direct positioning of the cursor location, providing scrolling windows, or displaying complex graphics, to mention just a few. Not all video terminals have the same functional capabilities, and even in those that do different terminals often require different commands to invoke the same function.

To activate a special display function, it is necessary for the program to send the terminal a special *control sequence* defining the desired change. These control sequences usually take the form of a special nondisplayable control character, optionally followed by additional characters. The first control character *primes* the terminal that the in-coming characters are to be interpreted as part of a control command, and not to be displayed on the screen. The <u>ESC</u> character (decimal value 27) is often used as the lead-in character for these command sequences, and the command strings are often referred to as *escape sequences*.

The number of characters that make up a device command depends both on the command and the terminal type. While the first character of the command string is usually a nonprinting control code (decimal value 1 to 31), other characters in the escape sequence are often graphic (displayable) characters. Even when graphic characters are transmitted as part of an escape sequence, they are not displayed, although they may affect the value of $X or $Y. After processing the appropriate number of characters for the command being received, the terminal automatically switches back to display mode; subsequent graphics characters will then be displayed.

Consider the escape sequence(s) necessary to clear the screen on a VT-100 terminal. Two sequences are actually required: the first is used to home the cursor; the second clears the display from the current cursor location to the end of the screen. Example 12.2 demonstrates two methods for clearing the screen on a VT-100.

```
o|>Write *27,"[H",*27,"[2J"←                                          |o
 |                                                                    |
 |      -or-                                                          |
o|                                                                    |o
 |>Write *27,*91,*72,*27,*91,*50,*74←                                 |
```

EXAMPLE 12.2. Clearing the screen on a VT-100

In both cases, the same characters are output to the device and the screen is cleared. However, the two techniques may have different effects on the updated values of the variables $X and $Y. The MUMPS standard specifies that all graphics characters output as string literals will cause the values of $X and $Y to be updated appropriately. It does *not* specify what happens to $X and $Y when the <u>Write</u> *char syntax is used; that decision is left up to the implementor, and many do *not* update $X and $Y when this syntax is used.

Example 12.3 demonstrates a simple technique that can be used to determine whether or not the <u>Write *char</u> syntax updates the value of $X under your implementation.

```
o|>Write !,$C(84,101,115,116,105,110,103) Set x=$X Write ?9,x←      |o
|Testing  7                                                         |
|>Write !,*84,*101,*115,*116,*105,*110,*103 Set x=$X Write ?9,x←    |
o|Testing        0                                                  |o
```

EXAMPLE 12.3. Effect of Write *char syntax on $X

If the Write *char syntax does *not* update the value of $X as graphic characters
are written, the output will look like Example 12.3. The characters "Testing" will
be output, but the value of $X remains zero. When tabbing out to the ninth column,
MUMPS assumes it still needs to output nine space characters. If $X is updated,
then both commands will produce identical output (that is, "Testing 7").

Regardless of the Write command syntax used to clear the screen in Example
12.2, *neither* results in the correct setting of $X or $Y. MUMPS does *not* recognize
the effect of either of the escape sequences and, consequently, does not set $X or
$Y to zero. Two methods can be used to reset $X and $Y: they can be explicitly
set after the Write command [Set ($X,$Y)=0]; or the # format control character
can be included as the last argument to the Write command (Write
*27,"[H",*27,"[2J",#).

> *Note*: the MUMPS standard does *not* permit alteration of system
> variables (those starting with a $) with the SET command, but most
> implementations permit Seting $X and $Y.

To facilitate device-independent programming techniques, most implementors supply utilities to define terminal display characteristics for use by applications.
While this represents a step in the right direction, the information maintained for
video terminals is usually limited to basic descriptions (that is, the number of lines
and characters per line) and a few control sequences (how to clear the screen or
position the cursor). One of the more commonly used approaches is to call a
terminal definition subroutine at the beginning of an application. This subroutine
returns a number of device-specific variables for the principal I/O device associated
with the process that can then be used within the application. Typical of the variables
returned is the list shown in Table 12.2.

These variables can then be used within the application when manipulating
the display. The next example demonstrates how these variables are initialized and
used.

In this example, the variables FF, RM, and XY returned from the utility
CURRENT^%TRM are used to clear the screen (Write @FF) and then to center
two lines of header information. The code should work on all terminal types defined
in the utility %TRM. The text lines will be centered correctly, regardless of the
terminal's physical line length (for example, 40, 80, or 132 characters) or the length

TABLE 12.2 VARIABLES RETURNED TO IMPROVE DEVICE INDEPENDENCE

Variable	Function and use
FF	A string to be used as an indirect argument to a <u>Write</u> command to clear the screen and set the system variables $X and $Y to zero (for example, <u>Write</u> @FF).
RM	A variable defining the terminals right margin (that is, the $X value of the last character that will fit on a line, 79 for most video terminals).
SL	The screen length (number of lines on the screen, 24 for most video terminals).
XY	A list of commands used as an argument to an <u>Xecute</u> command to position the cursor to a specified location on the screen and update $X and $Y appropriately. For a VT-100, the returned value of <u>XY</u> might be:

"Write *27,"[",dy + 1,";",dx + 1,*72 Set $X = dx,$Y = dy"

and it could be used with the following code:

"Set dx = 20,dy = 10 Xecute XY"

```
o|GetData ;Main entry point to enter/edit patient data        |o
 |        Do CURRENT^%TRM ;Get variables FF, SL, RM, and XY     |
 |        Write @FF,$$Center("XYZ Medical Clinic")             |
o|        Write !,$$Center("Patient Data Entry/Edit"),!        |o
 |GetID Read !,"Patient ID: ",PID Quit:PID=""                  |
 |          .                                                   |
o|          .                                                   |o
 |Center(txt) ;display "txt" centered left-to-right            |
 |        New dx,dy Set dy=$Y,dx=RM-$L(txt)\2                   |
o|        Xecute XY                                            |o
 |        Quit txt                                             |
```

EXAMPLE 12.4. Using FF, RM, and XY

of the text to be displayed. After invoking the subroutine <u>GetData</u>, the screen will appear as in Example 12.5.

```
o|                      XYZ Medical Clinic                     |o
 |                   Patient Data Entry/Edit                    |
 |                                                              |
o|Patient ID:                                                  |o
 |                                                              |
 |                                                              |
o|                                                             |o
```

EXAMPLE 12.5. Screen after calling executing Example 12.14

While this approach is a step toward providing a device-independent programming environment, it still leaves much to be desired. Section 12.5.1 examines a number of more advanced techniques that permit greater control of the terminal.

12.4.1.2 Keyboard Interactions In many respects, programming keyboard input is much less complicated than managing the display, especially if we restrict our consideration to the 128 ASCII character set defined by the MUMPS standard. While the actual key layout may differ between terminal types, all can generate the basic ASCII character set. The graphic characters are generated by pressing individual labeled keys (with or without the SHIFT key), and the nongraphic control characters can all be generated by holding down the <CTRL> key while pressing one of the other keys or by pressing the <DEL> key. See Appendix A for the key stroke(s) necessary to generate the entire 128 ASCII characters.

In general, there are two different types of READs in MUMPS: the multi-character READ (for example, Read Ans or Read Ans#10) and the single-character READ (for example, Read *char). There are a number of functional differences between these two types of READs.

The multicharacter reads (whether variable or fixed length) are used to input one or more characters into a variable. As characters are input from the keyboard, some of the control characters (Table 3.1) have special significance. These characters are *not* included in the input string, but, instead, act as commands to MUMPS. For example, the <CTRL>U character is often used to instruct MUMPS to delete all characters input since the READ started. Usually, characters are automatically echoed on the display as they are pressed. Automatic echo can be enabled or disabled on some systems with appropriate arguments to the OPEN or USE commands. On completion of the READ, the variable used as the READ argument contains the string of characters read from the keyboard. If the READ was terminated with the <ENTER> key, that character is *not* included in the input string.

In contrast, single-character READs can be used to input any character on the keyboard; the special control characters listed in Table 3.1 are not intercepted by MUMPS and are passed through to the variable. Usually the character being read is *not* echoed to the display, although this is implementation specific. On completion of the READ, the variable used as the READ argument contains the decimal equivalent of the ASCII character associated with the key pressed. While the fixed-length READ with a *readcount* of *one* also reads only one character, it is *not* the same as a single-character READ. The fixed-length READ responds to the control characters in Table 3.1 and returns an ASCII character, not to its decimal equivalent.

A READ command can be satisfied in a variety of different ways, depending on the READ syntax used. In general, three conditions are used to terminate a READ from the keyboard: when a special terminating character (such as <EN-TER>) is pressed; when the number of characters input matches the specified readcount for fixed length READs (readcount is assumed to be *one* for single-character READs); or, if timeout is specified, when timeout seconds have elapsed since the beginning of the READ. When a READ is terminated by timeout, the characters input up to the point where the READ is terminated are returned in the variable, and the system variable $TEST is set to zero. In addition, many implementations permit the programmer to designate other characters that will terminate a READ. Definition of terminating characters is usually accomplished by including an optional parameter to an OPEN or USE command.

TABLE 12.3 VT-100 SPECIAL KEY CODES
SENT TO THE COMPUTER

Keyboard key	Characters sent to the computer
Up arrow	\<ESC>[A
Down arrow	\<ESC>[B
Right arrow	\<ESC>[C
Left arrow	\<ESC>[D
PF1	\<ESC>OP
PF2	\<ESC>OQ
PF3	\<ESC>OR
PF4	\<ESC>OS

Unfortunately, things get more complicated when we expand our coverage to the special keys that are often available on the keyboard. These include such keys as *cursor control* (up, down, left, and right arrow keys) and special *function keys*. As with many of the special display functions described previously, there is no standard definition of these keys or the code(s) transmitted to the computer when they are pressed. Usually, terminals convert these special keys to single control characters or special escape sequences which are sent to the computer. Table 12.3 lists the characters sent to the computer by a VT-100 terminal when these special keys are activated.

If one of these keys is pressed during a normal READ (for example, Read Ans), the characters are simply inserted into the input stream and echoed on the display as if the individual keys had been pressed. For example, if the user presses the *right-arrow* key, three characters will be inserted into the input stream [*escape* (decimal 27) and "[D"], and the two graphics characters "[D" will be echoed on the screen.

Use of these special characters within a MUMPS application requires explicit programming; they are *not* handled automatically by the system. One method for interpreting special keyboard escape sequences available on some implementations involves the use of a special implementation-specific variable used to hold escape sequences received from the keyboard. With this method, the programmer first specifies (with an OPEN or USE command) that the \<ESC> character will also be interpreted as a READ terminator. When a READ is satisfied, a special system variable can be checked to see how the READ terminated. This variable will contain either the code for the \<ENTER> key (decimal value 13) or the *entire* escape sequence, if that was how the READ was terminated.

Unfortunately, this is not always enough. Consider the case where we wish to implement an editing keyboard READ (that is, allow the user to move through an existing answer using the left- and right-arrow keys and make changes in the answer). Using the technique just described, we can detect when an arrow key is pressed, and, using the cursor positioning techniques described in Section 12.4.1.1, can move the cursor left or right as indicated. But how can we resume a partially completed READ? We can't. MUMPS has no direct method for issuing a keyboard READ with the input buffer initialized to anything but an empty string.

One method for getting around this problem is to write an extrinsic function that mimics the normal MUMPS READ command, but with extended editing capabilities. An example of an extrinsic function to perform an editing keyboard READ is presented in Section 12.5.4.

12.4.2 Printing Terminals

Printing terminals are similar in many respects to video terminals, except that they generate hard-copy output. There is an enormous variety of printer types (line printers, dot matrix, daisy wheel, laser printers, and others), and an even wider variety of capabilities [character size, pitch, and font; page orientation (horizontal or vertical); type style (bold, underlined); and graphics capabilities]. The challenge of writing device-independent code for printers is even more difficult than for video terminals.

Printers are usually interfaced as either RS-232 devices (see Section 12.4.1 and Appendix H) or through a special *parallel interface*. Parallel interfaces tend to be faster than serial RS-232 interfaces; characters are transmitted seven or eight bits at a time rather than one bit at a time as found in the RS-232 interfaces. For the most part, the actual printer interface is immaterial and does not affect the programmer.

As with video devices, printers often accept *escape sequences* from the computer to alter basic characteristics such as horizontal and vertical pitch, print font, and so on. In addition, many printers can be interfaced to accept characters faster than they can actually print them. This is known as *buffering*. As in video terminals, it is usually necessary to provide *handshaking* between the terminal and the computer to permit the printer to inform the computer when its buffer fills (see Appendix H for a description of some handshaking conventions). Again, this is usually transparent to the programmer and is handled by the system.

While we will not directly address writing device-independent routines using printers, many of the techniques discussed in Sections 12.5 can also be applied to these devices.

12.4.3 Magnetic Tape Drives

Magnetic tape devices are designed to process large volumes of sequential data. They are typically used in MUMPS applications to archive data, to save and restore globals and routines, and to transfer data to or from other computer systems.

While the tape industry has standardized more than the video terminal or printer industry, there are still a number of important variations between the way data are physically stored on tape, as well as how they are logically organized. Most industry standard tape drives will read or write to or from 1/2-inch tapes using a nine-track format (each character is divided into nine bits with each bit written or read by a separate head). The data are usually recorded at one of three densities: 800, 1,600 or 6,250 bytes per inch (BPI). Tapes have to be read at the same density with which they were written.

Beyond the physical characteristics of a tape drive, one also has to consider the logical format of the tape. Tapes can be *labeled* or *unlabeled*, they can be written using different character sets, individual records can be fixed or variable length, and so on. Both the physical and logical characteristics of a tape drive are usually established through implementation-specific OPEN and USE commands. You are advised to check your system documentation for a more detailed description of these characteristics and how they can be established.

Input/output operations from or to magnetic tape are handled as strings of characters; binary data cannot generally be processed by MUMPS. In addition, MUMPS is usually incapable of deciphering the file-oriented directories written by some operating systems. For the most part, MUMPS treats magnetic tape I/O as streams of characters; normal reads will input characters from the tape until a <Carriage Return> character (decimal code 13) is encountered. Reading this character is analogous to pressing the <ENTER> key on a keyboard read; it signifies the end of the current record and the READ is terminated.

> MUMPS cannot generally READ or WRITE binary data from or to devices and is limited to ASCII (or EBCDIC) character sets.

Implementations supporting magnetic tapes often support translation between the ASCII character set used internally by MUMPS and the EBCDIC (Extended Binary Coded Decimal Interchange Code) character set used on many mainframe computers. This translation is automatic if it has been requested (that is, through appropriate OPEN or USE commands); on input, EBCDIC characters are translated to ASCII, and on output, ASCII characters are translated to EBCDIC. This translation is transparent to the MUMPS program performing the READ or WRITE operations.

When data are output to tape, they are written as *blocks* of information. The length of the block is established with an OPEN or CLOSE command and is usually 512, 1,024, or 2,048 bytes in length. These blocks are similar in nature to the disk blocks described in Chapter 11; they represent the smallest physical unit of information transferred between the magnetic tape and a memory buffer. Each block can contain many records or lines of characters. When processing a READ request, MUMPS goes to the magnetic tape buffer and inputs characters from there; if the buffer is exhausted, MUMPS reads the next block from magnetic tape into the buffer and continues extracting characters from the buffer until the READ is satisfied. This process is reversed for WRITE operations, with characters being output to the buffer until it fills and then written to tape.

But even after the basic operating characteristics have been established, magnetic tape operations differ significantly from video or printing terminals. Tapes can be rewound, blocks can be skipped (either backward or forward) and special error conditions can arise that need to be recognized and acted on. For example, one of the more common practices used to segregate logical files on magnetic tape

TABLE 12.4 HYPOTHETICAL MAGNETIC TAPE CONTROL SEQUENCES

MUMPS command	Control function
Write *-1	Rewind the tape and set to off line.
Write *-2	Rewind the tape. If output operations were in progress, the contents of the buffer are first written out and any tape marks or trailer blocks are also written, depending on the format established with an OPEN or USE command.
Write *-3	Write TAPE MARK to tape, first writing any data that are currently held in the buffer.
Write *-4	Write end of file (EOF) lable. First empty the buffer and then output appropriate trailer label.

is to separate them with *tape marks*. Tape marks are special blocks that do not contain data but, instead, act as markers on the tape. Reading a tape mark block is considered an error on most MUMPS systems. Another error condition that is different from terminal I/O is that it is possible to physically run out of data on a tape (we reach the end of tape or EOT). In general, there is a greater need to be able to interrogate and control the magnetic tape operation than is found in terminal operations.

Controlling the tape is often handled by a special format of the WRITE *CHAR syntax in which the decimal value of CHAR is interpreted in a different context when directed to a magnetic tape than to a terminal. Special values of CHAR initiate control sequences on the magnetic tape controller, rather than being sent to the tape as data; often *negative* values for CHAR are used to signify this control function (see Table 12.4).

It must be stressed that the control sequences listed in Table 12.4 are implementation specific and represent but a small subset of the commands needed to control tape operations; different systems may implement these functions in different manners.

In addition, it is necessary to be able to interrogate the status of the tape drive after an I/O operation. Most systems support one or more special system variables that contain the status of the current device, often as a series of bits (for a magnetic tape these usually reflect the magnetic tape hardware status register). Many conditions reflected in this status register will also cause an error condition under MUMPS and initiate a MUMPS error trap (error traps and error processing are discussed in Chapter 13).

Table 12.5 represents the contents of a system variable ($ZA), which holds the current magnetic tape status for one MUMPS implementation. The value of $ZA is interpreted as an integer number that can then be interrogated by a MUMPS program. Individual bits in the number can be examined using techniques shown in the next example.

This example demonstrates one technique for extracting individual bits from an integer. MUMPS does not have specific bit-oriented operators; the AND and OR operators return a logical value (zero or one), not a logical combination of

TABLE 12.5 MAGNETIC TAPE STATUS REGISTER—$ZA

Bit	Value	Trap?	Meaning
0	1	Yes	Logical error, mixed READ and WRITE operations
1	2	No	Tape in process of rewinding
2	4	No	Tape is write protected
3	8	No	Density 800 BPI
4	16	No	Density 1600 BPI
5	32	No	Density 6250 BPI
6	64	No	Tape is at beginning (BOT)
7	128	No	Tape is on line
8	256	Yes	Record length (block size) error
9	512	No	End of tape (EOT)
10	1,024	Yes	Bad parity or CRC error
11	2,048	Yes	Tape controller error
12	4,096	Yes	Tape mark (TM)
13	8,192	Yes	Tape not ready

```
o|Ready(MT) ;Return status of Tape ON-LINE (True/False)    |o
 |         New online Use MT                                |
 |         Set online=$ZA\128#2 Use 0                       |
o|         Quit online                                      |o
```

EXAMPLE 12.6. Check the status of bit 6 (on line)

the bits in the operands. The general formula to determine the value of a given bit is

$$Bit = integer\backslash(2**(pos))\#2$$

where *pos* is the bit number being checked (bit 0 is the least significant bit in the *integer*). This calculation shifts the bit to be checked to the right to make it the least significant bit (the integer divide eliminates all bits shifted to the right of the implied decimal point), and the modulo operator is used to see whether or not the result is odd (the least significant bit is on). Example 12.7 demonstrates a general-purpose utility to display the current status of a magnetic tape.

While MUMPS does not have specific bit-oriented operators, it is possible to examine individual bits in a normal decimal number using the integer divide (\) and modulo (#) operators.

```
o|MTstatus(MT) ;Display current status of MagTape MT.          |o
 |            New i,status Use MT Set status=$ZA Use 0           |
 |            Write !,"Status Word = ",status For i=1:1:14 Do Disp|
o|           Quit                                               |o
 |Disp        New bit Set:i>1 status=status\2 Set bit=status#2    |
 |            Write:bit !,$P($T(Status+i),";",2,99)              |
o|           Quit                                               |o
 |Status ;List of status bits and their meaning                 |
 |            ;Mixed Read/Write Operations                       |
o|           ;Tape REWINDING                                    |o
 |            ;Tape WRITE-PROTECTED                              |
 |            ;800 BPI                                           |
o|           ;1600 BPI                                          |o
 |            ;6250 BPI                                          |
 |            ;Beginning of tape (BOT)                           |
o|           ;Tape ON-LINE                                      |o
 |            ;Block Size Error                                  |
 |            ;End Of Tape (EOT)                                 |
o|           ;Parity or CRC Error                               |o
 |            ;Tape Controller Error                             |
 |            ;Tape Mark (TM)                                    |
o|           ;Tape Not Ready                                    |o
```

EXAMPLE 12.7. Display current magnetic tape status

12.4.4 Sequential Disk Files

Most MUMPS implementations support, in addition to global and routine files, access to more standard disk files. In dedicated MUMPS systems (those in which MUMPS is *not* running under the control of another operating system), the files are usually not named but simply refer to areas of the disk reserved for sequential data. The devices used to transfer data to and from these areas are usually referred to as *sequential disk processors*, and the files generated through them are temporary.

When MUMPS is running under another general-purpose operating system (such as MS-DOS on microcomputers), it is usually possible to create or use files compatible with the operating system. In general, there are special arguments to the OPEN command to indicate the file name to be used (including, where appropriate, disk and directory addresses) and special parameters to indicate what is to be done with the file (for example, read, write, append, and delete). Operations that are inconsistent with the established parameters (such as opening a nonexistent file for reading data or trying to write data to a file opened for reading) usually generate an error condition, which can be trapped by the program (see the discussion on error processing in Chapter 13).

As with magnetic tapes, the information written or read to or from the disk file is assumed to be strings of characters, not binary data. It is possible to open a binary file and read from that file, but the data are read in as eight-bit characters and will probably appear as garbage to the program.

To demonstrate the use of disk files, we will explore the creation of a disk file that can be used to export MUMPS data for subsequent processing by LOTUS-123. LOTUS expects import files to be of a specified format: they consist of logical

TABLE 12.6 DATA TO BE
EXPORTED TO LOTUS

Global Reference	Data
ˆSrch(1,1)	10,13,142,1,76,28
,2)	121,23,4,57,71,47
.	
.	
,25)	41,89,,14,62,101

lines of data [each line is terminated with a carriage return and line feed combination
(*13,*10)], with each *line* representing a *row* of data in the spread sheet. Within
each line, individual fields are separated from each other with commas, and each
field represents a new *column* in the spread sheet.

Table 12.6 shows the data that could have been created by a search program
for exporting to LOTUS. Assuming that each node in the global represents a logical
line of data to be exported, we can write a general-purpose subroutine to create
a file that can then be imported by LOTUS.

```
o|Export(gref) ;Create disk file of nodes under "gref"     |o
 |       New File,sub Set sub=""                            |
 |       Read !,"Output data as file: ",File,! Quit:File="" |
o|       Open 10:(FILE=File:MODE="Write") Use 10            |o
 |       For  Set sub=$O(@gref@(sub)) Quit:sub="" Do OUT    |
 |       Close 10 Write !,"all done."                       |
o|       Quit                                               |o
 |OUT    Write @gref@(sub),! Use 0 Write "." Use 10         |
 |       Quit                                               |
o|---------------------------------------------------------|o
 |>Do Export("ˆSrch(1)")←                                   |
 |Output data as file: A:LDATA.123←                         |
o|.........................                                 |o
 |all done.                                                 |
 |>                                                         |
```

EXAMPLE 12.8. Subroutine to dump global data to a disk file

On some micro-based MUMPS implementations, the CLOSE command automatically outputs a special terminating character (<CTRL>Z, decimal value =
26), which is used by the operating system to mark the end of a text-oriented file.
On reading external disk files into MUMPS, this flag can be used to terminate
input, as demonstrated in the next example.

```
o|Get    Open 10:(FILE="TEST.DAT":MODE="READ")             |o
 |Read   Use 10 Read data If data=$C(26) Close 10 Quit     |
 |       Do Calc Goto Read                                  |
```

EXAMPLE 12.9. Terminating input from disk file with <CTRL>Z

It must be emphasized that this is but one of many possible conventions for terminating files; such conventions may not be followed by all systems or even all files on a given system. Some implementations maintain special system variables that can be interrogated to determine the status (for example, End-of-File) of the device after I/O operations. Again, check your documentation.

What if we wanted to use the same data in Table 12.6, but now format it for export to a "canned" statistical package that expected fixed-field records instead of the variable-length records exported to LOTUS? The import file for this package consists of a variable number of records (each record is a logical line of data) with the individual fields within the record of fixed length (five characters wide, for example) rather than separated by commas as in the previous example. Example 12.10 demonstrates how we could take the same data and generate a new output file of this format.

```
o|Export(gref) ;Create disk file of nodes under "gref"        |o
 |        New File,sub Set sub=""                               |
 |        Read !,"Output data as file: ",File,! Quit:File=""    |
o|        Open 10:(FILE=File:MODE="Write") Use 10               |o
 |        For  Set sub=$O(@gref@(sub)) Quit:sub="" Do OUT       |
 |        Close 10 Write !,"all done."                          |
o|        Quit                                                  |o
 |OUT     New i,line,x Set line="",x=@gref@(sub))               |
 |        For i=1:1:$L(x,",") Set line=line $J($P(x,",",i),5)   |
o|        Write line,! Use 0 Write "." Use 10                   |o
 |        Quit                                                  |
 |_____|
o|>Do Export("^Srch(1)")←                                      |o
 |Output data as file: A:LDATA.EXP←                            |
 |......................                                        |
o|all done.                                                    |o
 |>                                                            |
```

EXAMPLE 12.10. Subroutine to create a fixed-field disk file

The only real difference between this subroutine and the one in Example 12.8 is in the part OUT, where we use the $JUSTIFY command to pad out each field to five characters. Example 12.11 demonstrates what the created file looks like.

```
o|>Open 10:(FILE="A:LDATA.EXP":MODE="READ")←                   |o
 |>For  Use 10 Read L Quit:L=$C(26)  Write !,L←               |
 |                                                             |
o|   10   13  142    1   76   28                               |o
 |  121   23    4   57   71   47                               |
 |                    .                                        |
o|                                                             |o
 |                    .                                        |
 |   41   89        14   62  101                               |
o|>                                                           |o
```

EXAMPLE 12.11. Sample dump of file created in Example 12.10

12.4.5 Print Spool Devices

Print spool devices are often used as alternative output devices for data being sent to a printer. One problem often encountered in a multiuser environment is gaining ownership of printers for output, since each device can only be owned by one process at a time. The spool device is unique in that it can be owned by more than one process at any given time. Output directed to the spool device is segregated from output from other MUMPS processes and is terminated when the device is closed. Usually, the lines output to the spool device are actually held in a global for processing by a general-purpose *un-spool* utility program.

Spool print devices can generally be shared among more than one MUMPS process.

The unspooler program (often a job running in the background) constantly monitors the spool file looking for completed jobs (that is, when a spool device is CLOSEd by a MUMPS process). At this time it checks for an available printer and begins printing the accumulated text. The application that originally spooled the text can continue processing data or even spool additional print jobs.

This approach to printing has many advantages over direct ownership of the printer by the application program. Often the printer is relatively slow when compared to the processing speed of the application, tying up the terminal (and the user) for more time than is necessary. Spooling reports, instead of printing them directly, allows many jobs to simultaneously create reports instead of waiting for a printer to become available. If the application is to generate multiple copies of a report directly on a printer, it must be run separately for each copy, whereas a report that has been spooled can be printed any number of times before it is deleted from the spool file. And, finally, the application program does not have to concern itself with printer malfunctions (such as the printer running out of paper); this is the responsibility of the unspool utility.

12.4.6 Miscellaneous Devices

The category miscellaneous is, by no means, designed to connote lower importance than devices covered in the previous sections. There are simply too many devices to cover them all completely. In this section we briefly discuss two broad categories of devices: networks and the wide variety of devices that can be attached to computers through RS-232 ports.

12.4.6.1 RS-232 Devices The RS-232 interface is one of the most popular and widely supported interfaces used for connecting peripheral devices to computers.

We have already discussed its use with video terminals and printers (Sections 12.4.4, 12.4.2, and Appendix H), but it is also used extensively with other devices. These include card embossers and readers, plotters, light wands, automated laboratory equipment, and other computers, to name just a few.

MUMPS, with its flexible I/O environment and powerful string primitives, is an ideal language to interact with character-oriented devices such as these. With its ability to transmit and receive the entire ASCII character set (as either blocks of data or as single characters) and its ability to issue timed READs, MUMPS provides the programmer with all the necessary components to control and collect information from these devices.

12.4.6.2 Networks   Networks come in a bewildering variety of forms with a broad range of features. Basically, networks are designed to communicate data between computers or between devices and computers. They can be implemented using relatively slow speed terminal lines or specialized high-speed hardware. Transmission of data can be over simple twisted-pair cable, coaxial cable, fiber cable, radio transmissions, or microwaves. Networks can be configured as buses, rings, stars, point-to-point connections, and others, and employ any of dozens of transmission protocols.

Almost all MUMPS implementations support networks and networking of data transmissions in one form or another. For the most part, this networking is transparent to the programmer, and it is not necessary to understand either the hardware or software protocol in use. One example of networking in MUMPS is the use of distributed databases and extended global syntax discussed in Section 10.5. Systems supporting networks usually permit the placement of globals and routines on different computers within a network. These data can be shared between users on different systems with either implicit references (that is, the MUMPS system automatically maps the references to the correct computer) or through explicit references using the square bracket ("[]") syntax.

Unfortunately, there is not yet a standard definition of either hardware or software networking protocol, and it is not usually possible to network different implementations of MUMPS. The MUMPS Development Committee is currently trying to establish a networking standard to facilitate the communication of information between different systems, but resolution is probably years away.

12.5 Advanced Topics on Device I/O

In the previous sections we examined a number of specific peripheral devices and their use under MUMPS. While devices in the same general category (for example, video terminals) all share common attributes, they differ substantially in their overall capabilities and how these capabilities are invoked. In this section we examine methods that can be employed to take advantage of special terminal characteristics while, at the same time, maintaining a high degree of device independence. We concentrate primarily on video terminals, since they represent the window into the MUMPS environment most often experienced by the end user. The principles and techniques developed to exploit the characteristics of video terminals can be expanded to cover other types of devices.

To develop high-quality interactive programs, we want to take advantage of all the capabilities inherent in most of today's video terminals. Unfortunately, as we have seen in the earlier sections of this chapter, the methods used to invoke these functions vary significantly from terminal-to-terminal and from system to system. One of the more vexing problems facing programmers today is the variety of control sequences required to activate the same function on different terminal types or to input special keys such as the cursor (arrow) or function keys.

Far too many times I have seen excellent MUMPS applications whose only major shortcoming is the method in which they interact with the user. Often question and answer sessions are processed as if the program were being run on a printer. Questions are presented sequentially, slowly filling the screen, while older questions and answers scroll off the top of the display. One wonders why programmers persist in writing line-oriented applications instead of taking advantage of the screen-oriented I/O. Often programmers attempt to write programs around the lowest common denominator (the "glass teletype") to improve the portability of applications between different terminal types and MUMPS implementations. This need not be the case. With MUMPS's flexible I/O environment, it is possible to write screen-oriented programs to enhance user interactions and still keep programs portable between different terminal types and systems.

We start this discussion by developing a set of extrinsic functions for device- and system-independent control of the display screen (Section 12.5.1). In Section 12.5.2 we explore a function to interface with the keyboard, translating special keys to a common format for use by an application. Section 12.5.3 demonstrates the use of the display functions and the single-character READ function developed in Sections 12.5.1 and 12.5.2, in an application designed to collect multiple choice and options from the keyboard. Next, we examine an editing keyboard READ function in Section 12.5.4. Section 12.5.5 explores the use of a screen-oriented question driver to manage the display and collect user answers, incorporating the functions developed in the earlier sections. These examples are not designed to be exhaustive solutions to the problems of managing video terminals. Instead, they should serve as a starting point for a collection of support utilities to match your environment and meet your specific needs.

A complete listing of the functions described in this section, along with their descriptions, can be found in Appendix I.

12.5.1 Screen Handling Utilities

In this section we explore a set of device functions that can be used in managing terminal I/O and then design a set of extrinsic functions that can be invoked to activate the functions. The first step is to define and name the terminal functions that we wish to control. Table 12.7 presents a set of device control mnemonics, along with a brief description of their function and their effect on the system variables $X and $Y.

TABLE 12.7 DEVICE FUNCTIONAL MNEMONICS

Device	Mnemonic functional description
Clr	*Control function:* Erase the screen, position cursor at upper-left corner; set $X and $Y to zero.
Cup(X,Y)	*Control function:* Position the cursor to location X,Y; update the values of $X and $Y to the values of X and Y.
Eol	*Control function:* Erase the screen from current location to end of line; $X and $Y remain unchanged.
Eos	*Control function:* Erase the screen from the current location to end of screen; $X and $Y remain unchanged.
Hoff	*Control function:* Turn intensity from HIGH (bold) to NORMAL (dim); $X and $Y unchanged.
Hon	*Control function:* Turn intensity from NORMAL (dim) to HIGH (bold); $X and $Y unchanged.
Len	*Descriptive function:* Contains the screen LENgth in lines. Performs no action and does not affect the values of $X or $Y.
Reset	*Control function:* Used to reset the terminal. Clears the screen (Clr), sets normal intensity (Hoff), normal video (Roff), and underlining off (Uoff); sets the values of $X and $Y to zero.
Roff	*Control function:* Turn reverse video OFF; $X and $Y unchanged.
Ron	*Control function:* Turn reverse video ON; $X and $Y unchanged.
Uoff	*Control function:* Turn underline OFF; $X and $Y unchanged.
Uon	*Control function:* Turn underline ON; $X and $Y unchanged.
Wid	*Descriptive function:* Contains the line WIDTH in characters. Performs no action and does not change the values of $X or $Y.

There are two broad types of functional mnemonics in this table: those that are used to *control* or change the display, and those that *describe* certain physical attributes of the terminal, such as the number of lines on the display or the length of each line. The control functions are used to alter the display and require sending one or more character sequences to the terminal. The descriptive functions are used within an application to make decisions concerning control of the display, such as the need to pause at the bottom of the screen or how to center (left to right) text.

Table 12.7 represents an expanded list of the device mnemonics originally presented in Table 12.2 and defines the minimum functional list for our utilities. The only *essential* function is Cup; we would be hard-pressed to perform sophisticated screen I/O without being able to position the cursor.

It is desirable to have terminals that support the Eol and Eos functions in hardware, but these features can be *emulated* in software, provided the terminal supports cursor positioning. The remaining functions (Hoff, Hon, Roff, Ron, Uoff, and Uon) all control display attributes that are used to highlight or accent the display; they are used to improve the video image, but are usually not essential to the applications. The functions listed in Table 12.7 could easily be expanded to include a variety of other terminal characteristics such as color (foreground and background) and blink.

Having defined the functions to be implemented, we now examine how they can be invoked by an application. We could use the general philosophy described in Section 12.4.1.1, whereby a single call is made to a terminal definition subroutine at the beginning of an application. This subroutine returns variables that are then used to control display characteristics. There are a number of problems associated with this approach. The variable names are generally fixed, and may conflict with variable names within the application. The number of functions (returned variables) may be large and increase the overhead of managing the local symbol table (in terms of its size and the time required to search for specific variables). Most important, the control functions may be used as arguments to either a WRITE or an XECUTE command, depending on the specific terminal type *and* the manner in which the system updates the values of $X and $Y. An application program must determine whether the command argument need be written or executed each time a function is invoked.

Another approach is to make each terminal control an extrinsic function to be used as an argument to a WRITE command. The extrinsic function is responsible for determining whether or not the terminal control sequence is output with a WRITE or XECUTE command, not the application program. Example 12.12 demonstrates how Example 12.4 could be rewritten using this method.

```
GetData ;Main entry point to enter/edit patient data
        Write $$Clr^%Tf,$$Center("XYZ Medical Center")
        Write !,$$Center("Patient Data Entry/Edit")
GetID   Read !,"Patient ID: ",PID Quit:PID=""
        .
        .
Center(txt) ;display "txt" centered left-to-right
        Write $$Cup^%Tf($$Wid^%Tf-$L(txt)\2,$Y)
        Quit txt
```

EXAMPLE 12.12. Terminal control using extrinsic function

The use of extrinsic functions to control display characteristics standardizes the manner in which they are invoked and improves the visual clarity of the program. Each extrinsic function is used as the argument to a WRITE command, clearly marking its function as I/O related. Also, the need for argument indirection (for example, the Write @FF shown in Example 12.4) is eliminated; the extrinsic functions perform all necessary indirection.

Each different terminal type is assigned a unique device name that is used to identify it (for example, "VT-100"). Since we may have many different terminal types on a given system, it is necessary to identify the correct type in order for the functions to send the appropriate control sequences. This can be accomplished by passing the terminal name each time one of the functions is invoked [for example, Write $$Clr^%T("VT-100")], but this is both cumbersome and space-consuming. Instead, we define the terminal name (**TN**) only for the Reset function; all other functions will use the terminal name used for the last reset operation for a particular MUMPS device ($IO).

The Reset function is used to establish the terminal name associated with a MUMPS device ($IO) and to initialize the display. Initialization involves clearing the screen, positioning the display cursor to the upper-left corner, and setting the system variables $X and $Y to reflect the cursor position (0,0).

Two alternative methods can be used to identify the current terminal name in the Reset function. The first is to pass the terminal name as an optional parameter to the function. The second is to rely on the reference global ^%Ti, which is indexed by each MUMPS device ($IO) on the system and points to the terminal name associated with that device. Once a terminal name has been established for a given MUMPS device in ^%Ti, it becomes the default name for the Reset function until it is explicitly changed. Each time the Reset function is called with a new terminal name, that name is entered in ^%Ti and becomes the new default name associated with the current MUMPS device ($IO). Figure 12.2 depicts the structure of ^%Ti.

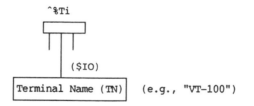

FIGURE 12.2. Terminal identification global

We also need to define a support global to hold the various terminal descriptions. The first level of this global is indexed by the terminal name (TN) and points to a free-text description of the terminal. The second level is indexed by the Device Function Mnemonic (DFM) and points to the data (indirect argument to a WRITE, argument to an XECUTE, or definition value) associated with the function mnemonic.

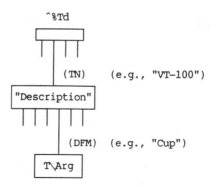

FIGURE 12.3. Terminal definition global

TN	TN is the terminal name, such as "VT-100".
DFM	The DFM is the device function mnemonic such, as "Clr" or "Reset".
T\Arg	This data node holds two separate pieces of information. The first (**T**) defines the Type of Arg that is held in the node (that is, whether it is an argument for a **W**rite command ("**W**"), an argument for an **X**ecute command ("**X**"), or a **D**escription ("**D**"). The second field of the node (**Arg**) is the actual data associated with the function mnemonic.

The definitions for the two descriptive terminal mnemonics (Len and Wid) begin with the characters \D. The definition of each control mnemonic begins either with \W or \X, depending on whether the control function is invoked with a Write or Xecute command.

For reference, Table 12.8 lists the data that could be used to define a VT-100 terminal.

The definitions provided in Table 12.8 assume that the Write *char syntax does *not* alter the value of $X as graphic characters are sent to the terminal (see discussion in Sections 3.4.4.3 and 12.4.1.1). If your MUMPS implementation does update $X with the Write *char syntax, the definitions for the functions Eol, Eos, Hoff, Hon, Roff, Ron, Uoff, and Uon will have to be altered to adjust $X after the control sequence has been sent to the terminal. For example, the characters sent to a VT-100 to erase to the end of line (Eol) are "<ESC>[0K". Three of the four characters in the sequence are graphic and may cause $X to be incremented. To adjust $X for any graphic characters output, we could redefine the Eol data node as follows:

$$^\%Td(\text{"VT-100","Eol"}) = \text{"X\textbackslash New x,y Set x} = \$X,y = \$Y \text{ Write } *27,*91,*48,*75$$
$$\text{Set } \$X = x,\$Y = y\text{"}$$

The "Eol" function leaves the cursor in its original position, and the XECUTE

TABLE 12.8 FUNCTIONAL DESCRIPTIONS FOR VT-100

^%Td Reference	Data
^%Td("VT-100")	DEC VT-100 CRT
^%Td("VT-100","Clr")	W\#,*27,*91,*72,*27,*91,*50,*74
^%Td("VT-100","Cup")	X\Write *27,*91,y + 1,*59,x + 1,*72 Set $X = x,$Y = y
^%Td("VT-100","Eol")	W*27,*91,*48,*75
^%Td("VT-100","Eos")	W*27,*91,*48,*74
^%Td("VT-100", "Hoff")	W*27,*91,*48,*109
^%Td("VT-100","Hon")	W*27,*91,*49,*109
^%Td("VT-100","Len")	D\23
^%Td("VT-100","Roff")	W*27,*91,*48,*109
^%Td("VT-100","Ron")	W*27,*91,*55,*109
^%Td("VT-100","Uoff")	W*27,*91,*48,*109
^%Td("VT-100","Uon")	W*27,*91,*52,*109
^%Td("VT-100","Wid")	D\79

argument sets $X and $Y to synchronize the system with the terminal. The other control functions could be altered in a similar fashion.

One might assume that we could simplify the previous XECUTE string by eliminating the New x,x Set x=$X,y=$Y ... Set $X=x,$Y=y and replacing it with ... Set $X=$X−3. Unfortunately, this may not always work. Some MUMPS implementations automatically perform a new-line sequence after outputting the last character on a line; a carriage-return, line-feed sequence is output to the terminal, $Y is incremented by one, and $X is set to zero. In such instances, the simplified code would not correctly establish the values of $X and $Y after the control sequence is sent to the terminal.

Some implementations take special steps when an ESC character is written to a terminal. In these systems, updating the values of $X and $Y is suspended from the ESC character to the end of the WRITE argument; the characters following the ESC character are transmitted to the terminal but do *not* alter $X and $Y. In systems that support this feature, both Write $C(27,91,49,109) and Write *27,*91,*49,*109 will successfully erase End Of Line on a VT-100, but the second form will incorrectly alter the value of $X. In the first form, all the characters in the escape sequence are part of a single WRITE argument; in the second form, each character in the sequence is a separate WRITE argument.

The choice of terminal definitions is dependent on both the terminal and on how the system handles updating of $X and $Y. Check your documentation.

Having defined the function mnemonics, let's look at the extrinsic functions required to perform the desired operation(s) on the display. Example 12.13 shows a listing of two functions: Reset and Clr.

```
^%Tf    ;JML-NYSCVM
        ;Extrinsic functions for terminal control
        ;
Reset(TN) ;Reset Terminal; "TN" is optional terminal name
        Set TN=$G(TN),TN=$S(TN="":$G(^%Ti($I)),1:TN)
        If TN="" Quit 0
        Set ^%Ti($I)=TN Write $$Clr,$$Hoff,$$Roff,$$Uoff
        Quit 1
        ;
Clr() Quit $$doit("Clr") ;Clear Screen, Set ($X,$Y)=0
        ;
doit(mne) ;common exit function
        New value Set value=$G(^%Td(^%Ti($I),mne))
        If value?1"W".E Write @$P(value,"\",2,999)
        If value?1"X".E Xecute $P(value,"\",2,999)
        Quit $S(value?1"D".E:$P(value,"\",2,999),1:"")
```

EXAMPLE 12.13. Reset and Clr functions

The Reset function is usually performed once at the beginning of an application, and it performs two distinct tasks. First, it establishes the specific terminal type to be associated with the current device and stores this value in ^%Ti($IO) for the other terminal functions. Second, it clears the screen and resets all display attributes (bold, reverse video, and underline) to OFF. If the optional parameter TN is not passed to the <u>Reset</u> function, the terminal name is established from ^%Ti($I). If the terminal name is invalid, the <u>Reset</u> function returns a FALSE (0) value. If the terminal name is found and the terminal is initialized, <u>Reset</u> returns a TRUE (1) value.

The <u>Clr</u> function is used to clear the screen of the current device ($IO) using the terminal name defined by the last executed <u>Reset</u> function for the current device. The character string used to perform the clear screen function is retrieved from the terminal definition global ^%Td.

All the extrinsic terminal functions, with the exception of <u>Reset</u>, use the common function <u>doit</u> to perform the specified action. Note, especially, the manner in which the extrinsic function <u>doit</u> is invoked. This function is used as the argument to the QUIT command of the requested function [for example, <u>Quit $$doit("Clr")</u>] to pass the name of the control function being performed. Within <u>doit</u>, the variable <u>mne</u> defines the function being requested. The variable <u>value</u> is set to the function code for the particular device and defines how the device function is to be performed, as well as what is returned as the function value. If <u>value</u> starts with a "**W**", the function is implemented with a <u>Write</u> command. If the first character is "**X**", the function is implemented with an <u>Xecute</u> command. In both cases, the function returns an empty string as the function result. When used as an argument to a <u>Write</u> command, the empty string causes no change to the display. If <u>value</u> starts with the character "**D**", then no action is performed to the display and the function returns the description (that is, <u>Len</u> or <u>Wid</u>). If either the device or requested function is undefined, the value returned by the function is an empty string and no change to the display is initiated.

The remaining functions from Table 12.7 are implemented in a fashion similar to the <u>Clr</u> function. See the listing of routine <u>%Tf</u> in Appendix I for the listing of these functions.

Example 12.14 expands on the earlier examples (12.12 and 12.4) to demonstrate the use of some of the extrinsic functions just described.

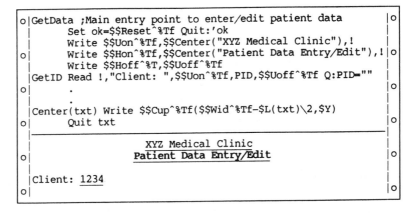

```
GetData ;Main entry point to enter/edit patient data
        Set ok=$$Reset^%Tf Quit:'ok
        Write $$Uon^%Tf,$$Center("XYZ Medical Clinic"),!
        Write $$Hon^%Tf,$$Center("Patient Data Entry/Edit"),!
        Write $$Hoff^%T,$$Uoff^%Tf
GetID Read !,"Client: ",$$Uon^%Tf,PID,$$Uoff^%Tf Q:PID=""
        .
        .
Center(txt) Write $$Cup^%Tf($$Wid^%Tf-$L(txt)\2,$Y)
        Quit txt
        ─────────────────────────────────────────────
                    XYZ Medical Clinic
                  Patient Data Entry/Edit

Client: 1234
```

EXAMPLE 12.14. Expanded screen handling with display control functions

TABLE 12.9 DEFINITION OF A "DUMB" TERMINAL

^%Td Reference	Data
^%Td("DUMB")	Aardvark glass teletype
^%Td("DUMB","Clr")	X\Write $$Cup(0,0),$$Eos
^%Td("DUMB","Cup")	X\Write *3,*x,*y Set $X=x,$Y=y
^%Td("DUMB","Eol")	X\New x,y Set x=$X,y=$Y Write ?$$Wid, $$Cup(x,y)
^%Td("DUMB","Eos")	X\New i,x,y Set x=$X,y=$Y Write $$Eol For i=$Y+1:1:$$Len Write $$Cup(0,i),$$Eol If i=$$Len Write $$Cup(x,y) Quit
^%Td("DUMB","Hoff")	[empty string]
^%Td("DUMB","Hon")	[empty string]
^%Td("DUMB","Len")	D\23
^%Td("DUMB","Roff")	[empty string]
^%Td("DUMB","Ron")	[empty string]
^%Td("DUMB","Uoff")	[empty string]
^%Td("DUMB","Uon")	[empty string]
^%Td("DUMB","Wid")	D\79

The extrinsic display control functions described in this section permit a high degree of device independence along with ease of use. Unfortunately, there are times when invoking certain display functions that the display is altered in unexpected ways. Refer to Table 12.8, which defines the character sequences necessary to alter the display attributes for a VT-100. Examine, especially, the character sequences used to turn off highlighting (Hoff), reverse video (Roff), and underlining (Uoff). They are all the *same*.

The fact that the same control sequences are used for more than one display function has serious implications when programming the display. Individual attributes cannot be turned off without turning off *all* attributes. This interaction between display attributes is not a problem on all terminal types; some permit individual attributes to be activated and deactivated without affecting the rest of the attributes. The application must keep track of the current display characteristics and make sure that the appropriate attributes remain active when one is turned off.

Earlier in this section we stated that the only essential hardware capability for these extrinsic functions is the ability to position the cursor. While display options such as high intensity, reverse video, and underlining are desirable, most applications will run substantially the same without them. Table 12.9 lists the terminal definition for a "dumb" terminal supporting only cursor positioning. While a terminal that supports the Eol and Eos functions in hardware may perform these functions faster than the terminal defined in Table 12.9, these functions will still work, even on this dumb terminal.

12.5.2 Keyboard Input: Single-Character READ Function

Next, we examine the problems associated with keyboard input, especially as it relates to recognizing special keys such as *arrow* (cursor) and *function* keys. In

TABLE 12.10 MULTICHARACTER SEQUENCES RETURNED BY SINGLE-CHARACTER READ

Key pressed	Characters returned	Key pressed	Characters returned
BACKSPACE	"<BS>"	Up arrow	"<AU>"
TAB	"<TAB>"	Down arrow	"<AD>"
ENTER	"<RET>"	Left arrow	"<AL>"
<CTRL>U	"<CAN>"	Right arrow	"<AR>"
ESC	"<ESC>"	Function Key 1	"<F1>"
DELETE	"<DEL>"	Function Key 2	"<F2>"
[timeout]	"<TO>"	Function Key 3	"<F3>"
		Function Key 4	"<F4>"

Section 12.4.1.2 we examined some of the problems associated with reading these keys. There is no established standard as to the actual characters sent to the computer when the special keys are pressed on the keyboard. In some instances, the keys are mapped to a single character (usually one of the control characters); in others, a multiple-character escape sequence is sent.

We need a method of reading characters from the keyboard and translating the special keys into a common format for use by application programs. To perform this action, we define an extrinsic function that emulates the single-character READ command in MUMPS. This function uses the single-character READ command available in MUMPS, but also converts all special keys (which may be received as multiple-character strings from the terminal) into a common format. Whenever special keys are read, the function returns a multiple-character sequence defined in Table 12.10. All graphic characters (decimal values 32 to 126) read will be returned as a single ASCII character.

Characters other than the graphic characters or those listed in Table 12.10 are ignored. The entry [timeout] in Table 12.10 does not represent a key, but rather that the read function timed out before a key was pressed. The single-character read function provides for a read timeout in a manner similar to the MUMPS Read command.

We need to expand on the terminal descriptions held in ^%Td to cover the definitions of special keys for each terminal type, as well as the characters returned to the application when those keys are pressed. Only the keys on the right side of Table 12.10 need be defined in ^%Td; those on the left side of the table correspond to standard ASCII characters and are the same on all ASCII terminals. For definition purposes, we use the mnemonics AU, AD, AL, AR, F1, F2, F3, and F4 for defining the special keys. The key definitions are held in ^%Td using the Terminal Name (TN) as the first-level subscript, the characters "keys" as a second-level subscript, and the key mnemonics (for example, "AU", "F1") as the third-level subscript. The data for each key mnemonic (KM) consists of the character(s) sent to the computer when that key is pressed. The characters used to define the KM subscript are those that are passed to the application by the single-character READ function. Figure 12.4 depicts the expanded structure of global ^%Td.

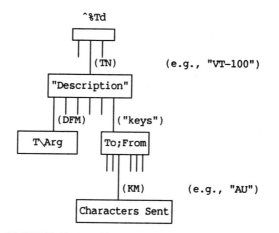

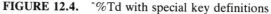

FIGURE 12.4. ^%Td with special key definitions

For example,

^%Td("VT100","keys","AU")=$C(27,91,65) <ESC>[A

^%Td("VT100","keys","F1")=$C(27,79,83) <ESC>OS

Not all terminals have the same capabilities, and key mnemonics for functions unavailable on a given terminal are not included in ^%Td. We now know where the information defining each special key is kept, but it is not in a form particularly well suited for our single-character READ function. We do not want to search through ^%Td looking for possible matches as characters are received from the keyboard; doing so would be too time consuming, especially for multicharacter sequences.

Instead, we maintain a composite set of character lists (To;From) at location ^%Td(TN,"keys"). The field To is a list of the KM subscript values with commas used to start and end the list, and to separate individual list elements (for example, ",AD,AL,AR,...,F2,F3,"). The field From contains a list of characters sent by the terminal for each of the key mnemonics defined in the To list. Individual subfields in the From list are bounded by DELETE characters [$C(127)]. Any complete character sequence received from the terminal found in the From list is converted to the associated field in the To list. The substring extracted from the To list (bounded by the characters "<" and ">") is the value returned by the single-character READ function as the result of reading one of the special keys. For example, see Figure 12.5.

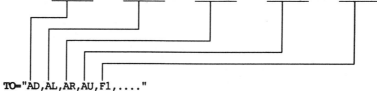

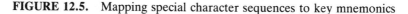

FIGURE 12.5. Mapping special character sequences to key mnemonics

The To and From lists can be built from the definitions held under `^%Td(TN,"keys")` with the following code:

```
o|^%Tf   ;JML-NYSCVM                                        |o
 |        ;Extrinsic functions for terminal control          |
 |        ;                                                   |
o|        .                                                  |o
 |        .                                                   |
 |BuildTF(TN) ;Builds To;From lists for ^%Td(TN,"keys")       |
o|        Set  TN=$G(TN) Quit:TN=""                          |o
 |        New from,km,to Set km="",from=$C(127),to=""         |
 |        For  Do  Quit:km=""                                 |
o|        .    Set km=$O(^%Td(TN,"keys",km)) Quit:km=""      |o
 |        .    Set from=from_^(km)_$C(127),to=to_km_","       |
 |        .    Quit                                           |
o|        Set ^%Td(TN,"keys")=to_";"_from                    |o
 |        Write !,"Key definition for ",TN," finished."       |
 |        Quit                                                |
```

EXAMPLE 12.15. Defining key translations lists

The To;From lists must be built once for each terminal on the system. If any of the key definitions are altered or additional key definitions are added, the subroutine BuildTF must be run again for that terminal name (TN).

The use of these two lists for translating characters received from the keyboard permits us to check incoming strings for possible matches with a simple contains operation ([), rather than having to search a global. The groundwork is now finished, and it is time to examine the actual read function.

```
o|^%Tf   ;JML-NYSCVM                                           |o
 |        ;Extrinsic functions for terminal control            |
 |        .                                                     |
o|        .                                                     |o
 |ReadS(timeout,echo) ;Single-character READ; Do $$EchoOFF      |
 |        New c,chars,d,find,from,n,to Set d=$C(127)            |
o|        Set from=$G(^%Td(^%Ti($I),"keys")),to=$P(from,";"),fr|o
 |  ---om=$P(from,";",2,999)                                    |
 |        Set Timeout=$G(Timeout) Set:Timeout="" Timeout=1E25   |
o|        Set Echo=$G(Echo) Set:Echo="" Echo=1                  |o
 |gchar Set chars="" Read *c:Timeout Goto readsx:c>31&(c<127)   |
 |  ---!(c<0)                                                    |
o|cchar Set chars=chars_$C(c)                                   |o
 |        Goto readsx:from'[(d_chars),more:from'[(d_chars_d)    |
 |        Set find=$L($E(from,1,$F(from,d_chars_d)),d)-2        |
o|        Set c=$P(to,",",find) Goto readsq                     |o
 |more  For n=1:1:$$RPT Read *c:0 Quit:c'<0                      |
 |        Goto ccharc'<0 Set c=$A(chars,$L(chars))              |
o|readsx If c>31&(c<127) Write:Echo *c Quit $C(c)               |o
 |        Set c=$S(c<0:"TO",c=13:"RET",c=21:"CAN",c=27:"ESC",c= |
 |  ---8:"BS",c=9:"TAB",c=127:"DEL",1:"")                       |
o|        If c="" Write *7 Goto gchar                           |o
 |readsq Quit "<"_c_">"                                         |
```

EXAMPLE 12.16. Single-character **ReadS** function

The optional timeout parameter is similar to a timeout parameter in a MUMPS Read command. The timeout parameter specifies the number of seconds the function will wait for keyboard input before aborting. If timeout expires before a key is pressed, the function returns the string "<TO>". If no timeout is specified, the timeout period is set to an arbitrarily large number (1E25 seconds).

The optional parameter echo defines whether or not graphic characters read from the keyboard are echoed (displayed) after receipt. If the parameter echo is TRUE (or if not passed to the function), graphic characters will be echoed on the display; if FALSE, they will not be displayed. The use of this parameter is demonstrated in future examples (the multiple-choice and option functions $$MC and $$Opt presented in the next section).

The basic operations performed by this extrinsic function are straightforward. A single character Read command is issued and, if the character entered is a graphic character, that character is echoed to the display (if echo is TRUE) and returned to the calling program. If a timeout was specified and a character was not entered in the specified time period, the function returns the characters "<TO>".

If the first character read is *not* a graphics character, the program checks to see if it is a lead-in character for one of the special keys [for example, from [$C(127)_chars]. If not, control is transferred to done, where additional checks are made for nongraphic characters. Those nongraphic characters that are recognized (for example, <ENTER>, <TAB>) are converted to multicharacter strings (for example, "<RET>", "<TAB>"), which are returned by the function. If the nongraphic character is not in the list of acceptable characters, it is ignored and the keyboard READ is reissued.

If the first character read is potentially one of the special keys, additional keyboard reads are performed (label more) until either a match is found or until a character is received that precludes the character sequence from representing any of the special keys. If a special key match is found, the function returns a multicharacter sequence identifying the key (for example, "<AU>", "<F1>"). If *no* match is found, the function returns the character that forced the match to fail.

Notice the additional function $$RPT used in line more. We may encounter special problems when reading multicharacter sequences sent by the terminal to the computer, especially when the terminal is operating at slow speeds (for example, 1200 baud). After determining that the first character may be part of a multicharacter sequence, the function may have to issue additional reads to collect the next character(s) sent by the terminal. It is necessary to wait long enough to guarantee that all characters of a multicharacter sequence are read, but not delay processing if the additional characters are not forthcoming. For example, we will want to use the <ESC> character in later applications to provide a panic button for the users. If the <ESC> character is also a lead-in character sent by the terminal for special keys, we wish to return control to the calling program as soon as we can determine that the terminal is sending no more characters.

The slowest terminal speed supported by most implementations is 110 baud

(10 characters per second). If the function waits up to $\frac{1}{10}$ second for the next character, we can be sure to collect all characters in a multicharacter escape sequence. Unfortunately, the MUMPS' Read command timeout has a resolution of $+/-$ one second; to guarantee not missing the next character, we would have to use a timeout value of **2**. Instead, the function uses a software loop to monitor for incoming characters for $\frac{1}{10}$ second. Since different hardware and software configurations execute instructions at different speeds, it is necessary to establish how many times the loop must be executed to provide a $\frac{1}{10}$second read. Example 12.17 demonstrates the use of the subroutine SetRPT which can be used to determine the value for the extrinsic variable $\$\$RPT$.

```
o|^%Tf   ;JML-NYSCVM                                         |o
 |        ;Extrinsic functions for terminal control          |
 |         .                                                  |
o|SetRPT ;Execute to establish Quit value in line RPT+1      |o
 |        New i,h,n                                           |
 |        Write !,"Establish loop value $$RPT for 1/10 sec."  |
o|        Set h=$P($H,",",2) For i=1:1 Quit:$P($H,",",2)'=h   |o
 |        Set h=$P($H,",",2) For i=1:1 Read *n:0 Quit:$P($H,","|
 |    ---,2)'=h                                               |
o|        Write "Edit RPT+1 to be  QUIT ",i\10,"  for 1/10 seco|o
 |    ---nd Read.",!                                          |
 |        Quit                                                |
o|        ;                                                   |o
 |RPT() ;Loop repeat count for 1/10 second                    |
 |        QUIT 10 ;Replace 10 with value from SetRPT          |
```

EXAMPLE 12.17. Single-character READ RPT count

The value for $\$\$RPT$ must be established for each MUMPS system (hardware *and* MUMPS implementation). The subroutine SetRPT should be run when there are no other jobs on the system to obtain an accurate value.

```
o|>Do SetRPT^%t←                                             |o
 |Establish loop value $$RPT for 1/10 second.                |
 |Edit RPT+1 to be  QUIT 14  for 1/10 second Read.           |
o|>                                                          |o
```

EXAMPLE 12.18. Establishing value for $\$\$RPT$ function

Use the value returned by the subroutine SetRPT as the argument to the QUIT command in line RPT $+1$ to establish a $\frac{1}{10}$second delay. This delay will not adversely affect keyboard input. It is used only in the case of input of possible multicharacter escape sequences. In most cases, the terminal will be operating at a much higher speed than 110 baud, and the number of loop iterations executed before the next character is input will be small.

Two additional system-related functions must also be established before we can use the $\$\$ReadS$ function. The function ReadS assumes that the system does *not* automatically echo characters input with the Read *char syntax. Unfortunately, some systems do echo characters read in this fashion, and it is necessary to turn

echo off <u>before</u> invoking $$ReadS. To turn echo ON and OFF we create two
additional extrinsic functions: $$EchoON and $$EchoOFF.

```
o|^%Tf      ;JML-NYSCVM                                         |o
 |           ;Extrinsic functions for terminal control          |
 |               .                                              |
o|               .                                             |o
 |EchoON() ;System-specific function to turn ECHO OFF           |
 |          Use 0:(0:"") ;Insert code to turn ECHO ON Here      |
o|          Quit ""                                            |o
 |EchoOFF() ;System-specific function to turn ECHO OFF          |
 |          Use 0:(0:"SI") ;Insert code to turn ECHO OFF here   |
o|          Quit ""                                            |o
```

EXAMPLE 12.19. Extrinsic functions to turn keyboard echo ON and OFF

It is necessary to edit these functions to include system-specific commands to
perform the <u>EchoON</u> and <u>EchoOFF</u> functions. The <u>Use</u> commands shown in Ex-
ample 12.19 demonstrate the way this is accomplished in *one* MUMPS implemen-
tation. If your system does *not* echo characters input with the <u>Read *char</u> syntax,
then both functions can consist of a single command: **Quit ""**.

Example 12.20 is a program fragment that should help clarify the general
approach toward using the $$ReadS function described previously. Other examples
using this function are provided in the following sections.

```
o|Test    ;Main entry point for TEST MANAGEMENT package.        |o
 |        ;                                                      |
 |        Kill  If '$$Reset^%Tf Write "NO Terminal Def." Quit   |
o|        Set opt=$$GetAns Quit:opt=""                          |o
 |            .                                                  |
 |            .                                                  |
o|GetAns() ;Read keyboard entry.  Return Part Number           |o
 |         New char,pn                                           |
 |         Set pn="" Write !,"Part number: ",$$EchoOFF^%Tf       |
o|         For  Do  If $L(char)>1 Quit:"<RET><TO>"[char        |o
 |         .   Set char=$$ReadS^%Tf(600)                         |
 |         .   If char?1E Set pn=pn_char Quit                    |
o|         .   If "<RET><ESC><AU><AD>"[char Set char="<RET>" Q |o
 |         .   Quit                                              |
 |         If char="<TO>" Write *7," No Response." Set pn=""     |
o|         Write $$EchoON^%Tf                                   |o
 |         Quit pn                                               |
```

EXAMPLE 12.20. Sample program using $$ReadS function

The function <u>Reset</u> is invoked once at the beginning of an application to
establish the current terminal type. Before beginning the loop to input individual
characters, keyboard echo is turned OFF. When finished with the single-character
keyboard input, echo is turned back ON, and execution proceeds.

Many MUMPS implementations offer additional system-dependent features
to aid in reading special escape sequences from the keyboard. Some, for example,
provide a special system variable into which the character(s) that terminated a read

is placed. If the <ESC> character is designated as a Read terminator, then the entire escape sequence is available in this variable. The $$ReadS function shown in Example 12.17 does not take advantage of any implementation-specific features (other than that found in the functions EchoON and EchoOFF) and should run on most systems with only minor modifications.

12.5.3 Option Lists and Multiple-Choice Questions

There are numerous occasions during the execution of a program when an application presents the user with a list of options or a multiple-choice question. We have already discussed a number of simple techniques for displaying an option list (Examples 7.11 and 8.33). In keeping with the screen-oriented I/O described in the previous section, the discussions in this section expand on these earlier examples and define general-purpose utilities to display and collect user options.

For the first example, we examine a utility to collect the results of a simple multiple-choice question from the keyboard. Consider, for example, the following question:

Read to SAVE Data ? [**Yes**] No

The valid options ("Yes" and "No") are displayed after the question and the current default answer is highlighted. To accept the highlighted choice, the user presses the <ENTER> key. To change the choice, users can either use the left- or right-arrow keys, or they can enter the first identifying character ("Y" or "N") of the desired option. An entry of "?" will invoke the display of HELP text associated with the question.

To simplify the processing of HELP text, we will assume that the application uses a divided screen for display; the top 19 lines (0 to 18) are used for questions and answers, and the bottom 5 lines (19 to 23) are reserved for the display of help text or error information.

It is necessary to pass the multiple-choice utility three types of information:

1. The list of choices.
2. The help text associated with the question.
3. The default answer (that is, the answer that will be highlighted at the beginning of the function).

If a letter or number is entered by the user and more than one choice starts with that character, the selector will advance to the next choice beginning with that character. The default answer parameter is optional; if absent, the first choice in the list will become the default.

The most convenient method for passing the option list and help text to the multiple-choice function is through an array. The top node of the array reference contains the list of options; individual options in the list are separated from each other with *semicolons*. The help text is held as lines of data under the option list. For example, see Table 12.11.

TABLE 12.11 INPUT ARRAY FOR MULTIPLE-CHOICE FUNCTION

```
^Opts(1) = "Male;Female;Unknown"
^Opts(1,1) = "Enter the SEX of the patient. Use the LEFT and RIGHT arrow"
^Opts(1,2) = "    keys of enter a 'M', 'F', or 'U' to select one of the"
^Opts(1,2) = "    choices. When done, press the <ENTER> key."
^Opts(1,3) = " "
^Opts(1,4) = "PLEASE use the 'Unknown' choice sparingly. In most cases"
^Opts(1,5) = "    it only requires asking a relative or friend to"
^Opts(1,6) = "    determine these data."
```

The information concerning the multiple-choice list is typically held in a global. The location (that is, the array or global name, the number of levels, and the subscripts pointing to the list) are passed to the function as a string literal. The function uses subscript indirection to access the data in the array. The default choice is passed as a separate parameter and is a number designating the field position within the choice list. The function will return the *option number* selected (for example, **2** for "Female"). The function is invoked in the following manner:

Write !,"Patient SEX: " Set opt = $$MC^%To("^Opts(1)",2,.term,600)

The first parameter passed is the *array reference* in which the multiple-choice data are held; this is the only required parameter. The second parameter is the *default choice* that is highlighted when the $$MC function is first invoked; if not passed, the first field in the choice list is used as the default selection.

The third parameter is passed *by reference* and represents the manner in which the option was terminated. In addition to returning the selected option, $$MC can also return *how* the read was terminated (that is, whether the user pressed the <EN-TER> key, the <ESC> key, and so on). This is important in the broader context of the application. For example, if the <UP-ARROW> key terminated the read, the application should back up to the previous question on the screen. The terminating character is represented by a string of characters bound by the characters "<" and ">"; the list of terminating keys is shown in Table 12.12.

The fourth parameter represents the number of seconds the function will wait before *timeout* occurs. If not passed as a parameter to the function, an arbitrarily long period (1E20 seconds) is used as a default. If the option timed out, the currently selected option is still returned as the function value, and the optional third parameter (the terminating sequence) is set to "<TO>".

The function $$MC automatically handles user requests for HELP text (entry of "?"). The help text passed with the multiple-choice list is displayed at the bottom of the screen. If there are more help lines than will fit, the function displays a message to that effect and waits for the user to press the <ENTER> key for the additional lines. If the user presses any key other than <ENTER>, that key is used as input to the function. The next key pressed after help text has been displayed causes the help text to be erased from the screen.

Also notice the method used to highlight the current choice; it is both in **boldface** and enclosed in brackets ("[. . .]"). Even on terminals that do not support

TABLE 12.12 INPUT TERMINATING SEQUENCES

Characters returned	Key pressed	Description
<RET>	<ENTER>	This is the normal terminating key for most applications and generally indicates that the application should continue with the next question.
<ESC>	<ESC>	The <ESC>ape key can be used by the application as a panic button. When pressed, the application can check to see whether or not the user wishes to abort the program. It could also be used to provide additional system-wide help, such as keyboard conventions and the like.
<AU>	<UP-ARROW>	The <AU> terminator indicates that the application (after checking the answer) should back up to the previous question.
<AD>	<DOWN-ARROW>	The <AD> terminator is similar to the <RET> terminator; the application checks the answer and then advances to the next question if the answer was valid.
<TO>		The <TO> terminator indicates that the function timed out before the user pressed one of the normal terminating keys.

two intensities, the selected choice will stand out from the others. On quitting the function, all choices are erased from the original line, and the selected choice is displayed at bold intensity.

Using the option list shown previously [^Opts(1)], Example 12.21 demonstrates the use of this function.

```
o|Test    Quit:'$$Reset^%Tf                                   |o
 |         Write $$Clr^%Tf,!,"Patient SEX: "                   |
 |         Set sex=$$MC^%To("^Opts(1)","",.trm)                |
o|         Goto Escape:trm="<ESC>",Prev:trm="<AU>"             |o
 |            .                                                |
 |            .                                                |
o|            .                                                |o
 |_____    |
 |Patient SEX:   [Male] Female Unknown                         |
o|                                                             |o
 |                                                             |
 |                                                             |
o|                                                             |o
 |                                                             |
o|                                                             |o
 |Enter the SEX of the patient.  Use the LEFT and RIGHT arrow|
o|   keys or enter a 'M', 'F', or 'U' to select one of the   |o
 |   choices.  When done, press the <ENTER> key.               |
 |                                                             |
o|<ENTER> for more                                             |o
```

EXAMPLE 12.21. Use of $$MC function

TABLE 12.13 INPUT ARRAY FOR $$OPT FUNCTION

Array reference	Contents
^Opt("Main")	"Aardvark Terminals!Financial System Options"
^Opt("Main",1)	"1) Billing options."
^Opt("Main",1,1)	"Brings up the Billing Option list that includes:"
^Opt("Main",1,2)	" 1) generate bills, 2) Print bills, 3) Print"
^Opt("Main",1,3)	" monthly reports."
^Opt("Main",2)	"2) Receivable."
^Opt("Main",2,1)	"Accounts-Receivable package . . ."
^Opt("Main",3)	"3) Payable."
^Opt("Main",3,4)	"Accounts-Payable . . ."
^Opt("Main",4)	"4) Payroll."
^Opt("Main",4,1)	"Brings up the Payroll option list . . ."
^Opt("Main",9)	"0) Quit."
^Opt("Main",9,1)	"Terminate the computer session."

This example shows the screen after the user has entered a question mark to display the help text. Users can move through the list with either the left- or right-arrow keys, or they can enter the first character (upper- or lowercase) of any of the choices.

A similar function can be developed to display larger lists of options vertically on the screen, rather than as a horizontal list. This type of multiple-choice screen is often used to display and collect main options within an application. We take a slightly different approach with these lists. Each option also has a short (one to four lines) description, and the function displays the description of the currently selected option in the help text area. As with the previous example, the option list is passed to the function as an array. The array reference points to a screen title (and optional subtitles); the next level under the title contains a list of the options; and under each option is a list of free-text lines describing the option. The choice of subscripts is arbitrary but determines the order of the displayed options and descriptive text and the value returned by the function. Table 12.13 lists an array structure suitable for input to the option choice function $$Opt.

The title node contains free text, which will be displayed at the top of the screen. The title consists of a primary title and one or more subtitles; each field is separated from the others with an exclamation point (!) and will be displayed on a separate line, centered left to right.

As with the $$MC function, the user will be allowed to select from the list using the arrow keys (up- and down-arrow) or by typing in the first character of the option. If more than one option starts with the same first character, the option selector will advance to the next option starting with that character.

As the user moves through the option list, a selector flag (the characters = = >) moves up and down the list to point to the currently selected option. In addition, the descriptive text associated with the currently selected option is displayed at the bottom of the screen.

The $$Opt function is invoked in the following manner:

```
Set opt = $$Opt^%To("Opt(""Main"")",3,.term,600)
```

The first parameter is the array reference pointing to the option list data; it is the only required parameter. The second parameter is the default option that is initially selected on entry to the function. It is passed as a *number* representing the option position within the list (that is, 1 for the first option displayed, 2 for the second, and so on); it is *not* directly related to the subscript pointing to the option, although the subscript will affect the order in which the options are presented. The third parameter is passed *by reference* and is used by the function to return the method by which the option was terminated (that is, whether the option was terminated when the user pressed the <ENTER> key, whether it timed out, and so on). The value returned in this parameter corresponds to those listed in Table 12.12 except that <AU> and <AD> are not returned, since the up- and down-arrow keys are used to move through the selections. The fourth parameter represents the number of seconds the function will execute before aborting. As with the $$MC function, if the timeout parameter is absent, the function will default to an arbitrarily long timeout (1E20 seconds).

The $$Opt function returns a value that corresponds to the *subscript* of the selected option (for example, 4 for "Payroll"). Example 12.22 demonstrates the use of the $$Opt function using the data presented in Table 12.13.

```
o|                     Aardvark Terminals                    |o
 |                   Financial System Options                |
o|        ==> 1) Billing options.                            |o
 |            2) Receivable.                                  |
 |            3) Payable.                                     |
o|            4) Payroll.                                     |o
 |            0) Quit.                                        |
 |                                                           |
o|                                                            |o
 |                                                           |
o|                                                            |o
 |                                                           |
o|                                                            |o
 |Brings up the Billing Option list that includes:          |
o| 1) generate bills, 2) Print bills, 3) Print              |o
 | monthly reports.                                          |
o|                                                            |o
```

EXAMPLE 12.22. Use of the $$Opt function

The extrinsic functions ($$MC and $$Opt) demonstrate two simple methods that can be employed within an application to select choices from option lists. Both use the display functions described in Section 12.5.1 and the single-character read function described in Section 12.5.2 to provide an interactive and screen-oriented approach toward data collection.

As with the other examples in this section, a complete listing of these utilities, along with a description of their use, is found in Appendix I.

12.5.4 Editing Keyboard Read

The <u>Read</u> command in MUMPS provides the means of inputting characters from a device (such as a terminal) for use by an application program. Despite the many syntactical variations permitted in MUMPS, the <u>Read</u> command has one serious drawback when viewed from the perspective of the end user; it cannot be used to modify an existing answer. To correct an entry, the user must usually retype the entire response, rather than edit an existing answer. In this section we explore the use of an editing keyboard read that permits altering an answer using the special keys (left- and right-arrow, <DEL>, <BS>, and so on) found on most video terminals.

The extrinsic function $$Read is used to emulate the READ command in MUMPS, but with additional editing capabilities. A complete listing is found in Appendix I. The $$Read function is invoked in the following manner:

Set ans = $$Read^%Tf(oldans,width,.term,timeout)

All the parameters are optional. When specified, they have the following meanings:

oldans	If there is an existing answer, it is passed in as the first parameter. The $$Read function will display <u>oldans</u> and allow the user to edit the displayed characters.
width	This parameter defines the maximum field width for the answer. If not passed, the $$Read function defaults to a width representing the characters remaining on the line (from the value of $X when the function is invoked to $$Wid).
.term	This parameter (passed *by reference*) is used by the function to return a string of characters defining how the read was terminated. See Table 12.12 for a list of the terminating sequences.
timeout	This parameter specifies the number of seconds the function is executed before it aborts. If not specified, an arbitrarily large timeout value is used (1E25 seconds). If the $$Read function times out before a terminating key is pressed, the function still returns the (edited) answer, but sets the <u>term</u> parameter to "**<TO>**".

The $$Read function displays the existing value for <u>oldans</u> (if passed) in a reverse video field of <u>width</u> characters. The cursor is then positioned after the last character in the answer, ready for user input. Using the left- and right-arrow keys, the user can move through the answer. Graphic characters are inserted to the left of the cursor location, and characters from the cursor to the end of the answer are shifted right. The <DEL> key can be used to erase the character at the cursor location; the <BS> key can be used to erase the character to the left of the cursor. Attempting to enter characters that would make the answer exceed the specified field width causes the bell to be activated and the character is ignored. The special character <**CTRL**>U is used to erase the entire field and has a toggle action. If the current field is the same as the original value passed to the function, the entire field is erased. If the current field is different from the original value passed to the function, the original answer is made the current answer.

The $$Read function terminates on receipt of an <ENTER>, <ESC>, <UP-ARROW>, <DOWN-ARROW>, or any of the function keys. The function also terminates if a <u>timeout</u> is specified and that period of time elapses since the $$Read function was invoked. The terminating condition is passed back in the parameter <u>term</u>. On completion of the function, the user entry is rewritten to the display in **bold** intensity without reverse video.

```
o|GetClient ;JML-NYSCVM                                                  |o
 |          ;get basic client demographic data                          |
 |          Kill  Quit:'$$Reset^%Tf                                      |
o|          Write ?15,"Client Data Entry/Edit",! Set ID=""               |o
 |GetID     Write !,"Client ID Number: "                                 |
 |          Set ID=$$Read^%Tf(ID,10,.trm,600)                            |
o|          Quit:trm="<AU>"!(ID="")                                      |o
 |          Goto Fk:$E(trm,2)="F",Esc:trm="<ESC>",TO:trm="<TO>"|
 |          Set x=$G(^Client(ID))                                        |
o|          For i=1:1:6 Set @$P("name,street,city,state,zip,pho|o
 |     ---ne",",",i)=$P(x,"\",i)                                         |
 |Name      Write !,"Client Name: "                                     |
o|          Set new=$$Read^%Tf(name,30,.trm,600)                         |o
 |          Goto GetID:trm="<AU>"                                        |
 |          Goto Fk:$E(trm,2)="F",Esc:trm="<ESC>",TO:trm="<TO>"|
o|          If new="" Write *7," Must answer this." Goto Name            |o
 |          Goto Street:new=name Set name=new                            |
 |          If name'?1A.E1","1A.E Write *7," Name not in the fo|
o|     ---rm 'Last,First', please VERIFY." Goto Name                     |o
 |Street    Write !,"Street: "                                          |
 |             .                                                        |
o|             .                                                        |o
```

EXAMPLE 12.23. Code fragment using editing keyboard READ

Example 12.23 demonstrates the use of the $$Read function to input answers from the keyboard. While it does provide the users with certain advantages over a normal MUMPS READ command, the code shown could hardly be called screen oriented. In addition, there is a considerable amount of redundant checking associated with each question. In the next section we explore a technique to automate the process of displaying questions, moving between the questions, handling basic functions such as display of help text, and verifying the answers to the questions.

12.5.5 Question Driver

In the previous sections we developed a number of low-level utilities to aid in the management of screen display and keyboard input. These functions provide us with the basic tools necessary to support a screen oriented approach in interactions with the user. However, as shown in Example 12.23, the tools developed so far do not go quite far enough; there is still considerable programming required even to handle a relatively simple question-and-answer application. In this section we investigate higher-level tools for managing dialogue with the user.

Before exploring specific techniques, let's examine some of the factors that affect a well-engineered dialogue between a computer program and the user. A number of important factors will enhance or detract from the user's acceptance of a program. Some factors to be considered include:

- Keep the screen *simple*. The less cluttered a screen is, the easier it is to understand. The use of display attributes (high and low intensity, reverse video, color, and the like) can aid in screen organization and visual impact. However, overzealous use of these features can add confusion rather than clarity.

- Organize questions in logical groups (frames) of related data; do not mix frames of unrelated material. Presenting two separate frames of questions rather than one combined frame may actually speed up data entry. When displaying option lists, try to keep the total number of options to ten or less; if the list is longer, break it into two or more separate lists.

- Frames of questions or options should always have a clear heading indicating where the user is and what functions are being performed.

- The question text should be clear and concise. Avoid wordy questions or option text; supporting information can be supplied as auxiliary help text.

- Always provide the ability to get additional on-line help for a question and provide a consistent means for invoking the help text. Typically, this involves defining a single character (such as "?") that can be entered for *any* question to get additional information.

- For those questions in which the answer may come from a *list* of possible answers, it is important for the user to be able to display that list. External code books or reference charts are cumbersome and often lost. For small lists, the entire list can be displayed; for larger lists, it may be necessary to provide the capability of searching by key word(s) or partial key word(s).

- Display existing or default answers where available, and provide the user with a simple means for accepting that answer (that is, pressing the <ENTER> key to accept the displayed value). When choosing values for default answers, use those most likely to be entered by the user.

- Provide the ability to move about in a frame of questions. Especially important is the ability to back up to previous questions and alter the answers. Other features might include the ability to back up to the first question in a frame or to skip ahead to the last question in the screen (providing that no mandatory questions are by-passed). In frames with large numbers of questions, it may be desirable to provide the capability of jumping to a specific question, especially if many of the questions are optional or have preassigned default values.

- Aim for a flexible data entry format that permits a variety of input values that are reduced (by the program) to a common format. For example, for a question on Sex in which the valid entries may be 1 - Male, 2 - Female, or 3 - Unknown, allow 2, F, f, female, and so on, as valid entries.

- Whenever appropriate, ensure case insensitivity (for example, permit "Yes", "YES", "yes", "NO", and so on, for a Yes/No answer). Although closely related to the previous factor, this is an important enough concept to warrant this separate entry.

- In data collection sessions, permit the user the ability to preanswer questions. This is often accomplished with the type-ahead features available in some MUMPS implementations. In other cases, it is question specific. Consider a question-and-answer session used to collect address data [Name, Street, City, State, ZIP, Phone(s)]. When collecting the City, it may be possible to accept a ZIP code. The subroutine verifying the city entry can then look up the ZIP code, supply the correct city and state, and skip ahead to the phone(s) question. The amount of time that can be saved during data entry using such features can be significant.

- Provide a panic button or other well-defined means of aborting an operation. The <ESC> key is one choice that is nicely mnemonic for the requested function ("ES-Cape"). Additionally, you may wish to provide a standard set of options if this function is invoked, such as 1-Ignore, 2-Restart current function from beginning, and 3-Exit the computer.

- *Be consistent.* Regardless of which of these features you choose to provide to your users, provide them for *every* question asked. If some questions use an entry of "?" to display help text and others accept the same entry as data, the users will quickly stop asking for help on *any* question. Even in cases where no help text is available, a message to that effect should be displayed. *Be consistent.*

After this quick review of the factors that affect a well-engineered question-and-answer session, let's turn our attention to the topic of *question drivers* to aid in implementing these considerations. A question driver is a utility program that cycles through a set of predefined questions; it controls the display of information, the asking and verification of questions, and the movement between questions. The listing of the question driver subroutine described in the following discussion can be found in Appendix I.

The question driver presented here assumes that the information pertaining to a screen's worth of data (a *frame*) is held in an array with a structure similar to that depicted in Figure 12.6.

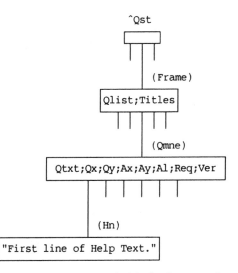

FIGURE 12.6. Structure of array suitable for input to the question driver

Frame	The subscript <u>Frame</u> defines a single *screen*'s worth of questions. It can be any valid subscript but is usually mnemonic for the screen (for example, "Registration" for a frame used to register a patient).

Frame The subscript <u>Frame</u> defines a single *screen*'s worth of questions. It can be any valid subscript but is usually mnemonic for the screen (for example, "Registration" for a frame used to register a patient).

Qmne Each question to be asked in a frame is defined by a question mnemonic (<u>Qmne</u>). The *Qmne* servers two purposes: (1) it is used as a subscript into the question array pointing to the description of the question, and (2) it is used by the question driver at run time to define the name of the local variable into which the answer associated with a particular question is stored.

Hn The subscript <u>Hn</u> is used to point to sequential lines of help text associated with a particular question. The value of <u>Hn</u> is not important except that it affects the order in which lines of help text are displayed.

Qlist <u>Qlist</u> holds a list of question mnemonics (<u>Qmne</u>) and defines the order in which questions are asked. The comma character is used to separate <u>Qmne</u> fields in <u>Qlist</u>.

Titles The <u>Titles</u> field contains one or more lines of free text that are displayed at the top of a screen. Individual lines within the <u>Titles</u> field are separated from each other with the exclamation point character (!). Titles are centered (left to right) when displayed.

Qtxt The <u>Qtxt</u> field represents the question text that is displayed for a particular <u>Qmne</u>.

Qx The starting $X value for display of the question text (<u>Qtxt</u>).

Qy The starting $Y value for display of the question text (<u>Qtxt</u>).

Ax The starting $X value for the answer field.

Ay The starting $Y value for the answer field.

Al The length (in characters) of the answer field. If <u>Al</u> is zero, the driver does not perform a read.

Req A TRUE/FALSE flag that indicates whether or not the question is REQUIRED. If TRUE, the question is mandatory and cannot be skipped.

Ver The address (LABEL^ROUTINE) of the MUMPS code that will be used to verify the answer. If omitted, no verification will be performed (that is, a free-text answer).

The global description shown in Table 12.14 will be used in the examples that follow.

For the sake of brevity, we have left out the help text nodes for all questions except <u>Name</u>. Once the question global has been defined, the question driver is invoked with the following MUMPS code:

```
Do Drv^%Qd("^CQst(""CREG"")",.Term,Exclude)
```

The first parameter [^CQst("CREG")] defines the array reference for the question frame to be processed. The second parameter (Term) is optional. It is used by the question driver to pass back the method in which the driver terminated (that is, <RET> indicates the user went through all questions, <AU> indicates

TABLE 12.14 TEST DATA FOR QUESTION DRIVER EXAMPLE

^CQst("CREG")	"ID,Name,Str,City,State,ZIP,Phone,Save;ABC Legal Services!Client Registration"
^CQst("CREG","ID")	"Client ID:;0;3;12;3;6;1;ID^CREG"
^CQst("CREG","Name")	"Name:;30;3;36;3;25;1;Name^CREG"
^CQst("CREG","Name",1)	"Enter client name in the form Last,First M."
^CQst("CREG","Str")	"Street:;4;4;12;4;30;1;"
^CQst("CREG","City")	"City:;45;4;51;12;1;"
^CQst("CREG","State")	"State:;5;5;12;5;2;1;"
^CQst("CREG","ZIP")	"ZIP:;30;5;36;5;5;1"
^CQst("CREG","Phone")	"Phone(s):;2;7;12;7;40;0;"
^CQst("CREG","Save")	"Ready to Save:;0;9;15;9;0;1;Save^CREG"

the user backed out, and so on). The parameter <u>Exclude</u> is optional and defines a single character that is to be excluded from input. This character is typically used as a delimiting character in the database. If the user enters that character as part of an answer, the driver will display an error message and repeat the question. Example 12.24 shows what the screen looks like after invoking the driver.

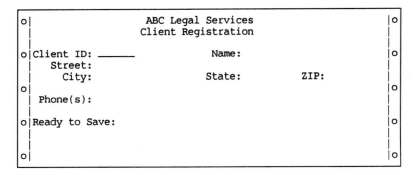

EXAMPLE 12.24. Screen display after invoking the question driver

The question driver clears the screen, displays the titles, and then displays each question and any existing answers. The question text for each <u>Qmne</u> is displayed at the location (<u>Qx,Qy</u>). In addition, a check is made to see if the variable name associated with the mnemonic is defined. If not defined, a new variable with the same name as the question mnemonic (<u>Qmne</u>) is defined as an empty string. The answer field for the question is then displayed at coordinates (<u>Ax,Ay</u>) as highlighted (bold) text.

To simplify the examples, the driver reserves the bottom of the screen for displaying help text and error information; only the top section of the screen (lines 0 to 18) are used for questions and answers.

The question driver uses the editing keyboard READ function described in the previous section to collect user input from the keyboard. As user responses are collected, the driver performs a number of checks on the data input.

- If the answer is an empty string, and the question is required (Req = TRUE), the driver displays an appropriate error message at the bottom of the screen and the question is repeated.

- If the new answer is identical to the initial answer for the question, the driver skips ahead to the next question to be processed (from the Qlist string).

- If the answer contains a question mark, the driver displays the help text associated with the question at the bottom of the screen and reasks the question. Help text and error messages are automatically cleared at the completion of the next READ.

- If the keyboard entry contains the character passed in the parameter Exclude, an error message is displayed and the question is repeated.

- If there is a verify part (Ver is nonnull), the driver dispatches control to the indicated part for verification. The verify part is used to check the validity of a particular entry. If the entry is invalid, the verify part passes an error message back to the question driver. The driver then displays the error message at the bottom of the screen and repeats the question.

- If there were no errors in the entry, the driver sets the variable name associated with the question to the value obtained from the editing keyboard read.

- The question driver then advances (or backs up a question if the READ terminator was an up-arrow) to the next question in the list Qlist. If there are no more questions in the list, the question driver quits. All variables containing question answers (that is, variables whose names are held in Qlist) are available to the calling program.

The question driver handles all display management and movement within a frame of questions. The programmer can concentrate efforts on the verification of answers and let the driver handle all the routine aspects, such as checking for null entries or for a required field or displaying help text.

Verification of keyboard entries is handled by verification subroutines (Ver). A verification subroutine is optional for each question; if not defined, no verification is performed and the answer field is assumed to be free text. Verification subroutines perform two important functions: (1) they are used to check an answer for a particular question, and (2) they can be used to pass back instructions to the driver. The driver invokes a verification subroutine in the following manner:

Do @(Ver(.ans,.err,.redisplay,.goto))

Parameter	Description
ans	The keyboard entry to be checked is passed to the verification subroutine in this parameter. If the answer is altered within the subroutine and no error is flagged (see description of err), the modified form of the answer will be saved in the variable name Qmne when control is returned to the driver. The modified answer will *not* be automatically redisplayed by the driver; see the description of the redisplay parameter for how to display altered answers. The verification subroutine also has access to all of the variables containing the values associated with the questions. If any of these variables are altered, the changes are in effect when control is returned to the driver. Redisplay of altered values must be accomplished explicitly with the redisplay parameter.

Parameter	Description
err	The err parameter is used to pass back error information to the driver. This parameter is initialized to an empty string by the driver before control is passed to the verification subroutine. If the verification subroutine sets err to a value other than an empty string, that value will be displayed as an error message when control is returned to the driver. Answers flagged as an error prevent updating of the variable associated with the question, and the question in error is repeated.
redisplay	If the verification subroutine changes the values of one or more of the variables associated with the questions in the frame, it is necessary to pass back a list of question mnemonics defining those answer fields that should be redisplayed by the driver. The parameter redisplay is used to pass this information back to the driver. Individual Qmnes are separated from each other in this list with commas.
goto	The goto parameter is used to pass information back to the driver concerning the next question to process when control is returned to the driver. If this parameter is not altered, the next question to be processed is the next from the question list (Qlist). To alter the flow of questions, this parameter is set to the Qmne associated with the new next question.

Using the test data defined in Table 12.14, Example 12.25 demonstrates how the question driver is invoked and also demonstrates a variety of verify subroutines.

```
o|Client ;JML–NYSCVM                                              |o
 |        ;Client Registration Module.                            |
 |        Do Drv^%Qd("^CQst(""CREG"")",.term,"\")                 |
o|        If term="" Write *7,"Illegal Terminal Definition."      |o
 |        Quit                                                     |
 |        ;                                                        |
o|        ;Verify Subroutines                                     |o
 |        ;                                                        |
 |ID(ans,err,redisp,goto) ;Client ID                              |
o|        If ans'?1N0.5N Set err="1-5 digit NUMBER" Quit          |o
 |        New i,y Set redisp="Name,Str,City,State,ZIP,Phone"      |
 |        Set y=$G(^Client(ans))                                  |
o|        For i=1:1:6 Set @$P(redisp,",",i)=$P(y,"\",i)           |o
 |        Set:y'="" goto="Save"                                   |
 |        Quit                                                     |
o|Name(ans,err,redisp,goto) ;Client Name                         |o
 |        Quit:ans?1A.E1",1A.E                                    |
 |        Set err="Last,First - please VERIFY answer."            |
o|        Quit                                                     |o
 |Save(ans,err,redisp,goto) ;Ready to SAVE question               |
 |        New yn,ans,trm Set yn="Yes;No"                           |
o|        Set ans=$$MC^%To("yn",1)                                |o
 |        If trm="<AU>" Set goto="Phone" Quit                     |
 |        If ans=2 Set goto="Name" Quit                           |
o|        New i,x Set x=""                                        |o
 |        For i=1:1:6 Set x=x_"\"_@$P("Name,Str,City,State,ZIP|
 |   ---,Phone",",",i)                                            |
o|        Set ^Client(ID)=$E(x,2,999)                             |o
 |        Quit                                                     |
```

EXAMPLE 12.25. Use of the question driver

This example represents all the code that needs to be written by the programmer to display the frame shown in Example 12.24, cycle through the questions, initialize the answers, and file the results. Only three questions are flagged as needing verification (ID, Name, and Save). The other questions are all free text and do not require verify parts.

The subroutine ID is used to verify the "Client ID" answer. If the answer is legal (that is, 1 to 6 digit number), the subroutine then initializes the variables associated with the rest of the frame questions from the main client database and flags them for redisplay by the driver. If data exist for the indicated client, the subroutine also advances the question pointer to the "Ready to Save" question (that is, Set goto = "Save"), assuming that the data do not need correcting.

The subroutine Name is used to verify the "Client Name" question. If not valid (for example, missing a comma), the subroutine passes back an error message to that effect.

The subroutine Save uses the multiple-choice function ($$MC) to collect a "Yes/No" response from the keyboard. Since the subroutine is handling its own I/O [the answer length for the question (A1) is zero], the subroutine must explicitly check for input of an up-arrow and alter the question flow. If the user response is NO, question flow is redirected to the "Client Name" question. If the keyboard response is YES, the data are filed in the main client database.

As stated at the beginning of this section, the scope of this question driver has purposefully been kept rather simple. Many valuable additions could be included to enhance its utility as a programming tool. The driver could be expanded to handle automatic translation of coded answers, lists of answers, and multiple-choice questions as part of the driver, to mention but a few possibilities.

12.5.6 Summary of Advanced I/O Topics

The utilities presented in this section are somewhat limited in capability; they are intended to demonstrate the advantages of using high-level programming tools for developing applications. Using techniques such as these, it is possible to develop sophisticated I/O applications without sacrificing portability between different terminal types or different MUMPS implementations.

The resulting applications present a uniform interface between the computer and the user. Subroutines such as the question driver permit rapid prototyping of applications which enhances communication between the programmer and the user as the application is being developed. The use of such techniques can dramatically reduce the time required to develop an application.

Considering all these factors, there is *no* excuse for programmers to continue writing interactive programs using old-fashioned line-oriented input and output approaches. The widespread use of microcomputers with high-quality display handling has conditioned the user community to expect such performance from computer programs. Do not disappoint them.

12.6 Chapter Highlights

- Each job initiated from a terminal is assigned a *principal device* to which I/O is directed until another device is made active with a USE command (12.2).

- The principal device can be referenced with the special device identification code of 0 (zero). For example, Use 0 (12.2).

- The MUMPS standard does *not* permit alteration of system variables (those starting with a $) with the SET command, but most implementations permit Setting $X and $Y (12.4.1.1).

- MUMPS cannot generally READ or WRITE binary data from or to devices and is limited to ASCII (or EBCDIC) character sets (12.4.3).

- While MUMPS does not have specific bit-oriented operators, it is possible to examine individual bits in a normal decimal number using the integer divide (\) and modulo (#) operators (12.4.3).

- Spool print devices can generally be shared among more than one MUMPS process (12.4.5).

13

Error Processing

It seems appropriate, somehow, that the discussion of error processing is handled in Chapter 13, a number not often associated with good luck. In any programming environment, errors are bound to be encountered as programs are executed. While not yet part of the MUMPS standard, virtually all implementations support one form or another of *trapping* when these conditions arise. It is possible to instruct the system to transfer control to a section of MUMPS code to process the error. The actual mechanisms for informing MUMPS where control is to be transferred and what happens after the error code has been executed vary significantly from system to system.

In the following sections we examine error processing in a somewhat evolutionary nature; we start by examining a relatively simple approach that is still used in some implementations and then expand our considerations to the more complex solutions that are currently being discussed by the MDC.

All these discussions concern nonstandard features of the language and are likely to be different from the actual mechanisms found in your implementation. As usual, refer to your system manuals for detailed information on error trapping and error processing.

When running a MUMPS program, there are four broad error conditions that can arise:

1. Programming Errors: Errors of this type are due to problems in writing the routines and are usually relatively easy to find and correct. They involve conditions such as <SYNTAX> errors (for example, Set x = 22//7), <UNDEFINED> variables (for example, Set x = var when you meant Set x = Var), and so forth. Most of these errors are discovered and corrected during the debugging of the program, well before they are released to the users. On the other hand, it is often difficult to check all possible execution paths of complex applications before they are released to the end user. Errors of this type can appear long after the application has been released. With careful testing, it should be possible to minimize their occurrence.

2. Logical errors: These are perhaps the most complex and difficult errors to resolve. Often, they are completely devoid of "hard" errors such as <UNDEFINED> data nodes or <SYNTAX> errors and only appear when programs do unexpected things or databases begin to hold logically inconsistent values. Often, they can be traced to poor programming practices, such as incorrect use of naked global syntax, or to faulty program logic.

3. Input/Output Errors: This type of error results from the use of input/output devices and can occur at any time and in the best of programs. I/O errors are initiated by factors external to the program (for example, Magnetic tape OFF-LINE or printer out of paper) and are not generally under the control of the programmer.

4. System Errors: These errors, too, are generally out of the programmer's control and often reflect hardware errors (for example, <DISK> error or <ILLEGAL INTERRUPT>) or errors generated by the operating system (for example, database degradation error). They often reflect a serious malfunction with the computer and usually require the intervention of the system manager (or help from hardware or system support specialists) to correct the problem.

13.1 Trapping Errors

All errors, with the possible exception of logic errors which may not manifest themselves immediately, are detected by MUMPS. If no trapping mechanism has been established, encountering an error condition results in a system-generated error message. After the message has been displayed, execution of the process is terminated. The error message displayed at the terminal is usually fairly cryptic (often an error number) and has little or no meaning to the user (for example, **<NAKED> ERROR** or **ERROR 52713**).

Recognizing the desirability of maintaining program control for processing errors, most MUMPS implementations permit error recovery to be handled by MUMPS code.

> A MUMPS job can bypass the system's normal error handling and process error conditions on its own.

This typically involves the use of a system variable (often named **$ZERROR** or **$ZE**) that serves two purposes. The variable can be set by the program to hold the address (label associated with a MUMPS subroutine) to be branched to in event of an error (that is, **LABEL^ROUTINE**). If an error is detected, the same variable is set by the system to hold information defining the error (for example, the type and location of the error) before control is passed to the error processing subroutine. Example 13.1 demonstrates this approach toward error trapping.

```
o|Test    ;Routine to demonstrate simple error trapping   |o
 |         Kill Write !,"Demo error trapping."              |
 |         Set $ZE="Err",a=22,b=7                           |
o|         Write A/b                                        |o
 |         Write !,"All Done."                              |
 |         Quit                                             |
o|Err      Write *7,!,"Serious Programming Error !!"        |o
 |         Write !,"Please give this info to the programmer:"|
 |         Write !,$ZE                                      |
o|         Quit                                             |o
 |_____|
 |>Do Test←                                                |
o|Demo error trapping.                                     |o
 |Serious Programming Error !!                             |
 |Please give this info to the programmer:                 |
o|<UNDEF>;Test+3                                           |o
 |>                                                        |
```

EXAMPLE 13.1.   Simple error trapping using $ZE

In line Test+2 we designate an error trap location by setting the system variable $ZE to a MUMPS label (we could also have set $ZE to a ^ROUTINE or LABEL^ROUTINE reference). During execution, MUMPS detects an error in line Test+3; the variable A is undefined. At this point normal execution stops; all *stacks* (nested FOR and DO commands) are cleared; the address to which control is to be transferred is picked up from $ZE; $ZE is set to hold information concerning the error type (<UNDEF>) and the location of the error (Test+3); and finally program control is transferred to the designated MUMPS code.

> Early error trapping mechanisms usually cleared all stacks (nested DO and FOR commands) before control was transferred to the error processing code.

This approach to error trapping, although limited, does provide some advantages over error processing by the system. In the first place, errors are interrupt driven, and it is unnecessary to constantly check error flags (especially when performing I/O operations) to see if a requested operation was successful. When an error occurs, MUMPS automatically interrupts the process and passes control to error processing code. The program can log information important for correcting the error and provide improved communication with the user concerning what has happened and what to do about it.

Unfortunately, it is not generally possible to make corrections (for example, put the magnetic tape on line) with this scheme and then continue execution where the program was interrupted. Since all stacks (nested DO and FOR commands) are cleared when an error is detected, quitting the error processor quits the entire program. You do not have to QUIT the error processor and can, instead, use a *GOTO* command to continue processing.

```
o|Save(MT) ;Save search results to Magnetic Tape (MT)       |o
 |        New sub Set $ZE="MTerr"                            |
 |        Open MT::0 Else  Write *7,"Magtape Busy" Quit      |
o|Rewind Use MT Write *-5 ;rewind tape                       |o
 |        Set $ZE="Err",sub="" For  Do Output Quit:sub=""    |
 |        Close MT Write !,"All Done"                        |
o|        Quit                                               |o
 |Mterr   Use MT If '($ZA\64#2) Use 0 Goto Err               |
 |        Use 0 Read !,"Put MagTape ON-LINE, press <ENTER>:",x|
o|        Set $ZE="Mterr" Goto Rewind                        |o
 |Error   Write *7,"Error=",$ZE                              |
 |        Quit                                               |
```

EXAMPLE 13.2. Recovering from a magnetic tape off-line error

If a correctable error occurs while $ZE = "MTerr" (for example, the tape was not on line; see Section 12.4.3), the user is requested to correct the problem and press <ENTER> to continue processing. Note the need to <u>USE MT</u> before interrogating the magnetic tape status held in $ZA; on entering an error processor, most implementations automatically perform an implied <u>USE 0</u> to make the principal I/O device the current active device. Also notice that it is necessary to reset the value of $ZE to the trap address before resuming execution; the system clears the trap address and reuses the system variable $ZE to hold information specific to the error. If a second error occurs before $ZE is reset to a trap address, error trapping is disabled and control will be passed to the system for error processing.

This approach allows a user to recover successfully from the tape off line errors and continue processing. However, when the subroutine QUITs, the entire application is done. If this subroutine is invoked from another routine, control will *not* be returned to the calling routine, since all stacks were cleared. In addition, establishing an error trap (setting $ZE) is *not* stacked. If the value of $ZE is changed in a subroutine, the new value supercedes any previous error trapping. On return to the calling routine, $ZE will still reflect any changes made to it by the subroutine. This approach presents a major problem in writing modular programs with calls to general-purpose subroutines.

The next evolutionary step taken by most implementors was to separate the error trap address from the error status information. Separate system variables are used to establish the error trap address (some systems use a system variable named <u>$ZT</u> for this information) from the error status (the system variable containing the type and location of the error). Some implementations have taken this concept one step further, using a system command rather than a system variable to establish the current error trap address (for example, ZETRAP MTerr^%Error).

A more profound development was the introduction of the concept of stacking error trap addresses when subroutines are invoked. This is analogous to issuing a NEW $ZT, but it is performed automatically each time a subroutine is called. The subroutine can then establish its own error trap address; when the subroutine QUITs, the value for the error trap address is popped off the stack and returns to the value it contained before the subroutine was called.

More advanced error trapping mechanisms permit the stacking of error trap addresses. This allows subroutines to set a new error trap without destroying previously set addresses.

At the same time, the method for invoking the error code is often different than that described earlier. The stacks for existing DO and FOR commands are left intact, and the error processing code is invoked with an implied GOTO (Goto @$ZT). If the error subroutine terminates with a QUIT command, the effect is the same as if the subroutine had QUIT (the Goto command extends the range of a subroutine); control is passed back to the command following that used to invoke the subroutine. Example 13.3 demonstrates this philosophy.

```
o|Main    Do Save("^Test(1)",47) Write !,"Finished."         |o
 |         Quit
 |Save(Gbl,MT) ;Save nodes under Gbl to MagTape MT            |
o|         New sub Set $ZT="Mterr"                            |o
 |         Open MT                                            |
 |Rewind Use MT Write *-5 Set sub=""                          |
o|Loop     Set sub=$O(@Gbl@(sub)) If sub="" Close MT Quit     |o
 |         Write @Gbl@(sub),! Goto Loop                       |
 |Mterr    Use MT If '($ZA\64#2) Use 0 Goto Err               |
o|         New x Read !,"Ready Tape, press <ENTER>:",x        |o
 |         Goto Rewind                                        |
 |Err      Write *7,"Error = ",$ZE                            |
o|         Quit                                               |o
```

EXAMPLE 13.3. Error processing without stack deletion

We will *always* get the "**Finished**" message in this example, whether or not an error was encountered and whether or not we could recover from the error. It does, however, point out some additional questions. On quitting the error code Err, control is returned to the command following the Do Save, even though the process did not complete successfully. The QUIT command in Err is handled exactly as the QUIT in line Loop would have been. In many cases, it would be desirable to clear all stacks before quitting, instead of retaining them. Implementations that employ this type of error trapping often include a special form of the QUIT command called **ZQUIT**. ZQUIT performs like the QUIT command *except* that it clears all stacks *before* quitting.

> These newer trap mechanisms also retain the current stacks (nested DO and FOR commands), which allows execution to continue if the error can be corrected.

While this approach permits execution to continue if the error can be corrected, it is not always possible to determine where or how to resume execution. Remember that the error code is invoked with a Goto @$ZT, and a Goto command must be used to continue execution. In Example 13.3 there was a convenient restart address (label Rewind), but in many cases this will not be true. While the system generally passes the error trap information (which line of code was in error) to the error subroutine, it is usually not possible to determine *where* in the line the error occurred nor how to resume execution at that exact spot.

Consider the problems associated with trapping interrupts generated from the keyboard (<CTRL>C). Assume we have a search program executing and wish to allow the user to interrupt the process. We may also wish, in some instances, to permit the search to resume after the interrupt. Consider the following code:

```
o|Search(Dx) ;Search for all patients with a diagnosis of Dx |o
 |         New ans,pid                                         |
 |         Set $ZT="Trap",pid="" Kill ^Srch($J) Break 1        |
o|         For  Set pid=$O(^Pat(Pid)) Quit:pid=""  Do GetDx    |o
 |         Quit                                                 |
 |Trap     If $ZE'='?1"<INTRPT>.E Goto ERROR^Util              |
o|         Write !,"Working on Patient number ",pid            |o
 |Read     Read !,"Stop or Continue (S or C): ",ans            |
 |         If "SsCc"[ans'=$L(ans) Goto Read                    |
o|         If "Ss"[ans Write !,"Aborting search." ZQUIT        |o
 |         Goto ?????                                          |
```

EXAMPLE 13.4. Trapping keyboard interrupts

Most implementations consider an interrupt generated by pressing the <CTRL>C key to be an error and, consequently, control is transferred to the error subroutine when this event occurs. But where can we Goto in the last line of the error trap to resume the search? The Goto command transfers control to the *beginning* of the labeled line, but what if we were interrupted in the middle of a line of code (for example, in the middle of the FOR loop in line 4)? To resolve this dilemma, many implementors allow the use of an argumentless Goto command

(Section 3.3.1.4) to resume execution at the command after the error condition was encountered. This form of the GOTO command does not conform to the MUMPS standard, but does provide restart capabilities in this situation.

An alternative solution for implementations that do not support the argumentless GOTO is to disable BREAKS and then periodically *poll* the status of the principal device to see if the user has pressed a key on the keyboard. One method for performing this task is demonstrated in the next example.

```
o|Search(Dx) ;Search for all patients with a diagnosis of Dx |o
 |          New ans,pid                                       |
 |          Set $ZT="Trap",pid="" Break 0                     |
o|          Write !,"Press ANY key to interrupt search: "     |o
 |          For  Set pid=$O(^Pat(pid)) Q:pid=""!$$Quit Do GetDx|
 |          Quit                                              |
o|Quit() ;Check for ANY key                                  |o
 |          Read *ans:0 Quit:ans=-1 0                         |
 |          Write !,"Working on Patient number ",pid          |
o|Read      Read !,"Stop or Continue (S or C): ",ans          |o
 |          If "SsCc"[ans'=$L(ans) Goto Read                  |
 |          If "Cc"[ans Quit 0                                |
o|          Write !,"Aborting search." Quit 1                 |o
 |Trap      Goto ERROR^Util                                   |
```

EXAMPLE 13.5. Polling the keyboard

This technique should work on all systems but assumes that keyboard type-ahead is enabled (see discussion in Section 6.1.5).

There is another problem associated with this method of error trapping when using extrinsic functions. If you remember, the QUIT command that terminates an extrinsic function *must* have an argument that equates to the value being returned by that function. Any QUIT command used in error processing code that terminates the extrinsic function must also have an argument that returns the result of the function or additional errors will occur.

> Error traps within an *extrinsic function* that issue a QUIT command must provide an argument to the QUIT or additional errors will occur.

But what happens when an invoked subroutine does *not* set up an error processing part? In such situations, MUMPS will unstack all DO, FOR, and NEW commands and extrinsic functions until it reaches a level at which the error trap was set. It then executes the error processor at this level. Example 13.6 demonstrates how this unstacking works.

```
o|Start  Do Lab1 Write !,"Done" Quit                        |o
 |Lab1    Set $ZT="Error" Do Lab2 Write "Lab1" Quit         |
 |Lab2    Do Lab3 Write " Lab2" Quit                         |
o|Lab3    Write " Lab3" Set; this Set causes an error        |o
 |        Quit                                               |
 |Error   Write !,"Error = ",$ZE Quit                        |
o|─────────────────────────────────────────────────────────|o
 |>Do Start↵                                                 |
 | Lab3                                                      |
o|Error = <SYNTAX>;Lab3                                      |o
 |Done                                                       |
 |>                                                          |
```

EXAMPLE 13.6.   Unstacking error traps

When the <SYNTAX> error is encountered in line <u>Lab3</u>, MUMPS begins unstacking DO levels until it reaches one in which the error trap was set (<u>Lab1</u>). It then executes the error code at this level and quits back to the next lower DO level (<u>Start</u>) where the "**Done**" message is displayed.

> When an error is encountered, MUMPS unstacks DO (and NEW) commands until it encounters a level at which an error trap address was established and then transfers control to that address.

There are ramifications to the unstacking of error traps, especially as it relates to the variable environment with parameter passing and the NEW command. As levels are unstacked to find one in which the error trap was set, all NEWed variables (whether explicit or the implicit NEW performed on variables in the formal parameter list) are also unstacked. When a level in which the error trap was set is finally reached, the variable environment may be considerably different than when the error actually occurred. This can greatly complicate the process of determining the conditions that caused the error. In general, it is better for each subroutine to establish its own error trap, although all can reference the same general-purpose error processing code.

In Example 13.7 we make use of a nonstandard form of the $ORDER function to find all the current variables in the partition and display their values. While there is no standard method for finding the names of all variables in the local symbol table, many implementations provide a method for doing so. Some use a nonsubscripted argument for the $ORDER function, others use a special form of the $VIEW function.

Typically, we would not perform a variable dump to the screen. Much of the data will probably scroll off the screen during display, and it serves to further confuse the user. A better method would be to save the variables in a scratch global indexed by the routine in which the error occurred (usually found in $ZE), then by the date and time ($H), and then followed by the variable names. This

```
o|Display(CID) ;display the data associated with client CID  |o
 |          Set $ZT="Error^Util" New cty,name,sta,str,type,x,y,i |
 |          Set x="cty,name,sta,str,type",y=$Get(^Cd(CID))     |
o|          For i=1:1:5 Set @$P(x,",",i)=$P(y,"\",i)           |o
 |          Set x=^Ref(type) If x="" Quit                      |
 |          .                                                   |
o|          .                                                   |o
 |          Quit                                                |
 |-=-=-=-=-=-=-=-=-=-=-=-=-=-=-=-=-=-=-=-=-=-=-=-=-=-=-=-=-=-=-|
o|Util   ;Utility parts for Client Info System (CIS)          |o
 |       ;                                                      |
 |Error Write !,"Programming Error, call X-3391",!,$ZE,!       |
o|      New %s Set %s="" For  Do ErrD Quit:%s=""              |o
 |      ZQUIT                                                   |
 |ErrD  Set %s=$O(%s) Quit:%s=""!(%s="%s")                     |
o|      Write !,%s,"=",@%s                                     |o
 |      Quit                                                    |
```

EXAMPLE 13.7. Establishing error trap in subroutines to preserve variables

approach has the advantage of recording the information for later examination by
the programmer. It also has the advantage that the programmer can reload all
these variables from the global and then test the offending code with the values
that actually caused the problem.

Remember that these examples represent an attempt to describe some of the
many error trapping techniques that are currently employed. At present, the MDC
is hard at work to define a standard method for trapping and processing errors,
although, due to the complex nature of the problems involved, a uniform approach
may be some time in coming. The final definition of the mechanisms for trapping
errors and the effect of errors on a given process will probably include stacking
error traps and unstacking levels when an error is encountered, although the specifics are still being debated.

13.2 Debugging Programs

The primary tool used in debugging MUMPS programs is the **BREAK** command
which is used to temporarily interupt program execution and put the user (hopefully
the programmer) in direct mode. While in direct mode the variable environment
can be examined and changed. Program execution can then be resumed, although
the standard does not define how this is accomplished. Many implementors resume
execution of an interrupted program when a direct mode ZGO or Goto command
is entered. Others, especially those with versions running on microcomputers,
provide special debugging environments making use of windows and function keys
to control execution after the BREAK has been executed.

Many implementations provide additional variations of the BREAK command that permit controlled execution of the program by command, by line, and
so on. In this mode, an implied BREAK command is executed after each command
or line is executed, permitting the programmer to single-step through the code.
These modes are usually controlled by arguments to the BREAK command (for

example, <u>Break "S"</u> to step through the code a single *step* at a time or <u>Break "L"</u> to step through by *lines*). Some microcomputer implementations put the programmer in a special debugging mode in which individual commands, lines, or parts can be executed as steps.

There are some warnings that should be observed when using the BREAK command. In many versions, the status of the last global reference and the values of the system variables $IO, $X, $Y, and $T are not stacked when control is transferred to direct mode. Code executed in direct mode that alters any of these values may cause unpredictable results when program execution is resumed. Also, there is an implied <u>USE 0</u> performed before the programmer is placed in direct mode. If another I/O device is currently the active device, it may be necessary to issue an appropriate <u>USE</u> command before program execution is resumed.

One last consideration: most MUMPS implementations ignore BREAK commands embedded in a program except under special conditions. This is to prevent an end user from being accidentally placed in direct mode while running an application. The conditions that regulate whether or not a BREAK command is executed depend on the implementation. Some rely on whether or not the program was initiated from direct mode (that is, by a programmer), while others rely on initiating a debugging session with special commands (for example, **ZDEBUG^TEST**).

13.3 Chapter Highlights

- A MUMPS process can bypass the system's normal error handling and process error conditions on its own (13.1).

- Early error trapping mechanisms usually cleared all stacks (nested DO and FOR commands) before control was transferred to the error processing code (13.1).

- More advanced error trapping mechanisms permit the stacking of error trap addresses. This allows subroutines to set a new error trap without destroying previously set addresses (13.1).

- These newer trap mechanisms also retain the current stacks (nested DO and FOR commands), which allows execution to continue if the error can be corrected (13.1).

- Error traps within an *extrinsic function* that issue a QUIT command must provide an argument to the QUIT or additional errors will occur (13.1).

- When an error is encountered, MUMPS unstacks DO (and NEW) commands until it encounters a level at which an error address was established and then transfers control to that address (13.1).

14

MUMPS: The Evolving Language

There is a saying that a computer program that is no longer evolving is one that is dying; that saying holds true, to an even greater extent, for computer languages. MUMPS is certainly evolving. Over the past two decades, the number of enhancements and additions to the language make it barely recognizable when compared to the original language that came out of Massachusetts General Hospital. Yet, during this period of extensive change, the basic flavor and overall design criteria have remained intact.

One reason for the success and continued growth of the MUMPS language is the process by which the language is changed. Of the ANSI standard computer languages, MUMPS is the only one in which most of the development committee members are end users, not product vendors. Changes to the language reflect real needs of the user community.

It is in view of this user-driven evolution that we explore the changes likely to be seen in the MUMPS language in the coming years. Many extensions to the language have a common theme: that of interfacing to other standards (networking protocols, other computer languages, other character sets, graphics interfaces, and so on).

The following discussions are speculative in nature. The techniques and examples shown represent the prevailing attitudes of the MDC, but the final resolutions may be quite different from those presented.

14.1 Networking

The topic of networking is an important consideration in a database management environment, especially given the increase in distributed computing systems brought about by the microcomputer revolution. There are numerous MUMPS implementations that currently support networking. Unfortunately, the networking supported is usually specific to a single vendor's MUMPS system; networked communication between different implementations is not usually possible.

A second problem concerns the nature of networking support typically found in MUMPS. Most MUMPS networks are used to support distributed databases *within* the MUMPS environment; they are not designed to communicate between MUMPS and non-MUMPS processes.

14.1.1 Networking between MUMPS Implementations

There is a major effort underway by the MUMPS Development Committee to standardize networking protocols. When in place, this standard will permit communications between heterogenous MUMPS systems and will have a major impact on the design and use of distributed MUMPS database applications.

With the advent of faster and cheaper microcomputers and with uniform networking protocols, it will be possible to take full advantage of a distributed hardware and software environment. Single processes (or groups of related processes) could be run on individual hardware systems to ensure a high throughput, regardless of the number of users on the entire system. Shared databases could be distributed throughout the network, or they could be maintained at file server nodes.

Networking between MUMPS processes would have an impact on the language standard, since it may be necessary to include network address information when referencing globals distributed on remote systems. This information will probably take the form described in Section 10.5.1. References to globals residing on remote systems will need to identify the network node(s) on which the globals reside. Such references might take the general form

<NetworkAddress>Global

where NetworkAddress defines the network address of the Global. The square brackets ([. . .]) currently used in many implementations will probably be maintained to ensure backward compatibility, and another pair of characters will be used to mark the NetworkAddress (possibly the "<. . .>" characters).

Networking will likely extend to referencing routines, and possibly even devices, located on other network nodes. When a different NetworkAddress is specified in a routine reference, that routine would be loaded from the specified network node for execution in the current node. To start a MUMPS process on another networked system, the extended network syntax would be used with the Job command.

Extended network capabilities will emphasize the need for additional security measures. At present, there is no standard method for limiting access to global data by user, function, or networked system. Many implementors do provide utilities that permit a rudimentary form of global security. These usually take the form of establishing READ, WRITE, or KILL access to particular globals by applications running outside the directory in which the globals reside. As processes and databases are distributed within the context of a network environment, the need for better protection schemes increases. The lack of adequate database security has been cited as a major flaw by critics of the MUMPS language.

14.1.2 Networking with Non-MUMPS Environments

At the same time that internal MUMPS networking protocols are being established, efforts are being undertaken to develop a standard interface for network communications between MUMPS and non-MUMPS systems. This mode of networking would enhance the transmission of data to or from the MUMPS environment and applications written in other languages.

The issues involved in networking between MUMPS and non-MUMPS systems are not as clear as those between MUMPS systems. It is likely that such communications will require invoking special system functions to access the network, but such changes may not require extensions to the MUMPS language.

14.2 Enhanced Device Control

In Chapter 12 we discussed many of the problems associated with creating application programs that are both device and system independent. A major area of concern being addressed by the MDC is an expansion of the MUMPS standard to facilitate device-independent programming.

These efforts are directed toward defining an extended set of *format control* arguments that can be used with the Read and Write commands. The basic approach under consideration is to:

- Identify the type of terminal being used with an optional parameter (the DeviceType) to the Use command. For example, the code

Use 0::"X3.64-1979"

would establish the principal device as being a terminal that conforms to the ANSI X3.64-1979 terminal definition standard (for example, a VT-100 terminal). A command of Use 47::"MAGTAPE" would define the MUMPS device 47 as being a magnetic tape drive.

- Special *format control* sequences would be defined for each DeviceType. The syntax of the *format control* sequences would be /controlmnemonic. The control mnemonics may be different for each DeviceType. For example, one would not be able to /REWIND a video terminal. The *format control* sequences could then be used as arguments to Read and Write commands in a manner similar to the format control sequences #, !, and ?nn.

Write /CUP(10,22)   Position the display cursor to location $X = 10$, $Y = 22$. Update the values of the system variables $X and $Y to reflect the changed cursor location.

The MUMPS system would be responsible for determining the appropriate control sequences to activate the controlmnemonic on any given device type. The system would also be responsible for updating the values associated with $X and $Y.

In addition to the extended format control syntax for the Read and Write commands, the following two system variables would be introduced.

$KEY $KEY would contain the control sequence that terminated the last Read command from the current device. If no Read command was issued to the current device, or when no terminator was used (for example, as the result of a timeout, a fixed-length READ, or a single-character READ), the value of $KEY would be an empty string.

$DEVICE   This system variable would reflect the consequences of the last Input/Output operation that was processed. If the last I/O operation requested was possible and successful, $DEVICE is set to TRUE (1). If the last I/O operation was not possible for the device, $DEVICE is set to FALSE (0).

The use of expanded device format control codes would provide a relatively simple manner to interface with a variety of devices and external standards. Implementors would provide definitions for a variety of existing DeviceTypes, such as the ANSI X3.64-1979 terminal definition standard, the ANSI X3.124-1985 Graphics Kernel System (GKS), and magnetic tape drives. In many respects, this approach mimics the extrinsic terminal control functions described in Section 12.5.1.

14.3 Access to Other Languages

An important aspect in the continued growth of the MUMPS language will be the ability to access other languages and standards. The original versions of MUMPS required dedicated computer systems; when MUMPS was running, only programs written in the MUMPS language could be executed. This single-language environment is becoming a thing of the past as layered MUMPS implementations and networking with non-MUMPS computer systems become more prevalent.

Traditional access to computing programs written in other languages has been through the exchange of data, either on magnetic tape or disk files. MUMPS provides an extremely flexible I/O environment that permits writing or reading datasets in almost any format. In earlier examples (12.8, 12.10) we examined techniques for creating sequential files in MUMPS for exporting data to external spread sheet or statistical analysis programs.

There are many possible advantages to be gained by allowing MUMPS applications to invoke non-MUMPS processes. One use would be to give MUMPS programs access to system-level "tool-kits" for manipulating system-specific information such as file directories (selecting files, deleting files, and so on).

Another use would be to take advantage of special hardware on the system that is not directly supported in the MUMPS environment (plotters, tablets, graphics packages, and the like).

A third use would be to interface with high-level "canned" applications such as spread sheets and statistical or numerical analysis packages or to other standards such as SQL (structured query language). This type of interface often involves the transfer of large amounts of data between the MUMPS and non-MUMPS process. Methods to enhance data communications between a MUMPS application and the non-MUMPS process are a difficult issue and may involve creating "hooks" to make MUMPS data structures accessible to the external application.

On the negative side, calls to external non-MUMPS applications, especially those involving system utilities or low-level hardware interfaces, are likely to be system specific. MUMPS applications using such features may not be portable between different hardware or software environments.

14.4 Use of Alternative Character Sets

The MUMPS standard defines the internal character set used for programs and data as the seven-bit ASCII character set presented in Appendix A. This is a limitation that affects the computer systems on which MUMPS can be implemented. Many systems, especially some of the larger mainframes, use the EBCDIC (Extended Binary Coded Decimal Interchange Code) for internal representation of characters. The internal use of the EBCDIC character set has some important implications. The EBCDIC character set collates differently than the ASCII character set. Commands and functions that rely on the collating order (such as the follows operator or the $Order function) may produce different results, depending on the character set used. Some functions (such as $ASCII and $CHAR) are defined specifically for the ASCII character set. While many vendors have implemented MUMPS on computer systems using the EBCDIC character set, these implementations do not always conform to the MUMPS standard.

An even greater problem exists when trying to support MUMPS in other countries. The seven-bit ASCII character set is inadequate for representing the non-English text used in many countries and severely limits the use of MUMPS in these situations. A partial solution is to expand the current definition of the seven-bit ASCII character set to include eight bits. This would permit the definition of 256 unique characters, rather than the current 128, and has already been implemented by some vendors. Unfortunately, this solution introduces its own problems with regard to the internal collating sequence used by MUMPS and the pattern match operator. Simply expanding the character set without addressing the associated problems is not an adequate solution.

The problem of supporting Japanese or Arabic character sets is even more complex. In these languages, it is necessary to use at least two bytes to represent all possible characters. This has major ramifications beyond those already mentioned. For example, which value does the $Length function return, the number of bytes in the string or the number of characters? In the Japanese character set, the width of the displayed character may vary. How should MUMPS update the variables $X and $Y?

The issues surrounding the use of alternative character sets are complex and will have a substantial impact on the MUMPS language. However complex, these topics must be resolved by the MDC in order for MUMPS to achieve widespread use outside English-speaking countries.

14.5 Standardized Error Processing

The MUMPS standard does not specify how errors encountered during program execution are processed or reported. Despite this omission, virtually all MUMPS implementations permit the trapping of errors and subsequent processing by MUMPS code (Chapter 13). The methods used to invoke the error trapping mechanism and the effect the error has on the application vary from system to system. To achieve full use and to maintain application portability between systems, these error processing mechanisms must be standardized.

14.6 Miscellaneous Language Changes

In addition to the broad topics discussed, a number of specific language changes are currently being examined. A sample of those being considered includes:

- *Bit manipulation:* A number of proposals are being considered that would allow MUMPS to manipulate individual bits within a bit stream. These manipulations would permit individual bits in a variable to be set, interrogated, or combined (and/or) with the bit streams in other variables.

- *Tree copy:* Another proposal concerns the implementation of a new MUMPS command (the Move command) that would provide the ability to copy one global branch (or an entire global) to another location. The results achieved by this command would be similar to the Copy function presented in Example 10.15.

- *Reverse $ORDER:* The $ORDER function returns the next higher subscript for a referenced array element. The reverse $ORDER function would return the next *lower* subscript value for a referenced array element. This function is already available as a nonstandard feature in many MUMPS implementations.

- *Tree search:* There are proposals to expand the ability to search through globals for specific data values or patterns of data values, rather than just the next physical data node provided with the $ORDER and $QUERY functions. These proposals include the ability to set both horizontal and vertical search limits to permit searching through selected branches and levels of a target global.

- *Increased pattern match capabilities:* There is a proposed extension to the pattern match operator that allows logical ORs of pattern codes without the need for restating the target string to be checked. Consider the problem of checking a social security number in which a "-", "/", or " " (space) is allowed as a delimiter between numeric fields (for example, 090-35-3004, 090/35/3004, and 090 35 3004 would all be valid entries). With the current pattern match syntax, it would be necessary to specify nine separate pattern match codes and logically OR them together.

(SS?3N1"-"2N1"-"4N)!(SS?3N1"-"2N1"/"4N)! . . . , (7 more patterns)

In the proposal under consideration, the same result could be achieved by enclosing the options for each pattern field within parentheses as follows:

SS?3N(1"-",1"/",1" ")2N(1"-",1"/",1"/")4N

The patterns to be ORed together are enclosed in parentheses and the OR fields within each group are separated from each other with a comma. If the first check within a combined pattern fails, the next field is checked. If the entire pattern field is processed without finding a successful match, the entire pattern fails. The first match encountered in a pattern field causes the rest of the field to be ignored, and the pattern match process continues after the closing parenthesis.

14.7 Concluding Remarks

The MUMPS language provides the programmer with an extremely powerful tool for managing data in a real-world environment. MUMPS has a built-in database management system supporting hierarchical, sparse, and shared data files in which the keys pointing to the data can be arbitrary strings of characters. As a language, it is interpreted and permits rapid development and debugging of applications. It supports an extremely flexible I/O environment, making it a simple matter to interface with a variety of devices and to import or export data to other programming languages. MUMPS also supports execution indirection, making it possible to execute instructions held as data. In short, MUMPS is an ideal language to develop database applications.

Does this book really achieve its rather pretentious goal of being the "Complete MUMPS"? In a word, *no*. It is impossible to convey all the nuances of this rich language. On the other hand, we have covered most of the basic elements of this unique language, and you should have a sound footing for developing programs in MUMPS. I strongly believe that once you have experienced MUMPS, you, too, will echo the statement presented in the preface: **But it's so much easier in MUMPS!**

A

ASCII Character Set

354

Dec	Character		Dec	Character	Dec	Character	Dec	Character
0	^@	NUL	32	Space	64	@	96	`
1	^A	SOH	33	!	65	A	97	a
2	^B	STX	34	"	66	B	98	b
3	^C	ETX	35	#	67	C	99	c
4	^D	EOT	36	$	68	D	100	d
5	^E	ENQ	37	%	69	E	101	e
6	^F	ACK	38	&	70	F	102	f
7	^G	BEL	39	'	71	G	103	g
8	^H	BS	40	(	72	H	104	h
9	^I	HT	41	)	73	I	105	i
10	^J	LF	42	*	74	J	106	j
11	^K	VT	43	+	75	K	107	k
12	^L	FF	44	,	76	L	108	l
13	^M	CR	45	−	77	M	109	m
14	^N	SO	46	.	78	N	110	n
15	^O	SI	47	/	79	O	111	o
16	^P	DLE	48	0	80	P	112	p
17	^Q	DC1	49	1	81	Q	113	q
18	^R	DC2	50	2	82	R	114	r
19	^S	DC3	51	3	83	S	115	s
20	^T	DC4	52	4	84	T	116	t
21	^U	NAK	53	5	85	U	117	u
22	^V	SYN	54	6	86	V	118	v
23	^W	ETB	55	7	87	W	119	w
24	^X	CAN	56	8	88	X	120	x
25	^Y	EM	57	9	89	Y	121	y
26	^Z	SUB	58	:	90	Z	122	z
27	^[	ESC	59	;	91	[	123	{
28	^\	FS	60	<	92	\	124	|
29	^]	GS	61	=	93	]	125	}
30	^^	RS	62	>	94	^	126	~
31	^_	US	63	?	95	_	127	DELete

Keyboard sequence for generating characters with decimal codes between 0 and 31 are shown as ^**char** where ^ represents holding down the <**CTRL**> key and **char** is the character then pressed. Some MUMPS systems act on some of these control sequences (such as ^S, ^Q, ^O) and do not pass them through to the READ command.

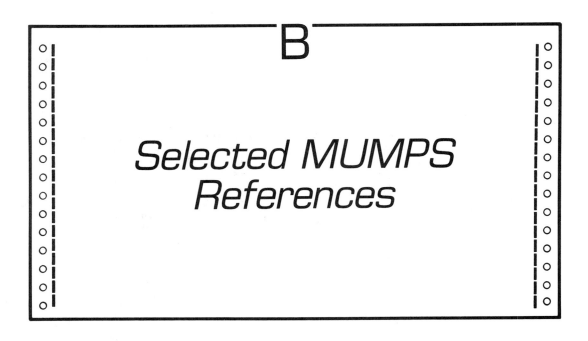

B

Selected MUMPS References

1. *American National Standard for Information Systems Programming Languages—MUMPS* (ANSI/MDC X11.1-1984 MUMPS Language Standard), MUMPS Development Committee, 1984. This document defines the formal specifications for the MUMPS language as approved by the American National Standard Institute (ANSI). It is a high-level technical text appropriate for experienced MUMPS programmers.

2. David R. Brown and Donald H. Glaeser, *A Cookbook of MUMPS: Programmer's Techniques and Routines*, Guidance Software, Kingwood, TX., 1984. An intermediate-level text demonstrating various MUMPS programming techniques. Numerous examples with line by line comments for all code presented.

3. Arther F. Krieg, *Computer Programming in Standard MUMPS*, MUMPS Users' Group, College Park, MD., 1984. An entry-level text for beginning programmers. The self-instruction format provides an excellent text for introducing the MUMPS language to nonprogrammers. The text is accompanied with numerous examples of MUMPS code.

4. Thomas Salander and Harlan Stenn, *MUMPS Programmers' Reference Manual 1985*, MUMPS Users' Group, College Park, MD., 1985. An intermediate- to high-level text designed for competent MUMPS programmers. Specific features of the language are explained in detail with limited examples. A copy of the language standard is included as an appendix.

5. Charles Volkstorf, *The MUMPS Handbook of Efficiency Techniques*, MUMPS Users' Group, College Park, MD., 1985. A text for advanced MUMPS programmers with over 100 suggestions and procedures designed to improve the speed and efficiency of MUMPS programs.

6. Richard F. Walters, Jack Bowie, and Jerome Wilcox, *MUMPS Primer Revised*, MUMPS Users' Group, College Park, MD., 1983. An introduction to the MUMPS programming language suitable for beginning programmers.

7. Richard F. Walters, *The ABC's of MUMPS: An Introduction for Novice and Intermediate Programmers*, Digital Press, Bedford, MA., 1988 (est.). This is a completely updated version of the MUMPS Primer scheduled to be published in the fall of 1988. As the name implies, it is designed for novice- and intermediate-level programmers. It contains all the proposed MDC Type A enhancements to the MUMPS language through June, 1988 and makes extensive use of examples.

8. Joan Zimmerman (revised by Tom Salander), *Introduction to Standard MUMPS*, MUMPS Users' Group, College Park, MD., 1984. An introductory text to the MUMPS language appropriate for beginning programmers. Numerous examples of MUMPS code are presented.

C

Summary of MUMPS Commands

BREAK (Section 3.5.1): Without arguments, the BREAK command is used to interrupt program execution and return control to direct mode for program debugging. Execution is usually resumed with an argumentless **GOTO** or **ZGO** command. With arguments (argument = True/False), it is often used to enable or disable keyboard breaks (<CTRL>C).

Examples:
> Set a = 22 **BREAK** Write !,A ;debug line
> Kill   **BREAK 0** ;disable keyboard BREAKS

CLOSE (Section 3.4.5, Chapter 12): Used to release device ownership established with the **OPEN** command.

Example:
> If ans = "Y" **CLOSE 47** ;done with mag-tape

DO (Section 3.3.2, Chapter 9): Used to invoke a MUMPS subroutine with the argument identifying the address of the MUMPS code to be invoked (LABEL, LABEL^ROUTINE, or ^ROUTINE). The subroutine is terminated with a QUIT command. On termination, program execution resumes with the command following the DO. Another method of invoking a subroutine is through use of **Extrinsic Functions** (Section 9.2).

Examples:

> If x>10 **DO Average^XYZ** ;call label Average in routine XYZ
> **DO Getrec(ID,.value)** ;call Getrec with parameters

ELSE (Section 3.2.2): Logical opposite of **IF** command, this command checks the true/false value of the system variable **$TEST** and is equivalent to the command **IF '$TEST**, but does *not* alter the value of $TEST. The $TEST variable is set on executing an IF command with arguments or timed commands such as OPEN, READ, JOB, or LOCK.

Examples:

> If a = b Write "equal"
> **ELSE** Write "not equal"
> Read a:10 **ELSE** Write "no response from keyboard"

FOR (Section 3.2.3): The FOR command is the primary loop control command with the arguments defining the number of times the rest of the commands on the line following the FOR command are executed. Both the **QUIT** and the **GOTO** commands can be used to prematurely terminate a FOR loop.

Examples:

> **FOR i = start:increment:end** Write Array(i),! Do test
> **FOR i = start:increment** Quit:'$D(Array(i)) Do Average
> **FOR** Read a Quit:a = "" Do ADDa
> **FOR i = "one","two","three"** Set x = x + 1 Do Convert

GOTO (Section 3.3.1): The GOTO command causes program execution to be passed to another MUMPS line. The argument (LABEL, LABEL^ROUTINE, or ^ROUTINE) specifies the line to which execution is to be transferred. Control transfer is absolute and does not return to the command following the GOTO. The GOTO command can be used to prematurely terminate a FOR loop.

Examples:

> If ans = "Y" **GOTO Done**
> **GOTO @$P("one,two^Edit,^three","'","','',ans)**
> For i = 1:1:100 **GOTO error:'$D(x(i))** Do Average(x(i))

HALT (Section 3.3.4): Used to terminate program execution, release all currently owned devices, clear all current LOCKs, and release the partition back to the system.

Example:

> If done **HALT**

HANG (Section 3.5.2): The HANG command is used to temporarily pause program execution for the number of seconds specified by the argument.

Example:

> Do Display(errmsg) **HANG 15** Goto Loop

IF (Section 3.2.1): The IF command is used to evaluate the true/false status of its argument and, if TRUE, execution continues with the remainder of the commands on the line; if FALSE, the rest of the commands on the line are ignored. The true/false results of the argument evaluation are saved in the system variable $TEST. Both the ELSE command and the argumentless form of the IF command can be used to subsequently test the status of $TEST. The timed form of the OPEN, READ, LOCK, and JOB commands also set the value of $TEST.

Examples:

> **IF a>10** Do init For i = 1:1:a Do GetRec
> **IF**   Do Check Goto End ;same as IF $TEST
> Read ans:30 **IF**   Do OutPut Goto Loop
> **IF ans' = "","Yy"[ans** Do Save Goto Start

JOB (Section 3.5.3): Used to start another independent MUMPS process. If timeout syntax is used, the system variable $TEST indicates whether or not the process could be started.

Examples:

> Set ^Que($J,$H) = PID **JOB** ^Print Quit
> **JOB UpDate^Save::5** Else   Write "Can't start now."

KILL (Section 3.1.2): Used to delete local and global variables and arrays (or branches of arrays). When array branches are killed, all nodes below the specified node are also deleted.

Examples:

> **KILL A,bc,X** ;deletes A, bc, and X
> If DEL = "Y" **KILL ^PAT(PID),^Temp(PID)** Quit
> **KILL Array,^Temp**
> **KILL (big,little)** ;delete everything but big and little
> **KILL**   Goto Start ;delete ALL local variables

LOCK (Sections 3.5.4, 10.4): Lock selected local or global variables or array branches. The LOCK command works *by convention*; it does not prevent other processes from accessing or changing the values of locked variables but does prevent them from being able to LOCK them or related array branches. The timed form of the LOCK command sets the system variable $TEST to indicate whether or not the LOCK was successful. The argumentless form of the LOCK is used to unLOCK all previously LOCKed variables.

Examples:

> **LOCK ^TEST(PID,"Lab")**
> **LOCK (^Pat(PID),^Lab(PID))**
> **LOCK +Inven(new),-Inven(old)**
> If done **LOCK**   Goto Next ;unlock all LOCKs

NEW (Section 3.1.3, Chapter 9): The NEW command is used to temporarily redefine variable names within the scope of a <u>DO</u> or <u>XECUTE</u> command or an <u>Extrinsic Function</u>. There is an implied NEW command issued for each variable in the formal parameter list of a subroutine or extrinsic function. A QUIT command terminating a subroutine or extrinsic function undoes all NEW commands (implicit as well as explicit) issued within the scope of that subroutine or extrinsic function.

Examples:

> **NEW a,b,c** ;new copies of a, b, and c
> **NEW (Array,X)** ;new copies of everything but Array and X
> **NEW**   Set a=22,b=3 Do Init ;completely new variable list

OPEN (Section 3.4.1, Chapter 12): The OPEN command is used to establish ownership of MUMPS devices such as terminals, printers, and magnetic tape drives. When used with timeout syntax, the system variable $TEST is set to true/false, indicating whether or not the device could be assigned to the process.

Example:

> **OPEN 47::0** Else   Write "Can't get MagTape" Quit

QUIT (Section 3.3.3, Chapter 9): The QUIT command is used to terminate a subroutine, extrinsic function, or FOR loop. For subroutines invoked with a <u>DO</u> or <u>XECUTE</u> command, the command is argumentless; the QUIT associated with an <u>Extrinsic Function</u> must have a single argument that evaluates to the value being returned by the function.

Examples:

> Sub If x>10 Write "Done." **QUIT**
> For i = 1:1:1 Read !,a **QUIT:a = ""**   Do Load
> Cube(x) **QUIT x∗x∗x**

READ (Section 3.4.3, Chapter 12): Used to input one or more characters from the current device (established with the <u>USE</u> command) into a variable. When the timed-read syntax is used, the system variable $TEST is set to true/false indicating whether or not the READ operation timed out.

Examples:

> **READ !,"Ready to save: ",ans** Do:"Yy"[ans Save
> **READ X#4** Goto Loop ;input up to 4 characters
> **READ ∗A** Goto Getnxt:a<32 ;single-character **READ**
> **READ !,"Name: ",name:10** Else   QUIT

SET (Section 3.1.1): Used to establish the value of a local or global variable name or an array node.

Examples:

> **SET A = 22,b = 33,ˆtest(A,10) = 1**
> **SET (X,Y,Z) = 0** ;initialize X, Y, and Z to zero

USE (Section 3.4.2, Chapter 12): Makes one of the currently owned devices (established with <u>OPEN</u> command) the current active device for subsequent <u>READ</u> and <u>WRITE</u> operations.

Example:

> If ans = "Y" **USE prt** Do Print USE 0 Quit

VIEW (Section 3.5.5): Implementation-specific command usually used to read or write disk blocks or to change memory locations. Not normally used in application programs.

WRITE (Section 3.4.4, Chapter 12): Used to output characters to the current device (established with the <u>USE</u> command).

Examples:

> **WRITE #,!,"Main Options" Do GetOpt**
> **WRITE !,Name,?20,Street,?40,City,?60,State,!**
> Read *A If a>32&(a<127) **WRITE *A**

XECUTE (Section 3.3.5, 7.1): Used to execute MUMPS commands held as data in variables or string literals.

Examples:

> **XECUTE "Set a = 33 Do GetPat^PAT(a) Quit:a = """""""" D Test"**
> For   Read !,"> ",coms Quit:coms = "" **XECUTE coms**

Z . . . (Sections 3.5.5-3.5.11): All commands starting with the letter **Z** are implementor specific, although most systems provide for the following:

ZINSERT	Insert a command line into the program currently loaded in the partition
ZLOAD	Load the named routine from disk into the partition.
ZPRINT	Print one or more lines of the routine loaded in the partition to the current device. Some implementations also use the nonstandard PRINT command for this function.
ZREMOVE	Remove (delete) the routine currently loaded from the *partition*; usually, the routine is *not* deleted from disk when using this command. To delete a routine from disk it is usually necessary to first issue a ZREMOVE command followed by a ZSAVE command.
ZSAVE	Save the routine loaded in the partition to disk.

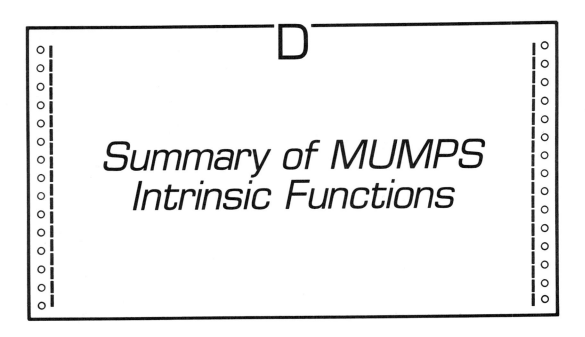

D

Summary of MUMPS Intrinsic Functions

$ASCII (Section 8.1.8): **$ASCII(string,position)** Returns the decimal value of the ASCII characters in string with the character position dependent on the argument position. If the argument position is absent, the value of the first character in string is returned. If the positionth character is not present, the function returns a value of -1.

Examples:

$A("123") = 49 ;default position = 1
$A("AbC1De",4) = 49

$CHAR (Section 8.1.9): **$CHAR(integer,integer, . . .)** Returns a string whose characters are the ASCII decimal equivalents of each of the integers in the argument list.

Example:

$C(97,98,99) = "abc"

$DATA (Sections 8.2.1, 10.2.2): **$DATA(Variable)** Returns a one- or two-digit

364

number defining whether or not the variable is defined and, if it is an array, whether it is a pointer node (has descendants), a data node, or both.

DATA
Present Absent

		Present	11	10
Descendants		Absent	1	0

$DATA values

In the following examples we will assume an empty local symbol table except for the following:

$$X = 22, Ary(1,2) = "1,2", Ary(1,2,3) = "1,2,3"$$

Examples:
$D(X) = 1
$D(Y) = 0
$D(Ary) = 10
$D(Ary(1,2)) = 11
$D(Ary(1,2,3)) = 1

$EXTRACT (Section 8.1.1): **$EXTRACT(string,from,to)** Returns the characters extracted from string from the fromth character to the toth character. Both from and to are optional: if to is absent, it is assumed to be the same as from; if from is absent, it is assumed to have a value of one (1). The following examples will assume that the variable X is defined as follows:

$$X = "abc12345ABC12"$$

Examples:
$E(X) = "a"
$E(X,3) = "c"
$E(X,1,3) = "abc"
$E(x,9,999) = "ABC12"
$E(X,55) = ""
$E(X,5,3) = ""

$FIND (Section 8.1.4): **$FIND(string,find,from)** Returns an integer number indicating the relative character position of the *next* character in string found after the characters specified by find; if the argument from is included, it represents the character location in string at which the search is to begin. If from is absent, the search of string begins at the first character. If the character string defined by find is *not* found, the function returns a ZERO (0). If found, the function returns the character position *following* the match. In the examples that follow, we will assume that the variable X is defined as

X = "0) Quit,1) Enter/Edit,2) Search,3) Print Results"

Examples:

$F(X,"E") = 13
$F(X,"E",13) = 19
$F(X,"E",19) = 0
$F(X,"2)") = 24
$F(X,"5)") = 0

$FNUMBER   (Section 8.1.7): **$FNUMBER(expression,code,decimal)**   Returns a formatted string in the form of a number based on the input expression and code with an optional specification on the number of decimal digits displayed to the right of the decimal point. The code argument can contain one or more codes, although some are mutually exclusive (for example, the "T" and "P" codes).

Code	Description
+	Leading " + ;; inserted in front of positive numbers.
−	Leading minus sign suppressed on negative numbers.
,	Commas inserted every third position to the left of decimal
T	Sign of number inserted at right end (*t*railing).
P	Negative numbers put inside parentheses ( ).

Examples:

$FN(22/7," + T",2) = "3.14 + "
$FN(22/7," + ",0) = " + 3"
$FN(10000.01,",",3) = "10,000.010"
$FN(− 5000,",P") = "(5,000)"

$GET   (Section 8.2.5): **$GET(variable)**   Returns the value associated with variable; if variable is undefined or only a pointer element [that is, '($D(variable)#2)], this function returns an empty string ("").

Examples:

```
$GET(^XYZ(123)) = ""          ^XYZ(123) is UNDEFINED
$GET(^XYZ(124)) = "data"      ^XYZ(124) is DEFINED

$GET(status) = ""             status is UNDEFINED or null
```

$JUSTIFY   (Section 8.1.6): **$JUSTIFY(expression,width,decimal)**   Used to right-justify a string or number (expression) within a field whose width is specified by width. The expression is padded with spaces on the left, if necessary. If the optional argument decimal is specified, expression is evaluated as a number that is right-justified within a field of width characters with decimal defining the number of digits to the right of the decimal point. The value of the number is rounded to decimal digits, not truncated.

Examples:

```
$J("Pad",8) = "     Pad"
$J("Pad",1) = "Pad"
$J(22/7,8,2) = "    3.14"
$J("Pad",5,2) = " 0.00"
```

$LENGTH   (Section 8.1.3): **$LENGTH(expression,delim)**   Returns the length of expression in either characters or subfields. If the optional argument delim is absent, the $LENGTH function returns the number of characters in expression. If delim is present, it is evaluated as a string of characters, and the $LENGTH function returns the number of subfields in expression using those characters as delimiters.

Examples:

```
$L("How now, brown cow?") = 19
$L("How now, brown cow?"," ") = 4
$L("How now, brown cow?","ow") = 5
$L("How now, brown cow?","*") = 1
```

$ORDER   (Sections 8.2.2, 10.2.2): **$ORDER(subscripted reference)**   Returns the next higher subscript (MUMPS collating order) above the last subscript specified in the subscripted reference. The starting point for any subscript level is an empty string and the value returned by $ORDER if there are no higher subscripts at the specified level is also an empty string. The examples that follow assume the following global definitions:

```
^X(1,2,3) = "1,2,3"
^X(1,2,4) = "1,2,4"
```

Examples:

$$\$O(^X(1,2,``")) = 3$$
$$\$O(^X(1,2,3)) = 4$$
$$\$O(^X(1,2,4)) = ``"$$
$$\$O(^X(1)) = ``"$$

$PIECE (Section 8.1.2): **$PIECE(expression,delim,from,to)** Returns a string extracted from <u>expression</u> using the character(s) in <u>delim</u> as delimiters. The returned string consists of all the characters between the <u>from</u>th occurrence of <u>delim</u> to the <u>to</u>th occurrence. If the optional argument <u>to</u> is absent, it is assumed to be the same as <u>from</u>. If the optional argument <u>from</u> is absent, it is assumed to be one (1).

Examples:

$P("How now, brown cow?"," ",2,3) = "now, brown"
$P("How now, brown cow?"," ",2) = "now"
$P("How now, brown cow?"," ") = "How"
$P("How now, brown cow?," ",4,99) = "cow?"
$P("How now, brown cow?,"*") = "How now, brown cow?"

Also, the $PIECE function is the only intrinsic function that can be used on the left side of an equals sign (" = ") when used with the SET command. In these cases, the first argument of the function must be a legal variable name.

If X = "1,2,3" then:

Example:

Set $P(X,",",2) = "test" then X = "1,test,3"

$QUERY (Section 8.2.4): **$QUERY(global reference)** The $QUERY function performs a "tree-walk" of a global from top to bottom and left to right. The value returned is a full global reference of the next global node containing data, regardless of the level of that data node. If there are no further data nodes following <u>global reference</u>, $QUERY returns an empty string. The examples that follow assume the definition of

$$^X(0) = "0"$$
$$^X(1,2,3) = "1,2,3"$$
$$^X(1,2,4) = "1,2,4"$$

Examples:

$Q("^X") = "^X(0)"
$Q("^X(0)") = "X(1,2,3)"
$Q("^X(1,2,3)") = "X(1,2,4)"
$Q("^X(1,2,4)") = ""

$RANDOM   (Section 8.3.2): **$RANDOM(range)**   Returns a uniformly distributed integer number from zero (0) to range − 1.

Example:

> $R(100) returns a random number between 0 and 99

$SELECT   (Section   8.3.1):   **$SELECT(expression:value,expression:value, . . .)** The $SELECT function scans the argument list from left to right evaluating each expression until one is TRUE (nonzero); it then returns the value (another expression) associated with the True expression. If no True expression is found, an error is generated.

If the variable T = 3, then

Examples:

> $S(T = 1:"one",T = 2:"two",T = 3:"three") = "three"
> $S(T = 1:"one",T = 2:"two") is an ERROR
> $S(T = 1:"one",T = 2:"two",1:"NEITHER") = "NEITHER"

$TEXT   (Section   8.1.10): **$TEXT(label + offset)**, **$TEXT(label^routine + offset)**, **$TEXT(+ offset)**   Returns the line of source code associated with the routine, label, and the optional offset (integer number). If the optional routine is omitted, the routine currently loaded in the partition is used. The function returns an empty string ("") if the referenced line does not exist.

Examples:

> $T(Start) returns line if label Start exists,
>   otherwise a null.
> $T(Start + 6)
> $T(+ 1) returns the first line of the current routine
> $T(+ 0) returns the current routine name

$TRANSLATE   (Section 8.1.5): **$TRANSLATE(expression,replace,with)** Performs a character by character replacement, replacing every occurrence of a character in expression that is also in replace with a character from with. For example, if the character "a" is in expression and is also the third character in the replace string, it is deleted from expression and replaced with the 3rd character in with. If the optional argument with is absent, it is assumed to be an empty string and causes the characters in replace to be deleted from expression.

Examples:

> $TR("a nice person","ae","AE") = "A nicE pErson"
> $TR("a nice person"," ") = "aniceperson"
> $TR(string,"ABC...Z","abc...z") converts string to
>   lowercase

$VIEW (Section 8.3.3): The $VIEW function is implementation specific; see the description under Section 8.3.3.

$Z . . . (Section 8.4): All functions starting with the characters **$Z** are implementation specific.

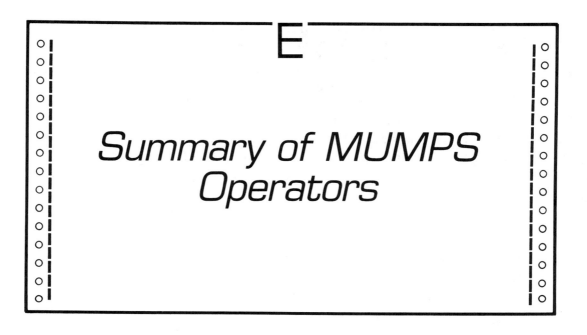

E

Summary of MUMPS Operators

See Chapter 5 for a detailed description of the operators.

+	Addition operator (e.g., 22 + 3 + ABC)
−	Subtraction operator (e.g., 22 − 3 − Sum)
*	Multiplication operator (e.g., Value*3.14)
/	Division operator (e.g., 22/7)
\	Integer division operator (e.g., 22\7 = 3)
**	Exponentiation operator (e.g., 2**4 = 16)
#	Modulo operator (i.e., remainder) (e.g., 7#4 = 3)
_	Underscore is the concatenate operator (e.g., "AB"_"CD" = "ABCD")
>	Greater-than operator (e.g., 2>1 = 1, 1>2 = 0)
<	Less-than operator (e.g., 1<2 = 1, 2<1 = 0)
=	String equals operator (e.g., "ABC" = "ABC" = 1, "0123" = 123 = 0)
[	String contains operator (e.g., "ABC"["BC" = 1, "ABC"["CB" = 0)
]	String follows operator (e.g., "BCD"]"ABC" = 1, "ABC"]"BCD" = 0)
?	Pattern match operator recognizing the following pattern types:

    A   Any of the 52 upper- or lowercase alphabetic characters

    C   Any of the control codes (decimal values 0 to 31, 127)

<u>E</u>	The entire ASCII character set (decimal values 0 to 127)	
<u>L</u>	Any of the 26 lower-case alphabetic characters ("a" to "z")	
<u>N</u>	Any of the 10 numeric digits (0 to 9)	
<u>P</u>	Any of the 33 punctuation characters (decimal values 32 to 47, 58 to 64, 91 to 96, or 123 to 126)	
<u>U</u>	Any of the 26 upper-case alphabetic characters ("A" to "Z")	

& The logical AND operator (e.g., $\underline{1\&3=1}$, $\underline{3\&0=0}$)

! The logical OR operator (e.g., $\underline{1!3=1}$, $\underline{3!0=1}$, $\underline{0!0=0}$)

' The apostrophe is the logical NOT operator (e.g., $\underline{'(2=3)=1}$)

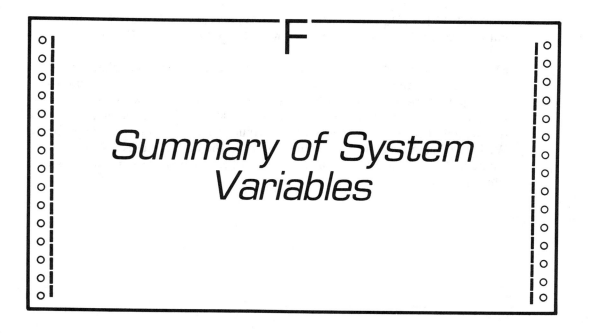

F

Summary of System Variables

$IO (Sections 4.4.4.2 and 12.2): Contains the device number of the currently active device (as established through the most recently executed USE command).

$JOB (Section 4.4.4.3): An integer that uniquely defines a job or process by identifying the partition in which the process is executing.

$STORAGE (Section 4.4.4.4): This variable reflects the amount of free space available in the partition. Partitions can be used as temporary storage for the current routine, the local symbol table, and system stacks, but not all implementations manage the partition space in the same way. In general, **$S** can be used to determine the amount (bytes) of free space available for variables. In implementations where variables and routines compete for partition space, the value of $S can change when different routines are loaded (that is, a subroutine is invoked).

$TEST (Sections 4.4.4.5, 6.1.5): $TEST contains a true/false (1/0) value reflecting the results of the most recently executed IF command with arguments or the status of the most recently executed OPEN, LOCK, READ, or JOB command with timeout syntax (if the command timed out before completion, $TEST = 0; otherwise, $TEST is set to 1).

$TEST is saved and restored during the execution of an extrinsic function, but *not* when subroutines are invoked with the DO or XECUTE command.

$X,$Y   (Sections 4.4.4.6, 4.4.4.7, 12.2): These variables hold the relative position of the cursor for the current active device (as established with the USE command). The upper-left corner of a screen or page has the coordinates $X = 0$, $Y = 0$. Each graphic character input or output to the device causes X to be incremented (with the possible exception of the input or output using either the READ *char or WRITE *char syntax). Each new line output to the device causes Y to be incremented. Both X and Y are reset to zero when a new-page sequence is issued (that is, Write #).

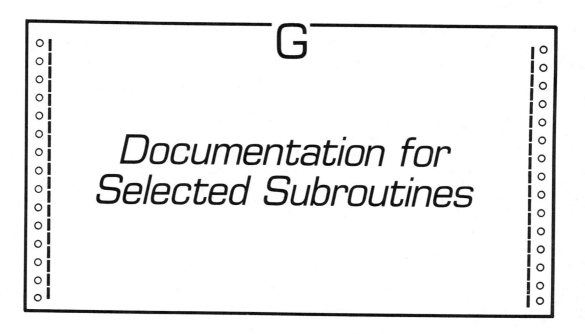

G

Documentation for Selected Subroutines

Example 9.11 Subroutine TimeFH

Subroutine name:	**TimeFH^%Zu**
Subroutine type:	**Extrinsic Function/Variable**
Calling sequence:	**$$TimeFH^%Zu(SECONDS,FORMAT) or $$TimeFH^%Zu**
Purpose:	Convert the parameter SECONDS from the number of SEC-ONDS elapsed since midnight ($H format) to a displayable format. The parameter FORMAT specifies whether the results will be in 12-hour (with an "AM" or "PM" indicator) or 24-hour format.
Input parameters:	Both the parameters (SECONDS and FORMAT) are optional.
SECONDS:	Can be an integer expression representing the number of seconds that have elapsed since midnight or the string "$H" to indicate the conversion of the current time from $H. If SEC-ONDS is *not* passed as a parameter, the **default** used is the number of seconds in $H.
FORMAT:	The parameter FORMAT is used to specify whether the time is to be returned in 12-hour format (FORMAT=12) or 24-hour format (FORMAT=24). If *not* passed or *not* equal to 12 or 24, it is set to the **default** value of 24.

Output: The results are returned as a string of characters in the general format **HH:MM** where HH is the hours and MM the minutes. In 24-hour format, both the hours and minutes are padded, as necessary, with leading zeros (02:09) while in 12-hour format, the minutes are padded with a zero, but the hour field is padded with a space (4:05). In 12-hour format the characters " AM" or " PM" are appended to the end of the HH:MM field. Strings returned for 12-hour format are eight characters long; those for 24-hour format are five characters long.

Error conditions: If SECONDS is an illegal value (less than 0 or greater than 86,400, which is 24 hours), the function returns an *empty string* ("""). An invalid FORMAT specification will result in the use of the default 24-hour format but does not return as an error condition.

Examples:

$$TimeFH^%Zu()	<u>17:05</u>
$$TimeFH^%Zu	<u>17:06</u>
$$TimeFH^%Zu("$H")	<u>17:06</u>
$$TimeFH^%Zu("$H",12)	<u>5:06 PM</u>
$$TimeFH^%Zu(82000)	<u>22:46</u>
$$TimeFH^%Zu(82000,12)	<u>10:46 PM</u>

Example 9.14 Subroutine DateFH

Subroutine name: **DateFH^%Zu**

Subroutine type: **Extrinsic Function/Variable**

Calling sequence: **$$DateFH^%Zu(Date)** or **$$DateFH^%Zu**

Purpose: Convert the parameter <u>Date</u> from a $H format (integer representing the number of days since December 31, 1840) to readable format (<u>MM/DD/YY</u>).

Input parameters: The parameter <u>Date</u> is optional, but if used it must be a nonnegative integer in the range from 1 to 99999.

Output: The returned value is a string of the general format "<u>Month/Day/Year</u>"; Month and Day are both one- or two-digit numbers and Year is a four-digit number.

Error conditions: If the input parameter <u>Date</u> is not a nonnegative integer in the range from 1 to 99999, the function returns an empty string ("""").

Examples:

$$Date^%ZuFH	<u>6/14/1987</u>
$$DateFH^%Zu(21608)	<u>2/28/1900</u>
$$DateFH^%Zu(+$H)	<u>6/14/1987</u>
$$DateFH^%Zu(53623)	<u>10/25/1987</u>
$$DateFH^%Zu(90007)	<u>6/6/2087</u>

Example 9.15 Subroutine NumChk

Subroutine name: **NumChk^%Zu**
Subroutine type: **Extrinsic Function**
Calling sequence: **$$NumChk^%Zu(Data,Range,Decimal)**
Purpose: Check the parameter Data for a valid number after stripping out all " " (spaces), "$" and ",". Optional tests on data Range and the maximum number of Decimal digits is also allowed. If Data is valid for all requested tests, NumChk returns the number in MUMPS numeric format. Otherwise, it returns an empty string ("").'Z
Input parameters: Parameter Data is required, while Range and Decimal are both optional.
Data: This is the string to be checked for a valid number. The characters " " (spaces), "$", and "," are removed from the entry before checking. Number can be real (that is, fractional digits allowed) or integer (Decimal can be used to force a check for an integer number).
Range: An optional parameter that specifies the minimum and/or maximum values that are permitted for the number being checked. The basic format for Range is a string consisting of "**LOW:HIGH**" (for example, " −100:100"). If *no* Range is specified, the *default* is −1E25 through 1E25. LOW and HIGH are optional (for example, a Range of ":100" would pass *all* numbers that did not exceed 100).
Dec: Optional parameter specifying the *maximum* number of fractional digits allowed in the number. If the string being checked contains more than the specified numbers, it is considered to be in error. If not specified, the *default* of up to 99 decimal digits is allowed.
Error conditions: If the number being checked fails any of the tests (valid number within the specified Range and with no more than Dec fractional digits), it is considered an error, and the function returns an empty string ("").
Examples:

$$NumChk^%Zu("$ +2,345.55")	2345.55
$$NumChk^%Zu(" −57"," −100:100",0)	-57
$$NumChk^%Zu(" −57.25","",0)	(empty string)
$$NumChk^%Zu("3300",":250")	(empty string)

Example 9.16 Subroutine Convrt

Subroutine name: **^%Convert**
Subroutine type: **Extrinsic Function**
Calling sequence: **$$Convrt^%Convert(num,from,to)**

Example 9.16   Subroutine Convrt   **377**

Purpose:	Convert the positive integer number <u>num</u> from base <u>from</u> to base <u>to</u>. Result returned as string in which letters ("A" to "F") may be present if the destination base was greater than 10.
Input parameters:	All three parameters (<u>num</u>, <u>from</u>, and <u>to</u>) are required.
num:	The positive integer representation of the number to be converted. It may contain uppercase alphabetic characters (A to F) if the <u>from</u> base is greater than 10.
from:	The *positive integer* base of the input number. Permissible range is 2 through 16.
to:	The *positive integer* base to which the input number is to be converted. Permissible range is 2 through 16.
Error conditions:	If any of the three parameters are in error, the result returned is an empty string ("").
Examples:	$$Convrt^%Convert(245,10,8) <u>365</u>
	$$Convrt^%Convert("EE",16,10) <u>238</u>
	$$Convrt^%Convert(238,10,2) <u>11101110</u>

Example 9.17 Subroutine Stats

Subroutine name:	^%Stats
Subroutine type:	**Invoked with DO command**
Calling sequence:	**Do ^%Stats(Array,.Results)**
Purpose:	To calculate simple statistics (MEAN, Standard Deviation, Standard Error, Low value, High Value, and Number of values) for an array or numbers.
Input parameters:	Both parameters (<u>Array</u> and <u>Results</u>) are *required*.
Array:	A string containing the array or global reference under which the data elements reside. It is used as part of a subscript indirection argument, and it is assumed that the data values reside *below* the reference. For example, if Array = "^TEST(1)", the data nodes might be found at "^TEST(1,2)", "^TEST(1,5)", and so on. Each data node should consist of a single number to be used in the calculations. Nonnumeric nodes are ignored.
Results:	A variable defining where the results of the calculations will be returned. The results are returned in the format:

Number;Low;High;Mean;Variance;Std Dev;Std Error

Where <u>Number</u> is the number of values processed, <u>Low</u> is the smallest value, <u>High</u> is the largest value, <u>Mean</u> is the average of values, <u>Variance</u> is the variance, <u>Std Dev</u> is the standard deviation, and <u>Std Error</u> is the standard error. If *no* values were valid numbers, <u>Results</u> is returned as an empty string. If <u>Num</u>-

ber is not greater than 1, <u>Std Dev</u> and <u>Variance</u> are returned as empty strings.

Error conditions: If no values were valid, then <u>Results</u> returned as an empty string. If <u>Number</u> not greater than 1, then <u>Std Dev</u> and <u>Variance</u> returned as empty strings.

Examples: For i = 1:1:10 Set Test(i) = i*i
Do ^%Stats("Test",.Ans) W !,"Stats = ",Ans

<u>Stats = 10;1;100;38.5;1167.83;34.17;6.2</u>

Example 9.18 Subroutine SQroot

Subroutine name: **<u>SQroot^%Zu</u>**
Subroutine type: **<u>Extrinsic Function</u>**
Calling sequence: **<u>$$SQroot^%Zu(Number)</u>**
Purpose: Calculate the <u>square root</u> of the absolute value of <u>Number</u>.
Input parameters: Parameter <u>Number</u> is required.
<u>Number</u>: Number whose square root is to be calculated. If negative, it is converted to positive before the square root is calculated. If zero (0), then a zero is returned as the square root.
Error conditions: If the <u>Number</u> to be converted is 0, returns a result of zero.
Examples: $$SQroot^%Zu(9)   <u>3</u>

$$SQroot^%Zu(-4*4)   <u>4</u>

$$SQroot^%Zu(5-5)   <u>0</u>

Example 9.18   Subroutine SQroot   **379**

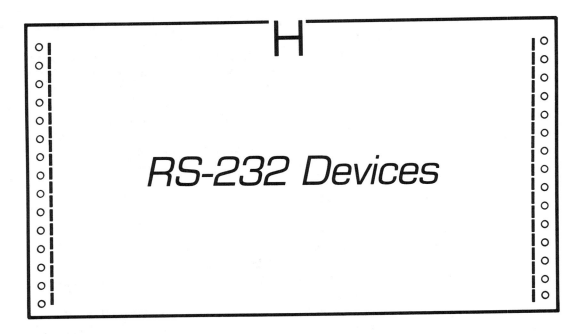

RS-232 Devices

The RS-232 Standard defines an electrical and connection interface for transmitting digital information between data terminal devices (DTE, devices such as computers and terminals) and data communications devices (DCE, or, in layman's terms, *modems*). This standard was established in the 1960s to standardize and improve the interchange of data between computers and peripheral devices connected via serial ports by the Electronic Industry Associates (EIA). A similar standard was established by the international standard organization Consultative Committee on International Telegraphy and Telephony (CCITT), which is essentially the same as the RS-232 standard established by the EIA.

Originally designed for interfacing terminals, modems, and computers, this standard represents the most common digital connection between terminals (and other instruments) and computers. Figure H.1 depicts a typical terminal-to-computer connection using the RS-232 interface definitions.

The RS-232 interface defines the type of connectors to be used, the pins within the connectors (25 signal lines, each terminating in a pin), and the electrical characteristics of the signals carried across the lines. While the standard defines all 25 connections, only pins 2 to 8 and 20 are typically used. Table H.1 displays these pin numbers and the names of the signals they carry.

The connections transmit data (TD, pin-2) and receive data (RD, pin-3) are used for data signals; an RS-232 connection can be transmitting and receiving data

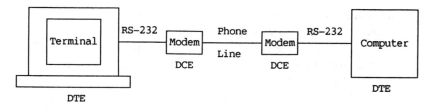

FIGURE H.1. Remote terminal-to-computer connection using RS-232 interface

simultaneously. The remaining pins are often referred to as *handshaking* signals and are used by DTEs and DCEs to determine whether or not the connected devices are ready. In normal operation a device or computer wishing to transmit characters over an RS-232 connection first *asserts* (sends a signal out) DTR to indicate that it is powered up and ready to go, and then checks to see if the modem is connected and ready (signals DSR and DCD are asserted). It then requests permission of the modem to transmit a character by asserting RTS; it will wait before transmitting the character until the modem acknowledges that it is ready by asserting the CTS line. As soon as CTS is asserted, the terminal or computer transmits the character.

TABLE H.1 MOST COMMONLY USED
RS-232 CONNECTIONS

Pin	Signal name	Abbreviation
2	Transmit Data	TD
3	Receive Data	RD
4	Request To Send	RTS
5	Clear To Send	CTS
6	Data Set Ready	DSR
7	Signal Ground	SG
8	Data Carrier Detect	DCD
20	Data Terminal Ready	DTR

There are also a number of other handshaking protocols commonly used when transferring characters over an RS-232 connection. These protocols are usually based on the values of the characters being sent and received. One of the more common protocols is the XON/XOFF convention. When a terminal or computer receives a DC3 (XOFF) character (decimal value of 19) it may, by convention, pause in transmitting characters until it receives a DC1 (XON) character (decimal value 17). The DC3 and DC1 characters can be generated at the keyboard by holding down the <CTRL> key and pressing either "S" or "Q".

This technique is often used at a terminal to suspend output and prevent the loss of data as lines scroll up. This convention is also used by terminals and computers to automatically signal the other device that their input buffers are full and they need time to empty these before more data are sent. Most MUMPS systems automatically handle this handshaking convention, sending XON and XOFF characters to prevent buffer overflows and responding to XON and XOFF sequences from the device. When DC3 or DC1 characters are received from a device, they are interpreted by MUMPS as control characters and are *not* generally put in the input string being read.

> Handshaking between an RS-232 device and the computer can be either in hardware (DTR and DSR signals) or through software conventions (XON and XOFF).

Data are transmitted over an RS-232 connection in a *serial, asynchronous* fashion; individual ASCII characters are broken into their constituent bits and transmitted one bit at a time. The speed at which data are transmitted over the line is usually referred to as the *baud* rate; the baud rate refers to the number of bits of data sent in one second. Each ASCII character sent generally consists of eight bits of data and two bits of framing information (to synchronize the characters). A baud rate of 9,600 translates to 960 ASCII characters per second.

When data are transmitted from a terminal to a computer through a modem, they are sent out the transmit data line (TD, pin-2) of the terminal, through the modem, over the phone line, and are received by the second modem. The transmitted and received data lines *cross* over the phone lines (when you speak into a handset your voice is received at the other end by the speaker) so that the signal sent via the transmit data line arrives at the computer on the received data (RD, pin-3) connection. In cases where modems are not used, it is necessary to wire the cable as a *null modem* to emulate this signal switching. Additionally, null modems are usually wired to bypass the normal hardware handshaking handled by the modem. Figure H.2 demonstrates a typical null modem configuration.

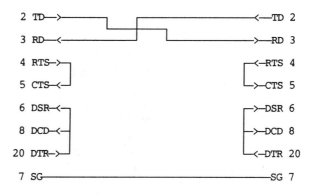

FIGURE H.2. Null modem connection

You should now be able to connect virtually any RS-232 device to your MUMPS system, correct? Wrong! Unfortunately, this standard is written in such a fashion that it can (and is) interpreted slightly differently by almost every terminal and computer manufacturer. Different pieces of equipment require different signals, and connecting these devices to your MUMPS system is often a hair-raising experience. However, most RS-232 equipment can be connected, and all that is usually required is some creative cabling (and lots of patience).

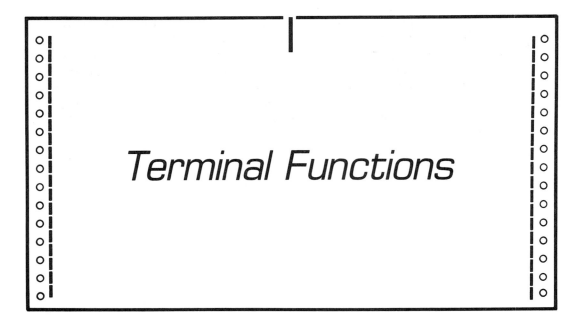

Terminal Functions

This appendix contains the documentation and listings for the video terminal functions described in Section 12.5, and for the question driver described in Section 12.5.5. The functions are held in three routines: routine %Tf contains the functions used to manipulate the display (for example, Clr and Hon) and to read characters from the keyboard (that is, the functions ReadS and Read); routine %To contains the multiple-choice function ($$MC) and the option-choice function ($$Opt); and routine ^%Qd contains the general-purpose question driver.

Before using any of these functions, it is necessary to define the terminal characteristcs for specific terminal types (initialize ^%Td; see discussion in Sections 12.5.1 and 12.5.2) and establish the terminal types associated with each MUMPS device number (^%Ti; see Figure 12.2).

Routine %Tf: Display and Keyboard Functions

The routine %Tf contains a number of basic functions needed to control the display characteristics of a video terminal and to input characters from the keyboard. An application using these functions should first *reset* the terminal using the $$Reset function; this need be done only once at the beginning of each application. The display functions are designed to alter the video display characteristics (for example, clear the display, position the cursor, and switch to high intensity). The keyboard functions are used to interface terminals with different characteristics to an application program. They convert all special keys (for example, cursor and function keys) into a common format for use by the application. Two input functions are provided: a single-character read ($$ReadS) and an editing keyboard read ($$Read). The editing keyboard read uses the single-character read function to input characters from the keyboard, and both use the display functions.

Display Function	Description
Reset	Set ok = $$Reset^%Tf or Set ok = $$Reset^%Tf(dev) Returns a truth value (0 or 1) indicating whether or not the RESET function was possible. If the parameter dev is passed, it defines the terminal type (for example, "VT100") to be associated with the current device (that is, $IO). If dev is not passed, the function uses the value of ^%Ti($IO) for the terminal type. The function establishes the terminal type for all other display functions, clears the screen, and resets all the display attributes ($$Hoff, $$Roff, and $$Uoff). This function is called once at the beginning of an application.
Clr	Write $$Clr^%Tf The Clr function is used to erase the display, position the cursor to the upper-left corner of the display, and set the system variables $X and $Y to zero.
Cup(x,y)	Write $$Cup^%Tf(NewX,NewY) Moves the display cursor to the specified location (x, y) and sets $X and $Y to reflect new position. The screen origin (upper-left corner) has the coordinates (0, 0).
Eol	Write $$Eol Erases the screen from the current cursor location to the End-Of-Line. Cursor and $X and $Y remain unchanged.
Eos	Erase the screen from the current cursor location to the End-Of-Screen. Cursor and $X and $Y remain unchanged.
Get	Set el = $$Get("Eol") ;el = "W*27,*91,*48,*75" for a VT-100 The $Get function returns the definition for the current terminal type for the specified function mnemonic. Can be used by programs that don't wish to go through the %Tf routine functions to manage the display. The first two characters returned indicate the type of data being returned.

Chars	Description
W	"W*27,*91,*48,*75" The remaining characters are used as an indirect argument to a Write command to invoke the function (for example, Write @$P(x,"\",2,999)).
X	"X\Write *27,*91,y + 1,*59,x + 1,*72 Set $X = x,$Y = y" The remaining characters are used as an argument to an Xecute command to invoke the function (for example, Set xy = $P($Get^%Tf("Cup"),"\",2,999) Xecute xy).
D	"D\79" The remaining characters describe a specific terminal characteristic (for example, screen Width).

Display Function	Description
Hoff	Write $$Hoff^%Tf Turns high intensity (bold) off. Characters displayed after this command will be at dim intensity. No change to cursor or $X, $Y.
Hon	Write $$Hon^%Tf Turns high intensity on. Subsequent characters will be displayed at high intensity (bold). No change to cursor, $X, or $Y.
Len	If $Y'<$$Len^%Tf Do more Returns the length of the display as (lines − 1) (that is, the value of $Y for the last line on the screen).
Roff	Write $$Roff^%Tf Turns reverse video off. No change to cursor, $X, or $Y.
Ron	Write $$Ron^%Tf Turns reverse video on. No change to cursor, $X, or $Y.
Uoff	Write $$Uon^%Tf Turns underline off. No change to cursor, $X, or $Y.
Uon	Write $$Uon^%Tf Turns underline on. No change to cursor, $X, or $Y.
Wid	Write ?$$Wid^%Tf-7,"Page ",p Returns the number of characters in a line as (chars − 1) (that is, the $X position of the last character on a line).

The display function lists could easily be expanded to control other characteristics, such as color or blink.

The keyboard read functions are designed to provide a uniform interface between an application program and both the system (MUMPS implementation) and a particular terminal type. Before they can be used, system-specific code must be inserted in three places within ^Tf: in the functions EchoOFF and EchoON and the extrinsic variable RPT.

The functions EchoON and EchoOFF are used to enable or disable the echoing of characters entered at the keyboard. The single-character read function ($$ReadS) uses a Read *c command to input characters from the keyboard. Some MUMPS implementations automatically echo characters read in this manner back to the display; others do not. For those implementations that do echo, the EchoON and EchoOFF functions must be modified to enable or disable the automatic echo feature. $$ReadS performs its own explicit echo, based on the characters received. Usually, the automatic echo feature is controlled with optional parameters to a Use command. If your system does *not* automatically echo on single-character Reads, then no special code needs to be used in these functions (that is, *remove* the Use commands shown in the listings).

The other system-specific item that must be adjusted is the extrinsic variable $$RPT. This variable is used in a single-character read loop and should be set to a value that provides for a $1/10$ second loop execution. This is necessary when reading escape sequences from the terminal to ensure enough time is allowed for terminals running at 110 baud. The special subroutine SetRPT is provided to calculate this value. Run the subroutine SetRPT (that is, Do SetRPT^%Tf) and record the value displayed as a result. Then edit the <u>QUIT</u> command in function <u>RPT</u> to reflect this value.

Read Function	Description
ReadS	Set char = $$ReadS^%Tf(tx,timeout,echo)
	All three parameters to the single-character $$ReadS function are optional. The first (<u>tx</u>) defines the values associated with the <u>special keys</u> (cursor and function keys). It is held in <u>^%Td($IO,"keys")</u>, but the overhead of a global reference can be avoided if it is passed in as a parameter. The second parameter (<u>timeout</u>) defines the number of seconds before the read is aborted; if not passed, it is initialized to a large value (1E25). The third parameter (<u>echo</u>) defines whether or not graphic characters will be echoed as they are entered from the keyboard. Some applications (see the functions $$MC and $$Opt) do not use character echo. The default is echo ON. The string returned from this function is either a single graphic character (decimal value 32-126), or a multicharacter string from the following list:

String	Description
\<RET>	Key was \<ENTER> (decimal 13)
\<BS>	Key was \<BACKSPACE> (decimal 8)
\<TAB>	Key was \<TAB> (decimal 9)
\<CAN>	Key was \<CTRL>U (decimal 21)
\<ESC>	Key was \<ESC> (desimal 27)
\<DEL>	Key was \<DEL> (decimal code 127)
\<TO>	Timeout expired before key was pressed
\<AU>	"Up-arrow" key
\<AD>	"Down-arrow" key
\<AL>	"Left-arrow" key
\<AR>	"Right-arrow" key
\<F1>	Function key 1 (also PF1)
\<F2>	Function key 2 (PF2)
\<F3>	Function key 3 (PF3)
\<F4>	Function key 4 (PF4)

Additional special keys can be handled with changes to the function $$ReadS and/ or changes to the terminal definition global <u>^%Td</u>.

Read Set x = $$Read^%Tf(oldans,width,.term,timeout)

Set x = $$Read^%Tf   ;no starting answer

Set x = $$Read^%Tf(oldans)   ;and so forth

The $$Read function provides for an editing keyboard READ. The function accepts up to four optional parameters: <u>oldans</u> is an existing answer that can be edited; <u>width</u> is the number of characters allowed for the answer (default is the rest of the <u>line</u>); <u>term</u> is a variable name (passed *by reference*) that the function uses to return information concerning how the read was terminated; and <u>timeout</u> is the number of seconds to read before aborting. If <u>oldans</u> is not passed, an empty starting string is assumed. The parameter <u>term</u> is set by the function to contain a designation of how the <u>Read</u> function terminated (for example, whether the \<ENTER> or function key was pressed). If <u>timeout</u> is not passed, the timeout is set to an arbitrarily large number (1E20 seconds).

Read Function	Description

When the function is invoked, the user can use the arrow keys, <BS>, <DEL>, and so on, to move around in the text and enter or delete characters. The function results passed back to the calling program contain the edited answer. If the optional parameter term is passed to the function, the condition terminating the read is passed back through this parameter. The terminating condition is bound with brackets ("<. . .>") and comes from the following list:

Terminator	Description
<RET>	User terminated the read by pressing the <ENTER> key
<ESC>	Read terminated with the <ESC> key
<AU>	Read terminated with "up-arrow" key
<AD>	Read terminated with "down-arrow" key
<F1>-<F4>	Read terminated with a function key
<TO>	Read timed out before terminated

Listing of ^%Tf%

```
%Tf        ;JML-NYSCVM ; 05 Nov 87  5:39
           ;Extrinsic functions for Terminal Control
           ;
           ;*****************************************************************
           ;*SYSTEM Specific functions. Must be rewritten for EACH system.  *
           ;*****************************************************************
           ;                                                                *
EchoON()   ;Turn ECHO ON for single-character Read                          *
           Use 0:(0:"") ;Enable ECHO for InterSystems M-11+                 *
           Quit "" ;                                                        *
           ;---------------------------------------------------------------*
EchoOFF()  ;Turn ECHO OFF for single-character Read                         *
           Use 0:(0:"SI") ;Disable ECHO for InterSystems M-11+              *
           Quit "" ;                                                        *
           ;---------------------------------------------------------------*
RPT()      ;Loop repeat count for 1/10 of a second single-character Read    *
           QUIT 10 ;                                                        *
           ;---------------------------------------------------------------*
SetRPT     ;Execute to establish Quit value in line RPT+1                   *
           New i,h,n ;                                                      *
           Write !,"Establish loop value ($$RPT) for 1/10 second" ;         *
           Set h=$P($H,",",2) For i=1:1 Quit:$P($H,",",2)'=h ;              *
           Set h=$P($H,",",2) For i=1:1 Read *n:0 Quit:$P($H,",",2)'=h ;    *
           Write !,"Edit RPT+1 to be  QUIT ",i\10," for 1/10 second Read.",! ;*
           Quit ;                                                           *
           ;                                                                *
           ;*****************************************************************
           ;*            End of SYSTEM Specific functions                   *
           ;*****************************************************************
           ;
BuildTF(TN) ;Builds To:From lists for ^%Td(TN,"keys").
           ;    run each time a new terminal is defined or if the special
           ;    character codes (cursor or function keys) are changed.
           Set TN=$G(TN) Quit:TN=""
           New from,km,to Set km="",from=$C(127),to=""
           For  Do  Quit km=""
           . Set km=$O(^%Td(TN,"keys")) Quit:km=""
```

```
              .     Set from=from_^(km)_$C(127),to=to_km_","
              .     Quit
                    Set ^%Td(TN,"keys")=to_";"_from
                    Write !,"Key definition for ",TN," finished."
                    Quit
              ;------------------------------------------------------------
      Reset(Dev) ;Called ONCE at beginning of application.
                    ;Reset current terminal ($IO) after establishing device type. If
                    ;"Dev" not passed, use default value in ^%Tio($I).
                    ;Return FALSE (0) if function fails, otherwise TRUE (1).
                    ;
                    Set Dev=$G(Dev),Dev=$S(Dev="":$G(^%Ti($I)),1:Dev)
                    If Dev="" Quit 0
                    Set ^%Ti($I)=Dev Write $$Clr,$$Hoff,$$Roff,$$Uoff
                    Quit 1
                    ;
              ;------------------------------------------------------------
                    ;
                    ;Terminal Display Functions
                    ;
                    ;Invoked as argument to a WRITE command (e.g., WRITE $$Clr^%Tf)
      Clr()         Quit $$doit("Clr") ;Clear screen, reset $X and $Y to zero.
      Cup(x,y)      Quit $$doit("Cup") ;Position cursor to (x,y)
      Get(mne)      ;Return value for "mne" for current terminal
                    If "<AU><AD><AL><AR><F1><F2><F3><F4>"[mne Quit $Get(^%Td(^%T($I),
              ---"keys",mne))
                    Quit $Get(^%Td(^%T($I),mne))
      Eol()         Quit $$doit("Eol") ;Erase from current cursor to END-OF-LINE
      Eos()         Quit $$doit("Eos") ;Erase from cursor position to END-OF-SCREEN
      Hoff()        Quit $$doit("Hoff") ;Set High Intensity (BOLD) OFF
      Hon()         Quit $$doit("Hon") ;Set High Intensity (BOLD) ON
      Len()         Quit $$doit("Len") ;Returns $Y position of last line on screen
      Roff()        Quit $$doit("Roff") ;Set Reverse Video OFF
      Ron()         Quit $$doit("Ron") ;Set Reverse Video ON
      Uoff()        Quit $$doit("Uoff") ;Set Underline OFF
      Uon()         Quit $$doit("Uon") ;Set Underline ON
      Wid()         Quit $$doit("Wid") ;Returns $X position of last character on a line
                    ;
      doit(mne)  ;Gets description for "mne" for current terminal type (^%Ti($I)). The
                    ;current terminal type is established with $$RESET function. Performs
                    ;requested function; returns "" for terminal control functions or the
                    ;value for terminal descriptive functions ($$Wid and $$Len).
                    ;
                    New value Set value=$G(^%Td(^%Ti($I),mne))
                    If value?1"W".E Write @$P(value,"\",2,999)
                    If value?1"X".E Xecute $P(value,"\",2,999)
                    Quit $S(value?1"D".E:$P(value,"\",2,999),1:"")
                    ;
              ;------------------------------------------------------------
                    ;
                    ;Keyboard Functions
                    ;
                    ;Single-character Read -  Set x=$$ReadS^%Tf(KeyTX,timeout,echo)
                    ;Editing keyboard Read -  Set x=$$Read^%Tf(oldans,width,.trm,timeout)
                    ;
              ;------------------------------------------------------------
   ReadS(Ktx,TO,Echo) ;Single-character Read; Do $$EchoOFF first.
                    New c,chars,d,f,find,n,t Set d=$C(127)
                    Set Ktx=$G(Ktx) Set:Ktx="" Ktx=^%Td(^%Ti($I),"keys")
                    Set t=$P(Ktx,";"),f=$P(Ktx,";",2,999)
                    Set TO=$G(TO) Set:TO="" TO=1E25
                    Set Echo=$G(Echo) Set:Echo="" Echo=1
      gchar         Set chars="" Read *c:TO Goto readsx:c>31&(c<127)!(c<0)
```

```
cchar      Set chars=chars_$C(c)
           Goto readsx:f'[(d_chars),more:f'[(d_chars_d)
           Set find=$L($E(f,1,$F(f,d_chars_d)),d)-2
           Set c=$P(t,",",find) Goto readsq
more       For n=1:1:$$RPT Read *c:0 Quit:c'<0
           Goto cchar:c'<0 Set c=$A(chars,$L(chars))
readsx     If c>31&(c<127) Write:Echo *c Quit $C(c)
           Set c=$S(c<0:"TO",c=13:"RET",c=21:"CAN",c=27:"ESC",c=8:"BS",
    ---c=9:"TAB",c=127:"DEL",1:"")
           If c="" Write *7 Goto gchar
readsq     Quit "<"_c_">"
           ;
           ;-----------------------------------------------------------
           ;
Read(Old,WID,Trm,TO) ;Editing Keyboard Read
           New ans,char,etime,i,sx,tx,wid,x Write $$EchoOFF
           Set Old=$G(Old),wid=$$Wid,Wid=$G(Wid),tx=$G(^%Td(^%Ti($I),"keys"))
           Set TO=$G(TO),etime=$P($H,",",2)+$S(TO="":1E20,1:TO)
           Set:Wid="" Wid=wid-$X Set Wid=$X+Wid Set:Wid>wid Wid=wid
           Set wid=Wid,ans=Old,sx=$X
start      Write $$Cup(sx,$Y),$$Ron,ans Set x=$X Write ?wid
getchar    Write $$Cup(x,$Y) Set char=$$ReadS(tx,1,0)
           If char="<TO>" Goto getchar:$P($H,",",2)<etime,readx
           Goto multi:$L(char)>1
           If sx+$L(ans)'<wid Write *7 Goto getchar
           Set ans=$E(ans,0,x-sx)_char_$E(ans,x-sx+1,999) Write char
           Set x=x+1 If sx+$L(ans)>x Write $E(ans,x-sx+1,999)
           Goto getchar
multi      Goto readx:"<AU><AD><RET><ESC><F1><F2><F3><F4>"[char
           If char="<AL>" Set:x>sx x=x-1 Goto getchar
           If char="<AR>" Set:x<wid&(x<(sx+$L(ans))) x=x+1 Goto getchar
           If char="<CAN>" Write $$Cup(sx,$Y),?sx+$L(ans) Set ans=$S(ans=Old:"",
    ---1:Old) Goto start
           If char="<BS>" Goto getchar:x'>sx Set x=x-1 Write $$Cup(x,$Y)
           Goto getchar:"<BS><DEL>"'[char
           Set ans=$E(ans,0,x-sx)_$E(ans,x-sx+2,999) Write " ",$$Cup(x,$Y)
           If x<(sx+$L(ans)) Write $E(ans,x-sx+1,999)," "
           Goto getchar
readx      Write $$Cup(sx,$Y),$$Roff,$$Hon,ans,$$Hoff,?wid,$$EchoON
           Set Trm=char Quit ans
```

Routine ^%To: Multiple-Choice and Option Selection

The subroutine %To contains two general-purpose utilities designed to display option lists and allow the user to select from the displayed choices. The two functions ($$MC and $$Opt) are screen-oriented, allowing the user to move between the displayed options with the keyboard cursor keys or by entering the first character of an option. They differ in how they handlle the displaying of the option list.

The function $$MC is designed to allow the user to select from a multiple-choice list of possible answers. The function displays the list of options on a single line and allows the user to move between choices using the left- and right-arrow keys. It is intended primarily for selecting between short lists of options (such as **Male Female Unknown** for a question on sex, or **Yes No** for a "Ready to Save" question).

The function $$Opt is designed to display longer lists, such as a primary function list at the beginning of an application. Unlike the $$MC function, $$Opt clears the screen, displays header information, and then lists the options, with each option on a separate line. The user can select between the options using the up- and down-arrow keys or by typing in the first letter of one of the displayed options. As the option selector (=>) is moved through the list, a brief description of the currently selected option is displayed at the bottom of the screen.

Both functions return an *option number* as a result of the function. In addition, an optional parameter can be passed to the function (the parameter *term*, which must be passed *by reference*) that will be set by the function to indicate how the function was terminated. The parameter term can assume the following values:

Term	Description
<RET>	The function was terminated by the user pressing the <ENTER> key.
<ESC>	The function was terminated by the user pressing the <ESC> key.
<F1>-<F4>	The function was terminated by the user pressing one of the function keys.
<AU>-<AD>	The function was terminated by the user pressing either the UP- or DOWN-ARROW keys. These keys are terminators only for the function $$MC; the function $$Opt uses the up- and down-arrow keys to move between selections.

Both functions are passed the option list and help or descriptive text as an array reference (local or global) that is used within the function with subscript indirection. The structure of the array is different, depending on which function is invoked. Consider the following array formats for input to the two functions:

Option List Format for Function $$MC

Ary(. . .)   = "Choice 1;Choice 2; . . . ;Choice n"
Ary(. . .,1) = "1st line of HELP text."
Ary(. . .,2) = "2nd line of HELP text."

.
.
.

Ary(. . .,n) = "nth line of HELP text."

Option List Format for Function $$Opt

Ary(. . .)   = "Header!Subheader . . ."
Ary(. . .,1)   = "First option text."
Ary(. . .,1,1) = "first line of descriptive text for first option."
          ,1,2) = "second line of descriptive text for first option."

.
.
.

Ary(. . .,2)   = "Second option text."

.

.

.

Ary(. . .,n)   = "nth option text."

In these examples, the "..." susbscripts are used to indicate "any valid list of prior subscripts." The array name is passed as a string of characters to the functions, which then use subscript indirection to access the data.

Both functions are invoked in a similar fashion. For example:

Set choice = $$MC^%To(AryRef,Default,.Term,Timeout)

Set opt = $$Opt^%To(AryRef,Default,.Term,Timeout)

where AryRef is a string pointing into the array holding the option list (for example, "^Test(1,2)"), Default is the option number automatically selected when the function is entered, Term is a variable name used to return an indicator defining how the function terminated (see preceding list), and Timeout is the number of seconds to attempt the function before aborting. Only the first parameter is required; the other three are optional.

The function returns the *option number* corresponding to the selection made.

Listing of ^%To

```
%To         ;JML-NYSCVM ; 05 Nov 87  6:34
            ;Multiple-Choice Utilities.
            ;
            ;Horizontal List (e.g., Sex:  Male [Female] Unknown)
            ;          Set opt=$$MC^%To(Ref,Default,.Term,Timeout)
            ;
            ;Vertical (new page, options on separate lines)
            ;          Set opt=$$Opt^%TOPT(Ref,Default,.Term,Timeout)
            ;
MC(Ref,Default,Term,Timeout) ;Horizontal Multiple-Choice
            New ary,cur,etime,ex,help,list,old,opts,n,sx,sy,tx,x,y
            Set Default=$Get(Default) Set:Default="" Default=1
            Set Timeout=$G(Timeout),etime=$P($H,",",2)+$S(Timeout:Timeout,1:1E20)
            Set opts=@Ref,sx=$X,sy=$Y,list=";"_$$UPPER(opts)
            For n=1:1:$L(opts,";") Set x=$P(opts,";",n),ary(n)=$X Write " ",x," "
            Set ex=$X,(cur,old)=Default,help=0,tx=$G(^%Td(^%Ti($I),"keys"))
            Write $$high,$$EchoOFF^%Tf
getmc       Set opt=$$ReadS^%Tf(tx,1,0)
            If opt="<TO>" Goto mcx:etime'<$P($H,",",2),getmc
gotmc       If help Write $$hlpclr Set help=0
            Goto mcs:opt?1E,mcx:"<RET><AU><AD><ESC><F1><F2><F3><F4>"[opt
            Goto getmc:"<AL><AR>"'[opt
            Set old=cur,cur=cur+$S(opt="<AL>":-1,1:1)
            Set:cur<1 cur=n Set:cur>n cur=1
            Write $$high Goto getmc
mcs         If opt="?" Set opt=$$hlpdis,help=1 Goto getmc:opt="<RET>",gotmc
            Set opt=$$UPPER(opt) If list'[(";"_opt) Write *7 Goto getmc
            Set x=";"_$P(list,";",cur+2,999),y=$F(x,";"_opt)
            If y Set y=cur+$L($E(x,2,y-1),";")
            Else  Set y=$L($E(list,2,$F(list,";"_opt)-1),";")
            Set old=cur,cur=y Write $$high Goto getmc
```

```
high()    ;Erase highlight from old, highlight new
          Write $$Cup^%Tf(ary(old),sy)," ",$P(opts,";",old)," "
          Write $$Cup^%Tf(ary(cur),sy)
          Write $$Hon^%Tf,"[",$P(opts,";",cur),"]",$$Hoff^%Tf
          Quit ""
hlpdis()  ;Display help text at bottom of screen
          New i,opt,s,x Set opt="<RET>",s=""
          For i=1:1 Do  Quit:s=""
          .    Set s=$O(@Ref@(s)) Quit:s=""
          .    If $Y+1'<$$Len^%Tf Do  If opt'="<RET>" Set s="" Quit
          .    .    Write $$Cup^%Tf(0,$$Len^%Tf),"<ENTER> for more: "
          .    .    Set opt=$$ReadS^%Tf(tx,1E25,0) Quit:opt'="<RET>"
          .    .    Set i=1 Write $$hlpclr
          .    .    Quit
          .    Write $$Cup^%Tf(0,19+i),@Ref@(s)
          .    Quit
          Quit opt
hlpclr()  Write $$Cup^%Tf(0,20),$$Eos^%Tf
          Quit ""
          ;
mcx       Write $$EchoON^%Tf,$$Cup^%Tf(sx,sy),$J("",ex-sx)
          Write $$Cup^%Tf(sx,sy),$$Hon^%Tf,$P(opts,";",cur),$$Hoff^%Tf
          Set Term=opt Quit cur
          ;
          ;-----------------------------------------------------------------
          ;
Opt(Ref,Default,Term,Timeout)  ;Vertical (new screen) Option Choice
          New ary,cur,i,list,old,opt,opts,n,titles,tx,x,y
          Set Default=$G(Default) Set:Default="" Default=1
          Set Timeout=$G(Timeout),etime=$P($H,",",2)+$S(Timeout:Timeout,1:1E20)
          Set titles=@Ref Write $$Clr^%Tf
          For i=1:1:$L(titles,"!") Write $$center($P(titles,"!",i)),!
          Set (opts,s)="",y=$Y
          For n=0:1 Do  Quit:s=""
          .    Set s=$O(@Ref@(s)) Quit:s=""
          .    Set y=y+1 Write $$Cup^%Tf(10,y),@Ref@(s)
          .    Set ary(n+1)=$Y_";"_s,opts=opts_";"_@Ref@(s)
          .    Quit
          Set list=$$UPPER(opts),opts=$E(opts,2,999)
          Set tx=$Get(^%Td(^%Ti($I),"keys")),(cur,old)=Default
          Write $$mark,$$EchoOFF^%Tf
getopt    Set opt=$$ReadS^%Tf(tx,1,0)
          If opt="<TO>" Goto optxx:etime'<$P($H,",",2),getopt
          Goto chkopt:opt?1E,optx:"<RET><ESC><F1><F2><F3><F4>"[opt
          Goto getopt:"<AU><AD>"'[opt
          Set old=cur,cur=cur+$S(opt="<AU>":-1,1:1)
          Set:cur<1 cur=n Set:cur>n cur=1
          Write $$mark Goto getopt
chkopt    Set opt=$$UPPER(opt) If list'[(";"_opt) Write *7 Goto getopt
          Set x=";"_$P(list,";",cur+2,999),y=$F(x,";"_opt)
          If y Set y=cur+$L($E(x,2,y-1),";")
          Else  Set y=$L($E(list,2,$F(list,";"_opt)-1),";")
          Set old=cur,cur=y Write $$mark Goto getopt
mark()    ;Un-mark old choice, mark new choice
          Write $$Cup^%Tf(6,+ary(old)),"    "
          Write $$Cup^%Tf(6,+ary(cur)),$$Hon^%Tf,"==>",$$Hoff^%Tf
          Write $$Cup^%Tf(0,19),$$Eos^%Tf Set s=""
          For i=1:1 Set s=$O(@Ref@(cur,s)) Quit:s=""  Write !,^(s)
          Quit ""
center(t) Write $$Cup^%Tf($$Wid^%Tf-$L(t)\2,$Y) Quit t
optx      Write $$EchoON^%Tf
          Set Term=opt Quit cur
          ;
UPPER(x)  Quit $TR(x,"abcdefghijklmnopqrstuvwxyz","ABCDEFGHIJKLMNOPQRSTUVWXYZ")
```

Routine ^%Qd: Question Driver

The subroutine %Qd contains a screen-oriented *question driver* used to display a predefined set of questions and then cycle through the questions, getting user input from the keyboard. The question driver handles all routine aspects of managing the question session, including the display of header information, display of question text, display of answers, reading input from the keyboard, dispatching control to verification subroutines, controlling the order of questions, and display of help text or error information.

The programmer must define an array (usually a global) containing the definition of the questions and then write verification subroutines for those answers requiring verification. The structure of the frame definition array is presented in Section 12.5.5, along with descriptions of how to invoke the question driver and how to write verification subroutines.

The question driver presented next uses the extrinsic display functions presented in Sections 12.5.1 to manage the display and the editing keyboard read (Section 12.5.4) to input answers from the keyboard.

Listing of ^%Td

```
^%Td        ;JML-NYSCVM
            ;Screen-Oriented Question Driver
            ;
Drv(%Ref,%Term,%Exc) ;Entry Point
            Set %Term="" Quit:'$$Reset^%Tf   ;Error in terminal definition
            New %al,%ax,%ay,%clrbot,%err,%goto,%i,%lst,%new,%qmne,%qlist
            New %qst,%qx,%qy,%redisp,%req,%ttls,%txt,%ver,%x
            Set %Exc=$E($G(%Exc))
            Set %x=@%Ref,%qlist=$P(%x,";"),%ttls=$P(%x,";",2,999)
            For %i=1:1:$L(%ttls,"!") Write $$center($P(%ttls,"!",%i)),!
            Set %lst="%txt,%qx,%qy,%ax,%ay,%al,%req,%ver"
            For %i=1:1:$L(%qlist,",") Do
            . Set %qmne=$P(%qlist,",",%i) Do getmne
            . Write $$Cup^%Tf(%qx,%qy),%txt
            . Write $$Cup^%Tf(%ax,%ay),$$Hon^%Tf,@%qmne,$$Hoff^%Tf
            . Quit
            Set (%qst,%clrbot)=0 Goto nxtqst
getans      Set (%err,%goto,%new,%redisp)="" Write $$Cup^%Tf(%qx,%qy)
            If %al Set %new=$$Read^%Tf(%new,%al,.%Term) Write:%clrbot $$clrbot
            If %new["?" Write $$dishlp Set %new=$TR(%new,"?","") Goto getans
            If %new'="",%Exc'="",%new[%Exc Do  Goto getans
            . Write $$err("Character """_%Exc_""" is NOT allowed.")
            . Set %new=$TR(%new,%Exc,"")
            . Quit
            Goto drvx:%Term="<ESC>" If %new=@%qmne,%new'="" Goto nxtqst
            If %new="",%req,%al Goto nxtqst:%Term="<AU>" Write $$err("Required An
        ---swer.") Goto getans
            If %ver'="" Do:%new'="!'%al @(%ver_"(.%new,.%err,.%redisp,.%goto)")
            Write:%redisp'="" $$redisp(%redisp)
            If %err'=""  Write $$err(%err) Goto getans
            Set @%qmne=%new If %goto'="" Set %qst=$$getqst Goto skpup
            ;
nxtqst      Set %qst=%qst+$S(%Term="<AU>":-1,1:1) Goto drvx:%qst<1
skpup       Set %qmne=$P(%qlist,",",%qst) If '%al,%Term="<AU>" Goto nxtqst
            Goto getans
            ;
```

```
redisp(%list) ;re-display answers in %list
          New %qmne For %i=1:1:$L(%list,",") Do
          .   Set %qmne=$P(%list,",",%i) Do getmne
          .   Write $$Cup^%Tf(%ax,%ay),$$Hon^%Tf,@%qmne,$$Hof^%Tf
          .   Quit
          Quit ""
          ;
getqst()  ;convert question mnemonic (%goto) to question number
          New x,y Set x=","_%qlist_",",y=","_%goto_","
          Quit x'[y %qst
          Quit $L($E(x,0,$F(x,y)),",")-2
          ;
center(txt) Write $$Cup^%Tf($$Wid^%Tf-$L(txt)\2,$Y) Quit txt
          ;
err(msg)  ;Display error message "msg"
          Write $$clrbot,$$Cup^%Tf(0,19),*7,"<<",%new,">>"
          Write $$Cup^%Tf(0,21) Set %clrbot=1
          Quit msg
          ;
clrbot()  Write $$Cup^%Tf(0,19),$$Eos^%Tf Set %clrbot=0 Quit ""
          ;
dishlp()  Write $$clrbot,$$Cup^%Tf(0,19)
          If $O(@%Ref@(%qmne,""))="" Write *7,"NO Help available." Goto dishlpx
          New Hn Set Hn="" For %i=1:1:5 Do   Quit:Hn=""
          .   Set Hn=$O(@%Ref@(%qmne,Hn)) Quit:Hn=""
          .   Write @%Ref@(%qmne,Hn),!
          .   Quit
dishlpx   Set %clrbot=1 Quit ""
          ;
getmne    New %i,%x Set %x=$G(@%Ref@(%qmne)),@%qmne=$G(@%qmne)
          For %i=1:1:8 Set @$P(%list,",",%i)=$P(%x,";",%i)
          Quit
          ;
drvx      QUIT
```

Index

Abbreviations
  commands   139
  functions   169
Absolute value   185
Actual parameter list   56, 204
Addition operator   123, 371
Alternate character sets   300, 351
AND operator   130, 371
Application compilers   282
Argument indirection   161
  with FOR command   163
Argument postconditioning   143
Argumentless commands   137
  DO command   57, 153
  FOR command   45
  GOTO command   49
  IF command   40
  KILL command   31
  LOCK command   92, 238
  NEW command   36
  QUIT command   58
Arrays   107
  branches   107
  $DATA of nodes   191, 364

Arrays (*Contd.*)
  deleting   32, 114
  global   3, 21, 114, 225
  hierarchical   107
  killing branches   32, 114
  nodes   108
  passed as parameters   56, 207, 212, 218
  searching with $ORDER   192, 226, 230
  sparse   4, 109
  Subscript indirection   165, 210, 218
  subscripts   108, 111, 227
  used in sorting   230
Arrow keys   298, 315
$ASCII function   186, 364
ASCII character set   187, 292, 300, 354
ASCII collating order   127
Assignment commands   27
  KILL command   30
  NEW command   35
  SET command   27
Asynchronous communications   293, 382
Attributes, display (bold, underscore, etc.)   293

B-trees   260
    deleting data   273
    entry order and size   267
    multiple subscript levels   271
    variants   268
Backup, globals   276
Balanced tree (B-tree)   260
Baud rate   293, 382
<BEL> key   79
Binary numeric operators   123
Bit interrogation   302
Bit manipulations   352
Block structuring   57, 149, 153
Blocks   261
    data   261
    links   268
    pointer   261
    splitting data blocks   263
    splitting pointer blocks   265
Boldface display   309
Boolean values   104
Branches, array   107
BREAK command   84, 345, 358
    resuming execution   50
BREAK, keyboard (<CTRL>C)   73, 76, 85,
    342
Buffering
    disk   273, 276
    keyboard input   76, 147
    magnetic tape   300

Calculations in context   9, 122
Canonic numbers   228
Carriage return character   73
Case (upper or lower)
    commands   138
    conversion between   181
    functions   169
    labels   149
    variables   105
$CHAR function   186, 364
Checking numbers   216
Clear screen   80, 294, 309
CLOSE command   81, 288, 358
Codes
    for data fields   253
    $FNUMBER   184
    pattern match   128, 352
Collating order
    ASCII   127
    MUMPS   128, 192, 228, 229
Combined operator types   132
Command line length   12
Command postconditioning   141

Command separators   148
Command summary, Appendix C   358
Command syntax   136
    abbreviation   138
    arguments   136
    case   138
    comments   147
    conditional execution   141
    implied commands   138
    timeout   145
Command types   26
    assignment   27
    conditional   38
    flow control   46
    input/output   64
    system and miscellaneous   83
Commands   24
Commas
    argument separators   138
    inserting into numbers   184
Comments   147
Compiled MUMPS   5, 17, 278
Compiler, application   282
Concatenate operator   125
Conditional commands   38
    ELSE command   41
    FOR command   42
    IF command   39
Conditional execution of commands   141
Constants
    numeric   102, 280
    string   100, 280
Contains operator   127
Conversions
    ASCII to decimal   186
    between number bases   217
    case (upper/lower)   181
    decimal to ASCII   186
    $H date to readable format   215
    $H time to readable format   213
    $H to day of week   124
    numbers   216
<CTRL>C   73, 76, 85, 342
<CTRL>O   73
<CTRL>Q   73, 76, 381
<CTRL>S   73, 76, 381
<CTRL>U   73
<CTRL>Z   304
Cursor keys   298, 315
Cursor positioning   62, 291, 309

Data
    encoding   253
    executing   62, 157

Data blocks 261
  adding data 261
  splitting 263
Data dictionary 164
Data element 246
$DATA function 191, 195, 233, 364
Data nodes 108, 261
Database design 246
Database errors 276
Databases 246
Date
  $H conversion 215
  $HOROLOG 114
Day of the week 124
Debugging programs 84, 345
Decremental LOCK 94, 239
<DEL> key 73
Deleting
  arrays 32, 114
  routines 97
  variables 30
Delimiters 248
Design, database 246
Device ownership (HALT command) 61
Device table 286
Devices 65, 286, 292
  current 69
  $IO 116
  magnetic tape drive 299
  networks 307
  ownership 65
  parameters 66, 67, 69
  principal 66, 288
  print spool 306
  printers 299
  RS-232 293, 306, 380
  sequential disk files 303
  video terminals 293
Dim display intensity 309
Direct mode 6, 12
Directories 17, 20
Disk buffering 273, 276
Disk files, sequential 303
Display attributes 293, 309, 310
  interactions between 315
  escape sequences 294
Distributed databases 240, 348
Division operator 123
DO command 13, 51, 203, 358
  argumentless 57, 153
  offsets 57
  parameter passing 203, 358
Documentation
  routine 214
  selected subroutines 375

Dynamic linking of routines 97

EBCDIC character set 300
Editing keyboard read 327
Editing routines 12, 96
ELSE command 41, 359
Empty string 100
Encoding data 253
<ENTER> key 73
EQUALS operator 126
Erase to end-of-line 309
Erase to end-of-screen 309
Errors 337, 352
  database 276
  reporting in compiled MUMPS 284
  resuming execution 50, 342
  trapping 337
Escape sequences 63
  display attributes 294
  keyboard 298
Exclusive KILL command 32
Exclusive NEW command 37
Execution level 154
Exponential numbers 102
Exponentiation 103, 123
Expressions 120
  numeric interpretation 122
  order of evaluation 120, 237
  string interpretation 122
$EXTRACT function 170, 365
Extrinsic functions 203, 210
  error handling 343
  $TEST 211
  QUIT command 60, 211, 343
Extrinsic variables 213

FALSE (boolean) 104
Field separators 248
Fields 246
$FIND function 178, 365
Fixed-length READ 71
Flow control commands 46
  DO command 51
  GOTO command 47
  HALT command 61
  QUIT command 58
  EXECUTE command 62
$FNUMBER function 183, 366
Follows operator 127
FOR command 42, 359
  argument indirection 163
  loop counter at termination 43
  terminating 48, 58

Form feed   78
Formal parameter list   34, 56, 204
Format control
 READ command   71
 WRITE command   78
Formatting
 numbers   182, 183, 366, 367
 strings   182, 367
Full duplex   293
Function keys   298, 315
Functions
 extrinsic   203, 210
 intrinsic   169, 364
 math   201
 nesting   202
 summary, Appendix D   364

$GET function   197, 366
Global copy utility   243
Global dump utility   243
Global variable names   106
Globals   3, 21, 114, 225
 backup   276
 buffering   273
 design   246
 distributed databases   240
 integrity   274
 inverted   250
 journaling   241, 276
 key   250
 locking   89, 238, 361
 naked reference   198, 236
 organization   249
 packing   275
 reference   253
 replication   241
 security   242, 348
 shared   5
 size   267
 storage efficiency   275
GOTO command   47, 155, 359
 with BREAK command   84, 342
 within FOR loop   44
Greater than operator   125

Half duplex   293
HALT command   14, 61, 360
Handshaking, RS-232   381
HANG command   85, 360
 alternative using timed READ   75
Hierarchical arrays   4, 107
$HOROLOG system variable   115, 213

IF command   39, 360
Implied commands   138
Inclusive KILL command   31
Inclusive NEW command   36
Incremental LOCK command   93, 239
Indexing   247
Indirection   157
 compiled MUMPS   283
 nesting   167
 operator   158
 XECUTE command   62, 158, 363
Indirection types   159
 argument   161
 name   159
 pattern   163
 subscript   165, 210, 218
Input/output   286
Input/output commands   64, 287
 CLOSE command   81, 288, 358
 OPEN command   66, 287, 361
 PRINT command   82, 97
 READ command   70, 287, 362
 USE command   69, 287, 362
 WRITE command   77, 287, 362
Input/output control characters   73
Integer divide operator   123
Integrity, global   274
Internals   259
 disk storage   260
 program execution   277
Interpreters   5, 17, 277
Interrupts (<CTRL>C)   73, 85, 342
Intrinsic data functions   169, 364
Inverted indexes   250
Inverting strings   180
$IO system variable   116, 290, 373

JOB command   86, 360
 with parameters   221
$JOB system variable   116, 373
Jobs   23
Journaling globals   241, 276
$JUSTIFY function   182, 367

Key compression   272
Key indexes   250
Keyboard breaks (<CTRL>C)   73, 76, 85,
 342
Keyboard buffering   76, 147
Keyboard input   297
 editing keyboard read   327
 single-character read function   315

Keys   246, 263
KILL command   30, 360

Labels   148
 case   149
 length   149
 tokens   280
Length
 command lines   12
 labels   149
 parameter list   205, 214
 screen   309
 variable contents   105
 variable names   105
$LENGTH function   176, 367
 nonoverlapping delimiters   220
Less than operator   126
Levels
 execution   154
 line   149, 154
 NEW command   37
 subroutine   213
Library subroutines   213
Line levels   149, 154
Line syntax   148, 154
Linestart character   149, 154, 188
Link pointers   268
Linking routines, dynamic   166
Literals
 numeric   102
 string   100
Loading routines   96
Local symbol table   19, 20
Local variables   106
LOCK command   89, 238, 361
 decremental   94, 239
 effect of HALT command   61
 incremental   93, 239
 unlock   92
Logical operators   130
Loops   42
Lowercase conversion   181

Magnetic tape drives   299
Math functions   200
MDC   8
Modems   380
 null   382
Modulo operator   123, 302
MUG (MUMPS Users' Group)   10
Multiple-choice function   322
Multiplication operator   123
MUMPS collating order   114, 128, 192, 227

MUMPS Development Committee (MDC)   8
MUMPS standard   8
MUMPS Users' Group (MUG)   10

Naked global reference   236
 order of evaluation   198
Name indirection   159
Name searches   250
Namespaces   21
Negative numbers, parentheses   184
Nesting
 functions   202
 indirection   167
 subroutines   37, 54
Networks   307, 348
NEW command   35, 55, 361
 implied   35, 205
 stacking and levels   37
 subscripted variables   36
 XECUTE command   63
New line   78
$NEXT function (obsolete)   195
Nodes (data and pointer)   261
Nodes, array   108
NOT operator   131
NUL character   100, 187
Null modem   382
Null strings   100
Numbers   101
 canonic   228
 checking   216
 comma insertion   184
 conversion   216
 conversion between bases   217
 exponential   102
 formatting   183
 random   199
 rounding   183, 185
 significance   102
Numeric constants   102
Numeric interpretation of strings   103
Numeric literals   102
Numeric operators   122

Offsets
 DO command   57
 GOTO command   50
 $TEXT function   189
OPEN command   66, 287, 361
Operator summary, Appendix E   371
Operator types
 binary numeric   123
 combined   132

Index   **401**

Operator types (*Contd.*)
  string   125
  unary numeric   122
Operators   99, 120
Option select function   322
OR operator   131
$ORDER function   111, 192, 226, 233, 367
  reverse $ORDER   352
Order of evaluation   120, 198
  naked global reference   237
Overlays, subroutines   23
Ownership of devices   66, 287

Packing globals   275
Parallel interface   299
Parameter list length   205, 214
Parameter passing   203
  actual list   56, 204
  by REFERENCE   56, 34, 207
  by VALUE   56, 206
  formal list   56, 204
  JOB command   87, 221
Parameters, device   67, 69
Parentheses
  negative numbers   184
  order of evaluation   121
Partitions   17, 18
  clearing   97
  $JOB command   116
Parts   151
Pattern indirection   163
Pattern match codes   128
Pattern match operator   128, 352
Percent (%)
  routines   213
  variables   105
$PIECE function   172, 368
  nonoverlapping delimiters   220
  SET $PIECE   29, 174
Point of reference, global design   249
Pointer blocks   261
  splitting   265
Pointer nodes   108, 261
Postconditioning   141
  argument   143
  command   141
  $TEST   40
Postfix notation   279
Precision (retrieval)   254
Principal device   66, 288
  with JOB command   87
PRINT command   82, 97
Print spool device   306
Printers   299

Printing routines   82, 97
Programming technique   222
Programs   152
  debugging   345

$QUERY function   195, 368
Question driver   164, 328
  verification subroutines   333
QUIT command   58, 362
  argumentless   58
  extrinsic functions   60, 211
  terminating FOR loop   44, 58
Quote character   100

$RANDOM function   199, 369
READ command   70, 287, 362
  editing read function   327
  single character function   315
  terminators   297
Recall (retrieval)   254
Records   246
Recursive programs   243
Reference files   253
REFERENCE, passing parameters by   34, 56,
    207
References, Appendix B   356
Relational operators   125
Replace strings   219
Replication of globals   241
<RETURN> key   73
Reverse Polish Notation (RPN)   279
Reverse video   309
Rounding numbers   183, 185
Routine documentation   214
Routine lines, $TEXT   188
Routines   151
  1st and 2nd line conventions   152
  debugging   84, 345
  deleting   97
  dynamic linking   166
  editing   12, 96
  loading   96
  name from $TEXT   189
  printing   82, 97
  saving   97
  size   19
RPN (Reverse Polish Notation)   279
RS-232 devices   293, 306, 380

Saving routines   97
Screen length   309
Screen width   309

Searches 192, 255
   name 250
   soundex 252
Security, globals 242, 348
$SELECT function 198, 369
   order of evaluation 237
Sequential disk files 303
Serial communications 382
SET command 27, 362
   order of evaluation 237
   $PIECE function 29, 174
Shell 158
Sign (numeric) 184
Significance, numbers 102
Signing onto MUMPS 11
Single character READ command 75
Single character WRITE command 79
Single character read function 315
Size
   globals and order of entry 267
   local symbol table 19
   partition 19
   partition ($JOB) 116
   routines 19
   variables 105
Sorting data 230, 255
   descending numeric order 256
Soundex code 252
Sparse arrays 109
Splitting
   data blocks 263
   pointer blocks 265
Square root 219
Stacking
   error traps 341
   NEW command 37
Stack execution 279
Statistics 217
Storage efficiency of globals 275
$STORAGE system variable 116, 373
String intrinsic functions 170
String literals 100
String literal tokens 280
String operators 125
String relational operators 126
Strings 100
   inverting 180, 181
   length 100
   literals 100
   null 100
   numeric interpretation 103
   replace 219
Subroutine parameters 203
   actual 56, 204
   arrays 56, 207, 209, 218

Subroutine parameters (*Contd.*)
   formal 34, 56, 204
   killing 34
   passed by REFERENCE 34, 56, 207
   passed by VALUE 56, 206
Subroutines 151
   exiting 51, 223
   extrinsic functions 203, 210
   invoking with DO command 51, 203
   levels 35, 37, 54
   libraries 213
   nesting 54
   overlayed 23
   parameter passing 55, 203
   QUITing 51, 223
Subscript indirection 165, 218
Subscripted variables with NEW command 36
Subscripts 4, 108, 111, 227, 247
   collating order 114, 128, 192, 227
   indirection 165, 218
   key compression 272
   multiple levels, B-tree 271
   null string 111
   searching with $ORDER 111, 192, 226, 233
   string 4, 111
Subtraction operator 123
Syntax 136
   command 136
   line 148, 154
   parts 151
   routines 151
System and miscellaneous commands 83
System variables 115, 373

TAB argument (READ and WRITE) 78
Table of variable addresses 281
Terminating
   extrinsic function 60, 211, 343
   keyboard read 297
   MUMPS 14
   subroutine 51
$TEST system variable 39, 116, 136, 373
   extrinsic functions 211
   postconditioning 40
   timeout 146
$TEXT function 188, 369
   compiled MUMPS 190, 283
Time
   $HOROLOG 115
   $HOROLOG conversion 213
Timeout
   command syntax 145
   JOB command 88
   LOCK command 92

Index   **403**

Timeout (*Contd.*)
   OPEN command 66, 68
   READ command 74
Timesharing 16
Token 278
Token streams 279
Trailing sign 184
$TRANSLATE function 179, 369
Trapping errors 337
Tree-structured arrays 4, 107
Tree walk, $QUERY 195, 368
TRUE (boolean) 104
Type-ahead 76
Typing variables 99

Unlock (global) 92, 238
Unary numeric operators 122
Underlining 309
Upper case conversion 181
USE command 69, 287, 362
Utilities
   display attributes 310
   editing keyboard read 327
   multiple-choice and options 322
   question driver 328
   screen handling 308
   single-character read 315
   statistics 217

VALUE, passing parameters by 34, 56, 206
Variable token 281
Variables 104
   arrays 107
   case 105
   extrinsic 213

Variables (*Contd.*)
   global 106
   in token stream 281
   interpretation 99
   length 105
   percent (%) 105
   system 115, 373
   typing 99
Verification subroutines (question driver) 333
Video terminals 293, 307
VIEW command 94, 362
$VIEW function 200, 370

Width, screen 309
WRITE command 77, 287, 362

$X system variable 63, 80, 117, 291, 374
XECUTE command 62, 158, 363
XOFF 73, 381
XON 73, 381

$Y system variable 63, 80, 117, 291, 374

$Z... commands 96
$Z... functions 201$
Z... system variables 117
ZGO command 84
ZINSERT command 96, 363
ZLOAD command 14, 65, 96, 363
ZPRINT command 82, 97, 363
ZREMOVE command 97, 363
ZSAVE command 65, 97, 363